Colchester People

The John Bensusan Butt Biographical
Dictionary of Eighteenth-Century Colchester

edited by

Shani D'Cruze

Volume 1
A-L

Second edition, 2010

ISBN: 978-1-4466-4621-2
Rights Owner: Shani D'Cruze and the estate of John Bensusan Butt
Copyright: © 2010 Shani D'Cruze and the estate of John Bensusan Butt, Standard Copyright License
Language: English
Country: United Kingdom
Edition: Second Edition

Contents

Acknowledgements	i
Editor's Introduction	iii
A Note on the Second Edition	xii
Abbreviations	xiii
Sources	xv

Dictionary Entries

A	1
B	37
C	130
D	186
E	242
F	254
G	280
H	321
I/J	391
K	400
L	430
Index to Volume 1	463

Acknowledgements

My thanks are due to the executors of John Bensusan-Butt who have funded this project for the publication of his historical research. Rita and Ken Sharpe and Elizabeth Long did valuable volunteer work on the Biographical Dictionary material. Bruce Neville's detailed knowledge of the local history and his collection of material on Colchester High Street has on several occasions been a source of valuable information. The Essex County Record Office has been very supportive of this project. Amongst the archivists and librarians who have provided assistance and clarification, I owe a particular debt of gratitude to Paul Coverley and Jane Bedford, the archivists at the Colchester and North East Essex branch of the Essex County Record Office (sadly now closed); their professional skills, their knowledge of the local historical sources and their advice and support have been invaluable. The Department of History at the University of Essex also provided office accommodation for several weeks.

Editor's Introduction

Scope and origins

In 1892 Charles E. Benham published *Colchester Worthies. A Biographical Index of Colchester*. It is a slim volume that selects for discussion some of the individuals whom to a late Victorian mind had made 'worthy' contributions to the history of the author's home town. *Colchester People* is a far fatter and less elegant project. While it confines itself to the eighteenth-century, *Colchester People* includes a much wider range of individuals. As well as the great and the good of the town there are some distinctly unworthy of civic merit and others merely mundane.

This biographical dictionary is compiled from the archive of eighteenth-century Colchester history compiled by John Bensusan Butt (JBB). His collection of primary source material was accumulated over forty years, and identifies over 1,000 individuals who lived in or were associated with Colchester in Essex. Through the accumulation of data from wills, property deeds, local institutional and Borough records, published histories, newspapers, correspondence, maps and visual material (including material not on deposit in a public archive), the JBB archive underpins several hundred extended individual and family histories of the middling sort and 'town gentry', as well as a quantity of less detailed entries. This collection is by no means a complete listing of Colchester traders, professionals and 'leisured' classes. It was accumulated over time through the overlaying of numerous smaller researches and its composition reflects the preoccupations of its compiler. Although some people listed date from the mid-seventeenth century and others had careers lasting well into the nineteenth, the archive is strongest for the middle decades of the eighteenth century. It privileges those with named occupations, who were involved in the Borough institutions or who used the local newspaper, the *Ipswich Journal*, to advertise their businesses. It is also stronger on the centre of the town than the Hythe or the liberties – not least because parish rates and Land Tax surveys were listed on a house-by-house basis for many town centre parishes, and alphabetically elsewhere. The material is slanted to the more visible Borough records, and pays scant attention to the labouring classes and the poor, though it has the great advantage of tracing individuals from outside the Borough who had Colchester associations and of tracking numbers of individuals who migrated out of or into the town. Though there is considerable information on women, the organisation of the data into a biographical dictionary tends to subsume Colchester women into the entries on their male kin. Despite these limitations, the JBB archive contains a very rich source of data on eighteenth-century Colchester, particularly for those social groups of at least small property.

In the eighteenth century Colchester was a sizeable provincial town of around 10,000 inhabitants, the largest urban settlement in north Essex and bigger than the county towns of both Essex and Suffolk. The cloth manufacture that had dominated the town in the seventeenth century was undergoing a long and uneven process of decline, whilst the growing prosperity of English agriculture (particularly within fifty miles of the huge London market) increased the importance of Colchester's market functions and its role in the coastal trade. Colchester's industrial centre of gravity shifted towards brewing, salt-making and other manufactures around its port at the Hythe and the more affluent were keener to sink capital into agricultural land than into the cloth trade. At the same time, secular economic growth and the development of markets meant that Colchester shared in the national trend towards domestic consumption and the making of cultures of gentility and politeness. Historians have recently shown an increasing interest in eighteenth-century urban society and culture, though London and the faster-growing industrial towns of the north and west have attracted most research. Colchester is interesting as an example of a town that was de-industrialising in an era of accelerating industrial growth, was near the cultural and social magnet of the giant metropolis yet was itself substantial enough to have its own cultural identity as well as its own political identity as an incorporated Borough. Therefore, not only do the three volumes of *Colchester People* contain information for those researching particular individuals and families, they build up a picture of social connectedness – between families, individuals, neighbourhoods and other kinds of networks – and therefore have something to say about English provincial urban society in the age of early modernity.

Readers looking for fuller discussions of Colchester's eighteenth-century history will find a succinct outline in the *Victoria County History of Essex*, Volume 9 (available online), which also clarifies much about the different parishes of the Borough, their character and location, local politics, the structure and organisation of Borough government, local charities and institutions etc. Philip Morant's 1748 *History and Antiquities of the Borough of Colchester* is also an invaluable source of information on the town and is available in a modern reprint in libraries, or online on subscription. For full details of availability of these two sources see Sources and Bibliography below. My own book-length study that draws on much of the JBB archive is *A Pleasing Prospect: Social Change and Urban Culture in Eighteenth-Century Colchester* (University of Hertfordshire Press, 2008).

John Bensusan Butt

John Bensusan-Butt was an artist, historian, sometime Borough and County Councillor and for many years a well-known figure in his native town of Colchester. His early career was as a water-colourist, then as an art critic for the local newspaper, and then in local public service as 'Councillor Butt' as well as Chair of the Colchester Civic Society. At the same time he was also beginning his historical research, initially through exploring the architectural and social history of the family's large eighteenth-century house (The Minories, 74 High Street). His enthusiasm for the eighteenth century, a period whose optimism and pursuit of progress he found highly congenial, fueled a further forty years of research. John followed the research trail to explore the artistic and cultural history of the region and significant figures with Colchester associations such as Thomas Gainsborough (see entry for Mary Gibbon (qv)). Nevertheless, he never exhausted the pleasures of delving into the minutiae of Colchester history made possible by the excellent survival of local records, as well as John's own position and contacts in the town. There was always something new and tantalising to find out - 'chasing hares' he called it. Consequently, despite his short articles in the *Essex County Standard* and a number of other pamphlets, lectures and articles, this core project - the *Biographical Dictionary of Eighteenth-Century Colchester* - never reached completion in his lifetime.

With the support of John's estate, it is now possible to publish much of this historical material. The first stage in putting into the public domain the fruits of John's prolific and detailed research was my own monograph *A Pleasing Prospect* (see above). As a second stage, a volume of historical biographical essays which John had himself selected for private publication in the late 1980s and early 1990s have been produced as *Essex in the Age of Enlightenment* (Lulu: 2009). Therefore these three volumes of *Colchester People: The John Bensusan Butt Biographical Dictionary of Eighteenth-Century Colchester*, are the final stage in this project. Volumes 1 and 2 contain alphabetically organised entries for individuals with an index listing of entries in each volume. Volume 3 has, as appendices, entries for inns, for the Colchester Medical Society and a transcription of the Anecdotes on eighteenth-century Colcestrians written by H. D. Bland, and also full indexes by name and occupation. The first edition of Volume 1 was published in 2009. This second edition, published alongside the other volumes, has been revised and contains a few extra entries and referencing.

Format and compilation

My connection with the JBB archive dates back to the work I did in the early 1980s as John's research assistant, tasked with compiling dictionary entries from his sizeable collection of notebooks and typescripts while I also pursued my own MA and PhD research on eighteenth-century Colchester. The dictionary entries in this and its sister volumes, in part originated from my early drafts which were added to over the intervening years by JBB and in part to a second stage of drafting by John in the early 1990s. During the final production of the dictionary, I have also written a further ten per cent or so of the entries appearing here to cover individuals who were originally targeted for inclusion, but whose entries had not as yet been drafted. Consequently the style and fullness of entries can vary. I have tried to abstain from John's example of 'chasing hares' and thereby infinitely delaying the completion of the project. John also made grateful use of the researches of others (of Keith Farries on millers, of G. O. Rickwood, Geoffrey Martin, or of Bernard Mason – whose wife acted as his research assistant – on clockmakers) and so has few notes on individuals researched elsewhere. Therefore some entries remain as 'stubs'. Readers are also referred on for those individuals who appear in the *Essex in the Age of Enlightenment* articles, or who are well discussed in the *Oxford Dictionary of National Biography* or elsewhere. My apologies to any readers looking for a particular individual whose entry is not as full as they might have liked.

In the final editing I have (I hope) removed the worst infelicities of drafting, particularly where those originally arose from my own postgraduate enthusiasms. Nevertheless, the dictionary remains very much a project that reflects JBB's approaches, interests and style, tempered somewhat by my input in the endless discussions we had when working on the material in the early 1980s. Entries often include commentary alongside the historical information, as well as the authorial and editorial choices made as to what to include and how to arrange it. I have not seen it as part of my role as editor to shift the perspective nor to smooth out John's 'voice' in the text.

I have included a comprehensive listing of Abbreviations in these preliminary pages, and hope that readers will therefore find even the more 'note form' entries fully comprehensible.

Early in this project, I was greatly helped by volunteer researchers Rita and Ken Sharpe and Elizabeth Long, who not only did some transcription but who also checked back many of the dictionary references to the original sources. My thanks to them for their invaluable work. Given the size of the project, not every primary source reference has been checked in this way, but the great majority have, and the balance have been verified against JBB's original notes. Attention had been focused on key sources such as the local newspaper (principally the *Ipswich Journal*), wills, apprenticeships, marriage licences and some Borough records. No systematic checking of parish registers (baptism, marriage and burial) has been undertaken, nor of poll books for Borough elections, free burgess admissions, parish rates and land tax. Births, marriages and deaths information is now much more freely available online, either through the *IGI* or through subscription sites. Likewise the Essex Record Office (ERO) online catalogue, SEAX, the National Archives catalogue and the A2A site have made it far easier for readers to track down information on specific individuals than was true at the time John was researching (from the 1950s to the 1990s). The urls of these and other relevant online catalogues and finding aids are included in the Sources section which also gives fuller information about the location and referencing of the main series of sources that underpin the entries. Unusually, I place this before the dictionary entries in this volume, so as to inform the reader for what follows.

The entries are fairly thickly referenced in (parentheses) in the text, however, given the volume of material, not every single item of information has a direct reference. My apologies to any reader looking for the origin of any specific item who has to search further, in SEAX, in A2A or in primary sources. The dictionary references primary sources in most cases, and where amplification might be helpful to readers I have included reference to John's original notebooks (now deposited in ERO C905, Boxes 16 and 17). Referencing John's notes has also been necessary for original documents not in any public archive, many of which are no longer accessible. The dictionary uses abbreviated references to the most-used published sources (e.g. Morant, *Colchester*) which are cited in full in the Bibliography. Sometimes, where the origins of JBB's comments have not been traceable, 'nfr' indicates that no further reference could be found. 'JBB note' often refers to his marginalia in the early drafts.

In general, the information presented in the dictionary entries falls into three categories. Firstly family history drawing on baptismal, marriage, burial and probate data. At this period, for the social sectors the dictionary is most concerned with, marriage licences as well as registers provide good information in many cases. Where available, wills are often transcribed fairly fully and describe material culture as well as social connection. Deeds of property and advertisements for house sales also bridge across between material and social position as well as mapping something of the social and cultural geography of the town, which is developed from use of parish rates and land tax assessments. Secondly, and most fully for men, the dictionary captures information about local public life. Information on individuals' trade or business comes from records of apprenticeship, advertisements in the *Ipswich Journal* and sometimes from petty and quarter sessions. JBB's interest in architecture had led him to trace payments for work done by the town's carpenters and builders in available sources. Particularly for eighteenth-century middling men, their occupation was complemented by office holding in their parish or Borough institutions and the membership of clubs and associations in framing their public social position. The membership if the local Medical Association (see also Appendix 2), the Castle Book Club and the town's freemasons lodges are documented.

The third category of information in the entries intersects with the second, and comprises the arena of local politics and government Dictionary entries record specific individuals' involvement in elections, the Corporation and its intermittent scandals, the Harbour Commissioners set up to regulate the navigation to Colchester's port at the Hythe, the trustees for local charities, such as the Free School and similar public bodies. There is also mention of the voting choices of free burgesses in parliamentary elections for the Borough. Readers unfamiliar with the outline of Colchester Borough politics, or with the mechanisms of eighteenth-century elections might find this information unhelpful (if not baffling). A 'balanced' representation means a vote for 1 Whig and 1 Tory candidate. When the local political context is especially salient for the carrier of a particular individual some further explanation is given, though this was not possible for every voter. Readers seeking explanation can find a succinct overview of local politics in *VCH Essex*, Vol. 9, 'Georgian Politics', available online.

Many entries conclude with a short paragraph generally beginning 'See also…'. Here are noted any particularly relevant sources (for example the clock and watchmakers' entries depend heavily on Bernard Mason's *Clock and Watchmaking in Colchester, England* (Colchester, 1969)). This is also the place where references are noted to individuals of the same surname which may or may not be connected with the main entry and which do not appear elsewhere in the volume.

The dictionary makes wide use of 'qv' (*quod vide* or 'which see') to cross reference between entries. For example, in the opening sentences for the entry for Thomas Boggis, baymaker, the reader is referred to four other dictionary entries, as follows;

> The eldest son of Isaac Boggis 1 (qv) and brother to Isaac 2 (qv) and James (qv). Attended the Writing School at Dedham (see under William Colchester (qv).

Where a particular piece of information appears in more than one entry (for example a legacy in a will is often included in the entries both for the testator and the legatee) the source reference will generally appear only once in the main entry (i.e. that of the testator) though where the reference has been repeated in the original drafts of both the relevant dictionary entries I have preserved it.

Dictionary entries are arranged alphabetically by surname. Each entry heading specifies name, trade or occupation (where relevant) and dates of activity (*floruit*, abbreviated to 'fl.').

Where not otherwise indicated the date range is from birth to death. Sometimes a single, terminal date (death, bankruptcy or will) is used. Where will dates are given in the form 1801/6, or 1756/9, this distinguishes the date the will was made (1801, 1756) and the date it was proved (1806, 1759). Generally a similar abbreviation is also used for dates before the calendar change (e.g. February 1733/4).

Each entry also has a reference number in square brackets. These may pose something of a puzzle, particularly to readers of a logical turn of mind. These reference numbers were allocated to the entries when the original drafts were being transcribed (or indeed written). Those early entries were not compiled primarily alphabetically but according to trade or occupational grouping, and as indicated, a fair proportion of entries were added later. Some of the original entries which referred to individuals insufficiently connected with Colchester have been eliminated. Also the original drafts included entries for many of the town's inns, which are listed separately in Appendix 1, Volume 3. Consequently, reference numbers do not follow the alphabetical sequence of the final dictionary, but have been retained as unique identifiers for each entry and also because they were cited in *Pleasing Prospect* and *Essex in the Age of Enlightenment*.

JBB, as I have said, hated finishing things. For him, research was never sufficiently complete and always a joy in itself. *Colchester People* is hardly the last word on the history of eighteenth-century Colchester, or of the myriad histories of the people who lived, worked and died there or thereabouts. There is much research for others to do, and inevitably corrections to be made. Nevertheless, it is a sizeable publication and represents the kind of extended research that is largely impossible for academic historians to undertake today. I hope that the final form that JBB's biographical dictionary has taken would not only be pleasing to him, but will also prove useful to historians of all kinds in the future.

Shani D'Cruze
Crete, 2010

A Note on the Second Edition

This edition of Volume 1 of *Colchester People* has been revised in the light of the final preparation of Volumes 2 (alphabetical entries M-Y) and 3 (appendices and indexes).

This volume is substantially the same as the first, 2009, edition, but has been re-formatted, and includes some improved referencing, correction of a few errors and a couple of additional entries.

Abbreviations

aet.	aged
app.	apprenticed (to)
Ass Bk	Borough Assembly Book
bapt.	baptised
bd	bound (as guarantor for marriage licence, recognisance etc.)
bkt	bankrupt
BL	British Library
bn	born
bur.	buried
ChCh	*Chelmsford Chronicle*
CPL	Colchester Public Library, Local Studies Section
dd.	deceased
d.	died
ECS	*Essex County Standard*
ER	*Essex Review*
ERO	Essex Record Office, Chelmsford
ESAH	Essex Society for Archaeology and History, previously Essex Archaeological Society
Eur. Mag.	*European Magazine*
ex. inf.	information provided by
fl.	*floruit* - recorded in the sources
gent	gentleman (style adopted by men who had become affluent and were retired from trade or profession)
Gents. Mag.	*Gentleman's Magazine*
IGI	*International Genealogical Index*
IpsJ	*Ipswich Journal*
m/s	marriage settlement
mess.	messuage
MI	monumental inscription
ML	marriage licence
mon.	monument (funeral)
NA	National Archives, Kew

ob.	obit (died)
occ.	occupied (by)
ODNB	*Oxford Dictionary of National Biography*
p.	proved (of will)
par.	parish
PCC	Prerogative Court of Canterbury
qv	*quod vide* (which see)
SRO	Suffolk Record Office, Ipswich
Thos	Thomas
tmt	tenement
Univ. Mag.	*Universal Magazine*
w.	will
wid.	widow
widr	widower
wits.	witnesses
Wm	William

Sources

The intentions of this section are threefold. Firstly the location and reference(s) of the main series of primary sources used in the dictionary entries are listed (alphabetically by name of source) and the referencing used in the dictionary entries is clarified. Sometimes archival arrangements have changed from when JBB made his original notes, and as far as possible the current location and references are specified. Secondly, a secondary source listing gives bibliographic (and where relevant online) information for published material. Frequently cited items of published material, given short references in the text (e.g. Morant, *Colchester*) are indicated in bold text. A concluding section gives information on (mostly online) catalogues and finding aids, which will be well-known to many readers but which indicate the sources of information I have drawn on as editor and suggest where readers in search of further details may turn to next.

Primary Sources, Location and References

ERO or NA references are given in dictionary entries. This section does not attempt to list all primary sources, simply those series often cited and/or where some further explanation is needed.

Alehouse Recognisances: Used in entries for innholders and inns to date various individuals' occupation of an inn. Not directly referenced in dictionary entries. Located in ERO.

Apprenticeships: JBB accumulated information on apprenticeships from a number of sources. Currently at NA, Kew on microfilm at IR 1, are the Inland Revenue Board of Stamps: Apprenticeship Books, 1710-1811. These supercede the 47 volumes, 1710-1774 indexed at NA IR 17. Copies of these were consulted by JBB at Guildhall Library and are now available online on subscription at www.britishorigins.net. Dictionary entries from this source are mostly referenced to NA IR 1, though some of John's early notes retain a reference to

Guildhall Library, Society of Genealogists, Index of Masters, 1710-1762, as IM, S929/1/…

JBB made wide use of Borough records of free burgess admissions to trace apprenticeships. Colchester burgesses were individuals whose fathers or grandfathers were free burgesses, or who had served an apprenticeship to a free burgess. Free burgesses were admitted at Borough Assemblies, or at its Monday and Thursday Courts. Having these sources readily to hand at first in the Castle strongroom and subsequently at the Colchester branch of ERO, JBB rarely noted the precise documentary source, and it has not been possible to re-examine and cross reference all these sources. Hence in many cases an apprenticeship identified in this way is not directly referenced in the dictionary entries, unless it has been traced in NA IR 1, where that reference is given. The Index to Admission of Freemen is also now viewable on SEAX at D/B 5 Fb2.

Court Records: Being a Borough, Colchester held its own Quarter Sessions and Petty Sessions, except for the period from 1741-1763 when the Borough Charter was in abeyance. All these records are in ERO. Quarter Sessions files (bundles) are in the series D/B 5 Sr. Quarter Sessions books are in the series D/B 5 Sb. Sessions Examination Books (Petty Sessions) are in the series P/CoR. For the 1750s, there are a few volumes of Lexden and Winstree Sessions (P/LwR) which cover the town.

Deeds: JBB was able to access, through friends, acquaintance and local booksellers, numbers of original deeds which are not on public deposit. Dictionary entries reference his photocopied or ms notes. Other deeds are on deposit at ERO. Some of them are hard to trace in the online catalogue, being part of the Record Office's acquisition of material previously held at Colchester Public Library, see reference C47. Where possible the dictionary entries also give the earlier CPL reference number, as listed on SEAX.

Free burgess admissions: See under apprenticeships above.

Maps and Plans: at ERO unless otherwise stated.

Marriage Licences: JBB very frequently resorted to Crisp's ms index to Essex marriage licences, still in CPL Local Studies section. These are well detailed indexes, often giving the name of the bond holder as well as the bride and groom, ages, occupations, and sometimes parish of marriage. These are referenced in dictionary entries to CPL Crisp ML(number). The number refers to the relevant page in Crisp's indexes, which occupy several (alphabetical) volumes, each of which begin at page 1. There will be more than one licence with the same ML reference, therefore, but the surname of the groom indicates which volume is relevant. These indexes also have an invaluable index by brides' surname. In editing the volume I also, with the assistance of Jane Bedford, consulted the marriage licence indexes at ERO (see references such as 'ERO ML D/ALL'). I have included both this and the Crisp reference where I have both available, to assist readers searching for the original licence. My thanks to Jane for chasing so many references.

Monumental Inscriptions: Some of these, of course, were noted by JBB from explorations of churches and churchyards. In this case dictionary entries mostly have no additional reference. Benjamin Strutt's *History of Colchester* (Colchester, 1803) contains a good listing of Colchester MIs in its second volume (cited as Strutt, *Colchester*). CPL also has Crisp's *Transcripts of Colchester Monumental Inscriptions* over several volumes, by parish (cited as CPL Crisp).

Newspapers: JBB made most use of the *Ipswich Journal*. He consulted this in hard copy at CPL, ERO and SRO, Ipswich and also later on microfilm. Confirmation of newspaper citations to original for the dictionary entries was undertaken on the microfilm copy at CPL. My thanks to Rita and Ken Sharpe who risked their eyesight undertaking most of this work. Some newspaper references in the dictionary entries, especially those to the *Chelmsford Chronicle* were compiled from my own MA and PhD researches.

Poll Books: JBB owned a full set of poll books for eighteenth-century Borough elections, including a photocopy of the ms poll book for 1735, then held in the ESAH library. CPL Local Studies holds a full set. Others are at ERO.

Rates and Land Tax: ERO holds a good run of late-eighteenth century Land Tax Assessments in the series Q/RPl. Survivals of parish rates are uneven. The most useful (for most of the town centre parishes) are listed in street order. They are in ERO amongst parish records in the D/P series'.

Sun Insurance: Viewed by JBB at Guildhall Library, where these records remain.

Trade Directories: The relevant directories for Colchester at this period are Bailey's *Directory* of 1784, the *Universal Directory* of 1791 and Holden's *Directory* of 1805.

Wills: Many wills cited in directory entries were those proved at the Archdeaconry Courts of Essex and Hertfordshire, held on microfilm and in original in ERO. Those for Colchester are mostly in the series' D/ACR or D/ABR, and so listed in F. Emmison's printed catalogues under secondary sources below. SEAX now invaluably lists alternative copies of the same wills in the D/ACW and D/ABW series', and is directly searchable online by testator's name. Where the JBB Dictionary entry or JBB's notes cited the D/ACR or D/ACR reference as in Emmison, I have retained it. On some occasions I cite the D/ACW or D/ABW reference extracted from SEAX.

These wills were proved locally and certainly by the second half of the eighteenth century tended to be wills of rather lower probate value. More affluent wills for the south of England were proved at the Prerogative Court of Canterbury (PCC). A pretty comprehensive series of these is at NA, catalogued at PROB 11. The catalogue is available online and documents can be downloaded for a small fee. JBB began exploring PCC wills in the late 1950s when they were held in the basement of Somerset House. They subsequently moved to what was then the Public Record Office at Chancery Lane. References under that system identified the register by the first surname appearing within it, and then the quire (folio) numbers.

Consequently the will of Thomas Boggis (qv), proved on 16 July 1790, is now at NA PROB 11/1193. The older PRO reference identified the will as Bishop 320. Generally the dictionary entries use the PROB 11 reference and date of proof only, since this is sufficient to identify the will on the online catalogue. Where the original draft dictionary entry used the older reference, sometimes the quire number is retained (in this case it would be NA PROB 11/1193/320). PROB 11 also includes wills proved in other small jurisdictions. The will of Revd Nicholas Corsellis (qv), for example was proved at Doctors Commons, reference Swabey 256. Here, the usual PROB 11 reference is given.

Secondary Sources

Benham, W.G., 'The Dunthornes of Colchester', *Essex Review*, 10 (1901) **(short reference, Benham, 'The Dunthornes')**

Bensusan-Butt, J., 'Jane and Ann Taylor as Engravers', *East Anglian Magazine*, 21 (1961)

Bensusan-Butt, J., 'The Gallant Story of Admiral (Sir Edmund) Affleck (MP)', *Essex County Standard*, 7 December 1962

Bensusan-Butt, J., 'A Gallery of High Stewards', *Essex County Standard*, 6 and 20 October 1967

Bensusan-Butt, J., *The House that Boggis Built*, revised edn. (Colchester, 1972) **(short reference, JBB, *The House that Boggis Built*)**

Bensusan-Butt, J., 'An Introduction to William Cole', *East Anglian History Workshop*, 2 (1981) (superceded by article in JBB, *EAE*:195-206)

Bensusan-Butt, J., 'A Friend to his Country: William Mayhew and the Recovery of the Colchester Charter, 1763', *Essex Archaeology and History*, 18 (1987) (the 1972, privately printed edition, deposited at ERO C905, is cited as **JBB, *A Friend to his Country*)**

Bensusan-Butt, J., S. D'Cruze (ed), *Essex in the Age of Enlightenment. Essays in Historical Biography* (Lulu, 2009) **(short reference, JBB, *EAE*)**

Blaxill, L., *The History of Lion Walk Congregational Church* (Colchester, 1939) **(short reference, Blaxill, *Lion Walk*)**

xix

Blaxill, L., *Nonconformist Churches of Colchester* (Colchester, 1946) **(short reference, Blaxill, *Nonconformist Churches*)**

Brown, A.F.J., *Colchester in the Eighteenth Century* (Colchester, 1969)

Brown, A.F.J., *Essex at Work 1700-1815* (Chelmsford, 1969)

Brown, A.F.J., *Essex People, 1750-1900* (Chelmsford, 1972)

Brown, A.F.J., *Colchester 1815-1914* (Chelmsford, 1980)

Burley, K.H., *The Economic Development of Essex in the Later Seventeenth and Early Eighteenth Centuries*, (PhD thesis, London 1957)

Cooper, J. et al., *The Borough of Colchester*, Vol. 9, *The Victoria County History of Essex*, (Woodbridge, 1994), available online at www.british-history.ac.uk **(short reference, *VCH Essex*, Vol. 9)**

Cromwell, T., *The History and Description of the Ancient Town and Borough of Colchester*, 2 Vols (Colchester, 1824) **(short reference, Cromwell, *Colchester*)**

Davidoff, L., 'Life is Duty, Praise and Prayer', *Fawcett Library Papers*, 4 (1981)

Davidoff, L. and Hall, C., *Family Fortunes, Men and Women of the English Middle Class, 1780–1850* (London, 1987)

D'Cruze, S., 'To acquaint the ladies'; Women Traders in Colchester c.1750–c.1800', *Local Historian*, 17 (1986)

D'Cruze, S., 'The eighteenth century attorney as political broker; the case of Francis Smythies', *Essex Archaeology and History, Transactions of the Essex Society for Archaeology and History*, 19 (1988)

D'Cruze, S., 'Our Times in Gods Hands', Religion and the Eighteenth Century Middling Sort, a Study of Colchester, Studies in Essex History (Chelmsford, 1990)

D'Cruze, S., *The Middling Sort in Provincial England: Politics and Social Relations in Colchester 1730-1800* (PhD thesis, Essex, 1990) **(short reference, D'Cruze, *Middling Sort*)**

D'Cruze, S., 'The Middling Sort in Eighteenth-Century Colchester: Independence, Social Relations and the Community Broker,' in Barry, J. and Brooks, C. (eds.), *The*

Middling Sort of People, Culture, Society and Politics in England, 1550-1800 (Basingstoke, 1994)

D'Cruze, S., *A Pleasing Prospect: Social Change and Urban Culture in Eighteenth-Century Colchester* (Hertford, 2008) **(short reference, D'Cruze, *Pleasing Prospect*)**

Farries, K., *Essex Windmills, Millers and Millwrights*, Vol. 2 (Edinburgh, 1984) **(short reference, Farries, *Windmills, Vol. 2*)**

K. Farries, *Essex Windmills, Millers and Millwrights*, Vol. 3 (Charles Skilton Ltd, 1984) **(short reference, Farries, *Windmills, Vol. 3*)**

Fitch, S.H.G., *Colchester Quakers* (Colchester, 1962) **(short reference, Fitch, *Colchester Quakers*)**

Foster, J., *Alumni Oxoniensis: The Members of the University of Oxford, 1715-1886: Their Parentage, Birthplace, and Year of Birth, with a Record of their Degrees; Being the Matriculation Register of the University* (Oxford, 1888) **(short reference, Foster, *Alumn. Oxon.*)**

French, H. *The Middle Sort of People in Provincial England, 1600-1750* (Oxford, 2007)

Gilbert, J, (ed.), *The Autobiography and Other Memorials of Mrs Gilbert*, 2nd edn (London, 1876) **(short reference Gilbert, *Mrs Gilbert*)**

Goose, N., 'The "Dutch" in Colchester: The Economic Influence of An Immigrant Community in the Sixteenth and Seventeenth Centuries', *Immigrants and Minorities* (1982)

Goose, N., 'The Rise and Decline of Philanthropy in Early Modern Colchester: The Unacceptable Face of Mercantilism?', *Social History*, 31 (2006)

Harrod, H., *Repertory of the Records and Evidences of the Borough of Colchester* (Colchester, 1865) **(short reference, Harrod, *Repertory*)**

Holman, P., 'The Colchester Partbooks', *Early Music*, 28 (2000)

Jephcott, J. A., *The Inns, Tavern and Pubs of Colchester* (Colchester, 2007) available at www.camulos.com **(short reference, Jephcott, *Inns*)**

Laver, H., 'The last days of baymaking in Colchester', *Transactions of the Essex Archaeological Society*, new series, 10 (1906)

Martin, G., *The History of Colchester Grammar School* (Colchester, 1947)

Martin, G., *The Story of Colchester* (Colchester, 1959)

Mason, B., *Clock and Watchmaking in Colchester, England* (Colchester, 1969)

Mason, S., *Essex on the Map* (Chelmsford, 1990)

Mason, S. and Bensusan-Butt, J., 'P. B. Scale: Surveyor in Ireland, Gentleman of Essex', *Proceedings of the Huguenot Society*, 24 (1988)

Morant, P., *The History and Antiquities of the Most Ancient Town of Colchester* (Colchester, 1748) **(short reference, Morant, *Colchester*)**

Morant, P., *The History and Antiquities of Essex* (Colchester, 1768) **(short reference, Morant, *Essex*)**

Namier, L. and Brooke, J., *The History of Parliament: The House of Commons 1754–1790* (London, 1964) **(short reference, Namier & Brooke, *House of Commons*)**

Penfold, J., *The History of Essex County Hospital, Colchester, 1820-1948* (Colchester, 1984)

Phillips, A., *Ten Men and Colchester* (Chelmsford, 1985)

Radcliffe, W., 'Thomas Tunmer and a Forgotten Spa', *The Practitioner*, 193 (1964)

Radcliffe, W., 'The Colchester Medical Society, 1774', *Medical History*, 20 (1976)

Rickwood, G.O., 'The Members of Parliament for Colchester', *Essex Review,* 7 and 8 (1899)

Romney Sedgwick, R., *The History of Parliament: The House of Commons, 1715–1754* (London, 1971) **(short reference, Romney Sedgwick, *House of Commons*)**

Royal Commission for Historic Monuments of England, *North East Essex* (London, 1922)

Sier, L.C., 'The Bluecoat School in Colchester', *Essex Review*, 54 (1940)

Sier, L.C., 'Charles Gray, MP of Colchester', *Essex Review*, 57 (1948)

Sier, L.C., 'The Ancestry of Charles Gray', *Essex Review*, 59 (1950)

Smythies, R.H., *Memorials of the Smythies Family* (London, 1912)

Speight, M.E., *Politics in the Borough of Colchester 1812-1847* (PhD thesis, London, 1959)

Spurrier, E., *Memorials of the Baptist Church, Eld Lane, Colchester* (Colchester, 1889) **(Short reference, Spurrier, *Eld Lane*)**

Spyvee, Henry, *Colchester Baptist Church - the first 300 years, 1689-1989* (Colchester, 1989)

Stephenson, D., *The Book of Colchester, a Portrait of a Town* (Buckingham, 1978)

Strutt, B., *The History and Description of Colchester*, 2 Vols (Colchester, 1803) **(short reference, Strutt, *Colchester*)**

Sweet, R., *The Writing of Urban Histories in Eighteenth-Century England* (Oxford, 1997)

Sweet, R., 'Antiquaries and Antiquities in Eighteenth-Century England', *Eighteenth-Century Studies*, 34 (2001)

Thorne, R.G., *The History of Parliament: The House of Commons 1790–1820* (London, 1986) **(short reference, Thorne, *House of Commons*)**

Twining, T., *A Selection of Thomas Twining's Letters 1734-1804: A Record of a Tranquil Life*, Walker, R.S. (ed.) (Lewiston, 1991) **(short reference, R. S. Walker (ed), *Thomas Twining*)**

Venn, J and J. A. Venn, *Alumni Cantabrigienses: A Biographical List of All Known Students, Graduates and Holders of Office at the University of Cambridge, from the Earliest Times to 1900*, (Cambridge, 1922-1954) **(short reference, Venn, *Alumn. Cantab.*)**

Finding Aids

The British Library catalogue is at http://catalogue.bl.uk.

Very many eighteenth-century English publications, including Morant's *Colchester* and his *Essex*, also Bailey's 1784 *Directory* are available with membership of a subscribing library (by Athens password) at *Eighteenth Century Collections Online* http://find.galegroup.com/ecco

The *IGI* and other genealogical data is available at http://www.familysearch.org

The *ERO*'s online catalogue is at http://seax.essexcc.gov.uk/

The extensive National Archives website, including catalogue, downloadable documents etc is at http://www.nationalarchives.gov.uk/ which also gives access to the large UK archives network A2A, and details of archive repositories at ARCHON (links on the 'search the archives' menu on main page).

The *Oxford Dictionary of National Biography*, (Oxford, 2004) is available online at http://www.oxford.dnb.com, with membership of a subscribing library.

Wills proved in the local Archdeaconry courts and deposited at ERO are catalogued online in SEAX and in, Emmison, F. G., *Wills at Chelmsford (Essex and East Hertfordshire)* (London, 1958-1969), Vol. 1. 1400-1619, Vol. 2. 1620-1720, Vol. 3. 1721-1858.

Colchester People

Volume 1

A-L

A

ABBOTT REVD JOHN DD [1]
Rector, All Saints
w. 1759/60

The father of Charles Abbott, the first Lord Colchester (*ODNB*).

Abbott's will (NA PROB 11/855 Lynch 180), made 16 July 1759, was not witnessed. Consequently at probate on 14 May 1760, Revd Thomas Skinner of St Botolphs, Bishopsgate, London (for whom see Jeremy Bentham, *The Correspondence of Jeremy Bentham*, I. Christie (ed), (London, 1968), Vol. 1:19) and James Bolton of the same place, merchant, made oath it was his writing. The will mentions Abbot's sons John Farr and Charles Abbott. The trustees were his wife Sarah, sister Elizabeth and father John Abbott together with his father-in-law Jonathan Farr.

See also: Matthew Abbott, All Saints, will 1786, ERO D/ACR 18/245; CPL Crisp ML340, ERO D/ACL 1754, Samuel Turner, West Mersea and Ephraim Shillito 2 (qv), Colchester, bound, Samuel (33) to marry Elizabeth Abbott (21) of All Saints.

ABBOTT WILLIAM [1280]
Woollen Draper, Tailor and Shopkeeper
w. 1804

Will NA PROB 11/1407, 14 April 1804.

See also: NA IR/17, William Abbott apprenticed to Thomas Haws jun., oyster dredger, Mersea, 3 gns, 1759; *IpsJ* 2 May 1777, auction of a messuage Black Boy Lane tenanted by William Abbott.

A

ABELL FRANCIS [4]
Saddler and Tanner
fl. 1762-1777

In 1760 Abell married Sarah Tillet (St Peters) of the family of High Street glovers (ERO ML D/ACL 1760). Francis Abell traded from premises owned by and next door to William Tillett (qv) at 149 High Street (rated 8), next the Foundry Yard, from 1760 until 1770 (*IpsJ* 14 April 1770) when Thomas Wood (qv) took over the saddlery as Abell was 'now engaged in the tanning business'. Abell had moved to Middleborough, a far more suitable site for a tannery being on the river by North Bridge. The premises were those left by Thomas Stevens (qv) carrier, to his daughter Sarah. Abell subsequently moved to East Donyland where on 29 March 1777 (*ChCh* 3 April 1777) he married advantageously to Mrs Bowman of Donyland Hall. The will of William Tillett (qv) made 6 September 1777 names Francis Abell, kinsman of East Donyland as an executor.

See also: 1766, Isaac Medcalfe app. to Francis Abell Colchester, saddler, £25 (NA IR 1/56/5); 1762, John Brock (qv) apprenticed to Francis Abell, £12 (NA IR 1/54/178); ERO Q/Sb 241/14, County Quarter Sessions Book, 12 July 1784, Gaol Calendar includes Martha wife Charles Baker, according to depositions of Francis Abell, Colchester, miller and Isaac Beardwell, Boxted, butcher, for having on 3 July 'stolen and carried away from off the stall of the said Isaac Beardwell in the open market in the parish of St Runwald ... six pounds of beef'.

ABELL FRANCIS TILLETT [3]
Attorney
fl. 1785-1838

The son of Francis Abell, saddler (qv) and Sarah *née* Tillett (daughter of Charles Tillett, hatter (qv)). He received £200 in the will of his grandfather Charles Tillett (qv) in 1785 and property at 150 High Street in that of his uncle William Tillett (qv) in 1787. Abell married Elizabeth Keep (22) daughter of the woolstapler of St Martins in 1804 (CPL Crisp ML89, ERO D/

ALL 1804) when he was described as a gentleman of St Runwalds aged 28. She died on 1 January 1807 aged 27 and was buried at Lion Walk though he himself was to receive an Anglican burial.

An entry in the Borough records (ERO D/B 5 Ta1), later crossed out, shows him apprenticed to Frank Smythies (qv) in 1785. He became a free burgess and voted from 1796 favouring a balanced representation. He was elected to the Corporation and served as Mayor in 1810 and 1819.

He died on the 25 May 1838 aged 74 and was buried at All Saints.

ABSOLON CHARLES [4]
Hythe Merchant
fl. 1786-1795

Nephew of Edward Snell (qv) merchant, from whom he inherited a corn and coal business at the Hythe (*IpsJ* 24 May 1794) that Snell had run in partnership with William Cook (qv). On taking over, Absolon solicited the favours of his customers, 'which he is determined to merit by a strict attention to their commands in the CORN and COAL TRADE.'

Sadly his career was short lived. In November, 1794 he made his will, just prior to a journey to Bristol for his health. He died on 10 March 1795 (*IpsJ*, 25 April 1795) apparently having never returned. His will (NA PROB 11/1260, Newcastle 214, proved 20 May 1795) left £100 to his father and £50 to his sister Martha. The bulk of the estate was to be sold, the proceeds to be divided between his father (thereafter to two other daughters by Absolon's father's second marriage) and Martha (thereafter to her children). The executor was John Eglonton Wallis (qv) who was married to Absolon's cousin Sarah (daughter of Edward Snell). Sarah was named as reversionary legatee of Martha's moiety. Wallis continued the business, as executor, advertising on 12 September 1795 (*IpsJ*).

A

JBB has also noted: William Absolon, pottery decorator and plant fancier of Yarmouth; William Absolon, victualler St Savior Southwark, NA PROB 11/1237, 7 October 1793.

AFFLECK SIR EDMUND, R.N., MP [5]
MP for Colchester Borough
ob. 1788

His family were of Dalham Hall near Newmarket. Their name was originally 'Auchinleck.' He was born 19 April 1725, fifth son of Gilbert Affleck, MP for Cambridge in 1737. An elder brother John was MP for Suffolk in 1743. On 15 July 1749 he married Hester Creffield *née* Hester Ruth (a widow) by licence, both then of Springfield (Springfield marriage register). This was a sound political alliance which connected Affleck with the leading Tory family of Creffield and with Charles Gray (qv) the Colchester MP who had married Hester's late husband's mother.

Affleck entered the navy as a lieutenant in 1745, was made captain in 1756 and commander the following March. He was later created rear admiral and 1st baronet.

In the American War he played a vital part in the British defeat of the French at St Kitts in 1782 fighting in the rear squadron which forced the attacking French to retreat. (French troops later forced the English garrison to surrender, however.) He earned further distinction on 12 April in the Battle of the Saints. Thereafter he served from 1782 to 1784 as Commissioner for the port of New York.

His absence did not prevent him from playing a leading role in Borough politics. At the 1780 election Charles Gray stood down and in default of an effective Tory candidate, Sir Robert Smyth (qv) was elected with Isaac Martin Rebow (qv) - two Whigs. Rebow's death the following year occasioned a by-election and Affleck, represented by his brother Philip, stood against Christopher Potter (qv), an outsider candidate. The campaign cost Potter £13,000 and he topped the poll with 634 votes to Affleck's 567. However he was later unseated on petition so Affleck gained the seat, whilst remaining on the other side of the Atlantic. He returned in 1784.

The *Ipswich Journal* reported that, 'Last Sunday arrived at his house in this town Commodore Edm. Affleck bart. one of the members for the Borough. He had arrived at Portsmouth last Friday afternoon in the *Assurance* Man of War from New York' (*Ips]* 16 January 1784; JBB NB Blue 1:28). His arrival was the occasion of a rumpus in the Borough Assembly. Though Affleck had paused on the way home to take his seat in the House of Commons, the Borough opposition maintained scruples as to whether his election was legal (*Ips]* 30 January 1784: JBB NB, Blue 1:28). A Corporation committee refused to add Affleck's name to a loyal address on the recent change of ministry, due to be presented by his fellow member Sir Robert Smyth. The Mayor William Seaber (qv), a brandy merchant, gave them a minute to change their minds but they would not so the Mayor ordered the town clerk to shut the book and dismissed the Assembly. The next week it was alleged to have been a put up job, a smart manoeuvre on the part of Seaber, who supported the defeated opposition candidate Christopher Potter. It was clearly the moment for Affleck to prove that he too was a generous benefactor. In a chilly winter, he gave £100 for distribution to the freezing poor (*Ips]* 7 February 1784).

Affleck silenced all doubts in the 1784 general election that April when he topped the poll with 665 votes. Potter came second with 425 and Smyth third with 416, Potter again lost the seat when after a petition the Commons ordered a re-run for second place, that July.

Affleck was only made a free burgess of the town after William Seaber was replaced as Mayor by Samuel Ennew (qv) in autumn 1784. He was sworn free burgess the first Monday in January of 1785 and gave a grand entertainment to the Corporation. A speech from Samuel Tyssen (qv) (another Potterite) to congratulate him concluded by Tyssen giving £50 to the freemen to 'drink the health of their worthy representative'. Either peace had been declared or Tyssen was

A

attempting to outdo the Admiral in generosity (*Ips*) 8 January 1785: JBB NB, Blue 1:32).

Affleck was on the committee of Jonas Hanway's benevolent Marine Society along with other local worthies Charles Gray (qv) and George Wegg 2 (qv). He had been named trustee in the will of Revd Richard Daniell (qv) (NA PROB 11/ 1049/46 Warburton, made 3 February 1779) together with Ambrose Godfrey, chymist, Covent Garden, James Round (qv) of Birch Hall (qv) and Edward Green of Lawford Hall Esq.

He had a London house and occupied another at 59 North Hill from 1764 till at least 1787. The North Hill house was rated 9 plus 20 personal estate (Notes on Deeds of 59 North Hill, JBB NB Blue 2:17-21). In 1784 or 5 he bought Fingringhoe Hall where he may have maintained a bear pit. Lady Affleck died in December 1787 and was buried at St Peters. She has a table tomb at the foot of the tower. The following May Affleck married a widow from New York, previously the wife of naval surgeon William Smythies 4 (qv). That November he died at his London house.

His will was made not long after his second marriage (NA PROB 11/1171, Calvert 513, Sir Edmund Affleck, bart., of Fingringhoe Hall, Essex and Queen Street East, Marylebone, made 28 June 1788, witnessed Allan MacMillan, Susannah MacMillan and Maria Short, servants to Sir Edmund, proved 24 November 1788 by his brother and nephew and again on 31 December 1788 by his widow).

He appointed his dearly beloved wife, Dame Margaret, his brother Philip Affleck and nephew William (both of Wimpole Street) as executors. He left £1,000 to his beloved niece Charlotte, the wife of Revd Thomas Sherrife; £1,000 to Elizabeth, the wife of Bower John Gibson of Mile End, Middlesex; £500 to his nephew Lieutenant William Affleck, RN, £100 each to his nephew Capt. William Affleck (the executor) and his niece Charlotte Metcalfe.

£5,000 was left in trust to his wife and 'much valued friend Captain Samuel Cornish', the interest 'to be applied to the Maintenance and Education of my natural daughter Charlotte

Brown as she now is called born in February 1785 and under the care of a Mrs Chandler, no. 9 in New Quebec Street', till her marriage with the Trustees' consent if living, or until she is twenty one. He further requested his wife, 'placing the utmost confidence in her', to take the girl 'under her guardianship and Protection as if she was her own and cause her to bear my Name'. If the girl should die before the age of twenty one, the trust money was left to his wife.

He left 'All my Capital Stock in the Long and Short Annuities' to his wife for the maintenance of her own son William Carlton Smythies until he was twenty one, or to buy him a commission in the army. Thereafter the money went to his wife. She also received absolutely his house in Queen Ann Street, and for life only the rents and profits of his estate and fisheries in Fingringhoe (from which last she had already £300 under her marriage settlement). After her death the Fingringhoe estate should go to whoever was the next baronet. The residue (chiefly consolidated stock) was left to his wife and brother Philip to divide share and share alike. Affleck asked to be buried at the family vault in Dalham Suffolk.

Philip Affleck was a full admiral at his death in 1799. The *Gentleman's Magazine* of that year described him as 'a zealous and brave officer and a firm advocate of the Christian religion. … An honest man and a faithfully affectionate friend.' He was made a Colchester free burgess the same day as Edmund Affleck.

See also: will of Elizabeth Affleck, widow (of Gilbert), Bury St Edmunds, proved 16 March 1775, NA PROB 11/1005/81, which appointed Edmund Affleck an executor; J. Bensusan Butt, 'The Gallant Story of Admiral (Sir Edmund) Affleck (MP), *Essex County Standard*, 7 December 1962; relevant entries in *ODNB*, L. Namier and J. Brooke, *The House of Commons 1754-1790*, (London, 1964).

A

AGNIS BENJAMIN [8]
Gardener
w. 1763/5

Second son of Thomas Agnis (qv). His will (ERO D/ACR 17/10) made 1763, proved 1765 leaves his lease of Middlewick Farm to his wife Elizabeth and son John, the executors and residuary legatees, to bring up his youngest son Robert. The other children; eldest son Benjamin, also Jacob, Elizabeth and Ann (see below), together with Robert at 21, received cash legacies of between £20 and £40. Agnis was a free burgess voting in 1747 for Nassau.

See also: William Cole, Wivenhoe, aged 25, to Ann Agnis, 20, St Giles 1766 (CPL Crisp ML134); JBB notes that the Lexden lands, part of Benjamin's legacy from his father Thomas (qv) were bought of Sarah and Elizabeth Cole.

AGNIS JOHN [7]
Gardener
fl. 1751-1808

Married Dorothy Mortier in 1751 (ML ERO D/ALL 1751). He was a free burgess and voted in 1768, 1780, 1781 and 1788, generally voting to obtain one Whig and one Tory MP.

Agnis occupied a house in East Street and garden ground called the Moores in St Botolphs which he owned. The Revd Richard Daniell's (qv) will of 1779 shows that Agnis also rented two fields called Golden Fields from Daniell. On 26 October 1771 (*IpsJ*) Agnis offered 100 pure apple plants for sale. He retired in 1807 and on 24 October (*IpsJ* 24 October 1807) his house and six acres of nursery garden were offered for rent. His will of 1807, proved in 1808 (ERO D/ACR 19/497, JBB NB 92/6) directed the rent to be paid to his two daughters, Hester the wife of Jeremiah Daniel (qv) customs officer and Dorothy Agnis, spinster who lived with her father. His trustees were James Mansfield the elder (qv) baymaker and Charles Heath (qv) gent of Colchester.

AGNIS ROBERT [9]
Gardener
w. 1782

Eldest son of Thomas Agnis (qv) from whom in 1733 he inherited the family house and garden ground called Childwell Moor, St Botolphs, where he then lived. This was in the valley beyond Moor Lane. His own will of 1782 (ERO D/ACR 18/155, JBB NB Feb 65) leaves this to his nephew and executor John Agnis (qv). Robert had no adult son, his boy Thomas being apparently young and sickly, receiving £5 only 'if living'. The bequest to John was also subject to cash legacies of £20 apiece to Robert's daughters Ann Wright, Mary Fiske and Abigail Agnis, as well as provision for his well beloved wife Ann in the form of £10 and two rooms in the house with their furniture. Robert and Ann had married in 1754 (CPL Crisp ML66, ERO D/ACL 1754) she being then Ann Manning, a widow of St Botolph's.

AGNIS THOMAS [6]
Gardener
w. 1733

The eldest of the Agnis dynasty of gardeners in St Botolphs. His will of 1733 (ERO D/ACR 14/398, JBB NB Striped:33) leaves a life interest in all his property to his wife Mary. Thereafter; to his son Robert, the garden ground in St Botolphs known as Childwell Moor (bought of Edward Raynham (qv)), the tenement in Queen Street (bought of William Carter) and £10; to his son Benjamin £10, 'Halfway House' St James (bought of Thomas Lucas) and lands at Lexden (bought of Sarah and Elizabeth Cole); to daughter Ruth Stace, two tenements on East Hill (bought of W. M. Carter); to daughter Ann Elliott £20; to daughter Elizabeth Wilder (wife of Francis Wilder (qv)) £50; £5 equally between the children of John Walker, carpenter and Sarah his wife lately deceased and £5 to daughter Priscilla Agnis.

A

ALDUS JOHN 1 [10]
Gardener
fl. 1741-1767

A free burgess voting in 1741 for Savage and Gray and in 1747 for Nassau and Gray. Was steward at the annual Auricula Feast at the Castle Inn in 1754 (*IpsJ* 4 May 1754). He died in 1767 and his wife and son advertised as follows:-

> Whereas JOHN ALDUS, gardener and Nursery Man, lately dwelling on EAST HILL in COLCHESTER, is now deceased. This is to acquaint those Gentlemen that used to favour him with their Custom, and others, that the business will be carried on by the Widow Aldus and her son John Aldus (qv); they hoping that such their friends will continue their favours to them, and may depend upon having their commands, duly expeditiously and carefully obeyed.... They have a great variety of choice Fruit Trees, as Peaches, Nectarines, and Apricots; with Apples, Pears, Cherries, and Plumbs, and all other sorts of Fruit Trees; fine young Virgin Quick, and Box for Edgings, & many Sorts of Evergreens, likewise a large Number of Mulberry-trees; all which are to be sold at a reasonable Rate (*IpsJ* 31 January 1767).

ALDUS JOHN 2 [11]
Gardener
fl. 1767-1807

Together with his mother, took over the business on the death of his father John Aldus 1 (qv) in 1767 (*IpsJ* 31 January 1767). His premises were partly in St Botolphs (rated 11) and partly at the bottom of East Hill (north side), St James, just below the Goat and Boot. Aldus was a free burgess and a regular voter from 1768 until his death. He supported Fordyce in 1768 and 1780, but did not subsequently vote for Potter.

ALEFOUNDER ALICE [15]
Schoolmistress
fl. 1750-1801

Née Hemstead of Great Cornard, she married Upcher Alefounder (qv) in 1750 (nfr); their son James was born some eighteen months later. Doubtless in order to augment her husband's income from the Customs following his bankruptcy in 1760, she opened a boarding school for Young Ladies in Trinity Street (when Mrs Lisle declined business, *IpsJ* 5 July 1760). Two years later, she advertised:-

> Mrs A. Alefounder, in Trinity Street, Colchester, begs leave to acquaint the Public, that her BOARDING SCHOOL for Young Ladies opens again on Monday the 28th of this Instant June; where due Care will be taken to instruct those entrusted to her, in everything requisite for a genteel and useful Education, to the utmost of her Abilities....

In 1764 she moved the school to Wivenhoe (*IpsJ* 17 March 1764) probably consequent on Upcher's appointment in Brightlingsea.

Alice inherited all her husband's estate on his death in 1781, including a house at the Hythe which was sold in May 1784 (*IpsJ* 15 May 1784, JBB Alefounder Notes, ERO C905, Box 2). In her later years she seems to have joined the Independent Meeting at Lion Walk and appears as a member there from 1797. She died in 1801. Her will (ERO D/ACR 19/248, made 15 December 1800, proved 6 April 1801) left the bulk of her estate comprising household goods and personal effects to her grandson George Alefounder, including various silver cutlery, a watch 'and the copper plate picture of him with his cousin Anna Maria Jane Alefounder. The same picture is framed and glazed and called 'Pleasing Intelligence' (and see also John Alefounder 3 (qv)). Her nephew Stephen Hemstead a surgeon of Market Ilsley, Berkshire received her silver tankard, it 'being family plate' and acted as executor with her friend Revd William Kemp, dissenting minister. Kemp was a baptist and

A

not a presbyterian minister, but her allegiance to Lion Walk was demonstrated in that she left Revd Giles Hobbes, also her friend, her 'Pebble Snuff box I usually wear in my pocket.' She requested to be buried, at St Leonards alongside her husband 'but not until my body shall begin to putrify'.

ALEFOUNDER JOHN 1 [1223]
Carpenter
1701-1763

Son of Edmund, apprenticed to Henry Bevan 1 (qv), 1714 for £8 (NA IR 1/43/156).

Free burgess by right of service, 1725. Common Councilman, 1734. Nominated Assistant in new Charter 1763, but died before it arrived in September. Buried, table tomb, St James, 14 June 1763.

His premises were 'opposite the Ship' on the lower corner of Land Lane, East Hill.

Records of payments – Chamberlains Vouchers: 1726, £8 15s 4½d; 1735 for East Bridge £31 1s 0½d; 1737, £4 19s ½d (ERO D/B 5 Ab1/27, 32); Winsleys Trustees, 1754, £7 13s 6d (ERO D/Q/30; JBB Report to Winsley's Trustees, ERO C905, Box 7).

Apprentices – (Guildhall Library, Society of Genealogists, Index of Masters, 1710-1762, hereafter IM, S929/1/5533), John Staines, 1731, £8 (notes on his will, of St Botolphs, 1780, JBB NB Jun64); Samuel Hartigrave, (made free 1734, votes from Greenwich, 1747, 1768, 1781); (IM S929/1/2283) Benjamin Gould (Gools), 1751, 12 gns. (created free burgess 29 February 1768, of Harwich, Assembly Book; *IpsJ* 28 February 1783, Harwich, Thursday last died Mr Benjamin Goules, mariner, aged 93 and oldest inhabitant. 'No apothecary ever attended him till within a few days of his death.'); (IM S/929/1/6244) George Wheeler, 1758, 12 gns.

Alefounder married at All Saints in 1724 to Elizabeth Upcher (ERO D/P 200/1/8. She died 10 March 1763, just before he did). They had eight children, as follows (legacies in his will of 1763 in parenthesis): (£25) John 2 (qv), bn. 1732, Free School

A

(ERO T/B 217/1) 1744, architect and surveyor in London; (£100) Robert (qv), bn. 1738, Free School 1748, grocer and quartermaster; (£25) Upcher (qv), bn. 1725, apprenticed to a baymaker, failed as one and later in Customs; (£150) James, bn. 1736, pawnbroker in London, dd. 1774; (£500 at 21) Lucy (qv), bn. 1745, married (1) Philip Havens, (qv) baymaker, in 1768, then (2) Capt. Robert Bass in 1789; (£300) Elizabeth, bn. 1734, married Peter Dawson, London, 'slop-seller'; (£300) Mary bn. 1730, married Kenelm Dawson in trade with Peter, above (for his trade card see Ambrose Heal, *London Tradesmen's Cards of the Eighteenth Century; their Origins and Use* (London, 1925), no. xvii); (£500 at 21) Sarah, bn. 1742, married (1765) Robert Kendall (qv), draper St Runwalds.

Alefounder's will, NA PROB 11/889, 21 July 1763, Caesar 319, also named son Robert and Isaac Green (qv) as executors, and left them £20 each for their trouble. The residue, if any, was left to Lucy and Sarah.

ALEFOUNDER JOHN 2 [1224]
Architect and Surveyor
1731/2-1787

Son of John Alefounder 1 (qv) and Elizabeth *née* Upcher. Baptised St James 19 March 1731/2. Entered the Free School aged 12, in 1744 (ERO T/B 217/1).

The following advertisement appears to refer to him: (*IpsJ* 8 March 1746) 'Mr William Penry, at Mr Lodge's, upholsterer, (Henry Lodge (qv)) in Colchester...who cures the impediment of Speach (sic) commonly call'd STUTTERING or STAMMERING.' Penry had claimed to have cured the son of Mr Alefounder of Colchester and also the son of Mr Richardson of Witham (also *IpsJ* 12 July 1746).

Apprenticeship not found – perhaps because the Country Registers are missing 1745-1750.

1752, a note on the back of an SPCK document addressed to the Revd Abbot Upcher at Bury St Edmunds says John Alefounder is 'at Mr Hillier, Lambs Conduit Passage, Red Lyon St.' An

A

Edmond Hilliard is listed in Holborn rate-book (nfr, but see London Metropolitan Archives, St Andrews, Holborn; JBB Alefounder Notes, ERO C905, Box 2).

1753, (ERO D/ALL 1753) married Sarah Vaughan (born 1733) of Greenstead Hall, who died 23 September 1762 aged 29, and is buried in the family altar-tomb at Greenstead. Her two children, John, born 1758, and George, born 1756, were cared for by their grandmother Ann Vaughn, who, dying in 1768 aged 72, passed the responsibility on to her sister Sarah Burdox 'untill they shall be fit to be put out apprentices to such trades as they shall take a liking to' (Will ERO D/ABW 103/1/25, spelt Vaughan; JBB NB Silver:66; see also Henry Vaughn (qv)). There is no mention of their father, of whom there is no certain visit to Colchester before 1775.

In County Elections, by right of freeholds in Colchester, John voted from London (1763), Homerton (1768) and Avemary Lane (1774). This involved traveling only to Chelmsford and not to Colchester.

Under the Building Act, 14 Geo 3 c.78, he was appointed District Surveyor of the parish of St Lukes Old Street and the Liberty of Glasshouse yard (parts of Finsbury) in 1774.

Thus, on 10 July 1775 he is finally admitted free burgess in Colchester, 'Architect and Surveyor' of Avemaria Lane, but he never voted in Borough elections.

In 1776 his son John entered the Royal Academy Schools as an architectural student, but George appears in all the Poll Books 1781-1796 as a farmer at Wenham Hall, Suffolk. From 1812 onwards he is of Colchester. He is buried with his mother at Greenstead, 1840.

Of John's architectural activity in London, nothing has been found. Only that 17 December 1776 he was called to report on progress of work on St Alphage, London Wall (architect William Hillyer).

1774, for the work of architect and surveyors under the Building Act of this year, see John Summerson, *Georgian London*, (London, 1945):125 ff. On p. 111 he mentions two carpenters, Cock and Hillyard who took some sites on Berkeley

Sq. in 1747, for development. Might this be the Edmond Hilliard, with whom Alefounder lodged in 1752? London research is beyond the scope of this Dictionary, but in 1962 I (JBB) explored St Luke's Rectory (1774 on rainwater heads). A large and interesting building, with columnar balusters etc. The biggest undertaking of the period in this parish was St Luke's Hospital by George Dance junior, 1782-9.

1776, Chancery case NA C12 1636/8, Alefounder v. Dawson. James Alefounder (brother of John 2), pawnbroker, died in 1774. John 2 intervened on behalf of his two children (aged 6 and 4) alleging that Peter Dawson who married his sister Elizabeth (see under John Alefounder 1 (qv)) had diverted £1,000 from their upkeep. Obviously a family quarrel. (I do not know the outcome.)

1779, a document at ERO D/DGn 17 is a draft agreement between William Jacobs Esq and John Alefounder re a passage on the east side of Alefounder's property on the corner of Land Lane. Alefounder gave up any claim on it, Jacobs making a paled fence along Alefounder's boundary, and Alefounder blocking it at its south end. Alefounder's tenant was a Mrs Sparling, but the house was empty after this between 1780-1785 at least, and only occupied again in 1790 when George Alefounder had succeeded to the premises and a Revd Mr Green occupied it.

He died intestate in March 1787, late of St Mary's Islington. Administration was granted in September to his son George (JBB NB Red I:92. However this appears to refer to John Alefounder 4, see NA PROB 31/767, exhibit 1787/644, and also also a will in NA PROB 11 for John 4).

This amount of attention to John Alefounder comes from the notion in Bensusan Butt, *The House that Boggis Built* (1978): 17-18, that he might have had a hand in the design of the Minories. But he gives the impression of avoiding Colchester, and not being popular in the family.

A

ALEFOUNDER JOHN 3 [1225]
Portrait Painter
1758-1794

Born 1758, son of John Alefounder 2 (qv) and Sarah *née* Vaughan of Greenstead Hall. She died 1762 and he was brought up by his grandmother Ann Vaughn until her death in 1768 then by her sister Sarah Burdox (see under John Alefounder 2 (qv); Henry Vaughn (qv)).

His father, taking his Colchester freedom in 1775, may then have taken charge of him, entering him in the Royal Academy schools as an architectural student. However John 3 turned to painting instead.

He took his freedom in Colchester 6 October 1783, but did not vote save in the second (July) election of 1784 when the outsider Christopher Potter lost his seat, in spite of a rally to him by a town party around Thomas Boggis (qv) and the last minute candidature of Samuel Tyssen (qv). Tyssen gained 26 votes, enough to enable him to petition. John 3's brother George from Wenham Hall in Suffolk, and his brother-in-law Robert Kendall 1 (qv) (draper married to Sarah *née* Alefounder) were both Tyssen voters.

As to his painting, J.T. Smith in his *Nollekens and his Times* (London, 1829, reprint, London, 1986):258, mentions his portrait of Moses Kean, actor and tailor.

Made his will 11 January 1785, (NA PROB 11/1266, Newcastle, proved 10 October 1795) when of Bow Street, Covent Garden, painter, 'intending shortly to depart to Bengal.' He left all his worldly estate in trust for his dear wife Maria Jane *née* Curd (? illegible) or Evans to have the interest, and after that to his brother George of Wenham Hall in trust for his godson George, son of the late John Alefounder 4 (qv), surgeon in the Navy (this John was son of Upcher Alefounder (qv)).

20 February 1789, Mrs Alefounder published a print by William Redmore Bigg (qv) called *Pleasing Intelligence* portraying her with this godson at 25 Bow Street, with a letter addressed to her 'per Swallow packet' reporting his prosperity

in Bengal (B.M. Catalogue of Engraved British Portraits, mezzo print. Subject, Mrs Alefounder holding letter with young son standing by her. pub. Mrs A. 1789. ERO C905, Alefounder notes, Box 2; JBB, *EAE*:192).

Gents. Mag. 55, (October 1795):880 reports his death in Calcutta 'thriving very well in his profession,' but sad to say, Sir William Foster's *British Artists in India 1760-1820* (London, 1931) gives a long account of his lack of success and suicide.

ALEFOUNDER JOHN 4 [1283]
Naval Surgeon
ob. 1787

The son of Upcher Alefounder (qv) and his wife Alice Alefounder (qv). Was apprenticed to John Fiske (qv) surgeon for £45 in 1767 (NA IR 1/56/38).

He died intestate in March 1787, late of St Mary's Islington. Administration was granted in September to his son George. (NA PROB 31/767, exhibit 1787/644, probate inventory, presented by wife Sarah Alefounder). But see also NA PROB 11/1132, will of John Alefounder, surgeon in the Navy, of Colchester, 6 June 1786.

His son George had a reversionary interest in the will of John Alefounder 3.

ALEFOUNDER ROBERT [14]
Linen Draper and Grocer
fl. 1738-1784

Attended Colchester Free School, admitted in July 1728 (ERO T/B 217/1). A free burgess admitted in the Monday Court on 16 January 1764 and described as a grocer and son of John Alefounder 1 (qv), carpenter. Announced in 1760 (*IpsJ* 28 July 1760, JBB NB 82/3:17) that he was the late apprentice of John Wallis (qv) (NA IR 1/52/7, in 1754 for £40) and had taken his shop opposite the Three Cups. Received £120 in his father's will (PROB 11/889, proved 21 July 1763, JBB NB Red I:61) of

A

which he was an executor. Later left Colchester and voted in 1781 from Woolwich, described as a 'gent'.

Alefounder was Quartermaster of the 25th Regiment of Foot in 1768 and later became surveyor in the Customs, Woolwich, where he made his will in 1784. (NA PROB 11/1121, Rockingham 488, made 22 June 1784, proved 24 September 1784, JBB Red 1:76). He left his sisters Mary Dawson, Elizabeth Dawson (see under entry for John Alefounder 2 (qv)) and nephew Philip Havens 2 (qv) £100 in 3% consolidated Bank Stock each. Philip Havens also received 'my Dressing table, Bason, Bottle and chamber pot china ware...' His brother John Alefounder 2 (qv) was left £5 for mourning. Nephews and nieces were remembered as follows: nephew George Alefounder, 25 gns; nephew Robert Alefounder, £100 in 3 per cents at 18 years - interest to be paid him annually till then by the executrix, who is to have the £100 if he died; nieces Ann Havens, Lucy Havens and nephew Robert Havens each received £50 in 3 per cents; nephew John Alefounder received £5 for mourning. He also left 'a very handsome mourning ring each' to Mr Thomas, Mr Isaac and Mr James Boggis (all qv). 'The residue and remainder of my Estate', was left to 'to my sister Lucy Havens' (see under Lucy Baas (qv)) who was named as sole executrix.

Was buried in St James, Colchester with his parents on 17 August 1784 (St James Registers, JBB Alefounder Notes). The nephew Robert Alefounder named in the will was the son of this Robert Alefounder's brother James. This nephew may be R.A. Esq Lieut in E Essex militia who married Miss Swale dtr of Mrs Swale of Ipswich (*IpsJ* 10 November 1798) and cf *IpsJ* 24 September 1809, sale of his furniture at Ipswich, 'as he is changing his residence.' The son of the nephew Robert was presumably Robt Swale Alefounder, created free burgess 3 April 1826.

ALEFOUNDER UPCHER [12]
Customs Officer, late Baymaker
1725-1785

The son of John Alefounder, carpenter (qv) and Elizabeth, *née* Upcher who had married in 1724. Upcher Alefounder was baptised at St James on 4 July 1725. He was apprenticed to Thomas Hills, baymaker, finished his training on 4 October 1743 (Essex Order Books ERO Q/508:9) and set up in the bay trade on his own account. He married Alice Hemstead at Little Cornard in 1750 (nfr) and their son John was baptised at St James on 16 February 1752.

Alefounder failed as a baymaker in 1756 (1 May 1756 *IpsJ*), but far from disappearing from town life, he made himself a new career and a modest competence in the Customs. In 1763 he received £25 in his father's will, and the following year he took up his Borough freedom with the renewal of the Charter (26 January 1764). In 1768 he was Tide Surveyor at Brightlingsea (Poll Book) and by 1778 he held two posts, that of Landwaiter at £40 p.a. and of Searcher at £8 (Land Tax). The Borough Poll Book of 1781 describes him as Tide Surveyor at Brightlingsea. He was an unadventurous voter supporting Rebow and Gray in 1768; Rebow in 1780 and Affleck in 1781 (posts in the Customs were in Isaac Martin Rebow's (qv) patronage). While far from a wealthy man he held a respectable place in the community and was active in St Leonards vestry. He died in the first quarter of 1784. His house (a 'two up, two down', rated 3 in 1783) was offered for sale described as well built, on 15 May 1784 (*IpsJ*, JBB Alefounder Notes, ERO C905, Box 2). His will of 1784/5 (ERO D/ABR 27/496) had left all his estate, including goods, chattels and securities as well as the house, to his wife Alice (qv). He was buried at St Leonards. (cf will Alice Alefounder (qv)).

A

ALVIS PETER [16]
Cordwainer
w. 1743

Tradesman and exciseman in All Saints. Witnessed the will of Nathaniel Barnes in 1740 with Peter Thorne, tallowchandler (ERO D/ACR 15/331), that of Elizabeth Summers, widow, All Saints together with Joseph Tanner (D/ACW 29/2/14, 1742), Ephraim Shillito 1 (qv) in 1741 (ERO D/ACR 15/115, 1742), and that of James Boys (qv) merchant, made in 1737 (NA PROB 11/737 proved 11 February 1745).

His burial records him as 'Peter Alvis, sometime an exciseman, universally esteemed a good Christian. ... a great minded man in low life whom future days will be found in a more exalted state (CPL Crisp MI; JBB Notebook 74/10:41). He left funding of £2 10s to support the Borough's Wednesday Lecture (see below) in his will (ERO D/ACR 15/139, 1742/3) as well as small legacies including £10 to his friend Ephraim Shillito 1 (qv) and £2 10s to Hester the wife of Samuel Phillips.

See Morant, *Colchester*, Book 1:100 for the office of Borough General Preacher and the (by the mid-eighteenth century, generally lapsed) Sunday and Wednesday Lectures. Morant also notes that the existing Sunday Lectures in the late 1740s were then kept up only by contributions.

ANDERSON THOMAS [18]
Linen Draper
fl. 1791

Advertised in April 1791 (*IpsJ* 9 April 1791) from the sign of the Hope and Anchor, the south side of the High Street, formerly Robert Kendall 1 (qv), just uphill from the Red Lion. The same year, aged 25, he married Martha Daniell (20) of St Peters, Colchester (*IpsJ* 23 April 1791, CPL Crisp ML75, ERO D/ACL 1791). In December 1791 his premises suffered an 'alarming fire' which 'raging with great violence, seemed to threaten devastation to the houses adjoining.' The damage was reckoned at £1,000, but the premises and stock were insured.

Anderson advertised his thanks to the public and that he hoped to resume trade shortly (*IpsJ* 17 December 1791).

In 1805 he married for a second time to Lydia Rutland, aged 25 of Hemptead (CPL Crisp ML89, ERO D/ALL 1805). The couple lived in a newly-built house, Beverley Lodge, on Lexden Road (now Gurney Benham House, Colchester Royal Grammar School. JBB notes on Deeds of Beverley Lodge, ERO C905 Box 10, under R. D. Mackintosh). Lydia Anderson lived there as a widow, but by 1813 the property had passed through two subsequent occupiers and was held by Benjamin Harris Esq.

See also NA IR 1/18/32 Thos son of Thos Anderson apprenticed to John Hopkins citizen and waxchandler, £21, 1747.

ANDREWS THOMAS [19]
Brewer
fl. 1769-1815

His mother was one of the Suffolk Cobbold brewing family (Jephcott, *Inns*:34, 40). Andrews was already trading as a brewer in 1769 when one William Trusson (cf Samuel Todd (qv)) drowned in a vat of Strong Beer 'at Mr Andrew's brewery' (CPL, *John Inman's Journal* 8 January 1769). Andrews established a very considerable business holding in Colchester, the extent of which is reflected in the insurances of his premises in 1776, which amounted to £2,300 (Sun Insurance 374368). These included his own dwelling on North Hill (rated 34), his brewery St Leonard (rated 43 in 1783) and a string of inns including the Star and Anchor, the Mitre (St James), Bishop Blaize (St Martin), Sun (St Nicholas), Coach and Horses (St Peter). Rate books also show him as owner of the Griffin (St Runwald), the Royal Oak (St Martin), the George (St Nicholas) between 1785-95, as well as property in St Giles (rated 9 and 4, 1786). He also rented granaries in St Botolphs (rated 44, 1793). The North Hill premises included a malting that was damaged by fire in 1799 (*IpsJ* 6 July 1799).

A

A portrait of Andrews by the Comte de Berenger survived in the Hollytrees Library photo collection. He married twice, to Miss Hussey, daughter of Napthali Hussey (qv) of Colchester in 1789 (ERO ML D/ALL) and to Miss Woodthorpe of Hollesley, Suffolk in 1801 (*IpsJ* 7 November 1801).

He was created free burgess on 27 July 1783 by right of apprenticeship to Samuel Todd (qv), beer brewer. Politically, he was a consistent Tory, voting in 1784, 88, 90 and 1812. His July 1784 vote for Tyssen implicates him in the pro-Potter faction. This and his election as Common Councillor on 5 September 1785 makes him a possible candidate as 'Tom Skylight' in the satirical notice of the Potterite petition committee in 1785 (cf James Green (qv)). He was made Assistant on 31 July 1789.

He died on 7 January 1815 (*IpsJ* 14 January 1815), 'in an apoplectic fit aged 75 ... universally beloved for his unbounded benevolence'. His will of 1798/1815 (NA PROB 11/1564, Pakenham, 21 January 1815) left a total of £2,550 in cash legacies to Mrs Jane Pattrick of Marks Tey, (cf Samuel Todd (qv)), the children of William Smith 2 (qv), Colchester wine merchant, Mrs Rebecca Hewitt Woodthorp, servant William Deeks, the widow of servant John Sparrow, and also £100 to the Bluecoat and £50 to the Presbyterian Charity Schools. The residue was distributed in small sums to various Cobbolds and Rouths, mainly of Ipswich.

ANGIER BEZALIEL 1 [991]
Miller
ob. 1783

Owned St Ann's mill, Harwich Road. An earlier post mill appears on maps from the late seventeenth century. Bezaliel Angier erected a brick tower mill on this site ('Goggle-fields'), which he had purchased in 1759 from Elizabeth Jackson of Aldham for £200 (ERO D/DEt T7). This mill burned down in 1767 (*IpsJ* 13 June 1767).

> On Saturday morning last, a windmill belonging to Mr Angier of this town, took fire, and notwithstanding all

possible assistance, and the engines having a tolerable supply of water, it burnt down to the roundhouse before the flames could be extinguished; the roundhouse is greatly damaged, and a considerable quantity of wheat and flour entirely destroyed (Farries, *Windmills*, Vol. 3:94).

A Colchester voter from 1768, voting so as to produce a one Whig, one Tory representation.

His will (NA PROB 11/1104) was made on 20 January 1783 and proved on 19 June 1783. He left his loving wife Ann the household goods, the interest on £200 in stock and annuities as well as on the proceeds of sale of messuages in St James, Colchester and other personal estate for life, plus a life interest in tenanted messuages and farms in Wivenhoe and St James Colchester (occupied in part by son-in-law Richard Cracknell), thereafter to be sold to pay cash legacies by his trustees, son Bezaliel Angier 2 (qv) and sons-in-law James Hague, merchant of St Anns, Middlesex and Bezaliel Blomfield ygr, Colchester, maltster.

On the death of his widow, his three daughters (Ann Blomfield, Sarah Cracknell and Mary Hague) were to receive £50 apiece from the sale of St James property, any remainder going to Bezaliel 2, the three daughters, the children of his late daughter Dorcas (who had married Joseph Posford) and grandson John Angier son of deceased son John.

Other trust monies were to be divided into six shares left to; Bezaliel 2, daughter Ann, daughter Mary, the children of Dorcas equally at age 21, grandson John Angier at 21, the interest of the remaining share to daughter Sarah for her sole use for life then to her children equally at 21.

On 18 August 1824, after the deaths of the original trustees, Joseph Cracknell one of the children of Sarah Cracknell received the residue of her sixth share.

A

ANGIER BEZALIEL 2 [1286]
Miller, Mayor 1788
ob. 1801

The son of Bezaliel Angier 1 (qv) and wife Ann. Married Mary Blomfield of Ardleigh in 1760 (CPL Crisp ML43).

Of St Ann's Mill, Harwich Road. Farries notes that 'Angier (probably the younger) insured the tower mill in 1796, for £100, the standing and going gears for £200 and the stock in trade for £200' (Farries, *Windmills*, Vol. 3:94).

Had been apprenticed to his father, as an 'oatmeal maker'. Created free burgess and Common Councillor on the same day, 5 September 1785. Angier was one of the group of tradesmen whose election to the Borough Corporation marked the coming to power of the Tory Corporation party, lead by Francis Smythies (qv) Town Clerk (Assembly Book 29 August and 10 September 1785, *IpsJ* 3 September 1785). Angier was created Assistant on 6 December 1787 and Alderman on 8 June 1788 – this last to enable him to serve as Mayor for that year. 1788 saw a heavily contested by-election when the radical George Tierney (qv) narrowly beat the candidate favoured by the Corporation Party, George Jackson (qv). Angier, as Mayor, acted as the returning officer. He and Francis Smythies (then the Recorder) manipulated the voting by opening and closing the poll *ad lib* and creating new burgesses by the score. They were severely challenged by a popular candidate and an organised opposition. Finally, the Mayor closed the poll with the votes at 640 apiece and returned BOTH candidates, hoping to secure Jackson his seat on petition (Namier & Brooke, *The House of Commons*, Vol 3:525, 668). The petition was unsuccessful and Angier (together with another Alderman Edward Capstack (qv)) also had to face a law suit from Tierney for misconduct at the election. The Corporation nevertheless voted their support to the Mayor (Assembly Book 20 July 1789). Tierney was beaten in the general election of 1790 and left Colchester to contest Southwark (for fuller account see D'Cruze, *The Middling Sort*, Chapter 8; D'Cruze, 'The Eighteenth-Century Attorney as Political Broker: the case of

Francis Smythies', *Essex Archaeology and History*, 19 (1988): 223-230).

Bland's Anecdotes (Appendix 3) are generally uncomplimentary about the Tory Aldermen who support Francis Smythies in the 1780s and 90s, and Angier is no exception.

> Bezaliel Angier once, as Chief Magistrate of Colchester, presented an address to the King. He was accompanied by the Corporation and the Town Clerk (Francis Smythies). They breakfasted together the morning of their admission to the King, and poor Beza was tutored by Frank how to go through the approaching ceremony. Amongst other cautions he told him he must not betray his want of breeding by misplaced timidity, but must kneel at the foot of the throne in presenting the address, which being received, he must rise and, with something like an air of confidence, take his silk handkerchief from his pocket and gently wipe his mouth. This he undertook to observe most religiously. Frank, who was a wag, contrived during breakfast to slip into the Mayor's pocket 'a hull of fat pork', which formed one of the delicacies of the morning's repast, and they all set off in proper trim to St James's Palace. The King received them graciously, and Beza went through the ceremony of presentation very well, and observed his instructions given him. Arising, he pulled out his handkerchief (a new silk one prepared for the occasion), when to his terror and dismay, out flew the unfortunate piece of pork, which rolled to the foot of the throne. Happily, however, for the worthy representative of the Colchester people, the circumstance passed unobserved by the Court, which was crowded, but not so by his own party, and he declared afterwards that he thought he should have swoonded when he saw the pork roll to the foot of the 'Kanopy' (quoted in Farries, *Windmills*, Vol. 3:94, see also Appendix 3, *Bland's Anecdotes*:47).

Ips] 14 January 1792 also notes that an 'enormous globular stone, spherical, 2ft circumference, 14lbs averdupoife' has been found in the body of cart mare which had died suddenly, belonging to Bezaliel Angier Esq.

Angier made his will on 23 March 1794 (NA PROB 11/1358, proved 17 June 1801). He left his son Henry a farm at Ardley (sic), several rented houses, a share in his granary at the Hythe and £500 to be paid by his son John out of the estate within 12 months. His son John received his water and windmills together with the working implements, his dwelling house and other land bought with the mills in Ardley. Daughter Mary Cooper and heirs received £400 (she married 13 November 1792 at Hadleigh to Edward Cooper, grazier, *ex inf* Bruce Neville). Henry and John, the joint executors, shared his interest in sailing sloops and the Hythe granary.

Henry, however, predeceased his father (died 26 October 1796, buried at St James). Bezaliel Angier died on 17 March 1801 and is buried at St James (*ex inf* Bruce Neville).

John Angier married Mary Parker in 1802 (CPL Crisp ML 98). He continued to operate St Anns mill, but being insolvent, mortgaged it for £1,100 and transferred his interest in it to John Angier jun in 1828 (Farries:94). The mill was for auction in 1834.

(*Essex County Standard*, 10 October 1834) by direction of Trustees for the sale of the estates of Mr John Angier;

> all that well-known capital brick TOWER WINDMILL – 6 acres – 'on a most commanding eminence just at the entrance of the town, and with a quarter of a mile from the Hythe' in St James. Apply Mr John Angier jun on the premises. At present works only two pair of French stones.

ARDLEY THOMAS [1255]
Carpenter
w. 1798

1755, carpenter of All Saints, married Sarah Till of St Runwalds (nfr, no marriage in St Runwald registers 1751-9, no ML in Crisps Indexes, CPL).

Worked for Winsleys Trustees, with Hitchcock 1778, 1780 and in 1774 with William Catchpool (ERO D/Q/30/2). Odd jobs in Chamberlains Accounts, 1778-1783 (ERO D/B 5 Aa2/1).

Will ERO D/ACR 19/137, proved 1798, 'yoeman.' Owns messuages in Black Boy Lane. A Baptist. George Rootsey and Isaac Diss (qv) executors. Annuity trust with Richard Patmore (qv), £30 p.a. for housekeeper Elizabeth Spooner. After her to sister Elizabeth, wife of William Perrie of Portland St, London, carpenter.

ARGENT WILLIAM [22]
Baymaker
fl. 1784-1820

Bland (*Bland's Anecdotes*, Appendix 3) is very uncomplimentary about William Argent, alleging he started his career as livery servant to Mrs Sperling of Dines (Dynes) Hall who retired to Colchester and died (cf will of M. R. Hills (qv)) thereupon Argent entered the bay trade as a rougher and sorter to some of the wealthier baymakers of the town. It is better documented that Argent rose under the auspices of Frank Smythies (qv) the Tory town clerk and was one of the group of honorary free burgesses rapidly promoted to Alderman 1785. (Assembly Book, admitted free burgess 29 August 1785, promoted to Alderman 5 September 1785). A Whig satire on this occasion in the *Ipswich Journal* also stigmatises Argent's liveried origins, as 'late footman to Mrs S. He too has commenced baizemaker and has raised himself to a degree of consequence that scarcely admits a parallel' (*IpsJ* 3 September 1785).

Argent became Mayor in 1816 despite Bland's allegation that he was,

> illiterate, but not quite so much as some of his predecessors, and I believe he could write his own name, but this was all he could do, some of their worships being capable of making their marks only (Bland:4).

A

Such civic honours are the more remarkable considering Argent's unsuccessful business career. In 1784 he married Hannah Robjent (St Peters registers, CPL Crisp ML74, ERO D/ACL 1784). Henry Johnson (qv) stood surety for the marriage licence. Hannah was the '..only survivor of a respectable family ... (of baymakers) ... now extinct.' (Bland:4) Their daughter Hannah was baptised at St Peters the following year. The family lived on North Hill (cf James Robjent (qv)).

Argent continued to trade as a baymaker until May 1793 when he became bankrupt (*European Magazine* 7 May 1793, D'Cruze, *Pleasing Prospect*:94). As part of a growing trend to refer local bankruptcies to the London court, the creditors meeting was convened at the Guildhall (*IpsJ* 11 May 1793) and one of the assignees was a Mr Bolton of Basinghall St London. His capital mansion on North Hill, his mill and a 1½ acre field were offered for sale during 1793 and 1794 (*IpsJ* 8 June 1793, 5 and 12 April 1794) not finding a ready purchaser in that period of high inflation and limited credit.

The family seem to have survived by changing trade. Holden's 1805 *Directory* lists William as a Porter and Cyder Merchant of St John's Green, Hannah Robjent was then running a Ladies Boarding School, doubtless due to their somewhat straightened circumstances but died in 1807 (St Peters registers). Argent seems to have continued in Colchester, his finances sufficiently repaired to serve as Mayor in 1816 and recording a Tory vote until 1820.

He died not long afterwards. His will was made in 1816 and proved in 1822 (ERO D/ABR 32/202, 'Alderman of Colchester'). Despite his bankruptcy he was able to retain ownership of the North Hill property, which was to be sold together with the bulk of the estate and divided between his two sons, William and James Underwood Argent. (James' middle name might indicate an otherwise untraced second marriage.) His daughter Hannah received his household goods, £400 and copyhold land in Greenstead. William Burgess (qv) grocer, who acted as executor with William Argent jun, received £100.

See also *IpsJ* 7 August 1789, John Baines, baker married Miss Argent.

ARNOLD JOSEPH [24]
Man Midwife
fl. 1786

IpsJ 7 May 1785: Mr Joseph Arnold, London, man midwife, elected member of Colchester Medical Society, 27 April (and see Appendix 2).

ARUNDELL ROBERT MONCKTON [25]
4th Viscount Galway
1752-1810

Galway occupied Berechurch Hall in the 1790s when it was vacated by Robert Smyth (qv). Charles Shillito (qv) dedicated his play *The Man of Enterprise* to him (1 December 1789) and Galway was present at the performance. Lord Galway also paid off the debts of the Colchester Oratorio in 1790 so that the receipts could go to the Charity School as was originally intended (9 October 1790 *IpsJ*, JBB *EAE*:96, 210, 213). He was MP for Pontefract 1780-83 and 1796-1802 and for York City 1793-90. Served as Comptroller of the Household 1764-7 and became a privy councillor in 1784 and KB in 1786 (Namier & Brooke, *The House of Commons*).

He married firstly Elizabeth the 3rd daughter of Daniel Matthew of Felix Hall Essex in 1779 and secondly Mary Bridget widow of Peter A. Hay Drummond in 1803 (she died 1835).

He was pro reform and a member of the Association Movement. Generally pro Administration after 1784 yet anti-Fox. Known for generally rising to address the house 'during long debates at late hours ... usually in a state which should have impelled him to silence.' He died on 23 July 1810 (Namier & Brooke).

A

See also *IpsJ* 22 October 1791, which reported that on Sunday afternoon a poor boy fell some 20ft from the top of chestnut tree in Lord Galway's park, Mistley. The boy broke his thigh. He remained on the ground some considerable time and no help offered except by a tar who offered to carry the boy on his back. A crowd assembled. His Lordship generously allowed boy to be brought into the house.

ASHFORD RICHARD [976]
Candlemaker and Grocer
fl. 1780-1815

In *IpsJ* 25 November 1780, Ashford advertised that he sold '… a peculiar sort of French hair powder at 1s a lb or 11s a doz.'

He occupied property in Crouch Street, St Mary-at-the-Walls with two other co-tenants, rated 30 overall (1783 rates). He was still in business making candles in 1815, when he advertised:-

> Richard Ashford
>
> Begs Leave to inform the Inhabitants of Colchester and its Vicinity, that he continues to manufacture, at his old-established OFFICE, in Butt-Lane, MOULD and DIP CANDLES: of which he had now ready for delivery, STORES of a superior quality, on the lowest Terms.
>
> R. A. avails himself of this opportunity of reiterating his sincere Thanks for the numerous Favours he has received for upwards of thirty-six years, and hopes for a continuance of that Support which it has ever been his Study to deserve.
>
> All Persons indebted to R. Ashford at the time of his (*illeg.*) the Grocery Business, in 1811, are requested to submit their Accounts within one month from the date hereof.
>
> Crouch Street, Colchester, October 6, 1815 (*Colchester Gazette* 7 October 1815).

ASHWELL JAMES [27]
Grocer and Wine Merchant
fl. 1754-1791

In 1754 Ashwell married Elizabeth Wallis (CPL Crisp ML66, ERO D/ACL 1754). The bondholder was Joshua Wallis of St Peters, Grocer. This alliance linked the Ashwells with other eminent nonconformist tradesmen (the Tabors and Thorns as well as the Wallis') whose businesses centred on the Hythe. In 1785 his daughter married John Collins Tabor (qv). During the 1780s Ashwell was a regular attender at St Botolphs vestry meetings.

James Ashwell received an anonymous letter dated 22 November 1772 (*IpsJ* 28 November 1772, JBB NB Check:57) threatening to attack his shop with 'bumshells'. The shop was newly brick fronted, in St Botolphs Street.

By 1783 he had prospered sufficiently to buy East Donyland Hall and acquired the family nickname of 'General Ashwell' since the Hall's previous occupant had been a General Gansel (David Gansel (qv); Tabor Papers, ERO D/DU/617). Bland describes Ashwell as 'a worthy brother of gluttony' due to his trips to Rotterdam with Henry Lodge (qv) in order 'to eat fish dressed in a peculiar way for which the Dutch were famous' (Appendix 3, *Bland's Anecdotes*: 42).

Ashwell died on 11 September 1791. His will of 1791/2 (NA PROB 11/1221 Fountain, 8 August 1792, of East Donyland Hall) names his second wife Ruth, dividing the proceeds of sale of Donyland Hall between her and the family. The Hall was offered for auction on 28 April 1792 (*IpsJ*) and again on 11 October and 1 November 1794 (*IpsJ*) when it was described as:

> Formerly the residence of Gen. Gansel and late of Mr Ashwell, deceased, situate at East Donyland in the County of Essex, within 2 miles of Colchester and 54 of London; bounded on the North and East by a navigable river.
>
> To be sold by Auction by Timothy Walford (qv)

A

In 5 separate Lots, at 12 o'clock, on Thursday next the 6th inst. at the Three Cups Inn, in Colchester, (unless previously disposed of by Private contract).

THE MANSION HOUSE, MANOR LANDS, and APPURTENANCES with the Perpetual Presentation to the Rectory of EAST DONYLAND, comprised in the five following Lots:

Lot 1: A substantial well-built Brick Mansion-house, in excellent repair; containing in the attic story, a very large laundry, 4 servants rooms, and other conveniences; first floor, 9 very good bed-chambers; principal entry, a drawing room 38 feet by 21 feet 6 inches, 18 feet high, with a bay window at the North end; 4 excellent parlours, all neatly fitted up with marble hearths and chimney pieces; a spacious kitchen, scullery, pantry &c. The basement consists of 4 dry cellars and a wine vault.

At a suitable distance, A handsome brick-built brewhouse and dairy, a storehouse and granary, 2 three-stalled stables and coach-house; a double barn, with stables on each side, bricked and sashed which makes one handsome front, on a rising ground, in full view of the house, and forms the East end of a noble farm yard, which is enclosed on the North and South sides with a lofty brick wall; to which is attached elegant and convenient accommodations for sheltering cattle from the weather; with cow house, pig sties, pens for calves and poultry, herdsman's house, hay barn, straw house, cart lodge, and chaise-house; a handsome dove house, summer house, 2 large gardens, walled in, and planted with choice fruit trees; extensive plantations, and 6 fish ponds; a lawn and park, with arable, pasture, meadow, and marsh land, containing about 195 acres, in a ring fence; all which is situate on the North East side of the road leading from Donyland Heath to Fingringhoe, the said road to belong to this lot, subject to a right of passage to lot 3; together with the manor, quit-rents, rights, royalty, and privileges, which extends over 2,000 acres. The fixtures of the mansion to be taken at a fair appraisement; and all timbers and trees, above 6 inches girth, to be taken at a fair evaluation.

The other lots – summarised briefly – were:-

- Lot 2: The Perpetual Presentation to the Rectory. 39 acres glebe. The present incumbent about 60.
- Lot 3: Farm House, Red Barn, and land on SW of road, about 160 acres, all freehold except 6 acres near church called Butlers.
- Lot 4: 12 acres and a cottage, north corner of Donyland heath, called Carters.
- Lot 5: Pilgrims, or Bulls Farm, in Wire Lane, 26 acres, copyhold.

For further particulars apply Messrs R. Tabor & Son, Mr J. W. Ashwell or Mr S. Daniell, steward to the said manor.

On 22 November 1794 (*IpsJ*), was advertised part of the furniture, including 'a capital fine-toned hall organ, with 5 stops, in a neat mahogany case', 70 stacks of firewood, and several very large wainscot bookcases.

ASHWELL JAMES WALLIS [28]
Merchant
ob. 1817

One of a network of substantial nonconformist trading families in the town, and connected to the Tabors, Thorns and Wallis'. Son of James Ashwell (qv). He took over the wine merchants' business on his father's death in 1791. On 14 December 1793, he advertised from 'the Wine Warehouse, St Botolphs Street':

> JAMES WALLIS ASHWELL begs leave respectfully to inform the public, he has on sale the following WINES which, upon trial, he doubts not but will be approved;
>
> Fine old rich or dry Raison at 3s 6d per gal or 10s per doz

A

>Best Old Wine of Smyrna or Mountain Kind, at 4s per gallon or 12s per doz
>
>Best old rum, of the Calcavella kind at 4s per gallon or 12s per doz
>
>Fine old Wine, of the Frontoniac flavour at 4s 9d per gallon or 16s per doz
>
>Fine Orange at 4s 6d per gallon or 14s per dozen
>
>Fine Cowslip at 4s 6d per gallon or 14s per doz
>
>Fine Raspberry at 4s per gallon or 12s per doz
>
>Discount 3d per gallon on 10 gallons and upwards.

He advertised on 1 November 1794 (*IpsJ*) that he had taken James Buxton's (qv) stock.

Ashwell became bankrupt and a series of property sales took place between 1807 and 1810. On 8 August 1807 (*IpsJ*) 14 substantial lots in various parts of the town were offered including a granary at the Hythe, shop on East Hill (occ. Thomas Best (qv)), dwelling in Bear Lane occupied Miss Dunthorne, etc. Donyland Place was advertised on 23 July 1808 (*IpsJ*), a farm of 160 acres and Ashwell's livestock on 17 September 1808 (*IpsJ*). On 27 October 1810 (*IpsJ*) James Wallis Ashwell's 'singularly pleasant and substantial Brick'd Mansion' in St Botolphs Street was advertised, including a Hall 22 x 15 feet, an elegant staircase and landing and lofty dining parlour 24 x 18 feet with handsome bow window, another drawing room in front 18 ½ x 13 ½ feet. The house offered 'a beautiful prospect'.

His will, made in 1812 (ERO D/ACR 20/17) irrespective of the bankruptcy, leaves all his messuages and tenements in Colchester and elsewhere to his wife for her own use together with all his personal estate including books. The will was finally proved on 22 November 1817 and meantime the mansion had been let to a Col. Morris (rated at £17) whereas Ashwell's widow was living in property rated at £4.

AUSTON EDWARD [30]
Gardener
fl. 1789-1806

A county freeholder. Bought the 'Castle Lands' from the executors of John Blatch Whaley (qv) on 28 November 1789. These comprised 10 acres of land east of Land Lane and stretching to the lane which led to the foot of East Hill; then Hop ground of 8 acres and a 2 acre Ash Plantation at the northern end, together with barns and a hop kiln with two cottages adjoining. (The property stayed in the family until 1922, and the two cottages remained standing until destroyed by bombing in the 2nd World War. JBB notes on Deeds of Maydays, Land Lane NB Jan 70, and report for Mrs Idris Carter, ERO C905, Box 10, General Notes M.)

Auston died on 25 January 1806, aged 68 and was buried at St Giles. His will (NA PROB 11/1441, 11 April 1806) provided £100 plus interest on £2,000 for life to his dear wife Elizabeth. She predeceased him on 26 May 1805 aged 65 so this legacy reverted to his son Edward in trust for his children. Edward jun also received £2,000 and the Castle Lands. His sister Mary (wife of Jeremiah Bartholomew) and brother Bartholomew Auston both received £20. Auston's wife Elizabeth, son Edward and esteemed friend Mr Samuel Cooke (qv), merchant were named as executors.

See also St Giles MIs (CPL, Crisp); Edward Auston 2, dd. 16 February 1820 aged 55; Susannah his wife, dd. 11 December 1842 aged 75; Henry his fifth son dd. 1827 aged 18; Joseph his fourth son dd. 1837 aged 31; Edward 3, bn. 19 January 1796, dd. 9 February 1877; his wife Harriet (*née* Holt of Lexden, married 1824, nfr) dd. 10 January 1845 age 46, son Edward 4 dd. 1844, aged 18, dtr. Helen dd. 22 January 1850 aged 18.

A

AYLMER MR [31]
Colchester Dancing School
fl. 1757

When John Wood (qv) resigned his dancing school in Colchester, Aylmer took it over, teaching on Mondays (*IpsJ* 2 and 9 April 1757).

See also burials St Peters, Mary Aylmer 24 June 1780.

B

BAAS LUCY [1278]
1745-1809

One of six surviving children of John Alefounder 1 and his wife Elizabeth *née* Upcher. Lucy Alefounder was baptised 2 October 1745. She married firstly (St Martins 1768) Philip Havens 2 (qv) of St Giles, gent and baymaker, who died 1782. Their son, William Upcher Havens died 29 November 1784 aged 9 years 9 weeks. Their daughter Lucy (bn. 1773) died unmarried on 28 May 1792. These two children are buried with their mother in the Havens family vault at St James. However, four other children survived to attend her second marriage at St Giles 9 April 1789 to Captain Robert Bass ('of Yarmouth', according to the marriage settlement ERO C47, CPL820). The wedding shows signs of having been a jolly occasion, no less than eight witnesses signing the register. These were Phillip Havens 3 (qv), Robert, Anna and Lucy Havens, Joseph Green (who also witnessed her brother Robert Alefounder's (qv) will), Margaret Mustard, Elizabeth Bass (who witnessed the will of Mary Mannall, widow of John Mannall (qv) carpenter on 12 August 1796, ERO D/ABR 29/1, proved 25 August 1796), and Mary Ann Mills.

Lucy Baas died a widow 13 November 1809 aged 64. Her will (NA PROB 11/1505) was made 18 March 1807 (witnessed by the lawyer William Mason 3 (qv) and J. Mason) and proved on 25 November 1809. It left:-

£5 to eldest son Philip Havens 3 of E. Donyland, Esq.

£1,200 in 3% Consols and £1,957 in 5% Bank Stock (both these sums having been transferred to her at late marriage with Robt Baas dd., when Charles Matthews (qv) of Colchester Esq and Joseph Green (qv), merchant were trustees) were to be divided equally between daughter Ann Pope wife of Revd James Pope of Gt Staughton, Hunts and son Robert Havens.

B

Robert Havens was also left £1,000 mortgage on copyhold estate Brightlingsea now held by him in trust for his children at 21.

Wearing apparel was left to Ann Pope.

The residue was also to be divided between Ann Pope and Robert Havens, who were named as executors.

BACON RICHARD [1301]
Upholsterer
w. 1733

His will is at ERO D/ABW 90/2/11, 1733/4. See also ERO D/DHt/T72/71, 98.

BACON SIR RICHARD [33]
Attorney
1695-1773

Richard Bacon was born on 22 February 1695. Then of Gislingham, he was apprenticed to Thomas Mayhew (qv) attorney of Colchester for £130 whose daughter, Bridget he married on 29 December 1720 when he was living in St Peters, Sudbury. He witnessed Mayhew's will in 1716 and, by a codicil of 1718 was made executor and guardian of the children. Bacon proved the will in 1728. After Bridget's death (6 January 1725/6) he married Lucy Gardiner (co-heir of the Barony of Fitzwalter) who died on 17 August 1765 (*Burkes Peerage and Gentry*).

Bacon served as Town Clerk for Colchester between 1725 and 1736. His bill of 1736 to the Corporation for services rendered amounts to £534 (ERO Chamberlain's Bills and Vouchers D/B 5 Ab1/33). He was created a free burgess on 9 December 1728. In 1741 he voted for the Tories, Savage and Gray, in 1747 for Gray and the Whig, Olmius and in 1768 for the sitting compromise candidates Gray and Rebow. He succeeded as 8th baronet of Mildenhall in 1753 and 7th baronet of Redgrave in 1755 due to his uncle and cousins dying early and without issue.

Bacon lived in Trinity Street and also occupied premises at 14 High Street rated 18 between at least 1764 and his death in 1773 which according to the *Chelmsford Chronicle* (8 April 1773) was 'much lamented by the poor to whom he was very charitable.' His will (NA PROB 11/986, 14 April 1773) directs he should be buried privately at Holy Trinity 'without any appearance of Pomp and Pagentry' and leaves the bulk of his property to his relations of the Schutz family (connected by marriage to the 5th baronet).

BAGNALL JOHN [1113]
Printer
fl. 1725 in Colchester

For a short time in 1725 Bagnall had premises the Red Lion Yard, before going on to Ipswich to found the *Ipswich Journal*. Between 1730-36 the *Ipswich Journal* included Colchester's Arms as well as Ipswich's in his heading.

JBB (NB Jan 68:24) cites G. C. [George Curlow?], *A Dialogue between a Sabbath Keeper and an Antinomian*, (Colchester, printed by John Bagnall at the Red Lyon Inn, sold by J. Marshal at the Bible in Newgate Street, London, or by W. Craighton, bookseller in Ipswich), c. 1725?

BAINES JOSEPH [992]
Baker
w. 1785

His will is at ERO D/ACR 18/217, made 1781, proved 1785, baker of Colchester.

See also will of Joseph Michael Baines, Gentleman, late Farmer of Saint Mary at the Walls, Essex, NA PROB 11/1539, 16 December 1812. This Baines was the subject of one of a collection of watercolour portraits by E. P. Strutt, now held by Colchester and Ipswich Museums.

BAINES PETER [34]
Innkeeper, George
fl. 1790-9

Tenant at the George from 1790, but in 1793 he also owned the Anchor, St Botolphs (cf Geo Smith (qv)). According to Bland (*Bland's Anecdotes*, Appendix 3) he had married Widow Sarah Smith the previous tenant.

BAKER JOHN 1 [36]
Baymaker
fl. 1759-74

A well known figure in the town, Baker was one of two clothiers who supported the radical parliamentary candidate Alexander Fordyce (qv) (*ODNB*), during the 1768 election and wrote an open letter to the *Ipswich Journal* complaining of the intimidation of voters by other baymakers and offering to employ any clothworkers dismissed for not voting as their masters chose (*IpsJ* 5 March 1768).

Baker had been admitted free burgess in 1764 (16 January) and was later elected Common Councillor on 3 September 1770 and Alderman (and Assistant) on 23 August 1774, just prior to becoming Mayor that autumn. Baker was innovative in his trade and on 9 November 1769 with London partners patented, 'A New Improvement of Making a sort of Bays for the Spanish & Portugal Trade Quite upon a New Invention Imitating those Manufactured in France, by which the French has, so considerable advantage over the English Manufactories' (*ER*, Vol. lvi (1958):20).

Baker's house was in Bear Lane opposite the Quaker meeting house and he offered to plaster and whitewash the wall of the chapel nearest the lane annually at his own expense (Fitch, *Colchester Quakers*:93-4). He was living there in 1759 when he married Mary Cole, sister of Edward Cole, tanner (qv) (CPL Crisp ML457, ERO ML D/ALL 1759).

Baker died in December 1774 (*IpsJ* 24 December 1774), 'a universal loss from his extensive trade' just a few months into his Mayoralty and was buried at St James with a great number attending. His will (NA PROB 11/1006, 4 April 1775), made in May 1774, leaves £100 to his wife Mary plus all household goods except the 'little China Bason given to my daughter Mary by Mrs Sparhawk at Gt. Coggeshall'. His executors, his wife and friends Phillip Havens 2 (qv) and Thomas Boggis (qv) both baymakers, should, 'in no wise presume to carry on the business at any rate whatsoever' and were to sell all real estate and place the profits out on interest for the benefit of his children equally at age 21. If all children should die minors then £50 was to go to each of the children of his late uncle Thomas Baker; £50 to his brother-in-law Edward Cole (qv); £500 and any residue to the children of William Swinborne of Tendring, Essex by Elizabeth (Cole) his wife. The £50 apiece left to Boggis and Havens was reduced by a codicil to £30.

On 2 January 1776 Baker's widow, Mary married at St Martins to Barwell Blower (qv) a baymaker of Bocking (ERO ML D/ACL 1776).

ChCh 17 May 1776 Baker's properties were offered for auction including three tenements in Bear Lane with a very large new-built warehouse adjoining.

BAKER JOHN 2 [35]
Carrier
fl. 1755

IpsJ 2 August 1755:

> Notice is hereby given, that JOHN BAKER doeth set out from his own House, over against the Rose & Crown in East Street, or from Stephen Mathaman's at the Fox & Dogs in St Mary's parish, Colchester and goes to the Spread Eagle in Maldon every Friday Morning at 5 o'clock till Michaelmas, and after Michaelmas every Thursday, with a light CART and one horse, who carries Passengers at one shilling each, and light Parcels at reasonable rates.

BANCILHON ANTHONY [1250]
Mason
fl. 1753

Mentioned in two marriage licences in 1753. CPL Crisp ML358, ERO D/ALL 1753, Bancilhon to marry Elizabeth Brewster of St Giles at All Saints, described as a mason of St Leonards. But compare CPL Crisp ML167, also of 1753, when he was of St Leonards stone-cutter, he was bound with Britton Lloyd of St Giles, Lloyd to marry Mary Hubbard of the same;

See also CPL Crisp ML254, John Luck of Willingdale Doe, farmer (26) to Jane Bancilhon of Chipping Ongar, 1782

BANISTER JOSEPH [38]
Watch and Clockmaker
1778-1875

Born in Lichfield in 1778, Banister came to Colchester in 1803 to work with Nathaniel Hedge 2 (qv) and entered into a full partnership with him in 1807. In 1809 he married Anne Maria Snell at St Marys. At the beginning of 1814 (*IpsJ* 22 January 1814) the partnership with Hedge was dissolved. Banister continued the watchmaking business at no. 19 High Street whilst Hedge specialised in jewellery next door at no. 18. When Hedge finally retired altogether in 1818, Banister purchased his premises and moved next door, renting out no. 19. Was manufacturing his own watches by at least 1821 (*Colchester Gazette* 17 December 1821). Banister continued as a leading tradesman and public figure in the town until his retirement in December 1853. Is notable for having invented an improved Dead Beat Escapement for clocks and watches, which he patented.

For a full account of Banister's career, see Bernard Mason, *Clock and Watchmaking in Colchester* (1969):354ff., in which see also illustration of his premises at 18/19 High St, c.1850, p. 373.

BARKER THOMAS [40]
Innkeeper, Castle, All Saints
fl. 1781-1787

Was living in All Saints when in 1781 he was elected overseer and soon thereafter was installed as tenant in the Castle Inn. He died in 1787 and an announcement was made on 2 July 1787 (*ChCh*) that his debtors should remit to his son Thomas Rutledge Barker (qv) who was to continue at the inn. He was a free burgess who voted from 1780. He supported Potter in 1781 but in 1784 voted for Affleck in April and Smyth in July.

BARKER THOMAS RUTLEDGE [41]
Victualler, Castle, All Saints
fl. 1787-1791

Son of Thomas Barker (qv), he succeeded his father at the Castle in 1787 (*ChCh* 2 July 1787). From thence until 1791 he was a regular attender at All Saints vestry meetings and was nominated as an overseer in 1790. He was a free burgess voting for Jackson in 1788 and Jackson and Thornton in 1790. He seems to have moved away from the town after 1791, when he was declared bankrupt (*London Gazette*, 27 August 1791, 27 January 1795).

BARLOW NATHANIEL 1 [42]
Upholsterer, Auctioneer and Appraiser
c. 1740-1798

The son of William Barlow, vicar of Elmstead (1731-c. 1755) and Margaret, *née* Lunn of Elsworth Cambridgeshire, who had married at Halstead in 1733. His mother was a widow when in 1755 he was apprenticed to Henry Lodge, upholder (qv) for £30 (NA IR 1/52/93) of which £10 was subscribed from the Fund for Relief of Poor Clergy and their children, a then newly founded Essex and Hertfordshire charity.

He opened a shop near the White Hart (no. 2 High St) in 1763 (*IpsJ* 26 November 1763) and in 1764 married Elizabeth Salter of St Giles parish when both were 24 (ERO ML D/ACL 1764). In 1767 he had moved next door, to no. 1 High St, at the corner of Head Street and High Street and had 'entered the cabinet way' (*IpsJ* 22 November 1767). He remained at these extensive premises (rated 46) for the remainder of his life. On 26 May 1787 (*IpsJ*) he had opened a 'warehouse' for upholstery and cabinet goods <u>'for ready money'</u> (underlining in original) as well as extending into grocery under the management of his son, Nathaniel 2 (qv). Barlow also had an extensive business as an auctioneer. In 21 May 1774 (*IpsJ*) he apologised for the inconvenience of a cancelled sale at West Bergholt for which he had distributed 500 handbills around the county. In spite of printing 700 notices of the cancellation, some prospective purchasers arrived nevertheless. In the 1780s and 90s Barlow handled sales all over north Essex and south Suffolk, generally in partnership with William Bunnell (qv) and the newspapers are full of their advertisements. Barlow & Son advertised for an apprentice 'in the Grocery, Tea and Upholstery business' in 1790 (*IpsJ* 13 November 1790).

Barlow was a free burgess by right of apprenticeship, voting from 1780-96. He was elected Common Councilman on 17 August 1781 and Assistant on 1 September 1783. In the two 1784 elections he switched vote from Smyth, the Whig, to the outsider Potter and remained thereafter with the (Tory) Corporation party under whom he served as Alderman from 27 August 1790 and as Mayor in 1792-3. He died in 1798 (*IpsJ* 14 April 1798; NA PROB 11/1307, Walpole 377, 1 June 1798), leaving all to his son, Nathaniel, who continued the business (cf *IpsJ* 2 and 9 February 1799).

See also ERO DE1/T423, copy will of 1798, plan of 1803 and sale catalogue; *IpsJ* 29 January 1803, description of premises, quoted under Nathaniel Barlow 2 (qv); these premises were earlier the Three White Naggs (qv). Picture of the premises in Benham's *Almanack* for 1900:94; 1780, John Chambers apprenticed to Barlow for £50 (nfr); *IpsJ* 12 June 1789, married at Writtle, William Barlow, son of Nathaniel to Miss Pool, only daughter of late Mr Pool 'formerly considerable brewer'.

BARLOW NATHANIEL 2 [43]
Grocer
fl. 1779-1802

Son of Nathaniel Barlow (qv), upholsterer. Was apprenticed to his father for the nominal sum of £5 for 7 years on 1 March 1779 (Register of Apprenticeship Indentures, ERO D/B 5 Ta1) and on 26 May 1787 (*IpsJ*) Barlow and Son, Grocers and Tea Dealers 'opened a warehouse' at their premises at the top of the High Street (no. 1). Nathaniel junior seems to have handled the grocery and his father carried on as an upholsterer and auctioneer. Nathaniel junior was a free burgess voting Tory like his father from 1788-96. He was elected Common Councillor on 5 September 1796. Nathaniel senior died in 1799 and Nathaniel junior, the main beneficiary under his father's will, took over the whole enterprise (*IpsJ* 9 February 1799). Shortly after, in 1802, however, he resigned from the Corporation, sold the premises and moved away from the town. The house and shop were advertised on 26 June 1802 and 29 January 1803 (*IpsJ*) and described in detail:-

> Lot 1: All that valuable, very desirable & substantial Brick freehold <u>Messuage</u> or <u>Mansion House</u>, at the corner of Head and High Streets, opposite North Hill, in St Peters Parish, Colchester, and nearly facing the new Corn-Exchange Market (35 feet north front, 66 feet west front); in the occupation of N. Barlow, tea dealer, grocer and upholsterer; and Mr John Worsley, comprising 2 excellent lofty shops, with circular sash windows, a large attached warehouse, convenient accounting room, a good keeping room, kitchen &c on the ground floor; excellent vaults and two dry cellars, a tea room (or withdrawing room) from which is a pleasant view of the fields; 2 dining rooms, 2 front chambers and 3 back chambers on the first storey; 6 front chambers and one back chamber on the second storey; with garrets on the same, terminating with a flat leaded turret, iron railed, commanding an extensive prospect of the surrounding country. Also will be

comprised in this lot a brick fronted vestibule with two tenements adjoining, with another shop, 41 feet in front (with occupation Mr Worsley and Mrs Pitt) containing altogether 107 feet front in Head Street (also yard, stables in Back Lane near White Hart).

Lot 2 : Two Freehold Tenements: occupied Mr Samuel Waterhouse and Mr William Payne in Head Street, 45ft. The premises are in substantial repair, and form a very compact estate, are not in the least inmated with other premises and have been in the tenure of the present proprietor for upwards of 30 years.

Mr Worsley under notice to quit on 29 September 1803, other tenants on 20 December 1802. Mr Barlow will sell the stock at a valuation and can give early possession, in the meantime trade will be carried on as usual.

BARNARD JOHN [45]
Surgeon
ob. 1768

In 1747 (NA IR 1/18/43), John Barnard, son of John was apprenticed to Henry Hall, citizen and apothecary for £100. Was himself working in Colchester by 1765 and took an apprentice, (NA IR 1/55/168) Edwin Godwin for £20. Two years later (Ips 7 March 1767) Barnard was in partnership with John Fox (qv), offering:

Inoculations

By Mr JOHN FOX; sen. Surgeon, at DEDHAM and Mr J. N. BARNARD, Surgeon in COLCHESTER

Who are now setting up, in a neat and convenient Manner a large and commodious House at ARDLEIGH late the seat of Sir Ralph Crefield (sic).

Gentlemen and Ladies may be inoculated in separate Apartments at Five and Four Guineas each and Servants at Three Guineas, all Necessaries found (Tea, Wine and

Washing excepted). Any Gentleman or Lady may bring a Friend or Servant, paying Half a Guinea a week for their Board.

Barnard's house was the old Queens Head Inn, High Street, St Peters (north side - the downhill neighbour of the Three Cups (cf Thos Bayles 1 (qv) and J. E. Wallis (qv) for the history of this house). The property is rated 16 in St Peters rates occupied by Barnard until 1768 and the following year after his death is listed in his wife's name. The house was offered for auction in the spring and summer of 1769 (*IpsJ* 6 May 1769) and described in detail (see under Henry Lodge auctioneer (qv)).

He died in 1769. His will (NA PROB 11/945) was made on 25 May 1768 and proved on 11 February 1769, leaving the whole estate to his wife Mary, sole executrix.

BARNARD REVD JOHN [44]
Clergy
ob. 1767

Colchester Corporation's mortgage of the Severall's estate, originally made to Daniel Defoe, was subsequently held by Revd John Barnard (ERO D/DC/5/18, JBB NB Yellow 2, NA King's Bench Indictments, KB/11/35).

After his death was advertised (*IpsJ* 24 October 1767) 816 acres of the Severalls estate, the lease having a further 55 years to run 'now let to good tenants at £510 per annum' and also a mortgage of other Corporation's estates at 4% or £2,600. The auction was to be held at the 'Great Piazze', Covent Garden by Mr Lanford & Son.

The estate was to remain in the Bernard family, however, since in 1813 (*IpsJ* 1 May 1813) were advertised 800 oak pollards for auction from the Severall's estate, the property of Revd James Bernard.

BARNES ANN [46]
Victualler, Cross Keys
w. 1792/3

Widow of William Barnes, the previous occupant of the Cross Keys. Her will of 1792/3 (ERO D/ABR 28/367, widow of St Nicholas) left the inn to her daughter Ann Bridges (wife of Theophilus (qv)) who was then living with her and the next door property to her son William, then a minor. Ann Barnes was sister-in-law to Thomas Wood (qv) of the Angel whom she named as her executor together with her daughter. Wood had married Widow Fow in 1776.

BARNS CLARK [49]
Brewer
w. 1783

Owned the brewery in Gutter Street at the foot of Sheregate Steps (now Sheregate Hotel, Deeds, ERO C47 CPL 680). Married Ann Sherman, widow in 1750 (CPL Crisp ML263 D/ALL 1750). His insurances with Sun Insurance in 1776 amounted to £2,100 on property and stock in various parishes. He died 12 March 1783. His will (CPL 680 as above) left the brewery with malting office, barns, stables &c to his son Thomas (qv) on condition that Clark's wife, Ann should have residence either there or in Thomas' house, together with an annuity of £50 per annum until her death or remarriage. Another messuage, St Mary-at-the-Walls was left to daughter Ann, being the house where she and her husband William Rouse (qv) baker lived (Rated 6 in 1783). Other cash legacies provide for his wife and daughters, Ann Rouse, Mary wife of John Hunt (qv), carpenter, Henrietta, wife of George Stevens, farmer, and Sarah Barnes (sic).

BARNS THOMAS 1 [50]
Brewer
ob. 1791

Also sometimes spelt 'Barnes' in the sources.

Son of Clark Barns (qv). A free burgess who voted from 1780-90, consistently supporting radical candidates. As well as the brewhouse in Gutter St, his St Giles property included several tenements and two inns, the Chequers and the Red Cow. He married Mary Stevens (qv) of St Peters (CPL Crisp ML310, brewer of Trinity). He died in October 1791 (*IpsJ* 15 October 1791). His will (made 6 June 1790, proved 18 October 1791, ERO C47, CPL 680, attested copy of will with deeds of Scheregate Hotel) provided for wife Mary for life, then daughter Elizabeth Ann. She later married James Thorn 3 (qv) (marriage settlement 19 May 1800, Deeds of Scheregate Hotel as above). Cole and Hales' plan of Holy Trinity in 1818 shows Mrs Barns as occupier of a small messuage in Trinity Street, owning and occupying a large house, yards and gardens at the beginning of Black Boy Lane, as owner of the 'Brewers' Arms' Inn and Gardens' between Black Boy Lane and Stanwell Street, as well as the extensive brewery on the corner of Lodder Lane and Gutter Street, occupied Mrs Keeling (cf Bland's story under John Hunt (qv)).

See reference to Barns' mortgages in D'Cruze, *Pleasing Prospect*: 85, 86, and for his assault of his servant Ann Cockerill, ERO P/CoR/12, 24 January 1789, discussed in *Pleasing Prospect*:171.

BARNS THOMAS 2 [51]
Saddler
fl 1794-1808

In 1794 succeeded to the business of Mrs Green in Headgate (*IpsJ* 12 April 1794). The death of Joseph Green (qv), an eminent merchant was announced in 1808 (*IpsJ* 31 December 1808) when Barns acted as agent for the sale of a messuage in Head Street, late occupied by Mrs Smith.

BARSTOW REVD THOMAS [52]
Rector, St Mary-at-the-Walls
fl. 1771-1788

Barstow is recalled by Bland as a frequenter of the King's Head Coffee Room and as the cleric who encouraged the innkeeper Daniel Manning (qv) to attend church. There, relating the Old Testament story of Daniel's call, Barstow thundered out 'Daniel, Daniel!' and roused Manning from dozing during the sermon (*Bland's Anecdotes*, Appendix 3).

Born in York, Barstow entered Clare College Cambridge in 1763 and obtained his BA in 1767, MA in 1770 and held a Fellowship between 1768-1770. He was Rector of Burnby, Yorks between 1769-71, of Aldham 1771-1820, of St Mary-at-the-Walls 1771-88 and St Lawrence 1788-1820 (Venn, *Alumn. Cantab.*).

He was a client of Richard Rigby (qv) of Mistley Hall, the Paymaster General, who apparently procured the rectory of St Lawrence worth £400 p.a. for him. Certainly both were amongst the members of the King's Head Club as was George Pickard (qv) wine merchant, Barstow's father-in-law and another Rigby connection. Barstow had married Mary Ann Pickard in 1778 (*ChCh* 10 July 1778).

Barstow's main residence was at Copford. He died aged 75 on 6 May 1820.

BARTHOLOMEW EDWARD [1247]
Carpenter
d. 1744

Important man in the earlier part of the eighteenth century. Not enough found about him.

Buried St Mary-at-the-Walls 25 December 1744. Rector Philip Morant (qv) noted in the register that he 'died of wounds rec'd the 22nd by the overturning of the Stage Coach in Ingatestone on his return from London to this town.'

Apprentices: John Gosnall, created free burgess at Monday Court by right of service, 1727; John Sherman, ditto, 1734;

Barker Holton (qv), £8, 1722 (NA IR 1/47/128); John Lince (qv), son of John, £7, 1741 (NA IR 1/50/227).

Work for Corporation (Chamberlain's Bills and Vouchers, ERO D/B 5 Ab1/33): 1736 (Voucher 96) £22 18s ½d; 1737 (Voucher 111) £10 17s 10d.

Winsleys Trustees (ERO D/Q 30/2/124):1734/5, £125 7s. The largest bill on accounts for building the Alms-houses.

BARTHOLOMEW JOHN [1249]
Stonemason
1711-1782

A settlement examination (ERO P/CoR/3, Borough Petty Sessions Examination Book, 19 January 1773, John Bartholomew, mason, now St Peters) shows that he was born at Rotherhithe, Surrey. Came to Colchester with his father when he was 14, to St Leonard's parish. He lived there with his father until he died and then with his mother. Has a wife Judith and two children, Judith aged 3 and Mary, 6 months.

IpsJ 8 August 1747:-

> John BARTHOLOMEW At the New Hyth, Colchester SELLETH Marble and Portland Slabbs for Hearths and Chimney-Pieces, of any Size; also Black Marble Tomb-Stones, Head and Foot-Stones, at the most Reasonable Prices.
>
> N.B. He employs a Workman in the Masonry Business who will undertake and perform in the neatest and most expeditious Manner, Work of any Sort belonging to his Employment.

See also *IpsJ* 12 December 1747, which says 'He also employs a Mason from London' (compare Bancilhon (qv)).

1765-7 was paid £62 6s for work for Lion Walk Octagon Chapel (ERO D/NC 52/5/2). *IpsJ* 23 October 1773, Declined lime trade at Hythe. Rebow accounts (ERO A6293 or C47) 27 June 1774 include a payment of 4 guineas 'for a Marble Grave Stone sold to him from Wivenhoe'. 1779 Isaac Slythe (qv) took his High St premises, also in 1782 the Hythe yard.

In 1758 he had apprenticed his son John to Thomas Bayles (qv) attorney for £100 (Guildhall Library, Society of Genealogists, Masters Indexes S/929/1/311). Bartholomew jun was a witness to Thomas Boggis' (qv) marriage settlement in 1763. And is perhaps the John Bartholomew junior, whose furniture and farming stock at Peldon was for auction for his creditors in 1780 (*IpsJ* 15 January 1780).

At the Hythe, Joseph Green (qv) was also in the lime and coal trade and there was a John Bartholomew whom Green says he has dismissed, December 1770, for taking money for coals and 17 August 1771 John Bartholomew, mason, says a foreman of the same name has been taking orders similarly (nfr).

24 March 1777 Sessions Books (ERO P/CoR/7) a John Bartholomew appears as a disorderly person.

Executor to Elizabeth Freeman (ERO D/DU 206/18, 1747). No will traced. Tombstone, St Leonard's; 'On a large black marble raised obliquely, chisseled very deep John Bartholomew of this parish, died May 9, 1782 aged 71 Also his two wives and nine children' (Strutt's *Colchester*, Vol. 2:67).

See also will Hannah Bartholomew, wife of John, Merchant, ERO D/ABR 22/223 made 1736, proved 1739.

BARTON ROYSTON [53]
Captain 67th Foot
ob. 1802

The husband of Thamar, daughter of Samuel Wall 1 (qv) attorney. As such was associated in various court proceedings arising out of disturbances created by Wall in the 1780s as the course of his insanity advanced (see under Samuel Wall).

The Bartons lived at no. 17/18 North Hill and later inherited the Wall family property in Angel Lane, St Martins after the death of Thamar's brother, Samuel Wall 2 (qv). In 1790 a friend of the Bartons died while staying at their house. He was Richard Bowyer Esq of London, presumably godfather to their son (see below). His obituary describes him as 'well known among the Dilettanti as an elegant performer on the German flute, a very sociable man and much regretted' (*IpsJ* 22 October 1790).

Barton died on 27 January 1802 and was buried in the Wall family tomb in St Martins where he was joined by his wife on 11 May 1806 and in 1813 by their son Royston Bowyer Barton, killed in action aged 26.

The family properties including 'several valuable and improveable freehold residences and small tenements on North Hill and Angel Lane' were for auction on 1 November 1806 (*IpsJ*). There seems to have been no sale, for, on 15 August 1807 (*IpsJ*) they were again offered, but this time for sale by private contract, and more fully described.

They comprised a capital modern-fronted dwelling house on the east side of North Hill. A 'cheerful' dwelling house adjoining the above, now occupied by Mr Candler (Stephen Candler (qv)) and two freehold tenements on the East side of North Hill occupied by Messrs Day and Morice as well as a ¾ acre close occupied by Mr Moore. In St Martins was a uniform freehold brick residence on the west side of Angel Lane with a very valuable safe underground, the iron door and lock of which cost £50. This was adjoined by another freehold cottage. There was also a 56 acre farm in Ardleigh and a capital residence in Hadleigh worth £30 p.a.

BATEMAN WILLIAM [54]
Innkeeper, Golden Fleece
fl. 1795-1805

His will (1805, ERO D/ABR 30/33, innholder, St Mary) gave a life interest in the estate to Isabella his wife (formerly Isabella Lingwood (qv) cf ERO ML D/ALL 1795). Thereafter the property was to be divided and half shared between the children of their marriage (Rebecca and William) and half to Isabella's children by her first marriage (John Lingwood jun. and Isabella Seaman). Thomas Andrews (qv) acted as executor.

B

The way in which the property was divided with a comparatively generous share for his step children reflects the fact that Bateman only came into the inn through his marriage with Isabella, and respects the association of the Golden Fleece with the Lingwood family.

BAWTREE JOHN [55]
Brewer
w. 1772/3

Of Wivenhoe. His will (ERO D/ACR 17/222, 1773) provides a £30 per annum annuity to his wife Sarah, charged on property at Brightlingsea, together with stock and tools of his trade to allow her to carry on the business for the benefit of herself and children. Other properties at Wivenhoe, Brightlingsea, Abberton, and Walton are divided between sons John, Samuel and William. Daughter Elizabeth was left £500.

His son John married Jane Ram of Berechurch in 1788 (CPL Crisp ML441).

BAYLES THOMAS 1 [58]
Grocer
w. 1726/7

Bayles' will (ERO D/ACR 14/9, Thomas snr, grocer) directed the sale of extensive properties, the proceeds to be held in trust for the benefit of his three sons, sister Pepper and five daughters. The property included the Queens Head and Falcon Inns in St Peters and St Runwalds*, other tenements in Angel Lane, Trinity Street and More (sic) Lane, a messuage in Aldham and land in Peldon and Mersea.

*Morant, *Colchester*, Book 2:49 reciting Edward Haverlands chantry in the church of Crouched Friars describes an 'Inn, called the Fawcon, with all the rentaries thereto annexed ... in the market place of this Town, and in the parishes of St Peter and St Runwald'. A footnote explains that these were 'Now the sign of the Queen Elizabeth's Head. There belonged then to it, three shops thereto adjacent, a garden joining to St Runwalds churchyard, and two other gardens...' The property was probably just westward from the Moot Hall and could well be the location of the new built house auctioned by Henry Lodge (qv) in 1769 later occupied by John Wallis (qv).

BAYLES THOMAS 2 [56]
Grocer
w. 1727/8

Died early within a year of his father Thomas Bayles 1 (qv). His brief will (ERO D/ACR 14/80, 1728, grocer St Runwald) simply left the messuage mentioned under his marriage settlement to his wife Martha, then to their children should they have any.

BAYLES THOMAS 3 [57]
Attorney
fl. 1745-1775

The son of Thomas Bayles 2 (qv) grocer and his wife Martha (qv), he was apprenticed to Jacob Vanderzee, attorney of Nayland, for the considerable sum of £105 in 1745 (NA IR 1/17/149). Created free burgess with the advent of the new Charter, he was in one day made up through Common Councillor and Assistant to Alderman on 27 August 1764. He served as Mayor in 1766 and 1773. Only one Borough vote is recorded for Bayles in 1768 when he supported the sitting candidates, Gray and Rebow.

Bayles administered his father's estate and in 1753 advertised for creditors to come forward (*IpsJ* 21 April 1753). He acted as agent for the sale of the late Mr Alderman Clark's (John Clarke (qv)) messuage and half acre in Maldon Lane in 1767 (*IpsJ* 19 December 1757) and also for the sale of James Robjent's (qv) extensive bankrupt properties in 1773 (*IpsJ* 19 January 1773). He was Robjent's main creditor, being owed more than £300. Bayles also drew up and witnessed at least 13 wills made between 1755 and 1778, most of them for Colchester residents including business proprietors, farmers, town gentry and widows.

He lived in Sir Isaacs Walk, Holy Trinity. Hortensia Richardson (22) married Bayles in 1756 (ERO ML D/ACL 1756) and after her death he married Mary Dennis (21) in 1771 (ERO ML D/ALL 1771).

Bayles died in July 1775 (*IpsJ* 14 July 1775) aged 47 at Romford while he was on his way to London to seek medical advice. His will of 29 July 1772 (NA PROB 11/1011, Alexander 335, proved 19 September 1775) left his house and other property in Holy Trinity as well as messuages in Moor Lane and elsewhere in St Botolphs, together with the bulk of his personal estate, to the children of his first marriage, Thomas and Hortensia. A life interest in the Isaacs Walk house and the plate and linen as well as £100, provided for his second wife Mary and a further £100 to their son William Dennis Bayles. A codicil of 31 August 1774 leaves the £600 Bayles had received in his father-in-law's will to another son Philip with the interest to his mother Mary for life. The executors were his friend Samuel Alston of Nayland, cousin William Brudenell Atkinson and brother-in-law Samuel Carr (qv).

See also will Thomas Bayles, gent, Colchester NA PROB 11/1157, Major 403-448, 23 October 1787.

BELL MARTIN [61]
Grazier, Broker and Rower
fl. 1734-1772

The master and relative of Henry Johnson (qv) who was admitted free burgess by right of apprenticeship to Bell on 26 January 1764 (JBB NB 79/2). Johnson later traded and was bankrupted as a baymaker. Bell's niece Sarah Draper (qv) was also half sister to Johnson.

Amongst other property Bell occupied, he leased New Fairfield near St Ann's Mill, St James from the Corporation (see *IpsJ* 14 April 1770, lease advertised, apply Mr Smythies Town Clerk (Francis Smythies 1 (qv)), now occ. Mr Martin Bell. On 6

October 1770 (*IpsJ*) it is offered for 21 years). He voted from at least 1734 until 1768 supporting the Tory 'Country' party in 1734 but voting for one candidate of each party thereafter.

His will, made by the nonconformist lawyer Peter Daniell (qv) (made 15 June 1772, proved 2 September 1772, ERO D/ABR 26/324, grazier and broker, St Nicholas) left property leased out to tenants in Greenstead and St James, to Mary Ann Gowen late of Colchester now Barnadiston. Otherwise, apart from two small cash legacies apparently to friends, the main beneficiary is Sarah Draper, his late wife's niece, who was living with him. She received all messuages in St Nicholas, St Botolphs and Lexden, extensive enough to be let to at least nine tenants, together with the residue of the estate. She was named as executrix together with Bell's 'esteemed friend' Thomas Boggis (qv) baymaker.

BERNARD REVD VALENTINE LUMLEY [63]
Curate Great Holland, Rector of Frinton and Stockton, Norfolk
1746-1816

Bernard was the son of William, a corn merchant and was born and educated at Bungay, Suffolk. Admitted sizar aged 19 at Emmanuel College Cambridge 3 July, 1765. He obtained his BA in 1769 and the same year became curate of Banningham, Norfolk (Venn, *Alumn. Cantab.*).

By 1779 he was curate of Great Holland when he delivered the Masonic Sermon at Ipswich. He was also Rector of Frinton between 1783-1801. After the death of his uncle, Valentine Lumley (qv) on 26 April 1794, he was instituted to the Rectory of Stockton in Norfolk (*IpsJ* 2 August 1794).

His finances were clearly not of the best for in 1795 (*IpsJ* 23 May 1795) his creditors were requested to meet at the Bell Inn, Thorpe and receive 12s 6d in the £, being the benefit of a certain assignment of February 1790.

His monumental inscription on a black slab in Stockton church, reads:-

B

To perpetuate the memory of the Revd Valentine Lumley Bernard who died in the performance of his duty on Sunday 24th March, 1816, aged 69 years. This stone is placed by his affectionate daughter Elizabeth Sarah Lumley.

BERNEY BOWN JOHN [93]
Innkeeper, White Hart
fl. 1773-1775

Berney Bown, for 'many years Butler to the Revd Dr Moore of Norwich and since to Sir Edward Astley, member for the County of Norfolk' took the inn in 1773 (9 October 1773 *IpsJ*) described as 'newly fitted up'. In 1774 (3 September 1774 *IpsJ*) the Colchester stage was advertised from the White Hart.

BEST CAPT THOMAS [1273]
Captain in East India Company
c.1715-1775

Baptist (Spurrier, *Eld Lane*). Formerly Captain of the *Prince Henry*, East India Company.

Married twice. 1) to Hannah daughter of Capt. Francis King, who dd. 1754 aged 40. 2) to Elizabeth Rootsey at Wivenhoe on 7 April 1760. She dd. Jan. 1778 aged 56 (Wivenhoe Registers, ERO DPP/277/1/4).

Ledger at Wivenhoe gives dates above and also commemorates Mary wife of Capt. Francis King, dd. 24 January 1720 aged 42; Capt. Francis King, dd. 29 March 1731 aged 52; son Francis, dd. 3 November 1738 aged 34; daughter Mary King dd. 25 March 1773, aged 66; Captain Thomas Best, dd. 9 January 1775, aged 60.

Best was executor of above mentioned Mary King, spinster (will ERO D/ACR 17/231, made 1769, proved 1773). She was cousin of Matthew Martin Esq (qv) and lived first with him (received £200 in his will NA PROB 11/772, proved 20 July 1749) and then with Samuel Martin Esq (received £150 in his will NA PROB 11/909, made 7 September 1761, proved 13 June 1765).

IpsJ 12 September 1761, when Queen Charlotte had stopped off at Sir Isaac Rebow's house Headgate on Monday 7th. 'Capt. Best attended her with Coffee, Lt. John Seaber with Tea.'

Capt. Best was a Winsley Trustee at the time of decease (ERO C905 Box 7, JBB report to Winsley's Trustees).

IpsJ 7 February 1778; To be sold ... genteel messuage on North Hill, built and occupied by late Capt. Thomas Best, with good cellars, two sorts of water, and a pleasant garden... enquire at house or of Mr Joseph Wallis (qv) ironmonger, Colchester (JBB Note: this was no. 2, 'Hill House', demolished 1910 for entry to Technical College, now the Sixth Form College).

Daughter Hannah 'last Tuesday married Mr Thomas Parsons, an eminent stonemason in Bath' (22 September 1770 *IpsJ*; ERO D/ALL 1770. CPL Crisp ML141 says he is of Linecombe in City of Bath, carver. See R. Gunnis, *Dictionary of British Sculptors 1660-1851*, revised edn (Abbey Library, 1951):293. Parsons was a baptist minister as well as a carver).

Best's will (NA PROB 11/1104/41 Alexander, made 29 November 1774, proved 14 February 1775 witnessed Samuel Smith (qv), Benjamin Hall (qv), Elizabeth Munsey) left son Thomas 2 (qv) the house in St Peter's in own occupation. A messuage in Holy Trinity occ. Mrs Catherine Butley and son, to was left to his wife for life, then to his son, failing whom to his daughter Hannah Parsons, who had the North Hill property. He also left £800 to wife for her own disposal as well as his share, a 16th part of East India ship called the *Thames*, estimated value £1,000.

Executor Mr Sanders Oliver of Cannon St, London stone mason, with £80 for trouble (see Gunnis:283). Executrix wife Elizabeth Best.

BEST THOMAS 2 [64]
Clothier
ob. 1789

Not free. Apprenticed to James Salmon, Clothier, Dedham in 1761 for £105 (NA IR 1/54/70). ERO ML D/ALL 1768 shows Thomas Best marrying Jane Blacksell of Kelvedon. Advertised on 30 May 1772 (*IpsJ*) as a clothier from Gutter Street. This house seems to have had a longer association with his family, since in 1768 (*IpsJ* 3 December 1768) a house with a new brick front and warehouse in Gutter Street 'designed for the bay trade' was advertised to sell or let, enquiries to Mr William Catchpool (qv) on the premises or Mr Thomas Best (qv) on North Hill. In 1773 (*IpsJ* 31 July 1773), Best jun was living on North Hill, when he acted as agent for the sale of property in the High Street, late occupied by William Munsey (qv). Was the son of Captain Thomas Best (qv), by whose will of 1775 he inherited property in Holy Trinity. In 1783 Thomas junior was listed as owner occupier of premises in Holy Trinity rated 16 with a personal estate of £10 2s. He died at age 43 and was buried on 17 December 1789 by Eld Lane Baptists (Spurrier, *Eld Lane*, obituary *IpsJ* 12 December 1789).

See also CPL Crisp ML413, ERO D/ALL 1768 of 1772 shows Thomas Best, clothier, St Botolphs married to Elizabeth Cooke (17) St Giles, but does not distinguish whether Thomas 2 or 3 was the bridegroom.

BEST THOMAS 3 [1193]
Grocer
fl. 1790-1809

1790-1 rated 3 in Black Boy Lane, St Botolphs.

IpsJ 9 July 1806 (JBB NB Jan 69:25) sale by auction on 13 July of four freehold dwellings on East Hill owned by James Wallis Ashwell (qv), occupied by Thomas Best, grocer and other sub-tenants. This sale was associated with the bankruptcy of James Wallis Ashwell. The following year (*IpsJ* 8 August 1807) a shop at the foot of East Hill occupied by Thomas Best, grocer, yearly tenant was amongst a number of properties for sale owned by Ashwell.

See also *IpsJ* 25 February 1809 advertised auction of furniture Thomas Best, general shopkeeper, Tollesbury.

BETTS STEPHEN [65]
Tinman
fl. 1764-1809

Betts is notable for his consistently anti-Tory politics. He voted in Borough elections from 1768 until 1807 supporting the most radical candidate on all occasions. He was elected Common Councillor on 10 August 1767, Assistant in 1781 and Alderman on 17 December 1781 during periods of Whig ascendancy. He was Mayor in 1782-3 when he presided, doubtless with approval, over the ceremonial which marked the end of the American Wars (1 March 1783 *IpsJ*). He was an active member of the Hand in Hand Club of 1788-90 in support of George Tierney (qv) and acted as steward. In 1792 he resigned from the Corporation together with Samuel Ennew in protest at the unruly piracy of Frank Smythies (qv) and the Tory Corporation party.

Betts was an auricula fancier and was steward at the 1770 feast at the Angel (5 May 1770 *IpsJ*). In 1771 he witnessed the will of William Daniel (qv) together with Henry Dobby (qv). At first, Betts occupied premises at 55 High St, next to Henry Lodge (qv) between September 1764 and 1767 (ERO C47 CPL629). He then moved uphill to no. 3 High Street until 1790 when, whilst keeping on that shop, he lived in All Saints at the lower end of the High Street (JBB note, 1983, Markhams). He died on 30 April 1809 aged 78 and 'much respected' (6 May 1809 *IpsJ*). Though earlier associated with the Baptists, he was buried in All Saints together with his wife Elizabeth (who had died on 19 April 1808 aged 70), his son William (qv) and his son's two wives.

BETTS WILLIAM [66]
Attorney
fl. 1784-1834

The son of Stephen Betts, tinman (qv) and his wife Elizabeth. A free burgess and consistent voter who shared his father's radical sympathies. In the 1780s and 90s he seems to have been resident in the Betts' family property in the High Street in All Saints and attended All Saints vestry from 1789. Newspaper items show him administering the deceased estate of William Townsend, attorney (qv) in 1790 (*IpsJ* 5 June 1790) and as agent for the sale of property in Moor Lane in 1799 (nfr). Henry Crabb Robinson says Betts was 'an odd man, a great reader' and heard that later he was insane (Henry Crabb Robinson, unpub. ms., *Material Reminiscences in Old Age*, Dr Williams Library).

Betts married twice, firstly to Sarah Kendall of St Nicholas at St Peters in 1784 (ERO ML D/ACL 1784), who died on 11 July 1794 aged 38. In 1801 (*IpsJ* 3 January 1801) he married Miss Sarah Keeling of St Runwalds who died on 7 June 1830 aged 62. Betts himself died on 13 January 1834 aged 72. All three were buried in the Betts family tomb at All Saints with Betts' parents and his children.

His first wife Sarah Kendall was daughter of the Quaker distiller Thomas Kendall (qv). The second wife Sarah, was daughter of John Keeling (qv), glass and chinaman of St Runwalds, by his first wife Grace Lees.

BEVAN ALBERTUS [1204]
Master Carpenter
d. 1766

No building work completed by Bevan can be identified. He took an apprentice John Whitaker for £15 in 1751 (Guildhall Library, Society of Genealogists, Masters Indexes, S/929/1/6256) and is witness to will of James Boys Esq of Layer Marney who leaves rings to seven county gentry (NA PROB 11/833, proved 11 November 1751). Bevan had no children.

Married second wife Sarah Fitch at All Saints 1741 (by banns, D/P 200/1/8).

Neighbour of Revd Philip Morant (qv) in St Mary's Lane, who is witness to both his will (made 1759, PRO PROB 11/924, Tyndal, carpenter St Mary-at-the-Walls, proved 11 December 1766) and his wife's (PRO PROB 11/995 Bargrave, Sarah, widow, St Mary-at-the-Walls, made 1770, proved 23 March 1774; she died in 1771). The wills are very similar, beneficiaries being his nephew Mark Leppingwell (qv) and nieces Sarah and Mary Leppingwell and Mary Bevan, nephews James Fitch and James Thorn 2 (qv), and nieces Grace Bawtree and Rachael Fitch.

He also left £10 to a brother Henry (not Henry 2 (qv)).

BEVAN HENRY 1 [1205]
Master Carpenter
1675-1728

Took four apprentices: 1714, John Alefounder (qv), £8 (NA IR 1/43/156); 1721, Gamaliel Carr, son of Gamaliel, £17 (Society of Genealogists, Masters' Indexes, IM S929/1/930), Carr was admitted free burgess 1728; 1743, Thomas Malden son of Isaac Malden, 20 gns (Society of Genealogists, Masters' Indexes, S/929/1/3759); James Nutman, admitted free burgess 1734, by right of service.

27 January 1708, 'formerly of Stanway, now of Lexden' bought Stanway inn 'Two-necked Swan' from John King (qv) (ERO D/DHt 250/8).

1720, Lexden Manor Court (ERO D/DEI/M), admitted to 'Cherry Orchard' estate on north side of hill down into Lexden (later Isaac Green's (qv) tannery).

27 September 1723, Borough Oath Book (ERO D/B 5 R1), appointed 'Inspector Terrarum' – 'land-looker' or surveyor in succession to James Deane (senr), deceased 1722.

Will ERO D/ABR 20/33, made 9 April and proved 29 April 1728. Left all estates in Stanway, Copford and Colchester to wife Thomasin (died 1761 aged 81) his executrix, for life, then those in Stanway and Copford to eldest son Henry 2 (qv), and those in Lexden to son Isaac (qv) (later an attorney), plus a mortgage on 'several tenements lying in Colchester called Downfall Alley' and £50 at 21.

To Henry was also left 'all the rough timber in my yards and my working Tools ... but my will is that all the Laths, Deals and Wrought Stuff shall be my Executrix's and also that the Planks and Joyce (sic) which are bespoke for Mr Green's Barn shall be made out of the same Rough Timber and that my Executrix have the same together with all Gates which shall be made at the time of my decease.'

To daughter Sarah £200 at 21 or marriage plus £100 at her mother's decease, or sooner if her mother thinks fit (Sarah married Samuel Ennew (qv) attorney).

To 'loving friend' Walter White a guinea ring, and to be supervisor of the will. Residue of real and personal goods etc. to wife.

See also William White, house carpenter of St Peter's Colchester, will of 1708 ERO D/ABR 7/16.

BEVAN HENRY 2 [1206]
Master Carpenter
1705/6-1766

Baptised Stanway son of Henry 1 (qv) and Thomasine, 10 February 1705/6; died Lexden 13 December 1766.

1737, Lexden Manor Court (ERO D/DEI/M) admitted to Horn Hall on north side of hill towards Colchester (JBB note: Hill House area).

1766, occupied Lexden Park at £55 p.a. owned by John Richardson (qv) apothecary.

Accounts of William Round of Birch Hall (ERO D/Dno T/11); include 5 cheques to Henry Bevan 1738-42, total £254 10s; and others to William Castells for £890. These may concern building of Birch Hall or William Round's improvements thereto (Morant, *Essex,* Vol 2:184; plate in *Gentleman's History of Essex,* 1772, see also James Round (qv)). Bevan also leased a farm from Round, Brockett's at Tendring (1733 for 99 years at £30 p.a).

Took apprentices; c.1735, Isaac Green (qv); 1743, Thomas Malden, son of Isaac (of Beeleigh Abbey, nfr).

IpsJ 25 September 1762; 'well timbered' Head St estates for sale, shortly afterwards rebuilt. These were (no. 54) Mrs Lidgould (recently (1990) Martins then Barclays Bank) and (nos. 7-9) John Osborne 1764-67 (Bakers, later Harpers Sports shop in 1990s). The former survives, very elegant.

Marriage Settlement, drawn up by Samuel Ennew (qv) (ERO D/DEl B24 1749) with Elizabeth Potter Everard of Wormingford and Brightlingsea. Married in 1751. (Two letters from Bevan to Ennew are surprisingly ill-spelt and bad writing. cf. extract from his will below).

The combined estates were considerable. In 1768, Morant (*Essex*, Vol 1:473) mentions Brockett's as his widow's and other estates including a farm on the London road at Stanway, and estate called Langham-valley in Langham which 'belonged to the late Mr Potter' (will 1738) 'now to his niece married to Henry Bevan Esq.' Also Little Beeleigh, part of the Abbey estate, late Henry now Isaac his brother's (JBB Note: an example of how Morant compiled his work over a period of years, and did not always update it). Mrs Elizabeth Potter Bevan dd. 1790, and Langham Valley, 102 acres, was for auction 10 September 1791 (*IpsJ*).

Free burgess 1727. Alderman in Charter of 1763, but resigned 27 August 1764. 1758 J.P. for County, 1750 Commissioner in Channel Act.

He had no children. His will (PRO PROB 11/1200 Bevor, proved 12 January 1791, merchant of Lexden, made 12 March 1756) was not proved till 1791 (after his wife's death). It has a codicil 21 November 1757 leaving £5 to two men and two maidservants unnamed. 'And a Giney apeace to twelf Workmen to carrey me the Grave which I desir maybe don in a very privett maner. Witness my Hand the day and year above. - H. Bevan - Viss. Mark Lepingwell (qv), James Notman (Nutman*), Thos Bimham (Burnham), Wm. Mills, Roger Hines,

Isaac Chaplen and the other six I love (sic) my executor within named to nominate and appoint. I give (three lines deleted) to my cosen Marrey Bevan daughter of Henry Bevan Twenty Gines - to Margat Petterken my cosen Ten Gines. H.B.

(*admitted free burgess by right of service to Henry Bevan 1, see also Benjamin Nutman, brickmaker and bricklayer, ERO will 1755 (nfr), W. Bergholt).

The story of the Lexden estate belongs to his brother Isaac (qv), left it by his father. Henry's will leaves residue to Isaac, and mainly concerns his wife and mother. £50 p.a. is left to sister Sarah Ennew after death of either and £100 when both dead.

It is clear from his last days (the will not mentioning Isaac Green (qv), but calling himself timber merchant) that building work was left to Green.

BEVAN ISAAC [67]
Attorney
fl. 1745-72

One of the Lexden family of that name. Bevan married Mary Carter (21) when he was a 22 year old gentleman at Witham in 1745 (ERO ML D/ACL 1745) He lived at Mistley. A house he owned in Manningtree was advertised to let in 1766 (*Ips]* 19 July 1766) and William Mayhew 2 (qv) attorney was agent for the transaction.

Bevan is chiefly important to Colchester's history as being the steward of Richard Rigby (qv) of Mistley Hall. He also managed property for Sir Robert Smyth (qv) MP who accused him of negligence during a legal action over the Pyfleet fisheries in 1785 (ERO D/Dfg/Z1, Smyth's correspondence; *VCH, Essex*, Vol. 9, Pyfleet fisheries:269).

Bevan's will, made on 12 December 1771 and proved on 8 January 1772 (NA PROB 11/974, Taverner 3, proved 8 January 1772), disposed of widespread properties in Essex for the benefit of his family. His wife Mary received £100 p.a. together with £200 cash and furniture worth £100. The bulk of the estate - much of it a reversionary interest on property to fall due following the death of his brother Henry's widow (Elizabeth Potter Bevan), was secured in trust for the benefit of his son and his daughter Sally (who was allowed a £4,000 dowry). The trustees were named as Bevan's 'friend and benefactor' Richard Rigby (qv) and brother-in-law Samuel Ennew (qv).

See also will Henry Ennew Bevan of Lexden, PRO PROB 11/1029, Collier, 29 March 1777.

BEVERLEY WILLIAM [68]
Farrier
w. 1782

Acted as executor to James Unwin, carrier (qv) in 1781 (will ERO D/ACR 18/113). Beverley's own will of 1782 (ERO D/ACR 18/147, farrier) left his real estate (a copyhold farm Great Bromley and the house where he lived in East Street) to William Bland, silk weaver of London, an executor. Sarah the daughter of Samuel Clay jun (qv) farmer of Greenstead received £200, and cash legacies of £10 were also left to Enoch King (qv) pavior, Samuel son of Edward Brown carpenter, and John son of Elizabeth Pilgrim. The other executor was Abraham Stradling (qv) (Unwin's son-in-law) who received £5.

BIGG WILLIAM REDMORE, RA [1179]
Painter
fl. 1749-1828

See full article at JBB, *EAE*:191-4.

BLACKWELL WILLIAM [72]
Innkeeper, Black Boy
fl. 1796-1805

Ended his life as a broker of St Giles, having been resident in St Leonards in 1796 (bill per Overseer's Accounts). His will of 1805/6 (ERO D/ACR/936, broker) divided his house into three parts, the middle (lower room and one chamber over) was left to his wife Sarah. The west and east parts were to be sold for the benefit of his wife and son-in-law James Prentice and comprised on the west, one cellar and two lower rooms, two chambers over, kitchen and a passage to the privy; and on the east one lower room, one chamber over, one small kitchen, large yard and small ground. Sarah was to make a choice from the household goods and the balance to be sold to provide for settlement of the estate and burial expenses, then £30 to James Prentice. The residue was to be divided between Prentice and Blackwell's son Richard who was also to receive his 'wearing apparell.'

In 1805 William and Richard Blackwell had acted as witness of John Willes' (qv) will. Willes was later landlord of the Black Boy.

BLAND CHARLES [1197]
Hosier
ob. 1775

A vault in St Nicholas used to contain Charles Bland dd. 10 March 1775 aged 54 – his beloved wife of 21 years, Alice, dd. 22 October 1767. The ledger over it survives, much worn, in remnants of the churchyard, with the curious addition; 'He beareth Field Ermine A Bend sable charged with three Pheons Head or ... Crest A Lyons Head Argent Issuing out of a Ducal Coronet or name of Bland' (CPL Crisp MIs). Joan Corder, *A Dictionary of Suffolk Arms*, (Suffolk Records Society, 1965):98 has similar arms for Bland, Visitation of 1664-8, but on ground Argent, at Eye. But the Carleton arms have ground Ermine.

Premises in St Runwalds opposite Three Cups, rated 14, 1766.

His will is at NA PROB/11/1006, Alexander made 29 November 1768, proved 4 April 1775. No children, so property is left to:-

- Elizabeth, eldest daughter of late brother Andrew, £400 in 3% annuities.
- Mary, her sister, copyhold 'Cocks' at Stanway plus £300.
- Edward, son of brother John, (Edward Bland (qv) hosier), freehold in St Runwalds occ. Mr John

Pilborough (qv) and bond for £300 on said John Pilborough 'and this house of Mr Pilborough's shall descend in the male line of the Blands forever and never be mortgaged.'
- Elizabeth widow of bro. John to be paid £50 in 2s weekly installments by Edward.
- Joel Bland (qv), son of brother Joel, reversion of half part of estate in St Runwalds (Mrs Rebecca Burgis's) and £200 at 21.
- Joel, wearing apparel, watches, buckles and buttons.
- Michael Gray, farmer at Canewdon, four tenements in St Peters, and £50 to his son Charles at 21, 'and if there is a daughter of the said Michael Gray that is named Alice' £10 to her, but if not to his eldest daughter.
- Some other £10 legacies including poor of St Runwalds and St Nicholas at 50s a year in bread, and to executors Joel and 'good friend John Pilborough' (qv) (who died however before it was proved).

See also: will William Bland, silk mercer, St Runwalds, NA PROB 11/1610, Cresswell, 18 November 1818; will Revd Thomas Bland, clerk, Colchester, NA PROB 11/1177, Machan, 8 April 1789; apprenticeship, NA IR 1/14/89, Charles Bland, son of Edward, Colchester, pipemaker, to John Farrow of Colchester, cutler, 4gns, also NA IR 1/21/75 William Bland to Joshua Crickett, citizen and weaver, 3 gns, 1757.

BLAND EDWARD 1 [74]
Hosier
fl. 1775-1797

Son of John Bland. In 1775 inherited 16 High Street (occupied John Pilborough (qv)) from his uncle Charles Bland, hosier, together with some family silver, bonds and mortgages worth £450, £100 cash when 21 and a fifth share of the residue of the estate. He was to pay his mother Elizabeth £50 in installments of 2s per week from the rents of 16 High St (will Charles Bland NA PROB 11/1006, Alexander 94-139, made 29 November

1768, proved 4 April 1775, died March 1775). He was a free burgess, voting first in 1790 and supported establishment candidates. On 8 April 1797 (*IpsJ*) a mansion house, St Runwald, opposite the Three Cups, late occupied by Edward Bland, was offered for auction at the Red Lion (auctioneer Stephen Candler (qv)) and no. 16 High Street was sold to Alexander Fordyce Miller (qv).

BLAND EDWARD 2 [73]
Tobacco Pipemaker
fl. 1735-55

Bland's son Charles was apprenticed to a cutler John Farrow in Colchester for £4 4s in 1735 (NA IR 1/14/89). Bland died in 1755 leaving his premises in George Lane to his wife Mary who sublet them as follows;

> To be LETT and Enter'd upon at Lady Day next. A messuage with convenient outhouses, formerly occupied by Edward Bland and now by John Randall, Tobacco Pipe Maker situate in George Lane, near the Market Place in Colchester and at the same time will be sold, the Moulds, Screws, and other Utensils in the said Business. Enquire further at the said house or of Mr Ennew attorney in Colchester (Samuel Ennew (qv), *IpsJ* 17 March 1759).

The premises continued as a pipemakers. In 1821 Stephen Chamberlain, pipemaker, directed in his will (1822, ERO D/ACR 32/154) that they should be rented by his nephew Stephen Chamberlain Rand for the benefit of his common law wife and two young children. There also appears to have been a long term connection between the Chamberlains and the Blands since in 1745 (NA IR 1/50/290) Stephen son of Stephen Chamberlain was apprenticed to Elizabeth Bland of Colchester, tobacco pipemaker for £4.

BLAND HENRY DANIEL [1198]
ob. 1851

Henry Daniel Bland grew up in Colchester, left for London as a young adult, but returned later in his life. He was the author of a series of scurrilous *Anecdotes* about the late-eighteenth century town, some of which still survive in manuscript in the John Bensusan Butt Collection (ERO C905, Box 2) and are transcribed below, in Volume 3 at Appendix 3.

Monument at St Nicholas records; William Bland of St Runwalds, dd. 20 August 1818, aged 75; Mary, dd. 1 September 1825, aged 80; Henry Daniel, dd. 16 April 1851, aged 79.

The exact identity of his father, William, is unclear. William Bland, staymaker, voted twice in 1784 for Potter and seemingly not again. A William Bland who was named Common Councilman in the 1818 Charter and promoted to Assistant in 1820 is a different man. Henry Daniel Bland was created free burgess of Colchester, 18 July 1799, the son of William 'of the City of London in service of East India Company'.

Ips] 4 October 1794 contained a public notice by baymaker Philip Havens 2 (qv):

> POACHERS & UNQUALIFIED PERSONS
>
> Whereas Bland junr of Colchester and Vince junr of Langham Essex, both unqualified persons have lately made improper use of the names of proprietors and stewards of manors; and have lately killed game ... near Donyland Hall ... and Bland junr did ... shoot a hare in the plantation adjoining the Church.
>
> A reward of FIVE GUINEAS is hereby offered to anyone who will give information....

This may explain something of why Bland left town (Vince jun. has not been identified).

Henry Daniel Bland, gent, voted from London in 1807 and 1812 but not later. His collection of poll books of 1820 were at one time in the JBB collection. Was appointed Alderman in Colchester 1836-1841.

Once back in Colchester he lived in St Mary's Terrace; Pigott's *Directory* of 1835 lists him at 1 St Mary's Terrace West (also in 1845, at St Mary's Terrace. In 1852, Miss Bland, 1 St Mary's Terrace). Bland died 18 April 1851 'in London suddenly, of Brighton and St Mary's Terrace' (nfr).

The typescript of *Bland's Anecdotes* in the JBB collection (at Appendix 3) was identified by JBB as being in Charles Benham's hand, 'given me by James Williams of Endsleigh School'. However, the collection seems to be incomplete, for example one about Francis Smythies and Headgate House (see *ECS* 24 February 1934 'from anecdotal writing in 1844'). A few entries in the anecdotes refer to nineteenth century figures and events, for example the death of Roger Nunn, 1844 or a reference to the *Weekly True Sun* of 26 August 1838.

BLAND JOEL [1285]
Salesman
w. 1780

Son of Joel Bland and nephew of Charles Bland (qv) whose executor he was (will proved 1775). His own will (salesman of Colchester, NA PROB 11/1060, Collins, made 1777, proved 7 January 1780) left everything to his son Joel, salesman, except £5 to Edward Bland (qv) and his mother.

See also Sessions Examinations, ERO P/LWR4, August 1759, gave evidence concerning a dog of his that had been hanged.

BLATCH JAMES ESQ [75]
(formerly Smythies)
fl. 1770-1812

The son of William Smythies, surgeon (qv) and his wife Elizabeth, *née* Blatch. She was one of the daughters of John Blatch (qv) merchant. Is notable for changing his surname by deed poll in 1772 to inherit £2,000 from his aunt, Sarah Edwards (NA PROB 11/975 made 13 December 1770, proved 27 February 1772, copy ERO D/DC5/37). Created a free burgess in 1781. He was Captain in the East Essex Militia in

1776 and subsequently a Major in 1778. He subscribed to Charles Shillito's (qv) *A Country Bookclub*.

He was executor to his father's will together with his brother Yorick Smythies (qv) and John Round (qv). He inherited copyholds in East Mersea, lands in Hitcham, Wattisham and Brightlingsea as well as oyster layings in the last. He also received a house built new in St Mary's parish, later known as Crouched Friars, and its neighbour (notes on deeds, ERO C905 JBB NB Dec 65). He renovated this mansion house. An inscription on the pump reads:-

B
J E
17

His servant was Maria Lay who had deposited her savings (some £100) in his hands. He witnessed her will on 7 June 1799, which distributed this amongst her relations (ERO D/ABR 29/246).

He made his own will on 27 February 1808 (NA PROB 11/1529, 30 Oxford, 7 January 1812, 'formerly James Smythies') which was drawn up by William Mason 2 (qv) attorney (who had also made Maria Lay's will). Blatch left his mansion in St Mary-at-the-Walls, the land there known as the Priory, and farms in Essex and Suffolk to his wife for life. Thereafter the St Mary's property was to be left to his son James Blatch and the rest to be sold and divided between his daughters Elizabeth Beevor and Mary Ann Hoblyn. The furniture and china were left to his wife.

The will was proved on 7 January 1812 by the executors Elizabeth Blatch, widow, Revd James Blatch his son and Revd Richard Hoblyn his son-in-law.

Blatch had married a second time to Elizabeth *née* Dennis. The couple are buried at St Michael Mile End. James Blatch Esq of St Mary-at-the-Walls, dd. 18 December 1811 aged 65, and his wife, dd. 22 October 1815, aged 72. After her death the family properties were sold.

On 27 July 1816 (*IpsJ*) Martells and North House Farm, East Mersea property of James Blatch Esq deceased were advertised for sale, followed on 3 August 1816 (*IpsJ*) by 27 acres in Peldon called Rose Farm and a further 80 acres in West Mersea and Peldon occupied by Charles Tiffin. The family lawyer William Mason (qv) was agent for the sales.

His widow's will is NA PROB 11/1574, 6 November 1815. Her son, James Blatch became a clergyman. Fellow of Magdalen College, Oxford and Vicar of Basingstoke (1814) (Venn, *Alumn. Cantab.*).

See also will of Jane Blatch, spinster, Witham, 10 May 1810, NA PROB 11/1511.

BLITHE FRANCIS [1114]
Bookseller
d. 1718

These trades have not been explored before 1730. However G. O. Rickwood (nfr) says Blithe was 'a well-known man.' He was listed as 'bookseller in Colchester' in the very long subscription list for John Walker's *An attempt towards recovering an account of the numbers and sufferings of the clergy of the Church of England, ... who were sequester'd, ...* (London, 1714) which includes a number of subscribers from Colchester and area.

BLOMFIELD BEZALIEL [76]
Farmer and Maltster
fl. 1755-1799

One of the extensive nonconformist family, mainly of Colchester, Ardleigh and Dedham, notable for wide ranging kin links with other nonconformists, (e.g. Tabor, Rouse, Robjent etc). He was apprenticed to Timothy Shorey, (qv) baymaker (his brother's father-in-law) for £50 on 27 May 1755 (Borough Register of Apprentices, ERO D/B 5 Ta1, NA IR 1/52/93) and was a practicing baymaker in 1768 when he took John Walton apprentice (no fee) for Rowing, Combing & Dressing of Wool (ERO D/B 5 Ta1, 25 April 1768). Bezaliel Blomfield the younger was bankrupted in 1772 (*London Gazette*, 20 June, 3 October, 1772, 27 March 1773, 13 September 1774, 12 September 1775, 2 July 1776) but he seems to have recovered from this setback.

Blomfield and many of his family were lifelong members of Lion Walk Meeting. A cousin, Samuel Tabor of Dedham, had been a pastor during the ministry of John Collins and the family's connection with the congregation was to continue well into the nineteenth century (Blaxill, *Lion Walk*). A ratepayer, by virtue of his malting at the Hythe he was active also in St Leonards vestry. (Premises rated 8, owner occupied including stock in 1783.)

He died in 1799 and was buried at Lion Walk. His will of 1797/9 (farmer, St Michael, Colchester, ERO D/ACR 19/167) distributed his property between his children, Bezaliel, Benjamin and Elizabeth, wife of Isaac Blyth, Boxted. Provision was also made for his granddaughter Mary Stammers (£200 at age 21 and £200 at 24) who sadly died soon after her 21st birthday, then living with her uncle, Bezaliel jun (will ERO D/ABW 119/1/27, 1811). She left her legacy to her uncles and aunts as above, according to the terms of her grandfather's will.

Other Blomfield wills include, Henry, gent, Dedham, 16 August 1777, NA PROB 11/10333 Collier; Bezaliel, Minister of the Gospel, Colchester, 5 January 1814, NA PROB 11/1551 Bridport; Bezaliel, maltster, 2 August 1811, NA PROB 11/1524 Crickett.

BLOWER BARWELL [77]
Baymaker, Bocking (Essex)
fl. 1752-1776

Married Mary the widow of John Baker (qv) at St Martins Colchester on 2nd January 1776 (ERO ML D/ACL 1756). Thomas Boggis (qv) was both a witness at this wedding and an executor of the bride's first husband. This was Blower's second marriage, having first married Ann Strutt of Felsted at Little Leighs in 1752 (CPL Crisp ML54, ERO ML/D/ALL 1752). Earlier in 1768 (*IpsJ* 10 September 1768) Blowers had set up as a wool factor at The Wool Hall in Bocking.

Blower's daughter Ann married Joseph Strutt on 16 August 1774. Blower was described in the marriage licence (nfr) as a dyer of Bocking. Ann died in September 1778 and her widower was then inspired to compose an Elegiac Poem '..in different measures and without rhime to the memory of an amiable and virtuous wife, her disconsolate husband offers this grateful proof of his sincere affection'. It was published in quarto, in London in 1782. Strutt was an antiquarian who lived 1749-1803 and died in London aged 55 (*ODNB*).

BLYTH ANN OATHWAITE [86]
Merchant
fl. 1777-1814

Born Ann Oathwaite Hazleton, the niece of John Oathwaite. (qv) mariner, she married Daniel Blyth (qv) merchant at St Leonards on 21 January 1777. Oathwaite died in 1788 leaving her his shipping business as well as confirming the £1,000 to be paid her after her husband's death per their marriage settlement. Blyth drowned in 1799 (*ChCh* 21 June 1799) but the shipping business continued, preserving the name 'Oathwaite & Co.' It had been shipping to Hull and Grimsby for forty years according to a later advertisement of 4 January 1817 (*IpsJ*). Ann remained in formal control of the vessels and real estate but it is unclear how much active part she took in the running of the business, for example it was her son Daniel Oathwaite Blyth (qv) who advertised he was continuing the trade after his father's death (*ChCh* 14 June 1799). She died in 1814, by that time having retired to her farm in Elmstead, her husband's birthplace. Perhaps a reflection of the inflation and embargoes of the war years, in 1802 (12/13 February, deeds of Stonehouse Farm, ERO C47 CPL933, JBB NB Yellow 1) a mortgage of £1,600 was raised on part of the family property,

Stonehouse farm (Hythe) with John Willes, gent of London (co-executor of John Oathwaite with Daniel Blyth).

Ann's property was sold swiftly after her death in 1814, (*IpsJ* 24 September 1814) including the farm at Elmstead, Stonehouse Farm (13 acres and 3 fishponds opposite Hythe church); a brig called the *Oathwaite* and two lighters the *Ann* and the *Dorothy* (the second named after Daniel Oathwaite Blyth's first wife). Although her will directs that these properties and also a messuage, yards, quay, wharf, granary and warehouse etc. be applied for the benefit of her daughters, Ann Oathwaite, Elizabeth Dorothy and Margaret Sophia Blyth, her estate was found to be insolvent with debts of £2,033 6s 8d. The daughters had to be provided for by annuities of £50 each purchased by Daniel Oathwaite Blyth.

BLYTH CLARK [82]
Cabinetmaker and Joiner, later Woolcomber
fl. 1754-1768

Had been bound apprentice to Thomas Grigson, ironmonger. Moved from St Botolphs to open a shop in All Saints (ERO D/P/200, All Saints Certificate Book). He advertised on 12 October 1754 (*IpsJ*) as follows;

> CLARK BLYTH, Joiner, Cabinet and Chairmaker, over against Mr Nathaniel Hedge's, Watchmaker in the Parish of All Saints, Colchester.

> Makes and Sells, at the most reasonable Prices, all Sorts of Mahogany, English and Foreign Walnut-tree Double Chests, Buroes (sic), Desks and Book-cases, Whist and Buroe Tables, Oblong and Oval Dining-Tables. Tea-boards, Waiters and Tea-Chests, common Chests of all Sorts, Fire Screens, and Tea Kettle Stands, Slat-Frames, Dumb Waiters, Beaufets (sic) and Corner Tables, Tea-Tables, plain and plate Fashion &c.

The following year Blyth married Ruth Stacy (25) (CPL Crisp ML219, ERO D/ALL 1755) who was later named as a legatee in Susannah Smith's (qv) will of 1774. The same year he took an apprentice, John King, for 13 gns (NA IR 1/52/134, 1755). Apparently the cabinetmaking business did not answer, for on 1 May 1756 (*IpsJ*) was advertised Henry Lodge's (qv) sale of Blyth's stock of furniture and wood. The apprentice was transferred to John Butcher in 1758 (NA IR 1/53/56, £15). Blyth was created free burgess on 10 December 1767 (Thursday Court) and voted on 16 March 1768 as a comber. He died very shortly after and was buried in All Saints on 27 March 1768.

BLYTH DANIEL 1 [81]
Merchant
1753-1799

Baptised on 29 September 1753, the son of Daniel and Elizabeth (*née* Kendall) of Elmstead. He established himself as a Hythe merchant and on 21 January 1777 married Ann Oathwaite Hazleton the niece and heir of John Oathwaite (qv) who ran a coastal shipping business. Blyth was active in St Leonards parish vestry from at least 1780 and built up a respectable property holding (see Ann Oathwaite Blyth (qv) for the sale after her death). In 1790 he and John Minter dissolved their partnership as coal merchants, each continuing business separately (*IpsJ* 3 April 1790). Blyth was to be applied to when the sloop *Trades Good Hope* plying between Colchester and Gainsborough (Master Edward Bateman) was for sale at the Hythe (*IpsJ* 26 May 1792). By 1799 he also had a yard at Wivenhoe from which he advertised coals, being then in short supply and fetching 46s per chauldron due to snow and a frozen navigation up to the Hythe (*ChCh* 8 February 1799). Blyth was not able to enjoy a prosperous old age, however, for later that same year (*ChCh* 7 June 1799) when traveling from Colchester to Harwich on the Colchester paquet, the vessel ran into a sudden squall two miles below Wivenhoe. Both Blyth and John Swan the master of the paquet were drowned. His son (unnamed, but described as a 'lad') and a Lieut. Wootton of the East Norfolk Grenadiers, who were also on board, survived by clinging to the mast for an hour until they were rescued by a passing collier. It was some time until Blyth's body was found and he was buried at the Hythe in the week of 21 June 1799 (*ChCh*).

His will, made 17 November 1787 and proved on 21 August 1799 (NA PROB 11/1328, merchant, St Leonards) named his wife Ann, his brother William Blyth of Kirby (gent) and John Bawtree (qv) brewer as executors. He provided a £10 annuity to his mother and £84 to his sister Martha; then after settling an outstanding £500 on a bond to his father-in-law, John Oathwaite (qv), left the balance for the benefit of his children. He shared a wall tablet outside Hythe Church with John Oathwaite (qv).

BLYTH DANIEL 2 and MARY [85]
Perukemaker and Milliner
fl. 1765-1780s

Daniel was a leading tradesman who held premises on the corner of High Street and North Hill, rated 8. He was admitted free burgess in 1764, by right of descent from his father John Blyth (JBB NB 88/8:29). He was elected Common Councillor on 10 August 1767 and Assistant on 7 December 1781. A political supporter of the outsider parliamentary candidate, Christopher Potter (qv).

Married Mary Brown of Sible Hedingham in 1766 (CPL Crisp ML334, ERO D/ALL 1766). He died in 1784 (All Saints MI, 24 August 1784 aged 55). His will (NA PROB 11/1131, made 24 May 1783, proved 7 July 1785) left Mary a life interest in all his property, including the stock in trade of the millinery, mercery, linen drapery and haberdashery business which she ran, thereafter to their nine children. He also left £20 apiece to apprentice each of the children (Daniel, Elizabeth, Robert, Mary, Ann, Thomas, John, Charlotte, George). In 1785 (*IpsJ* 5 February 1785) Mary advertised for a journeyman to carry on the business after her husband's death.

See also Peter Banyard apprenticed to Daniel Blyth, £15, 1773 (nfr); Thomas Blyth, baker, admitted free burgess by right of

B

descent from Daniel 1798, also son Daniel, perukemaker in 1788 and son Robert, hairdresser in 1796 (JBB 88/8:29).

BLYTH DANIEL OATHWAITE [87]
Merchant
fl. 1799-1835

Son of Daniel and Ann Oathwaite Blyth (both (qv)), he took over the merchants and shipping business owned by his mother on his father's death by drowning in 1799 (*ChCh* 14 June 1799). He married Dorothy Schofield of Alresford in 1804 (m/s Stonehouse Farm deeds, 2/3 November 1804, ERO C47 CPL933) and they had three children Daniel Oathwaite (bn. 1808), Harriett (bn. 1810) and Elizabeth Charlotte (bn. 1809), though it is unclear whether these were all Dorothy's children or those of his second wife Charlotte. The family's difficult financial affairs are shown in that Ann Oathwaite Blyth's (qv) estate was in debt after her death and are further evidenced by Daniel Oathwaite Blyth selling off on 4 February 1804 (*IpsJ*) tenements on the south of the street and opposite his granary, the granary itself and the crane in the quay as well as the Three Goats Heads inn.

The problem was one of trade fluctuations and insecurity. In 1814 his maltings at Rowhedge were described as the 'largest in the kingdom' (A. F. J. Brown, *Essex at Work* (Chelmsford, 1969): 126) and in 1824 Blyth was able to buy Hill House from the Ordnance (now (1983) the site of Paxman's club). However, he was bankrupted in 1833 (*ECS* 16 April 1833) and his household goods, four properties and three vessels were advertised for sale. His will made in 1835 and proved in 1839 left all his personal estate to his wife Charlotte, leaving her to make a division between their children at her death, something which itself may indicate that there was little left to divide.

BLYTH JOHN [80]
Perukemaker
d. 1803

Between 1763 and 1801 he occupied no. 88 High Street next to Hollytrees. Rated 7 next to Mrs Bream (see Ann Wilder (qv)) in 1787. Voted for Tierney in 1788 and 1790. In 1799 (*IpsJ* 31 October 1778) he acted as agent for the sale of stock in trade of Robert Brown (qv) deceased. He had three sons Daniel (qv), Thomas (qv) and Samuel (qv), all admitted free burgesses (JBB NB 88/8:29).

IpsJ reported his death in December 1802 (*IpsJ* 1 January 1803) aged 82, 'after a long affliction born with Christian patience'. His will is at NA PROB 11/1385, 29 January 1803.

See also Robert Brown son of Robert deceased apprenticed to John Blyth, 1719 (NA IR 1/46/49); John Blyth of Boxted Essex farmer and Nathaniel Cole (qv) of Colchester gunsmith bd John 22 to Dorothy Winkle of St Michael Mile End (CPL Crisp ML274, 1738).

BLYTH SAMUEL 1 [79]
Tailor
fl. 1756-1782

Son of John (qv). Admitted free burgess 1764. Married in 1756 to Susan Fox of St Martins in 1756 he being of All Saints (CPL Crisp ML310, ERO ML D/ACL, index names her as 'Fop'). Buried at All Saints 23 November 1782.

See also Samuel Blyth, butcher, admitted free burgess 1788 by right of descent from Samuel.

BLYTH SAMUEL 2 [84]
Innkeeper, Castle, All Saints
fl. 1763-68

A free burgess voting in 1768 for Rebow and Gray. May be the same person as Samuel Blyth 1 (qv), tailor.

BLYTH THOMAS [83]
Perukemaker
fl. 1759-1802

Son of John Blyth (qv) and brother of Daniel Blyth (qv), perukemaker (All Saints MI JBB 88/8:29). Married Susannah Clark of St Martin in 1754 at St Peters (CPL Crisp ML435). Advertised on 3 March 1759 (*IpsJ*) when he succeed Mr John Parker at premises next door to the George Inn, St Nicholas (probably 117 High Street, JBB NB Jan 63:59). In 1778 he was established across the road at no. 55 High Street (rated 9) where he remained till 1797. Was elected Common Councillor on 10 September 1765 and Assistant on 21 August 1780. Tended to vote for radical candidates, supporting Potter in 1781 and Tierney in 1788. A vocal and instrumental benefit concert followed by a ball was held in his honour at the Three Cups in 1792, tickets 3s (*IpsJ* 20 October 1792).

He died on 29 April 1802, aged 77 and was buried in All Saints with others of his family (MI).

See also: Free School Admissions, ERO T/B/217/1, Thomas son of Thomas, 1769 aged 5. Free burgess admissions, 1781, Thomas, Ensign in E. Suffolk militia, son of Thomas Blyth, grandson of John. Thomas jun, schoolmaster, Weathersfield voted in 1790 (Poll Book). Susannah Blyth, dd. St Nicholas 28 July 1775 (JBB NB 88/8:29, 34)

BOAD HENRY [88]
Schoolmaster
fl. 1732-1759

A local schoolmaster who compiled innovative English and Mathematics textbooks for children which followed his own methods and were designed to make the subjects more accessible to a wider audience. His *Artium Principia, or the Knowledge of the First Principles of Mathematics made Easy and Intelligible to the Meanest Capacity* was published in 1733. A lengthy and detailed newspaper advertisement (*IpsJ* 8 March

1739/40) proposes subscriptions to *The Art of Computing by Numbers, or, A Treatise of Arithmetic, both Vulgar and Decimal, in Theory and Practice* (15s to subscribers).

He refers to the sources for his various methods, and continues:-

> Also, that the Learner may the better proceed in each Step, with Certainty and Judgement, he has also given plain and easy Demonstrations of every Part thereof, without the tedious and unnecessary Pomp of Words used by some Writers, or the more scanty Provision of others; The one serving only to amuse and confound the Learner, and the other so mock him with a bare Pretence of Knowledge.

An appendix gave lists of problems, 'chiefly related to trade and business' together with, 'Some Directions for Book-Keeping after the Italian Manner, very useful for Teachers of Accompts and their Pupils.' Boad's approach was entirely practical and intended to 'expeditiously' qualify 'Youth' (whom he boarded) 'for clerkships or other Employment'.

By 1744 (*IpsJ* 22 September 1744) The *Treatise* was ready for the press and Boad also proposed (should he receive sufficient encouragement) to publish in weekly parts at 3d each, 'sticht (sic) in blue covers, and deliver'd to the subscribers at their own Houses by the News Carriers'.

Boad's English Spelling Book and Exposition had reached 23 editions by 1805, this last being enlarged by a Revd Thomas Smith who had also expunged all 'obsolete and indelicate words.' The school was clearly not a select establishment and Boad's advertisement of 1744 (above) also indicates something of its composition and the background of the pupils:-

> Whereas I find a Report has prevail'd to my Disadvantage, tho' without Foundation, That the great Number of Free Boys in my School, must necessarily take up too much of my Time, and hinder my giving due Attendance to the rest of my Scholars; and this has even

been intimated to me by some of my particular Friends, as a Reason for their not sending their own Children. It is therefore judg'd proper to acquaint the Publick, That the Time for teaching Ten Free Boys, now under my Care, by the charitable donation of a Gentleman, late of London, expires at Michaelmas next, when they will be dismiss'd; and the Numbers of the other Free Children belonging to my School, is diminished to Twenty Boys. If therefore those Gentlemen, who have made the Objection, will now give me their Encouragement, they may depend upon it, that all proper Care shall be taken of their Children, both with regard to their Learning and Morals, and the favour will be gratefully acknowledged, by

Their oblig'd humble Servant   HENRY BOAD.

Boad died in 1759 and is buried at St Nicholas. His son, Fauntleroy continued running the school (*IpsJ* 4 August 1759) and his widow Sarah settled debts and claims on his estate the following year (*IpsJ* 12 May 1760, untraced in *IpsJ* issues for May 1760, but cf notes in JBB NB 86/6, 88/6).

BOGARD CORNELIUS [89]
Draper
ob. 1756

Son of Josias Bogard, baymaker, St Peters, who died in 1684/5 (ERO D/ABR 11/404, made 15 December 1684, proved 18 January 1684/5). His brother Josias received the family property in St Peters, subject to a right of residence to their mother Mary for life, but Cornelius took a share in the personal estate alongside his sisters Susan and Martha.

A free burgess who voted in 1747 for Nassau, and a substantial tradesman. He died on 24 January 1756, aged 82, and according to his monument in St Peters was 'an honest man'. Inscriptions also record his wife Susannah (ob. 28 November 1722 aged 43) and daughters Hannah Bogard (ob. 1747 aged 38) and Susannah the wife of William Daniel (qv) (ob. 19 October 1747 aged 39) (JBB NB Oct 67:49).

Bogard's shop was taken over in 1757 by Robert Walker (qv) (*IpsJ* 29 January 1757).

See also CPL Crisp ML397, ERO D/ALL 1743, William Daniel, Colchester, 37, to Susannah Bogard, 33 at Lexden, 1743; CPL Crisp ML233 1700 (in ERO index but no reference given there), Samuel Langley of Colchester 'raser maker' and Josias Bogard of Colchester, baymaker, bd, Samuel to marry Martha Bogard; CPL Crisp ML 240, ERO D/ABL 1681, John Wilbore of Colchester, baymaker and Abraham Freemantle of Colchester, baymaker bound, John to marry Abigail Bogard, Colchester; Isaac Buxton app. to Cornelius Bogard, Linen draper, £70 in 1713 (NA IR 1/42/175); Wm. Dyer, son of Benjamin app. to Cornelius Bogard, Linen Draper, £80 in 1728 (NA IR 1/49/22).

BOGGIS ISAAC 1 [1118]
Baymaker
fl. 1731-1762

The son of John Boggis 1 (qv) baker. Was apprenticed in 1715 to Francis Lince (qv) baymaker for £20 (NA IR 1/44/38).

Bought the property later known as the Minories (74 High Street) from Robert Havens, London, merchant in 1731 (Lease/Release 28/29 September 1731). In 1737 he married Elizabeth Truston of Playford, Suffolk, spinster, daughter of Thomas Truston, gent. The marriage settlement made provision for her of both the Minories and property in Sudborne (sic) and Orford contributed by her father (Marriage Settlement, 31 May 1737). There were three sons of this marriage, Thomas (qv) born 1739, Isaac 2 (qv) born 1740 and James (qv) born 1744. Elizabeth Boggis died (20 August 1745) aged 30, and in 1751 Isaac Boggis married for the second time, at Witham, to Ann Tennant (38) widow. Both she and Isaac were described in the marriage licence (nfr) as being of All Saints Colchester and Edward Morley (qv) of St Leonards stood bond.

In 1751 (Lease/Release 25/26 November 1751) Boggis bought tenements and gardens to the east of the original Minories property (where the bus park entrance at the top of East Hill

B

now is (2008)) from Mrs Hannah Coe. These buildings were later used as a counting house and warehouses by James Boggis (qv) and it may be assumed that Isaac and later Thomas Boggis (qv) made the same use of them.

When the Dutch Congregation's monopoly over the bay trade broke up, Boggis and Joseph Duffield (qv) were Hall-keepers of the Wool Market for a year with first refusal of the lease (Ass Bk 27 January 1728). Was created Common Councillor on 10 December 1727, Assistant on 11 August 1730 and Alderman on 31 December 1739 for the short period of time until the Charter was lost in 1741. Was one of the trustees of Naggs Bequest to the Charity Schools (Morant, *Colchester*, Book 3:17).

Isaac Boggis made his will on 30 September 1761 (NA PROB 11/882, proved 1 December 1762). This confirmed his marriage settlement and left his wife all her wearing apparel and (for life only) 32 diamonds. His two younger sons Isaac 2 and James (both qv) received £6,000 apiece 'to be paid them respectively by my executor when and as they shall respectively come out of their times of their Apprenticeship'. The interest meanwhile was left to the eldest son, Thomas (qv) except for £50 each per annum for their clothing and use. On his wife's decease Isaac and James were to have a further £800 each out of the £3,000 of her marriage settlement. In case of dispute, 'it is my Will and request ... that they do consult and be advised therein by their Uncle Jeremiah Daniel Esquire (qv) and Mr Thomas Truston of Ipswich, Merchant.' Truston was his first wife's brother, of St Lawrences Ipswich, died 1772 leaving mourning rings to all three Boggis brothers (nfr). It is unclear why Jeremiah Daniel should be named as uncle. However see CPL Crisp ML 306, 1746, for Daniel's marriage to Judith Edlyne, widow, when Boggis stood bond.

Boggis left his brothers Josiah and Joseph £50 each for mourning. 'And I give to much esteemed Friends Charles Gray Esquire, George Wegg Esquire, John Cole, Michael Hills, Charles Whaley and William Smithies (*sic* – William Smythies, surgeon) (all qv) to each of them a Ring of a Guinea Value in Memory of me.'

Thomas Boggis received the residue.

Isaac Boggis died 11 November 1762 aged 62 and is buried in St James churchyard.

Unless otherwise cited, the sources used here are JBB's transcriptions of Minories Deeds and contextual information, ERO, C905, Box 2, A2. See also JBB, *The House that Boggis Built*, (1978).

BOGGIS ISAAC 2 [1119]
Merchant
1740-1801

Middle son of Isaac Boggis 1 (qv) and brother to Thomas (qv) and James (qv) Boggis. Apprenticed in 1756 to John Readshaw of London, fishmonger for £280 (NA IR 1/20/184). Was 'of the City of London, Merchant' acting as trustee in his brother Thomas' marriage settlement of 31 August 1763. Admitted Colchester free burgess 2 April 1764. Traded as a Hamburg merchant. Married in 1764 to Ann, daughter of William Rolfe of Langenhoe Hall. Rolfe left his daughter £5,000 and his son-in-law £3,500 in his will of 1775. Boggis lived firstly on 60 North Hill and later 9-10 East Hill. This house had been bought in September 1775 by his brother James Boggis (qv) for £1,380 but occupied from this point by Isaac Boggis (NA PROB 11/1012, 3 October 1775; *House that Boggis Built*:14-15).

IpsJ 29 November 1794, 'Saturday last died, very much lamented, Mrs Boggis, wife of Isaac Boggis Esq of this town.'

IpsJ 25 December 1794:

> This morning a letter was received by Isaac Boggis Esq of this town, sent by command of his Royal Highness the Prince of Wales, to inform him he had given orders to Commodore Paine, to convey her Royal Highness the Princess of Wales to Greenwich or Harwich; and that if she could land at the latter place, he will avail himself of the polite and obliging offer made by Mr Boggis in October last and that her Royal Highness (in that case) will certainly call on Mr Boggis.

B

> If Mr Boggis should have timely notice of her arrival she will be entertained in a stile of elegance and magnificence that cannot fail to astonish and please her Royal Highness, as Mr Godwin, of the Strand, has nearly finished a superb service of plate, ordered by Mr Boggis for this occasion. Mr Birch, of Cornhill, has received directions to conduct the entertainment; and Mr Boggis has desired him to procure every delicacy and luxury that this season and this country can afford.

This was the future Queen Caroline, on her way to marry George, later George IV. In fact she landed at Greenwich the following spring. The entertainment seems to have been planned to take place at the Minories, then vacant following the death of Thomas Boggis (qv) in 1790. Isaac Boggis also offered the Minories as accommodation to the Prince of Orange then a refugee from Holland (*House that Boggis Built*:32-3, from a letter in the possession of the family).

IpsJ 31 March 1798 gave £60 voluntary subscription for the Defence of the Country, the largest amount in the long list from Colchester. His servants gave 10s 6d.

His will was made 4 April 1799 and proved on 25 June 1801 (NA PROB 11/1358/359). He left his Capital Mansion house (9-10 East Hill), stables, gardens, furniture and household goods as well as his farm in Woodham Ferris, Essex (occupied by James Brewster) and £1,000 to his eldest son Isaac Rolfe Boggis. To his second son James he left his capital mansion in the parish of All Saints (i.e. the Minories) and its contents as well as the option to take at a fair valuation 'as much of my Stock in Trade of a Baymaker' as will make his share of the property equal to that of his elder brother. The residue were left to the two elder brothers in trust to sell and distribute shares equivalent in value to James and Isaac's legacies. These children were Ann Carthew, wife of Revd Thomas Carthew, Woodbridge, Suffolk; William Boggis; Edmund Rolfe Boggis; Charlotte, wife of Robert Douglass Esq Major of HM 56th Regt of Foot (whose share was to be diminished by the £1,500 her husband had received on their marriage).

All of Isaac Boggis 2's Colchester and Essex property was offered for auction in 1801 (*IpsJ* 18 July 1801, extensive listing) but evidently not sold since a later sale 'pursuant to the Will of Isaac Boggis Esq' took place at Garraway's Coffee House, Change Alley, Cornhill, 20 July 1809 by Messrs Skinner, Dye, Tuchin and Forrest, of 'Eligible Freehold Estates' comprising farms at Steeple and St Lawrence (called Motts and Hodges), Bures Hamlet (Ravensfield Farm) and Great Holland (Jenkins Farm) (nfr). See also *IpsJ* 8 July 1809, when his 'commodious mansion house' at 9-10 East Hill, including 'offices, pleasure grounds, gardens about four acres' were offered for auction.

Regarding the children of Isaac Boggis, JBB notes the following, mostly from letters and documents owned by the Boggis Rolfe family at Wormingford.

James did take up the trade of Baymaker, but quickly got a commission in the West Essex Militia (Letter to Lt. Col. Douglass, 1 March 1803, transcribed ERO C905, Box 2, A2) and was only in Colchester 'for a few days for the purpose of collecting the rents of the Estates' in February 1804. A deed of 1802 shows James buying the land and premises between the Minories and East Hill House from the Estate. He resigned his commission in 1821 because of financial difficulties (Letter to Douglass, 10 July 1821, transcribed by JBB as above). He was a Colchester Alderman.

Ann Carthew (1770-1834) had married in 1794, and raised a family by Revd Thomas Carthew, R.N.

Col. William (1776-1834) of W. Essex militia died at Southend.

Lt. Col. Edmund (1783-1808) died at Barbadoes (sic).

Charlotte's marriage to General Douglass ended tragically following her clothing catching alight. She died 22 April 1816 (Letter from James to Douglass, 4 August 1816, transcribed as above).

A sister Lucy (1771-1798) died unmarried.

A brother Thomas (1774-1794) died in action. *IpsJ* 13 September 1794, 'It is with regret we repeat the disagreeable intelligence of the death of Ensign Boggis, second son of Isaac Boggis Esq of

Colchester, who fell on the 31 July, at Fort Mozelle in Corsica, by a cannon shot from the enemy's works, whilst gallantly supporting the honour of his King and country, universally esteemed by all who knew him.'

Thus the whole generation seems connected with the Armed Forces during the Napoleonic Wars, including Capt. Revd Isaac Rolfe Boggis (1 February 1768 – 6 July 1825). He was created free burgess at the age of 17 on 29 September 1784. Voted in Colchester in 1812 and 1820 elections. MA Cantab. 1793. He was Captain in the W. Essex Militia, 1803-7 and curate of North Ockendon 1809-17. Lived at Berechurch Lodge in 1810 then at Fox Hall, Upminster and later at Langham Hall, Essex. In 1825 left England with his family intending to settle in the south of France. Died 6 July 1825 at Calais and is buried there (Venn, *Alumn. Cantab.*). Isaac Rolfe Boggis' marriage settlement to Elizabeth Mayor Stubbs, daughter of George Stubbs, Great George Street, Westminster, is in ERO D/DC 23/E. See subsequent family burials at St James Colchester. Descendants of this marriage were existing in the mid-twentieth century (*Burkes Landed Gentry*, 1952, 'Boggis, formerly of Edwardstone').

Unless otherwise cited, the sources used here are JBB's transcriptions of Minories Deeds and contextual information, ERO, C905, Box 2, A2. See also JBB, *The House that Boggis Built*, (1978)

BOGGIS JAMES [1292]
Gent
ob. 1787

Youngest son of Isaac Boggis 1 (qv), born 1744. Apprenticed in 1759 to Samuel Spatemen, a London grocer for the large fee of £450 (NA IR 1/22/30). Admitted free burgess 20 August 1765. He was a grocer in London at the time that his uncle Joseph Boggis (qv) made his will in 1765, but later lived with his brother Thomas (qv) at the Minories.

The brothers shared the same voting patterns in Borough elections. James and Thomas voted singly for Affleck (Tory) in April 1784, whilst Joseph Boggis (qv) (their uncle) and Isaac Boggis 2 (brother) voted for Affleck and Smyth (one Whig, one Tory). In the by-election of July 1784 Joseph, James and Thomas Boggis all voted for the outsider Christopher Potter (qv), whilst Isaac Boggis 2 voted for Samuel Tyssen (qv), a candidate put up at the last minute in order to enable a petition against the likely winner, the Whig Smyth. Hence the Boggis family seem unanimously to move away from supporting the increasingly radical Whig, Smyth.

His will (ERO D/ACR 18/294) was made 1 June 1787 and proved 31 December 1787. He died 22 June 1787 aged 43 and is buried with his father and other kin in St James. He left his brother Thomas 'the Diamond Ring he heretofore gave me' with all his pictures and prints, 'my Table Clock, Weather Glass and Silver Guggler' (presumably a narrow-necked wine decanter), as well as all furniture not otherwise disposed of. His sister (in-law) Ann Boggis, the wife of Isaac 2 received all my plate and rings 'except that above mentioned' to divide among her children. His goddaughter and niece Ann was left his gold watch, steel chain and gold seals. His nephew, Isaac Rolfe Boggis received 'my Horse with his saddle, bridle and other furniture, and also my Writing desk Beureau (sic) Bookcase and all my Books.' Uncle Joseph Boggis (qv) was left 4s per week and decent mourning. Martha Wenlock and James Brooker, 'servants living in the house with my Brother Thomas', received £10 each. Other servants, Sarah Squires and Thomas Fenton received £5 each.

5-guinea mourning rings were left to William Mayhew 2 (qv) and Revd Nicholas Corsellis (qv). One guinea rings went to John Debonnaire Esq, Ann his wife, Miss Ann Debonnaire, Francis Smythies 1 Esq (qv), John Morley Esq (qv), Allington Morley Esq (qv), John Cole Esq (qv), Joseph Green (qv), Robert Newell (qv), Thomas Andrews (qv), Thomas Hawes, George Reynolds (qv), Samuel Winnock (qv) and Isaac Samuel Clamtree (qv).

B

The residue was shared equally between the executors, brothers Thomas and Isaac.

It is evident from the similarities between this will and that of his brother Thomas that the two lived in the same house and had the same circle of friends. The only people named here who do not appear in his brother's will are the servant Thomas Fenton who went into service with Michael Robert Hills (qv) (Fenton is named in Hills' will) and William Mayhew 2, who died before Thomas Boggis. John Cole's father also appeared in Isaac Boggis 1's will, made 1761.

Unless otherwise cited, the sources used here are JBB's transcriptions of Minories Deeds and contextual information, ERO, C905, Box 2, A2. See also JBB, *The House that Boggis Built*, (1978).

BOGGIS JOHN 1 [1294]
Baker
ob. 1728

His will, made 1 April 1720, ERO D/DU/457/11, left a tenanted house to his wife Susan for life then to his son Josiah and heirs who also received £50. Son Isaac Boggis 1 (qv) received £150 and son Joseph Boggis received £162 at age 21. Grandson John Boggis (son of John 2) received £50 at age 21.

Died 28 October 1728, buried St James.

Unless otherwise cited, the sources used here are JBB's transcriptions of Minories Deeds and contextual information, ERO, C905, Box 2, A2. See also JBB, *The House that Boggis Built*, (1978).

BOGGIS JOHN 2 [1293]
Baker
ob. 1752

Eldest son of John Boggis 1 (qv), hence brother to Isaac Boggis 1 (qv). His will (ERO D/ABR 24/104, made 24 May 1752, proved 12 June 1752) left copyhold lands and tenements in East

Donyland to his son-in-law Stowers Carter (qv) on condition that he pay £200 to Boggis' daughter Hester Boggis. £200 was also left to daughter Lucy and the two daughters received his windmill in St Mary-at-the-Walls in his own occupation and the remainder of his lease of Drury farm on condition that they pay 5s per week to son John Boggis. Stowers Carter also received all the milling and farming stock and household goods. Residue to daughters Lucy and Hester. Lucy was named executrix together with Isaaac Boggis 1 (qv).

Unless otherwise cited, the sources used here are JBB's transcriptions of Minories Deeds and contextual information, ERO, C905, Box 2, A2. See also JBB, *The House that Boggis Built*, (1978).

BOGGIS JOSEPH [976]
Baker
fl. 1760s

Brother to Isaac Boggis 1 (qv). Headman for East Ward in 1764 (Assembly Book). Voted in the Borough poll of 1768.

His will (ERO D/ACR 18/320, made 9 February 1765, proved 25 June 1789) left his nephews Thomas Boggis (qv) baymaker and Isaac 2 Boggis (qv) merchant of London, all his messuages in St James parish, both in his own occupation and tenanted to sell and pay interest and dividends to 'my loving brother Josiah'. Mary Fidgett 'singlewoman now living with me' was left £5. The capital funds were to be divided between the brothers Thomas, Isaac 2 and James, then of London, grocer. Thomas and Isaac were executors.

Unless otherwise cited, the sources used here are JBB's transcriptions of Minories Deeds and contextual information, ERO, C905, Box 2, A2. See also JBB, *The House that Boggis Built*, (1978).

BOGGIS THOMAS [1120]
Baymaker
1739-1790

The eldest son of Isaac Boggis 1 (qv) and brother to Isaac 2 (qv) and James (qv). Attended the Writing School at Dedham (see under William Colchester (qv)).

Married Frances Hills, daughter of baymaker and merchant Michael Hills (qv) who lived near the Minories, in Queen Street. They married at Frinton (registers). Their marriage settlement of 31 August 1763 specified a settlement of £3,000 from her father and the conveyance of the Minories to trustees, Isaac Boggis 2 and Michael Robert Hills (qv) (brother of Frances), for her use if she survived her husband, or to their children.

In 1771, Thomas Boggis extended the Minories property with further purchases of tenements to the east and south (Lease/Release of 27/28 June 1771, Henry Francis of Castle Hedingham saymaker, to Thomas Boggis). In 1775 his wife Frances died in London and was buried in the family vault of her mother's family, the Dingley's at St Helen's Bishopsgate. JBB is of the opinion that the marriage had broken up (JBB, *The House that Boggis Built* (1978):14). Her death, childless, released the Minories, and the £3,000, from the provisions of the marriage settlement. The fortunes of the baytrade were also (temporarily) improving at this period and it seems that Thomas Boggis took advantage of these circumstances to thoroughly remodel the Minories in the then fashionable style, as it substantially remains (see *The House that Boggis Built* for the architectural alterations and also for observations on the material domestic culture and servants in the Boggis brothers' household. *IpsJ* 21 March 1795 and 9 November 1799: two almost identical advertisements for the sale of household goods of 'Two GENTLEMEN deceased', identified by JBB from similarities with the Boggis wills as James and Thomas Boggis).

Boggis was elected an Alderman on 24 August 1775 and on 29 September a Justice of the Peace for the Borough. He also served as Mayor in 1776-7 and 1780-1. In 1782 he was among the Colchester delegation presenting a Loyal Address to the King 'on the Success of H.M. Forces in various parts of the World' (*House that Boggis Built*:28, Ass Bk 31 May 1782). Politically, Thomas Boggis can be associated with the rise of the local Tory Corporation party in the 1780s. In the two elections of 1784, his and his brother James' votes demonstrate opposition to the Whig Sir Robert Smyth (see details under James Boggis).

Another facet of Boggis' public life was his important role in freemasonry in Colchester and Essex. Both Thomas and his brother James were Royal Arch masons. Thomas was originally member of the Angel Lodge and its Master in 1770. In 1777 the eminent freemason Thomas Dunkerley Esq visited Colchester for a meeting of the Provincial Grand Lodge. Boggis was created Deputy Provincial Grand master for Essex and seems to have been central in the creation of a new, and more socially prestigious lodge, the Lodge of Unity, in Colchester. This new lodge did not long survive Boggis' death in 1790. For a discussion of freemasonry in Colchester at this period and Boggis' influence, see D'Cruze, *Pleasing Prospect*:102, 110-11, 114-5.

Thomas Boggis was also the holder of one of the silver tickets for Colchester Theatre (*The House that Boggis Built*:17).

Boggis died 4 April, 1790. An obituary in the *Gents. Mag.*, lx:375 described him as 'an eminent baize-manufacturer, and one of the Aldermen of Colchester'. His will, made 19 March 1790 was proved the 16 July following (NA PROB 11/1193). He wished '... to be buried in Lead and in the same Vault with my late Father and the Names on the present Tomb Stone being wrong spelt I desire the Stone may be turned and polished and the present Names fresh cut thereon together with my own and then raised two feet and no more from the level of the Earth on Stone the railing round repaired and painted and in such repair and painting hereinafter kept by my Executors.'

He left:

B

to 'my good sister Ann the wife of my dear Brother' Isaac Boggis 2 Esq (qv) 'my Playhouse Ticket and the sum of Fifty pounds in token of my regard for her.'

Nephew Isaac Rolfe Boggis (eldest son of Isaac 2) received 'my Ivory Cabinet which I desire him to accept in remembrance of me'.

Cousin Mr William Truston (of his mother's family, see Isaac Boggis 1 (qv)), £100 and £20 each to those of his brothers and sisters then living.

Peter Devall 2 (qv), 'my faithful Servant' who managed the bay making business for Boggis received £100 and was asked to assist Isaac 2 in the business.

The Church of England Charity Schools 'of which I am now Treasurer' received £50 (see also ERO D/P 200/8/2, All Saints Vestry Meeting 13 August 1788 conveyance of part of the parish garden to the Charity Schools Trustees).

Servant, Martha Wenlock received £30, the 'Bed, Bedding and furniture which belong to the Room in which she sleeps and also of the Yellow Room adjoining with suitable linen to the same likewise the little roasting Jack a Dozen of Pewter Plates two Pewter Dishes and all the Stone Ware in common use in the Kitchen and her own Store Room' and a pension of 10s per week for life. (See also legacy to her in James Boggis' will. She had a small house next Peter Devall and Henry Johnson jun, opposite the Minories till 1813).

Old servant Thomas Brown received a pension of 2s per week.

Henry Johnson (qv) was left £25 to repay the bond for which Isaac Boggis stood surety for him for Whites Charity (for which charity see, Morant, *Colchester*, Book 3:1; Cromwell *Colchester*, Vol. 2:336).

Servant James Brooker received £25 and the right to remain in the house he now occupied 'he keeping the same in tenantable repair.' (He had been given this house since the death of James Boggis. It was in a court between Winsley's and Grey Friars across the road from the Minories. This is probably the same individual as James Brooker (qv) innkeeper, and compare John Brooker (qv) in the same trade.)

Servant Sarah Squire received £10 (see also CPL Crisp ML 225, Thomas Brooker of St Botolphs, victualler and Peter Devall of All Saints baymaker bound, Thomas, widr. to marry Sarah Squires of All Saints (25), 1792. Devall, as manager of the business, seems to have paid these pensions, nfr).

Mourning rings of the value of 5 guineas were left to John Debonnaire Esq, Ann his wife, Miss Ann Debonnaire, Revd Robert Dingley (qv) and Elizabeth (qv) his wife, Mr Thomas Andrews (qv), Mr Isaac Samuel Clamtree (qv).

One-guinea mourning rings were left to John Jacob Morley, Allington Morley (qv), Shaw King (qv), Francis Smythies 1 (qv) (all Esq) and to Revd Nathaniel Forster (qv), Revd Charles Hewitt (qv), Robert Richardson Newell (qv), Mr George Reynolds (qv), Mr Samuel Winnock (qv).

The remainder was left to his brother Isaac Boggis 2 (qv) and heirs, who was nominated executor together with Ann his wife and Isaac Rolfe Boggis, his son.

A codicil of 25 March 1790 increased James Brooker's legacy to £30 and added Mr Thomas Hawkes of Mersea to the recipients of one-guinea rings.

The list of those receiving mourning rings virtually duplicates that in his brother James' will of 1787 (see under James Boggis).

Unless otherwise cited, the sources used here are JBB's transcriptions of Minories Deeds and contextual information, ERO, C905, Box 2, A2. See also JBB, *The House that Boggis Built*, (1978) for a fuller discussion of Thomas Boggis.

BORROWS WILLIAM [90]
Corkcutter
fl. 1759-1806

Was born in the Isle of Ely (Borough Examination books, ERO P/Co R10B, January 1785) but by 1784 was resident in Colchester and married to Ann Griffin. He occupied property at no. 8 East Hill rated 15 from 1788 where his widow remained living until 1817. Their son William Griffin Borrows died on 19 February 1797. William Borrows' marriage related him to the Wilder/Griffin/Shillito group of families. He acted as guardian to George Shillito on the death of his father Charles (qv) and taught him the corkcutting trade. Borrows was a witness at George's wedding in 1803 to Harriet Herbert (ERO ML D/ACL 1803). This led to another family connection to the interrelated Marsden/Waynman/Herbert group of families, which was strengthened when his daughter Catherine Borrows married John Marsden, hosier (qv) in 1809 (ERO ML D/ACL 1809).

Borrows was buried at St Peters on 19 September 1806. His will (NA PROB 11/1450 Pitts 763-818, 31 October 1806) entrusted property on East Hill and Moor Lane for the benefit of four daughters, two brothers and two nephews. His trustees and executors were his wife Ann, Revd Robert Storry (qv) and Charles Great Keymer (qv).

See also JBB, *EAE*:100, 101.

BOUTELL EDWARD [91]
Innkeeper, Bricklayers Arms
fl. 1783-90

Continued in occupation over three years. In 1783 the inn was owned by Clark Barns (qv) (rated 4), thereafter it was inherited by Thomas Barns (qv), rated 6 in 1790.

BOWLAND JOHN KILLINGWORTH [1180]
Hatter and Wine-Merchant
fl. 1789-1818

Origin not found. Married Sarah, sister of Thomas Barns (qv) brewer and maltster, at St Mary-at-the-Walls, 22 September 1789.

IpsJ 29 January 1790 accused servant John Davies of stealing gold and silver lace. *IpsJ* 5 March 1791 was hatter in Head St at 'Princes Feathers, opposite the Fleece'. But at same date S. Ball, 'late-shopman to Mr Bowland, and hat-maker,' took a shop across the road in Head St 'next Mr Barlow', that is on the corner of Head Street and High Street (cf Nathaniel Barlow 1 (qv)).

There was a fire at his premises in 1792, when 'Last Monday night, between 11 and 12 o'clock, a fire was discovered in the cellar of <u>Mr Bowland, hatter,</u> Colchester, which by ... timely assistance was extinguished without doing any material damage (*IpsJ* 4 February 1792).

Land Tax St Peters, 1795 – was the proprietor of the Three Cups, rated 50, John Nunn occupier. He also owned 55 Crouch St (JBB: Notes on Deeds in ERO C905, Box 8, 17/18 August 1795, sale to John Pattrick (qv) gent).

Was bankrupted in 1798 (*London Gazette* 28 April, 7 July, 24 November 1798). However, seems to have recovered financially. *IpsJ* 21 May 1803, sold off 'Foreign Wines' at the Cross Keys, St Nicholas. In 1816 (11 November 1816, innholder) he paid £66 0s 3d for two pieces of Common Land, divided by the new cut Ipswich Road, just north of the Rose and Crown, of which he was then licensee (ERO C47, CPL787, 1815-1818; part of the sale of rights of common instituted by the Borough in 1807, for which see T. Cromwell, *Colchester*, Vol 2:261).

In 1804 he had been before the local Petty Sessions for the sexual assault of a soldier's pregnant wife in the street (ERO P/CoR 24, 9 February 1804).

BOWLER RICHARD [92]
Cardmaker
fl. 1717-1754

Whig, cardmaker and part of the town elite at a time before the decline of the bay trade was far advanced. He was named at a Channel Commissioner in the Act of 1749. One of almost half a dozen Bowlers who recorded Whig votes from at least 1734 and beyond Richard's death (cf 1768 poll).

B

Bowler is recorded first as occupier of part of the premises later the Minories (cf Thomas and Isaac Boggis (qv)) in the will of Robert Havens (made 1717, proved 3 November 1719, NA PROB 11/571, baymaker, Colchester) and though he subsequently moved (JBB note) seems still to be living there in 1748 when his daughter Rachel married John Abbott a woolcardmaker of Coggeshall (at Marks Tey, 28 March 1748; R. H. Brown Transcripts, ERO T/R80). On 10 March 1746 Bowler witnessed the will of Joseph Duffield, merchant (qv).

Two of Bowler's apprentices are known to have later become free burgesses; John Taylor who was admitted on 8 December 1740, and Philip Sansum (qv) admitted 16 January 1740/1 (JBB NB 76/7). Sansum was to succeed his master as the leading Whig cardmaker and Alderman in the town. Bowler died in the winter of 1753/4. His will made on 21 June 1753 (NA PROB 11/806, 16 February 1754) left his son-in-law Abraham Mortier (qv) £120. His daughter Mary Waller, widow, received £10 'and my silver cup.' His daughter Abigail wife of Joseph Turner, baker received £10; grandson Richard Waller £60 and granddaughter Dorothy Taylor £10 each. The main beneficiary and sole executrix was his single daughter Hester Bowler who received a tenement near Magdalen Green, all stock, securities and 3% annuities and also 'all my estate, money debts and effects abroad in New England and Philadelphia or elsewhere in America'. She was to be assisted by Bowler's friend Philip Havens 1 (qv) and proved the will on 16 February 1754.

See also CPL Crisp ML365, where the bride is named Canc'ler; Boyd's Index, ERO D/ALL 1739, John Taylor of All Saints and Philip Sansum bd John (22) to Ann Chancellor of St Runwalds, married 8 July 1739 at Stanway; CPL Crisp ML326, ERO D/ACL 1723, Abraham Mortier of Colchester baymaker and John Verlander bound, Abraham (21) to marry Eliz Bowles (sic) of Colchester, at Gt Horkesley, 1723 (Boyd's Index names her as Bowler); William Waller of Colchester, carrier and John James baymaker bound, Wm (28) to marry Mary Bowler (21), 1726, CPL Crisp ML 264. Boyds Index has this marriage at Colchester St Martin, 1725).

BOYLE MICHAEL and MARY [94]
Ribbon and Silk Manufacture and Millinery
fl. 1775-1809

Michael Boyle, 24, an Irishman from County Mayo, schoolmaster and Mary Walford, 22, were married in 1775 (St Mary-at-the-Walls registers 28 December 1775; CPL Crisp ML 332). Mary had traded as a milliner from the Old Three Crowns before her marriage (took Sarah Gardner apprentice in 1773 for £26 5s, NA IR 1/58/200; *IpsJ* 8 May 1775; she offered Millinery, Linen Drapers & Stuffs, N.B. Funerals furnished) and continued to do so when married. In 1780 Mary supplied the Rebow election campaign with eighteen yards of ribbon made up into twelve favours at 1s each (ERO C47, Rebow Papers: Samuel Ennew's Account Book, 8 September 1780, JBB Dec 65:74). In 1783 (*IpsJ* 16 January 1783, JBB Blue 1:34), M. Boyle, just returned from London, offered mercery and millinery at the Old Three Crowns, so the couple had evidently remained at the Walford premises (cf Timothy Walford 1 and 2 (qv) and Fisher Walford (qv)). François de la Rochfoucauld mentions 'a small ribbon manufactory' in Colchester in 1784 (*Melanges sur l'Angleterre*, (CUP, trans. 1933):161) but confirmation that this refers to the Boyles does not exist until 1790 when advertisements appear (*IpsJ* 8 May and 23 October 1790, 12 May 1792). In April 1791 Mrs Boyle ... (had) ... just returned from London with a fashionable assortment of millinery' (*IpsJ* 14 May 1791). In 1795 (*IpsJ* 31 October 1795) Mary Boyle again advertised from the Silk & Ribbon Manufactory offering millinery, haberdashery, Muffs and Tippets from London and 'a large stock of every breadth of black Modes and Gown Silks &c, which are chiefly made at Colchester'. On 5 April 1799 (*ChCh*) Mrs Boyle is mentioned as the Colchester supplier of Mills Corsets and French and Italian stays.

In 1793 (CPL Harvey Scrapbook, *IpsJ* 19 January 1793, JBB Sept 63:54) Michael Boyle stood surety for £200 with other leading tradesmen, for Richard Patmore (qv) who was indicted for distributing the Second Part of Thomas Paine's *Rights of Man*.

B

On 12 November 1808 (*Ips J*) Michael Boyle advertised the sale of his Mercery Hosiery and Haberdashery stock in the High Street prior to retirement after upwards of thirty years. He retired to Friday Street, Cheapside, London where he died in March 1809 (*Ips J* 25 March 1809). His will (NA PROB 11/1501 Loveday 604, made 20 December 1806, proved with several codicils 25 August 1809) left over £17,000. He named his wife, Mary, his brother-in-law Timothy Walford (qv), Revd Richard Storry (qv) of St Peters Colchester, Robert Tabor (qv) and William Hale of Wood St Spitalfields, silk manufacturer, as his executors. He left the lease of his house in Friday St to Mary then to his son Michael Walford Boyle at age 21. Mary also received £2,000 for her own use and all the household furniture. Son-in-law George Wooley received £1,500 over and above £500 he had already received. £500 was to be divided in equal portions at age 21 to Boyle's grandchildren, George and Mary Wooley, failing whom to his daughter Mary Honour Wooley. £2,000 each was left to his other children (Michael Walford Boyle, Maltilda Boyle and Sarah Boyle) at age 21. His brothers James and Patrick Boyle, then living in County Mayo were to receive the interest on £400. His executors were to receive £50 each and his servants were to be given mourning at the discretion of his executors. Boyle directed that his half share in properties in St Giles, held jointly with Timothy Walford (qv) were to be sold and added to his personal estate, from which £6,000 was to be held in trust, the interest for the use of his wife Mary for life. If she remarried this income was not to be used to pay her new husband's debts. After her death his son was to receive three quarters of this sum and the remaining quarter was to be divided between his three daughters Mary Honour, Matilda and Sarah.

BOYS JAMES [1289]
Merchant
w. 1745

One of the group of Tory Aldermen who seized control of the Corporation in 1728, at the time of the collapse of the Dutch

Bay monopoly. They rotated the office of Mayor between them and were later ousted through litigation which deemed them to have been improperly elected, when the Whigs gained ascendancy in the 1741 parliamentary election. Boys, along with Joseph Duffield (qv), the then Mayor James Blatch (qv) and the High Constable, William Seaber (qv) were tried at King's Bench for extracting 'foreign fines' to allow innkeepers who were not free burgesses to trade (NA KB 28/154/16 Trinity 1740; *IpsJ* 26 July 1740; Ass Bk 17 March, 21 July and 22 September 1740). The following March the Corporation formally agreed to defend the action and pay the legal expenses of the accused Aldermen and Seaber. Although they were fined £100, the case became a popular Tory cause in the town, and the Aldermen were treated to a triumphal entry when they returned:-

> On Wednesday last ... evening ... the Justices of this Corporation, who were at the last Assizes convicted of Extortion, on account of their altering the Method of taking 10s Foreign Fine of Alehouse keepers not free, pursuant to ADVICE and which had been taken many years before they were magistrates ... came to Town in the Stage Coach from London, where they had been OBLIGED to attend TEN DAYS, to receive the sentence of the Court of Kings Bench, and were all three fined £100 and a fourth [Seaber] person £120. .... And when the Inhabitants of the Town heard of the said Magistrates being on the road, several Hundreds of them who knew the TRUE GROUND of the prosecutions, in order to shew the Esteem they had for those Gentlemen, met them several miles out of the Town, and, to the no small Mortification of their REAL PROSECUTORS accompanied them into the Town with loud Huzzas: The Coach was lighted with a great Number of links; several Houses were illuminated, and the Evening concluded with Bonfires and ringing of Bells (*IpsJ* 29 November 1740).

B

(I assume that altering the method of taking the fine means that they demanded the money up front rather than asking for a recognisance or bond. For more detailed accounts of the complex politics of this period see *VCH Essex*, Vol. 9; D'Cruze, *Middling Sort*, Chapter 6 (Ed.)).

Boys died in the winter of 1745. He had made his will on 24 April 1737 (NA 11/737, proved 11 December 1745). He left his Colchester messuage, a tenanted farm and meadows in Fordham and West Bergholt and Partridge Fenn in Colchester to his son James at 21. His wife Elizabeth was left a life interest in his Colchester mansion and the £2,000 named in her marriage settlement. The residue was left equally to son James and daughter Elizabeth, failing whom to his brother Richard Boys. His 'well beloved friend' Charles Gray (qv) (neighbour in All Saints and Tory MP) was left the option to buy Partridge Fenn for £100. Richard Turner, his brother-in-law and wife Elizabeth were named executors and guardians of the children, if either should die Charles Gray was asked to take their place. A codicil of 21 September 1744 left 20 guineas to Richard Turner for his trouble as executor. The writing in the codicil was attested to by William Jackson, St Peter le Poor, London, gent.

Boys' wife Elizabeth *née* Turner, died 5 September 1745, aged 60. Her will is at NA PROB 11/741, proved 25 September 1745. See altar tomb, St James and other MIs for family connections (Strutt, *Colchester*, Vol. 2:42-3, JBB NB 85/4:47).

BOYS MARY [1141]
ob. 1792

Was the unmarried sister of Revd Richard Boys (qv) of West Bergholt. She died 'Monday last died at an advanced age' in 1791 (*IpsJ* 5 November 1791). Her will is at NA PROB 11/1210, proved 23 November 1791. Her furniture was sold off in Back Lane the following year (*IpsJ* 20 October 1792).

BOYS REVD RICHARD [1291]
Rector, W. Bergholt
ob. 1784

The son of Richard Boys, London bay factor and hence nephew of the previous Rector of West Bergholt, William Boys 2 (qv). During the 1760s the Boys' were friendly to the newly installed curate of Fordham, Revd Thomas Twining (qv) and his wife, Elizabeth (R. S. Walker (ed)., *Thomas Twining*, Vol. 1, Letter 16 22 February 1764, reports that the Twinings had stopped with the Boys' for ten days and the visit had been returned, also that Mr Boys was looking after the Twinings' dog, Friday, whilst they were away; Letter 13, 28 September 1764 reports that the Twinings dined with Mr Boys; Letter 18, 17 May 1765, describes Revd Nathaniel Forster (qv) visiting Mr Boys, and further dinner engagements).

His mother, Elizabeth also lived at West Bergholt where she died, December 1762 (will ERO, D/ABW 101/1/6, made 1761, proved 1763, mother of the Rector of W Bergholt, JBB NB Nov 67). His unmarried sister, Mary (qv), who died in Colchester in 1791, presumably was also part of the household at this point.

Boys had married Mary Seaber of St Peters in 1754 (CPL Crisp ML 448). She died 11 February 1782 aged 51. Richard Boys died 17 April, 1784 aged 53. They are buried at St James (ML Strutt, *Colchester*, Vol. 2:42-3). His will is at NA PROB 11/1116, clerk of Colchester, proved 5 May 1784.

See also the Boys families of Layer Marney (e.g. will of James, Layer Marney, proved 11 November 1751, NA PROB 11/833), of Coggeshall (JBB NB 85/4, 85/5) and Finchingfield (will of William, gent, Finchingfield, proved 10 August 1768, NA PROB 11/941).

BOYS WILLIAM 1 [1288]
Alderman
w. 1714

The Boys family had been numbered amongst prosperous Colchester traders since the seventeenth century, see for

B

example the will of Richard Boys, gent, Alderman of Colchester ERO, D/ABR 7/290, 1666.

This William Boys was father to James Boys (qv), the Colchester Alderman and to William Boys 2 (qv), Rector of West Bergholt. His will (NA PROB 11/540, proved 25 May 1714) was made on 21 March 1714. He left his messuage in All Saints to son James and cash legacies to his other offspring, viz; William 2 £800, Richard £1,000, Sarah £800, Martha £800. His son-in-law John Grimwood was left £200 in addition to the £400 he had received on marriage to Boys' daughter Elizabeth on condition that Grimwood should leave her £600 in his will. Boys' daughter Mary and her husband William Rush received £20 for mourning. Other tenanted messuages in St Marys went to son Richard. The residue was left to sons James and William 2, the executors.

BOYS WILLIAM 2 [1290]
Rector W. Bergholt and Easthorpe
w. 1734

The son of William Boys 1 (qv) and brother of James Boys (qv), Colchester Alderman. Entered St John's, Cambridge, 1698 aged 15; MA 1705. Rector of W. Bergholt 1706-34 and of Easthorpe 1725-34. He died January 1734 (Venn, *Alumn. Cantab.*). His will is at NA PROB 11/668, proved 26 November 1734.

BRAME BENJAMIN [96]
Innkeeper, Marquis of Granby
fl. 1778-1789

Buried St Peters, 7 June 1789.

BRAMSTON THOMAS ESQ and son [1276]
Gent
fl. 1729-1802

A number of rural gentry were created Colchester free burgesses in the Tory Borough takeover of 1729, but most then retired from Borough politics. Of the few that remained interested (cf John Moore (qv) of Kentwell Hall) the most notable is Thomas Bramston of Skreens, Roxwell, who voted 1734/5, 1741 and 1747, and his son Thomas Berney Bramston who only missed 1780, between 1768 and 1790. Skreens (their country house) is also notable for its annual musical and social week in the first days of January, regularly attended by Revd Thomas Twining (qv) from 1770-1801. Thomas Berney Bramston was also MP for Essex 1779-1802, the Tory in a regular Whig/Tory compromise arrangement.

The inter-relations of the Abdys and Bramstons can best be studied in Morant, *Essex*, Vol. 2:73 for Roxwell and Vol. 1:177 for Stapleford Abbot, especially the former.

BRASIER MARY [97]
Hatter
fl. c.1750

IpsJ of 24 November 1753 advertised the premises she lately occupied in the High Street. Enquiries were directed to Charles Tillett (qv) breechesmaker next door to the Three Cups.

BREAM JAMES [98]
Saddler
1730-1780

Was baptised at Little Ellingham, Norfolk 10 May 1730 and later apprenticed to Thomas Driver of Hingham, Norfolk for £7 10s in 1744 (NA IR 1/50/210). Bream seems to have come to Colchester thereafter and married Ann Wilder (qv) in 1757. They traded from 90 High Street, premises held by the Wilder family between 1689 and 1790 (JBB ms note). He died in 1780 and the business was continued by his widow.

See also JBB *EAE*:81, 102.

BREE REVD JOHN [100]
Rector, Marks Tey
fl. 1753-1780

The nephew of William Bree (qv) and recipient in his uncle's will of 1752/3 of £450 to continue his Oxford education and the reversion of William Bree's marriage settlement (failing any issue of his aunt).

He was the son of Robert Bree of Hampstall Ridware, Staffs and had matriculated at Balliol, Oxford from June 1751. He obtained his BA in 1755 and his MA in 1759 (Foster, *Alumn. Oxon.*).

He had financial problems in later life since on 16 December 1780 (*IpsJ*) the creditors of Revd John Bree late of Marks Tey were requested to send their accounts to William Suddell (qv) attorney. The estate was assigned to Revd Nathaniel Forster DD, Mr William Townsend and Mr Isaac Green (all (qv)), 'in trust for themselves and the rest of his creditors.'

BREE REVD WILLIAM [99]
Rector, Marks Tey
fl. 1721-1753

Bree became incumbent at Marks Tey in 1721 where,

> He built a very good parsonage house which stands conveniently near the London road, and made parks and other great improvements (Morant, *Essex*, Vol. 2:204).

In 1727 he married Elizabeth Puplett at Mile End, sister-in-law of Revd Palmer Smythies (qv), the Rector there (CPL Crisp ML 258, ERO D/ABL 1727). He later made a second marriage to Hester, *née* Rawstorn (see will below).

Bree's will was made on 25 October 1752, a few months before his death on 25 April 1753 (NA PROB 11/802, Musgrave, proved 9 June 1753). It was witnessed by Ann Wallis, Thomas Halley (qv) and George Wegg (qv). It was proved by his second wife Hester, the residuary legatee and sole executrix.

The will requested that Bree should be buried in the chancel of Marks Tey church near his 'late loving wife.' Lands in Warwickshire, Gt. and Lt. Wigborough and £400 in New South Sea Annuities in the name of Thomas Rawstorn Esq (qv) and Edward Arrowsmith clerk, as per his marriage settlement to Hester (*née* Rawstorn) were secured to her together with £100, his coach, harness and two coach mares. If Hester died childless the reversion of the marriage settlement was directed to John Bree (qv) the son of his late brother Robert who was also left £450 to finish his Oxford education until gaining his MA.

£10 apiece for mourning was left to his nieces Susannah Smythies and Ann Bridges (who also received a further £50 each), Aunt Edwards of Kenelworth, sister Bree widow of late brother Robert, brother and sister Eales, nephew John Bree of Warwickshire and wife, niece Elizabeth daughter of late brother Thomas Bree, nephew Thomas Bree Rector of Hanstall Ridware, nephew Robert Bree of Solyhull (sic), nephew Robert Mallory Woodcote, Warwickshire, niece Elizabeth Mallory and nephew Thomas Eales.

£100 each was left to nephew William and nieces Ann, Elizabeth, and Frances, children of late brother Robert Bree.

Further recipients of £10 legacies for mourning were brother and sisters Rawstorn, Arrowsmith, Bullock, Kilner, Smythies, sister Eldred and niece Sarah Arrowsmith. The wives of these families were, together with Hester Bree, all sisters and daughters of Samuel Rawstorn Esq (qv) of Lexden Manor. Messrs Kilner, Bullock, Arrowsmith and Eldred as well as Bree were all clerics.

£10 each was left to the successors of the Rectories of Marks Tey and Tendring for dilapidations and £5 to the poor of each parish. £2 2s was to provide for a sermon in each church within a month his decease. £50 was left to Revd Mr Anthony Gibson and £50 to Balliol Chapel, Oxford with a 1 gn. ring each to the Master and Fellows. £50 was also given to the Rector of All Saints Colchester (Nathaniel Forster (qv)) to repair and enlarge the Parsonage under the direction of Bree's friends Charles Gray Esq (qv) and George Wegg 2 (qv).

Three ledgers now in the tower at Marks Tey church record Elizabeth the loving and beloved wife of William Bree, Rector of this parish who died on 23 February aged 52 ('She had too much sense to desire a longer Epitaph and too much Merit to want one'), Hester, widow and relict of Revd William Bree died 13 October 1761 aged 65 and William Bree, fourth son of Robert Bree of County Warwick died 7 April 1753 aged 61. Bree has a Latin inscription.

See also will of Hester Bree, wid. Marks Tey, NA PROB 11/871, 12 December 1761.

BRIDGE JOHN [1221]
Carpenter
1778-1845

Parentage not found. Was 22 of St Mary's parish when he married Elizabeth Herbert, aged 22, at St Peters, 1800 (ERO ML D/ALL 1800). She died 1831. He is buried with her, at Lion Walk, died 21 August 1845, aged 67. At the time of his death was resident in St Botolphs St (*ECS*, 22 August 1845).

IpsJ 19 July 1806 (JBB Feb65:64); carpenter and joiner, moved from St Mary's parish to Lion Walk.

IpsJ 4 April 1812; has large quantity of slate of the best quality, which he intends to sell at London prices. All kinds of slating done at the shortest notice. This is the first mention seen locally of slate, so finely used by Henry Hammond Hayward (qv) in St Mary's Terrace, Lexden Road in the 1830s. The advertisement was illustrated with a drawing perhaps necessary to familiarise local builders and clients of the way it is used. Tiles and M-roofs are soon out of fashion. In the drawing it looks as if a strong wooden structure was expected to take the weight of the roof, and the width of the eaves accommodated brick or stucco below? (JBB note, 28 July 1995).

IpsJ 4 May 1816. Thanks his patrons for supporting him in his building business 'for the last sixteen years.' New room in the

Lion Walk now open as an Auction market. He re-built 6 Lion Walk (Notes on Deeds, JBB NB Mar 67:22-3, 26).

IpsJ 5 July 1817, advertisement. 'From 12 to 20 joiners can have employment. J. Bridge, Lion Walk.' See Blaxill, *Lion Walk*:28. This advertisement coincides with the Revd John Savill's (qv) move up East Hill while his new mansion was built at the corner of Land Lane, and the pitch of the hill was reduced by 8 ft.

Bridge's properties were for sale after his death, Advertised in the *Essex County Standard* of 12 September 1845. These included his premises in Lion Walk with the ladies school adjoining, cottages in West Stockwell Street, in Dromedary Yard and in Greenstead.

BRIDGES THEOPHILUS [103]
Victualler, Cross Keys
fl. 1792-1800

Son of William Bridges of All Saints and his wife Sarah. Theophilus can have had only limited expectations from his father's estate since the property was to be divided between five siblings after his mother's demise. However, he improved his prospects through marriage. He became proprietor of the Cross Keys because it had been left to his wife Ann by her mother Ann Barns (qv). He and Ann had been living and doubtless working at the inn during her mother's lifetime, and continued thereafter. As well as selling porter, wine, brandy, rum, geneva to both in and outdoor customers the Bridges were bakers and made and sold bread. Theophilus also joined the Loyal Colchester Volunteers during the French invasion scare (for the Loyal Colchester Volunteers, ERO D/DRb/02).

Ann Bridges died sometime during the 1790s for at the beginning of February 1799 (*ChCh* 8 February 1799) Theophilus married at Elmstead to Miss Powel, the eldest daughter of Mr Powel of the Academy there. His good fortune was short lived, however, for a year later he was declared bankrupt for debts contracted to his beer and wine suppliers (ERO D/DA T/714A,

25 February 1800). His beer supplier was John Hunt (qv) brewer, husband to Mary the sister of Thomas Barns (qv).

BROCK JOHN [104]
Saddler
fl. 1768

Brock had been apprenticed to Francis Abell (qv) in 1762 for £12 (NA IR 1/54/178), but only traded for a short while in Colchester. He advertised on 20 August 1768 (*IpsJ*) from Mr Dunthorne's shop near the Buttermarket, but the parish rates show no change in occupation (from James Dunthorne 1 (qv)) at this time.

BROCKWELL JOSEPH [106]
Baker
w. 1755/7

A free burgess voting for Grey and Olmius in 1747. His will (ERO D/ABR 24/422, 1757) left a messuage Holy Trinity and a tenement on the east side of 'Shiergate' which, together with his tools, were to be divided between his wife Joanna and sons Revd Joseph Brockwell (qv) and Isaac, who received the largest share.

BROCKWELL REVD JOSEPH [105]
Rector, W. Mersea and Steeple
fl. 1735-1797

Resident in St Martins, Colchester (rated 5, owner occupier in 1783) he made his individual contribution to the town's genteel society. He was one of those to play for James Dunthorne's 2 (qv) subscription concerts (Nathaniel Forster (qv) correspondence in BL Add Mss 11277, 1 March 1782, JBB NB Feb 69:37) and participated in the controversies surrounding the Free School elections in January 1779. Thomas Twining (qv) mentioned him in his report of the proceedings to Samuel Parr (qv):

> Oh! and pray now give Brocknell (sic) a hitch up. 1st Seeing he is Mr Hutchinsons relation (see below); 2ndly For that he voluntarily accompanied us in our triumphant procession ... (in support of Hewitt the successful candidate) ... with a long beard, a dirty shirt, a threadbare coat, and a blue cockade in his hat. Tis fact. No man more zealous.' (J. Johnstone (ed.), *The Works of Samuel Parr LLD*, (London, 1828), Vol. 8. For an account of these elections, D'Cruze, *Pleasing Prospect*:160-5).

Brockwell (then aged 38) had married Sarah Hutchinson (37) of St Runwald at Gt. Horkesley in 1751 (CPL Crisp ML451, ERO D/ACL 1751 bound by Charles Lind (qv) of Holy Trinity, Colchester). She was daughter to Richard Hutchinson, goldsmith (qv) who later moved to Ipswich (as did Samuel Parr). Sarah received a third of the residue including clothes in the will of her mother Jane (ERO D/ACR 16/324, 1762, widow of Colchester).

Joseph Brockwell was son of Joseph (qv) baker and Joanna. He was admitted free burgess by descent in 1734 (his brother Isaac was admitted in 1740). He voted in Borough elections from 1734, showing initially a preference for Tory or one Whig/one Tory voting. After 1784, however, he was a supporter of Whig or radical candidates.

He was ordained deacon at Chelmsford in 1735 (CPL Wire Collection, W5 no. 1 EAS Catalogue:63). He was Rector of West Mersea from 1748 and of Steeple (the adjoining parish) from 1750. These livings were in the gift of the mother of Shaw King Esq (qv) (Morant, *Essex*, Vol. 1:360).

Brockwell made his will on 9 September 1796 (NA PROB 11/1286, 130 Exeter, proved 18 March 1797) witnessed by William Shakeshaft, Joseph Cole and Thos Harrison. Samuel Cooke (qv), fisherman of Rowhedge was named executor and residuary legatee. The chief beneficiary, however, was the daughter of Alderman Lilley (qv) of Bear Lane who was left £10,000.

Bridget Carwin, widow of Abberton received a farm at Peldon and her daughter Bridget another in Tolleshunt Major and

Goldhanger. Harriet, daughter of the late Daniel Harvey (qv) Captain of the Wivenhoe cutter, now married to Mr Parrey of Aldermanbury, London, received £200 and her mother then of Stanmore Middlesex, £100. £200 was left to Mr Newell (Robert Richardson Newell (qv)), surgeon of St Mary-at-the-Walls 'in lieu of the little matter I owe him.'

The managers of the Charity Sunday Schools were left £100 for 'cloathing' for the children. The wife of John Smith late Sarah Potter received 6s per week for life. Mr John Kendall (qv) 'if he doeth scittle his house at the corner of the Town field upon ye Poor Widows' received £100. A bond held of Mr Rowles (Rolle (qv)) cooper of East Hill was cancelled.

The will was proved on 18 March 1797 by Samuel Cook.

BROOKER JAMES [115]
Innkeeper, Chaise and Pair, later Castle, St Peters
fl. 1795–1802

Was innkeeper at the Chaise and Pair, St Peters in 1795 before moving to the Castle in 1796, where he remained until 1802.

BROOKER JOHN [110]
Innkeeper, King's Arms, and Tulip Grower
fl. 1753-1802

Was apprenticed to Abraham Oliver, cooper in 1752 for 5gns (NA IR 1/51/24). Brooker was innholder at the Red Cow (North Hill) from at least 1765 whence he advertised 'A border of fine Tulips now in Bloom' comprising 300 plants for sale on 13 June 1769 (*IpsJ*, JBB NB Blue 1:102). Varieties included Baggot Rigo, Baggot Primo, Vareports, Incomparable Alexandras, Georges of Triumpher Royals, Violet, Lebecks etc.

In 1783-4 he had moved to the Bell in St Botolphs and from at least 1788 until his death in 1802 he occupied the Kings Arms (originally the King's Head) in St Mary-at-the-Walls. His will leaves his property to a 'dear and loving wife' Jane Brooker, subject to a charge on the personal estate and effects, especially the stables he erected (with owner's permission) on land where he now resides, owned by Mr Skingley. The charge is for debts outstanding to Robert Wright (qv) brandy merchant. The Kings Arms was occupied in 1803 by Jane Brooker and in 1804 by Samuel Brooker.

See also Coopers Arms, St Giles, occ. John Brooker, 1780-6, rated 4, owned Samuel Tabor (qv), see also the Bell (qv).

BROWN EDWARD [1215]
Carpenter
1721-1790

Baptised Soham, Cambs., 20 December 1721 son of John and Martha (*IGI*).

IpsJ 10 August 1765, one of the Colchester carpenters who advertised jointly for sawyers.

1757, work for Winsleys Trustees £13 17s 6¾d (ERO D/Q 30/2/22).

Overseer for the Poor in St Peters, 1772/3.

Quite good written hand as Land Tax assessor for St Peters, 1778.

1782, Repairs King Coel's Pump £2 1s 7d (Chamberlains Accounts, ERO D/B 5 Aa2/1).

His will (ERO D/ABR 28/197) made 7 January 1789 (witnessed by John and Jabez Willis who also witness the will of William Taylor 3 (qv) glazier 1786) proved 31 July 1790 by executors, brother John Brown of Soham, Thomas Stoneham, and William Stanes.

He owned tenements near Shire Gate, occ. Wm. Walker, Joseph Sacra, and;

(1) Jacob Willes, Henry Wolf, Robert Sadler, Joseph Spinks the widows Manning, Sacra and Noon, and - Chapman (to be sold and mortgage paid off).

(2) Tenements and messuages on Balcon Hill, St Peters occ. Thos Harvey, Wm. Dines, wids Sizey and Hodgskin (bought of wid. Sarah Robjent 'sometime since').

B

(3) Tenements on North Hill occ. myself, Wm. Stanes, Thomas Stoneham (his executors) Benj. Bennet, and wid. Bocking.

(4) Tenement in St Nicholas, occ. Wm. Wright, to be sold.

Brother John Brown of Soham, £40 (baptised 31 October 1715, *IGI*).

Sister Elizabeth Barnes 5gns and 5gns per annum. (She married Richard Barnes 16 October 1769, *IGI*).

But main Beneficiary is 'well-beloved granddaughter Sarah Clay who has the tenements (2) and (3) and the interest on proceeds of sale of (4) and eight spoons.

Edward Brown's second marriage, St Peters, 9 July 1770 (CPL Crisp ML 402) was to Mary Savill of St Runwalds, witnesses Martha Brown, Eliz. Noone, John Edwards jun. No mention of this second wife in will.

Brown's first marriage to Elizabeth Feast was 18 December 1744, (*IGI*) and she is buried St Peter's 2 October 1768. Their daughter Martha (bapt. St Peters 5 August 1753) married Samuel Clay*, and their one surviving child Sarah was baptised Holy Trinity, 3 November 1774. Martha is buried at Greenstead, 1 March 1781 aged 27, with 4 children who died in infancy. (William Beverley (qv) farrier, will ERO D/ACR 18/147, 1782 left £200 to Sarah, dd. of Samuel Clay the younger of Greenstead, farmer, at 21).

*This Samuel Clay the younger is the small boy whom James Deane (qv) painted, and whose mother Deane refers to as 'my cousin Sarah' (*née* Owen - connection not found).

BROWN JACOB [119]
Staymaker
fl. 1768

Advertised from Trinity Street, 4 June 1768 (*IpsJ*).

BROWN JOHN 1 [124]
Victualler
w. 1793/4

Occupied messuage St Botolphs rated 18 (1793) owned by Mrs Barnes (cf Thomas Barns (qv)) and himself owned another tenement in St Botolphs rented out to tenants (rated 5). His will of 1793/4 (ERO D/ACR 19/29, junior, victualler of Colchester) left these properties and other rentaries in St Giles plus all personal estate to his wife Mary. Her will of 1795 (ERO, D/ACW 36/4/4) directed the real estate to be sold and the proceeds disbursed in cash legacies to numerous relatives.

BROWN JOHN 2 [123]
Innkeeper, Duke of Marlboro
fl. 1780-9

Named in the rates as John Brown jun. There appear to be several John Browns engaged in the drink trade in Colchester towards the end of the eighteenth century. Though it is likely that more than one of these entries refers to the same man and/or that these individuals are related, no conclusive identification can be made. However, compare Joiner's Arms (qv), John Brown, distiller (qv).

BROWN JOHN 3 [120]
Innkeeper, Joiner's Arms
fl. 1783

Owner occupier per parish rates. cf John Brown 2 (qv).

BROWN JOHN 4 [121]
Distiller
fl. 1808

Brown's house in Moor lane and his furniture were sold in 1808 (*IpsJ* 30 August 1808) as he was leaving his situation. cf also John Brown 1 (qv) victualler, who died in 1793.

BROWN JOHN 5 [1254]
Stonemason
fl. 1812

IpsJ 8 August 1812

> J. Brown
> Statuary and MASON
> No. 22 East Hill
>
> BEGS Leave to return his sincerest Thanks to his Friends and the public for the support he has experienced for several years, and humble solicits continuance of their favours, assuring them of the greatest assiduity and attention will be paid to the execution of their orders.
>
> Chimney pieces fitted up for inspection in modern and approved style.
>
> Barn Floors, Rick stones, Roman Cement, Tarras &c &c on reasonable terms.

This John Brown, said to have been born in Braintree, 1780, and to have carried on his business for about 25 years, became famous as a geologist, dd. 1859. (Reach Smith's reminiscences in *Essex Naturalist*, Vol. 4:158, Vol. 8:155.) He was a charming character. Gunnis (R. Gunnis, *Dictionary of British Sculptors, 1660-1851*, revised edn (London, 1951) notes an 'Hellenic tablet' to Robert Torrin at Kelvedon (1823). There is a tablet to Revd Applebee (1826) at Easthorpe. In 1819 he held a £130 contract for stonemason's work on the new Essex County Hospital building. His house at Stanway with Chinese veranda was for sale as 'Bob Collier's' in 1968 (JBB Note).

The tombstone at Stoke-by-Nayland to his first wife who died 10 April 1810, aged 26, has charming carved top, and in so good a stone that it looks clean cut to this day.

BROWN ROBERT [122]
Perukemaker
fl. 1719-1778

The son of Robert. Apprenticed to John Blyth (qv) in 1719 for £8 (his father then deceased) (NA IR 1/57/27). Received a legacy of £20 in the will of William Naggs (qv) (ERO D/ACR 16/152, 1758). He occupied premises at 71 High Street from at least 1763 (JBB note, NB Jun 64:71). He voted in 1747 and 1768. George Wegg 2 (qv) numbered amongst the customers of 'honest Robin Brown' (Wegg to Gray, 5.3.1769, ERO D/Drg 4/35/61).

Brown's will (ERO D/ACR 18/41, made, 11 January 1774, proved 7 October 1778) names his brothers-in-law, Samuel and John Fitch of Sible Hedingham as executors. The will directs the sale of the house in All Saints and other goods and a division of the proceeds between his eldest son Edward and other four children (Mary, Henry, Elizabeth and John). The will was witnessed by John West, Thomas Cutter (his next door neighbours in All Saints) and Joseph Harvey. The sale was advertised in *IpsJ* of 16 and 31 October 1778 (JBB NB Jun 64:67, 75/1:15):-

> To be SOLD in small lots under PRIME COST
>
> All the remaining part of the Stock in Trade of MR ROBERT BROWN, deceased, at his late dwelling house in the parish of All Saints, Colchester, consisting of a variety of hairs ready prepared, and some unprepared; Any person desirous of purchasing any part of said stock, is requested to apply to Mr John Blythe, opposite All Saints church, Colchester, who is authorised to sell the same.
>
> There remains unsold, a good deal clothes press, a chest of drawers, a jack, a sign and a sign post, and sundry other things.
>
> Enquire of Nathaniel Barlow (1 (qv)), upholsterer, appraiser, and cabinet maker, Colchester.

BROWNE ABRAHAM [125]
Baymaker
w. 1729

Browne (will ERO D/ABR 20/ 232, 1729, baymaker, Colchester) left his wife Elizabeth £300 and the household plate. His brothers Nicholas, James and Peter received £100 each and together with his brother-in-law John Knockard, husband of his sister Susan, shared equally the stock etc. of the business. The Revd John Collings (*sic*) (Revd John Collins (qv)) of Lion Walk received £5 together with £5 for the poor of his meeting house. Cornelius Bogard (qv) linen draper and Timothy Shorey 1 (qv) baymaker (both Lion Walk) were executors and received £10 each for their trouble.

BRUNWIN LAYZELL [128]
Surgeon, Apothecary and Man Midwife
fl. 1752-62

IpsJ 11 December 1762: Advertised he was taking the shop late Mr Tweed's, Bocking. He was witness to the will of Richard Dawes' (qv) sister-in-law Anna Mayhew on 5 May 1762 (ERO D/ABR 24/130, transcribed JBB, *EAE*:136-8) so perhaps was apprenticed to Dawes.

BUFFETT JOHN [1166]
Clockmaker
1692-1758

Baptised 20 April 1692, St Mary-at-the-Walls, the eldest son of John Buffett, musician, Holy Trinity and wife, Bridgett. Apprenticed to Charles Ward, cordwainer on 25 July 1707 (Monday Court), but, given the coincidence of chronology and style of Buffett's early clocks, Mason is of the opinion that rather than continue with the apprenticeship he trained in clock making with John Smorthwait (qv) (Mason:252). Was in trade from 1715 in Gutter Street, abutting the town wall.

Swore the Oath of Allegiance in 1723. Was fined in Borough Sessions (22 March 1725) for trading as a 'Foreigner', having not been admitted as a free burgess. He took the status of Honorary Freeman on payment of a £10 fine in 1728. Served on the Law Inquest (petty jury) on 18 April 1729 and 11 January 1739 and on the Grand Jury six times between 1737 and 1740. Elected headman for Head Ward 6 October 1730 and is recorded in the Assembly Books on other occasions (1 October 1734, 30 September 1735). Voted in parliamentary elections in Colchester in 1734, 1741 and 1747.

Mason notes (256) that most of his output was aimed at the more expensive end of the market, since other Colchester clockmakers (John Smorthwait (qv), Nathaniel Hedge 1 (qv)) were producing larger numbers of comparatively cheaper 30-day clocks.

Advertised in 1756 (*IpsJ* 7 February 1756) to contradict rumours that he intended to leave off trade. The following week Edward Houghton advertised claiming that Buffett had indeed said he was ceasing to trade. (Mason had traced a single clock signed by Houghton and assumes him to be a journeyman clockmaker). Buffett, however, did close the pawnbroking branch of his trade in November 1756 (*IpsJ* 16 November 1756). John Bartholomew (qv), Hythe merchant, Buffett's cousin and later his executor (*IpsJ* 31 May, 1 July, 5 August 1758) acted as agent for the closure of the pawnbroking business.

Buffett died on 9 May 1758. His sister Mary had predeceased him in 1754. His will (ERO D/ABR 25/121, made 1757, proved 1761) left a number of monetary legacies to cousins, as well as his freehold property, three messuages in Gutter Street and one in St Martin's Lane.

Summarised from B. Mason, *Clock and Watchmaking in Colchester*, (Colchester, 1969):250-264. Edward Houghton had been apprenticed in Norwich in 1740, Mason:291.

BULLOCK WILLIAM ESQ [131]
Attorney
c.1749-1822

Free burgess by right of birth from his grandfather Edward Bullock Esq who on 20 August 1698 was 'pleased to honour this Corporation soe farr as to accept a freedom there...' before Ralph Creffield jun. Esq., Mayor (Colchester Oath Book:232). The Bullock family held Faulkbourne Hall near Chelmsford since 1637 (Morant, *Essex*, Vol. 2:117). The Edward above was MP for the county in 1698 and for Colchester with Sir Isaac Rebow (qv) in 1705 but died that year. His younger son Richard D.D., prebendary of Westminster Abbey, died in 1754, his wife being Whalley Berney of Norfolk (will NA PROB 11/931, 12 August 1767, of Colchester). Their children included the Revd Richard Bullock Rector of Dry Drayton, Cambs (created free burgess 6 July 1767, ob. 1809), John, Rector of Radwinter (1758-1794) and Boreham (created free burgess 29 September 1767) and Edward, plantation owner of Kingston Jamaica (will, NA PROB 11/1084, made 28 October 1770, certified as being in his hand on 19 December 1771. Copy proved at PCC by William as attorney for surviving executors on 12 December 1781).

Meantime the senior branch at Faulkbourne produced William's first cousin John Bullock, MP for Maldon 1754-1774, for Essex 1784-1809 and colonel of E. Essex Militia in succession to Isaac Martin Rebow MP (qv).

William Bullock therefore had impeccable Whig connections. Though no apprenticeship fee has been found it seems he was apprenticed to Samuel Ennew (qv) as shown by his being a witness (with Frank Smythies 1 (qv)) to the will of John Sebborn (qv) (1766/80, ERO D/ABR 27/175) and with Ennew alone to that of William Round (NA PROB 11/983, 24 November 1772).

William Bullock was admitted free burgess on 27 July 1772 (Ass Bk) then of 'Kingston Jamaica' (see will of Edward Bullock above). Held office on the Borough Corporation for a few years. Assisted by the resignation of Henry Johnson (qv) to give him place, he was promoted in all stages to Alderman on 24 August 1775. Johnson was re-admitted as Common Councilman in the same proceedings. Bullock was proposed as Mayor on 2 September 1776 but Thomas Boggis (qv) was preferred. Bullock resigned on 27 August 1778, 'now of Copt Hall Court in the City of London'.

In accord with his Whig sympathies, Bullock voted from London for Rebow (1780), Affleck (1781), Affleck and Smyth (April 1784, from Colchester), Smyth (July, 1784), Tierney (1788). No later vote is recorded. However, his brother John of Boreham voted for Tierney in 1790.

Married Charlotte Hossack daughter of Dr Colin Hossack (qv) and his wife Abigail (Charlotte was baptised Hadleigh 17 January 1748 and apprenticed to Lucia and Hanna Reeve (qv) milliners of Colchester, 9 August 1762 for £20 (NA IR 1/54/143) for 7 years). In 1773 Dr Colin Hossack (qv) named Bullock as his executor (will ERO D/ABR 27/351, made 13 March 1773, proved 1782).

Bullock advertised from Colchester, offering to lend money on land security in amounts between £500 and £1,000 in 1787 (*IpsJ* 17 March 1787). He had an office at Chelmsford and was in partnership with Thomas Lowten (qv) at Grays Inn when the firm was administering the deceased estate of Drigue Olmius, Lord Waltham (qv) (will NA PROB 11/1150, Major 100, 27 February 1787, Revd John Bullock a trustee). In all was witness to four Colchester wills and one in West Mersea including: Mary Scarlett (ERO D/ABW 105/2/62, made 1768, proved 1775); Daniel Manning (qv) of the King's Head Inn (ERO D/ABR 27/111, made 1779, proved 1779); John Blatch Whaley (qv) (NA PROB 11/1167, Calvert 333, proved 17 June 1788 and see *IpsJ* 16 August 1788 – re sale of Whaley's property, apply Bullock and Lowten).

Samuel Ennew (qv) (NA PROB 11/1268, Newcastle 683, proved 31 December 1795) left £10,000 in funds in the names of 'my friends William Bullock Esq of Lincoln's Inn and John Vernon the younger' of the same, in trust for an annuity of

£300 to Ennew's dear wife, Ann as well as Colchester properties to Bullock subject to £40 rent to her.

William and Charlotte Bullock had three children (1) Charlotte married Robert Gibson of Gt. Burstead clerk at Little Burstead, 1797 (Foster, *Alumn. Oxon.*). (2) Elizabeth married James Sperling, clerk on 2 May 1797, vicar of Great Maplestead (1797-1850) and Lamarsh (1803-50). She died 1858 aged 85. He died 31 October 1850 at Monk's Lodge aged 78. For their son George leaping a ditch see *Mrs Hurst Dancing, and Other Scenes from Regency Life*, watercolours by Diana Sperling, text Gordon Mingay (London, 1981):11. John Sperling of Dynes Hall was James' elder brother, and died 27 April 1851. (3) Sarah, married Capt. John Jingling R.N., died 1848.

Gents. Mag., 1 June 1822 records that William Bullock, 'a person of rare excellence', of Shelley House near Ongar was 37 years Clerk of the Peace for Essex (Wright, *Essex*, Vol 2:357). Hence Bullock may have succeeded Samuel Ennew (qv) in this office. Bullock's will (of Shelley, Essex) is at PROB 11/1659, 6 July 1822.

Sources: *Memoirs of the Family of Bullock*, Lt. C. W. Bullock, 1905 (ERO); Morant, Venn, Assembly Books, Wright's *Essex*, Namier and Brooke, *House of Commons*; *Essex Review*, Vol. 48 (1939): 12 ff., Alfred Hills on armorial china at Dynes Hall and the Reynolds' portrait there.

BUMSTEAD JOHN [133]
Colchester Academy
fl. 1784-1796

Probably the son of John Bumstead, broker and salesman (ERO D/ABR 28/280, made 1790, proved 1792) and his wife Alice. A free burgess, voting from 1784 to 1796 and like his father a supporter of radical candidates. He ran the Colchester Academy in Gutter Street, whence he advertised in 1790 and 1791 (*ChCh* 24 December 1790; *IpsJ* 1 January and 25 June 1791).

See also Holy Trinity Rates of 1783, showing Frederick Bumstead, tailor plus a tenement, rated 4 each.

BUNNELL WILLIAM [132]
Upholsterer, Auctioneer &c
fl. 1785-1808

Of a Witham family of glovers, a grandnephew to one Thomas Sandford (carpenter, Witham, 1796, ERO D/ACR 19/82). Married Mary, daughter of James Unwin, upholsterer (qv) of All Saints in 1780 (CPL Crisp ML314, ERO D/ACL 1780). Advertised paperhanging and carpets from opposite the Red Lion, High Street (probably in Middle Row) on 5 March 1785 (*IpsJ*). This appears to have been a short term let since no trace appears in the parish rates. Shortly after, Bunnell set up at his father-in-law, James Unwin's (James Unwin 1 (qv), 107 High Street) at the corner of Tenants Lane (St Helens Lane) and the High Street, where in 1787 (*ChCh* 2 November 1787) he advertised as 'newly entered into the cabinet branch'. In 1790, this property was taken by James Cross (qv) and Bunnell cannot be located until he took 111 High Street in 1793 where he remained. That year he expanded his business and advertised for two journeymen (*IpsJ* 20 April 1793) shortly before being promoted to Alderman in one day on 31 July 1793. Ten months later (14 June 1794 *IpsJ*) he took James Unwin jun (James Unwin 2 (qv)), his late apprentice, into partnership. Bunnell did not actually vote in Colchester until 1807 when he supported Thornton and Hart Davis, since at the time of the 1796 election he was acting as Mayor, which office he also held for the subsequent election.

When Unwin snr died in 1795 Bunnell was executor with R. R. Newell (qv). On 5 June 1795 (*IpsJ*, reference not confirmed) John Unwin (qv) plumber and glazier also advertised as a partner of William Bunnell. On 31 October 1795 (*IpsJ*) Bunnell took on Michael Lavallin (qv) to undertake the cabinetmaking side of the business. From 1790 Bunnell was in active partnership with Nathaniel Barlow 1 (qv) as an auctioneer. The association continued, carrying on an extensive business over a wide area until Bunnell entered into a new partnership with William Jackson after Barlow's death in 1798.

In 1797 Lavallin took over 111 High Street. Though Bunnell also owned a house in Helens Lane he may have returned to Witham without severing his business connections in Colchester, for he was 'of Witham' when in 1801 (4 February) he married his second wife, Mrs Sarah Farran (*née* Waynman) (ERO ML D/ACL 1801). Two months later his daughter Mary Ann (who benefited under Thomas Sandford's will, see above) died (5 April 1801) and was buried with the Unwins at All Saints. In 1806, William's daughter by his first wife married Roger Nunn surgeon (qv). Three years later, after his wife's death, Nunn then married Harriet the daughter of Bunnell's second wife. Bunnell died in Bath in August 1808 (*IpsJ* 6 June 1808). On 10 September (*IpsJ*) the firm of Bunnell and Jackson advertised his furniture at his house in St Helens Lane with the 'back gate to the Castle Bailey'. His real estate was sold on 10 December 1808. His will (ERO D/ABR 30/243, auctioneer, St Nicholas) directed that the proceeds of the sale was to provide £100 p.a. to his wife Sarah, residue to daughter Elisabeth wife of Roger Nunn.

Bunnell had succeeded sufficiently to end his life as one of the town's leading citizens. One wonders whether there was a grain of truth in Bland's opinion that Bunnell was 'an openhearted gentleman, a cheerful companion but miserably deficient in learning'. According to Bland, when auctioning books he misnamed Homer's *Illiad* as 'Homer's Eyelids' (*Bland's Anecdotes*, Appendix 3).

BURNHAM JOSEPH 1 and 2 [1191]
Drapers
fl. 1726-1775

Premises St Runwald, 30 High St. Father and son of a quaker family (Fitch, *Colchester Quakers*). Joseph Burnham, senior, was apprenticed to George Wegg 1 (qv) merchant taylor, and admitted free burgess by right of that service in 1726 (Assembly Book). He married Sarah Hewers (1705-1782) in same year. Voted for Nassau 1747, and died that year.

Joseph Burnham 2 was born 1727. Admitted free burgess on 30 January 1764 (ERO D/B 5 Fb2/4, Mason's Index of Free burgesses, 1801). In 1762, married Mary Lawrence (she dd. 1772, aged 46) and in 1781 Rachel Day (dd. 1808 aged 65). He died 1786 aged 59, of Kelvedon.

Traded as a draper at 30 High St 1766-1770 after which he moved to the shop next to William Keymer (qv) which his mother had after his father's death. Was rated 19 in those premises in 1775.

Voted for Rebow and Gray 1768, for Rebow only 1780, and for Affleck 1781. Not in 1784. On 12 July 1784, John Alexander, woolen draper of Inworth was admitted free burgess by right of apprenticeship to Burnham (ERO D/B 5 Fb2/4).

BUTCHER JOHN [1256]
Carpenter
fl. 1768

Of St Peter's parish. Free burgess, son of George, a baker, 22 February 1768. Voted for Fordyce 1768, and regular voter up to 1796. Supported Potter in 1784. 1756 married Rachel Fairbrother of St Botolphs. Barker Holton (qv) was a witness (registers). Is himself a witness at a double wedding when Stephen Kerridge (qv) cabinet maker marries Jane Rudge and Osborne Betts, carpenter married Elizabeth Till, 21 July 1755, St Peters (registers). No record of independent payments to him for work. NA IR 1/53/55, John King was apprenticed to John Butcher of Colchester carpenter in 1758, for £15.

BUTLER [134]
Brasier
fl. 1807

A dwelling house and shop occupied by Mr Butler at £60 per annum was for auction at the Red Lion, opposite the obelisk on the south side of the High Street, St Nicholas (*IpsJ*) 3 October 1807). This was probably 47 High Street occupied by Robert Davis in the 1790s.

BUXTON JAMES [135]
Wine Merchant and Distiller
fl. 1746-95

The son of James and Sarah Buxton of Burnham. Described as a 'dredger of Burnham', he married Margaret Hunt of Goldhanger in 1746 (ERO ML D/ACL 1746, where she is named as Hart) In 1756 he launched himself in business in Colchester, thus:-

> To be sold by the IMPORTER
> James Buxton, Distiller of Colchester Essex
>
> Old Coniac Brandy and Jamaica Rum, with all other sorts of spirituous Liquors, and all sorts of foreign wines; also British made wines, of a fine flavour, little inferior to the foreign wines. I have also a large quantity of fine old Geneva made just the same as Mr Todd's in every respect and equally as good, having acquired the art by my partnership with my brother* (who served his apprenticeship with Mr Todd) and as Mr Todd's affairs** call him aside for the present, take this Opportunity of informing the Publick, that I shall be obliged to all persons who will favour me with their orders, and doubt not but shall give all customers (who shall make Tryal of me) such satisfaction as will induce them to become constant customers.
>
> JAMES BUXTON (*Ips]* 4 September 1756).

*John Buxton (son of James) was apprenticed to Samuel Todd, grocer in 1744 for £100 (NA IR 1/17/105). He appears to have returned to live in Burnham. He is describes as resident there in his mother's will (ERO D/AER/35/175, made 1764, proved 1792) which names him as equal legatee with his sister Sarah (wife of John Tabor, Brightlingsea). James, whose fortune was then assured, though a 'dear son' received only a token guinea.

** Todd was bankrupt. (cf Samuel Todd (qv)).

James Buxton lived on the west side of Head Street, 2 doors uphill from the King's Head, rated 11. His son, James Buxton jun, though a baymaker, was involved in the wine merchants' business. In 1787 (ERO P/Co R11A, Sessions Examinations, 26 May 1787) James jun was examined at Borough Sessions. He had drawn five gallons of brandy from a cask in his father's dwelling house, St Marys and replaced these with water. He then left the said five gallons in a passage that the customs officer took them without examining the stock that had been watered 'and that the examinant cautioned him to be very particular and not to take it away without his being right, but that the officer was determined to take it and serve all alike as he had done Mr Hunt.' James jun. married Mary Abney on 22 December 1786 (St Peters Registers).

James snr. died 31 May 1795 aged 73 and was buried (presumably 'in linnen', as his will directed) at St Mary-at-the-Walls. His monument also includes his wife Margaret (d. 25 March 1808, her will NA PROB 11/1482, 19 July 1808) and daughter Sarah, wife of Charles Hills (qv) (d. 22 March 1788 aged 36). Buxton's will (NA PROB 11/1261, 25 June 1795) distributes property between his son James, farmer at Layer de la Haye and granddaughters Cecilia, Susannah and Frances Hills (cf Cecilia and Susannah Hills (qv)). Buxton had retired earlier, when James Ashwell (qv), wine merchant of St Botolphs had taken on his stock (*IpsJ* 1 November 1794) though his furniture and other goods were not sold off until 1809 (*IpsJ* 25 February 1809) at the Head Street premises. This sale included remnants of James jun's baymaking activities in the form of the wheels and barrel of a rowing mill.

C

CAGE JOHN [123]
Collarmaker
w. 1760

He took John Green as apprentice in 1754 for a fee of £15 (NA IR/1 52/7).

His will is of 1760 (ERO D/ABR 26/25).

CAMPLIN BISHOP [136]
Coachmaker
fl. 1773-76

May be the Bishop Campling who married Susanna King 14 June 1757, St Martin-in-the-Fields, Westminster (*IGI*). Advertised in Colchester 'from London' opposite the White Hart in 1773 (*IpsJ* 1 May 1773, see also *IpsJ* 12 March 1774). Camplin seems to have occupied one of the shops leased from the Winnock's Trustees. From 1775 he also occupied a house and yard behind North Hill near the Wagon and Horses (Deeds of the Bowling Green, ERO D/DE T162 - property known in the 1980s as the 'Tudor House'). In 1776 (*ChCh* 14 June 1776) his daughter married a Mr Harris of Colchester (probably Robert Harris, druggist (qv) who arrived from London in 1774). An affidavit in Borough Sessions of 3 March 1777 notes a case against Camplin for £3 16s 8½d, in which James Taylor 2 (qv) carpenter ,was plaintiff. He was imprisoned for debt (D'Cruze, *Pleasing Prospect*, 8, 89). From 1777 the North Hill premises were vacant and Camplin seems to have left the town. They remained vacant until taken over by John Malby (qv) several years later.

C

CANDLER STEPHEN [1222]
Carpenter and Auctioneer
1738-1812

Three sons of Robert Candler, weaver (viz Robert, Stephen and Wiseman) first voted in the election of 1734. Four to six Candlers vote in each eighteenth-century election, some being carpenters, others still weavers, and never all of one mind. The names Robert, Stephen and Wiseman are repeated, but only Stephen, son of Robert, carpenter (admitted in 1734) appears frequently in the local sources. He was admitted free burgess in Thursday Court, as son of Robert on 10 March 1768.

Candler was established in business by the time of his father's death in 1771. On 19 January 1771 (*IpsJ*), carpenter and joiner, he advertised that he was moving from Angel Lane (St Martins) and opening a shop in St Helen's Lane (St Nicholas) for household goods. He also asked that debts and claims on Robert Candler deceased to be sent to him. There is no sign of him ever having moved again.

Samuel Ennew's (qv) accounts for Isaac Martin Rebow's (qv) election expenses in 1780 include Rebow's share of the cost of building the hustings, to Candler & Hearson £4 14s 6d (ERO C47, Rebow Box 2). That year (*IpsJ* 1 April 1780) Candler auctioned the furniture and apparel etc. of late Mrs Elizabeth West (qv) cardboard maker, decd. at her late dwelling house, All Saints. On 25 July 1780 Candler witnessed the will of John Smith, carpenter of St Botolphs (ERO D/ACR 18/99, proved August 1780). Smith's wife Elizabeth, daughter of James Taylor 1 (qv) remarried to William Hitchcock (qv).

The Borough Sessions Minute Book 1787-94 (ERO D/B 5 Sb6/8; JBB Note, no precise date given) notes Candler amongst the sureties for Thomas Rowe, shoemaker, to keep the peace with Lt. Edward Thomas Hussey of the West Norfolk Militia. Rowe's sureties were Jeremiah Nevard of Colchester, wheelwright, Stephen Candler of Colchester, carpenter, William Nevard, wheelwright each £20. Others to appear, Thomas Nevard, writing clerk, Robert Candler the younger carpenter, Henry Mason of Colchester, turner. Case discharged.

C

In his trade as carpenter, he is listed in the Directories for 1783 and 1792. In 1792 he was rated 7 and personal estate £10 in the Land Tax assessments for St Nicholas. The list was signed by him with Henry Johnson (qv), another Assistant on the Corporation and Bezaliel Angier 2 (qv) Alderman. In Black Boy Lane, in the part just into St Botolphs (see John Hunt (qv)) two Stephen Candlers, Wiseman Candler and Candler junior, were rated 2, 3, 2 and 1 in 1791 (Overseers rates). Land Tax for St Botolphs, 1793, gives Stephen as proprietor rated 6 of John Hedge and others, and Wiseman next door as tenant of Philip Hast, rated 4.

He was an active auctioneer in the 1790s. For example, in 1794 he auctioned a 'Substantial House on North side of East Hill', late occupied Mr Francis Snell (qv) dd. (*Ips]* 22 March 1794. One of Candler's daughters had married James Snell, see below). In 1797 he auctioned the 'well accustomed Public House', the Joiner's Arms, with stables etc, at Shire-gate, Colchester, now occ. John Smith. (This is still (2009) a public house, for many years called the Duke of Clarence, at the top of Scheregate Steps. See below for other connections between Candler and the Smiths). Also included in this auction was a small bricked tenement adjoining, occ. Michael Merry (*Ips]* 17 June 1797). The same year at the Red Lion, Candler auctioned a Mansion House opposite the Three Cups in High Street, late occupied Edward Bland (qv) hosier, parish St Runwalds. This is 16 High Street. Alexander Fordyce Miller (qv) took it (*Ips]* 8 April 1797).

Candler's electoral behaviour is interesting. In 1768 he voted for Gray (Tory) and Fordyce (the radical interloper); 1780, no vote; 1781 Affleck (Tory); April 1784, Affleck and Smyth (radical Whig), July 1784 Smyth; 1788 Jackson (Tory - not Tierney, the radical supported by Smyth). The switch from Whig to Tory in the 1780s indicates Candler as a supporter of the Tory Corporation party, under the leadership of Frank Smythies 1 (qv). In fact on 22 February 1788 Candler was created a Common Councilman and promoted to Assistant on 31 August 1792. In July 1790, he again voted for Jackson against Tierney. Robert Candler was at that time the Serjeant at

C

Mace. During this period Stephen Candler obtained some substantial carpentry commissions from the Corporation, viz in 1788 and 1791-2 on the Exchange and Moot Hall and also in 1794 (£46 with John Taylor and others) (Smythies' account book with the Corporation, ERO D/B 5 Aa2/2, JBB NB Blue 4:23). Similarly he had acted as auctioneer when Smythies was involved in the sale of some small properties around the town centre, twenty three properties sold at The Angel in twelve lots, apply Francis Smythies, attorney (*IpsJ* 6 August 1785). In 1796 Candler was more politically independent, and voted for the Whig Shepley, as well as the evangelical Thornton, similarly giving a vote to Tufnell in 1807. He died before the poll in 1812.

In 1768, the same year he was admitted free burgess, he married Elizabeth Nunn of St Nicholas, aged 25. He was then of St Martins, aged 29 (ERO D/ACL 1768).

The 1782 will of William Hunt, butcher, St Runwalds (ERO D/ACR 18/153) refers to Candler as brother-in-law, making him with Robert Candler, sheriff's officer, trustee for Hunt's five children. Hunt is buried at All Saints, having died 4 September 1782 aged 45, together with his wife Hannah, who died 15 May 1779 aged 38. His relationships to Candler and to John Hunt (qv) not traced.

Candler's own will (ERO D/ABR 31/6), naming him 'Stephen Candler, carpenter and joiner, St Nicholas' was made 30 June 1807, and proved 2 March 1813. Witnesses were William Francis (qv), William W. Francis and Stephen Cawley (attorneys in Trinity St.). He left:-

£50 to youngest daughter Sarah.

Houses and hereditaments left to him by late brother-in-law Giles Nunn (qv), copyhold of Lexden, in or near Middleborough, to be sold for dear wife Elizabeth absolutely.

To Elizabeth for life, freehold St Nicholas where I now reside, and freeholds in Black Boy Lane or elsewhere, then to son-in-law Matthew Hewes of Mile End Colchester, miller (cf. Byam Hewes (qv)), in trust to sell and divide among my children:-

C

- Mary wife of James Snell of St Martins (they married 1782, when he was 22 and she was a minor; merchant taylor in 1788 poll).
- Stephen, to whom also joiner's working tools (created free burgess 24 June 1790, carpenter of St Peter's St, Westminster).
- Elizabeth was the wife of Matthew Hewes (married 1797).
- Robert (?fruiterer in 1812 poll, when 5 Candlers vote in Colchester and 6 in London).
- Sarah (Sarah Gooch Candler, who was named executrix with his wife, Matthew Hewes being removed, in a codicil of 1810).

Giles Nunn's (qv) will (ERO D/ACR 19/450 made 1801, proved 1806) refers to Sarah as Sarah Gouge Candler. Nunn had also asked Stephen to auction 16 North Hill for him (*IpsJ* 8 and 22 September 1792). 'A complete new-built Brick Freehold Mansion on centre of North Hill' rated 8, 'elegantly finished in the present taste.' 2 well-proportioned rooms in front, 5 over. Apply Mr Isaac Slythe (qv) opposite 3 Cups, Mr Giles Nunn near the spot, or auctioneer Stephen Candler. Nunn was bankrupt 1795. He entered Winsley's Gift Houses 1799 and died there 1806.

There is also a marriage 1810 (ML ERO D/ALL 1810) of Stephen Candler widower, fruiterer of St Dionis Backchurch, bound by Francis Snell to Sarah Candler aged 26, of St Nicholas Colchester. (presumably cousins, but precise connection not traced).

Candler died in early June 1812. (*IpsJ* 13 June 1812, JBB NB Jan 63:45) '... yesterday se'nnight died Mr Stephen Candler, one of the Assistants of the Corporation of Colchester.'

Burials, St Nicholas churchyard. Stone may not have survived when the church was demolished. Stephen Candler, 3 June 1812, aged 74. Elizabeth his wife, 25 June 1826 aged 90. (CPL, Crisp MI Transcripts: 90; JBB NB 91/5:15)

C

See also: (*Ips*) 1 November 1806 and 15 August 1807, JBB NB Jun 67:1) auction of properties owned by Royston Barton (qv) (identified by JBB through Land Tax assessment) included property on North Hill and a close in St Nicholas with tenants. The 'capital modern-fronted dwelling house' was on the east side of North Hill. 'A cheerful dwelling house adjoining above now occupied by Mr Candler.' JBB also notes a complaint against Stephen Candler for 'ill orders for nine whole playing and card laying till ten or eleven o'clock at night'. (JBB NB Jan 63:22, Photo in North Committee Room, Town Hall, no other reference given).

CANNING FRANCIS [1143]
Gent
w. 1783

Of Abberton Manor. The brother-in-law of Nicholas Corsellis (qv) of Wivenhoe, having 'married Bridget daughter of Thos Goodell gent and eldest sister of Mrs Mary Corsellis of Wivenhoe'. (Morant, *Essex*, Vol. 1:413, entry for Layer de la Haye, the seat of the Corsellis family where the manor was also held by the Cannings).

Francis Canning's will (ERO D/ACR 18/187) was made 31 May 1783, proved 13 September 1783. Canning named as trustees, John Ram (qv) of Berechurch farmer and Abraham Royllett of Basinghall St London gent. He left a life interest in his estate to his wife Bridget, the sole executrix, then divided the property between son John Goodall Canning and daughter Bridget Canning.

Canning was buried at Berechurch on 29 August 1783 in the Audley Chapel vault as he was a descendant of that family. His mother was a daughter of Thomas Audley (Strutt, *Colchester*, Vol. 2:77 and Morant as above).

See also: Will of Francis Canning of Foxnal, Warks NA PROB 11 920/262, made 1760, proved 1766, father of Francis Canning of Abberton. JBB NB 82/9:24-5 and 85/2:54 have notes and sketches of staircases at Abberton Manor.

CANT GEORGE 1 [138]
Gardener
fl. 1728-1747

The first of the Cant dynasty of gardeners who became prominent in the nineteenth century and remain in the town to this day. Was sworn free burgess on 9 December 1728 and voted in 1741 (Saville, Gray) and 1747 (Nassau).

CANT GEORGE 2 [139]
Gardener
fl. 1740-1780

Created free burgess as the son and apprentice of George Cant 1 (qv) in 1740. Voted for the same candidates as his father in 1741 (Saville, Gray) and 1747 (Nassau) and for Rebow and Gray in 1768. In 1759 he took William Frances apprentice for 2 gns (NA IR/17 58/175). He apparently died before the 1780 election when only his son voted.

CANT GEORGE 3 [143]
Gardener
fl. 1772-1809

Son of George Cant 2 (qv), became a free burgess on 31 August 1772. Voted from 1780 to 1807 but displayed no clear political preference except, perhaps a tendency to vote for well established candidates. He was elected Common Councillor on 17 August 1781.

He also occupied 5 acres of garden ground, Holy Trinity in 1780 per will of William Maples (qv) (1780/98).

Though a regular attender at St Botolphs vestry meetings in the 1780s he was nevertheless in sufficiently straightened circumstances to draw on the parish overseer for support when a son (unnamed) was ill and later died (1799-1800).

Cant died in 1809. His will, made in 1805 (ERO D/ACR 19/518) left his house rated 11 in St Botolphs which was mortgaged, to his son William Samuel (qv) subject to a weekly provision of 4s to his wife Elizabeth and on her death £100 to his second son George 4 and £10 to daughter Elizabeth Balls. The sons inherited equally the Moor ground in St Botolphs (rated 20 in 1793 when leased from Thomas Adams Esq) also subject to 2s weekly to his wife and £10 thereafter to his daughter. The sons were also charged with the purchase from the estate of Cant's tools, stock, plants etc. It seems that Cant was finally unable to make this slender provision for his family for early in January 1809 his bankrupt estate was auctioned (*IpsJ* 21 January 1809).

CANT JOHN [137]
Coachmaster
fl. 1718-1741

Acquired a mortgage on no. 3 East Hill on 17 June 1718 from John Taylor, plumber and his wife Abigail. (JBB Notes on Deeds) The interest persisted until 1746 when his nephews and executors disposed of it back to the Taylors). His will (ERO D/ABR 22/339) made in 1739, proved 1740, besides cash legacies of £900 to various nieces and 50s to the poor of St Peters and St Martins, left a farm in St Giles and Donyland plus £300 to his nephew John, later of Brightlingsea, and the coachmaster's business to nephew Thomas Cant (qv). John and Thomas acted as their uncle's executors.

CANT MARY [142]
Coachmaster
fl. 1760–1768

The widow of Thomas Cant (qv). She continued the coaching business and is named as proprietor of the London coach in Boswell's account of his and Johnson's visit to Colchester *en route* for Harwich (James Boswell, *The Life of Samuel Johnson, L.L.D comprehending an account of his studies and numerous works,*

Vol 1 (London, 1791):254, 255). In 1768, a widow of Colchester, she married William Taylor (qv) of Lexden, also a coachmaster (CPL Crisp ML336, Isaac Phillebrown, Mistley, merchant also stood bond) and they continued to run the business. She died on 1 March 1772 aged 49 and was buried in the Cant family tomb at Fingringhoe.

CANT THOMAS [140]
Coachmaster
fl. 1741-1760

Cant inherited his coachmaster's business at the top of North Hill next the Wagon and Horses (rated 23) from his uncle John Cant (qv). In November 1753 he bought from George Wegg (qv) for £25 a nearby piece of land and cottage known as Bowling Green (later occupiers Bishop Campling (qv), John Malby (qv)), situated between North Hill and the town wall. His will (ERO D/ABR 25/373) made 1760 proved 1765 left the main property and business to his wife in trust for his son Thomas who died intestate on 11 December 1792 aged 38. The Bowling Green (Deeds ERO D/DE T162) and adjacent properties were left to his daughters Mary (later wife of Mark Keymer (qv), who died 1812 aged 70) and Elizabeth (died 1810). Cant died on 1 November 1760 aged 44 and was buried in the family vault at Fingringhoe.

CANT WILLIAM 1 [141]
Gardener
1742-1805

Son of George Cant 2 (qv) and brother of George 3 (qv). Created free burgess in 1765 and voted from 1768, from East Bergholt. Thereafter he remained a Colchester voter and his voting pattern was similar to that of his brother George 3.

His house and garden ground were leased on the south of Gutter St, St Mary-at-the-Walls. On 25 July 1803 (ERO C47 CPL547) he also took on a 21 year lease at £15 p.a. for a piece of ground at the Hythe (rated 7 St Botolphs 1793). On 8 October

C

1791 (*IpsJ*) a case was tried at Quarter Sessions where 2 men were tried for 'feloniously stealing 4 ducks, 30 nectarines and 12 peaches' from William Cant. They were convicted and sentenced, one to 7 years transportation to Botany Bay, the other to be publicly whipped then 1 month hard labour. The differences in sentence were made because one of the men was employed by Cant, and therefore to the crime of theft had added 'the still greater one of basely betraying the trust and confidence reposed in him by his master.'

Cant died on 27 October 1805 aged 63 and was buried at St Mary's. Rather more prosperous than his brother, he left his house and ground to his son William 2 (qv) subject to a £40 annuity to his wife Mary (ERO D/ABR 30/61, 1806). Mary also received a selection of household goods. Cant's daughters Sarah Minks (wife of Robert) and Fanny Pollard (wife of James) were left £500 each but in Fanny's case this was reduced to £200 as she had already received an advance of £300.

His widow, Mary Cant, died on 13 July 1816 aged 77 and was buried with her husband.

CANT WILLIAM 2 [144]
Gardener
fl. 1779-1831

Son of William 1 (qv). A free burgess who voted from 1807. He married Mary Ann Revett (1791-1856). He continued his father's business at Gutter Street though part of the stock of nursery goods was sold off 23 September 1815 (*IpsJ*). On 26 July 1817 the freeholder of the Gutter St land sold off 40 acres, though Cant, whose lease ran till 1824 at £42 p.a., continued in residence and the business continued there until the 1880s. (ERO C47 CPL547) Cant was created an Assistant in the Charter of 1818.

He died aged 52 on 18 January 1831 leaving a wife and 7 children. His will (NA PROB 11/1787 13 July 1831) made provision for them and his sisters Fanny Pollard and Sarah Minks (see William Cant 1 (qv)). His widow married Richard

Jenkins, builder, of Holy Trinity in 1836. She died on 15 December 1856 and was buried with her first husband, their daughter Mary Ann Cross (ob. 19 April 1843 age 32) and her infant son.

CANT WILLIAM SAMUEL [145]
Gardener and Sergeant-at-Mace
fl. 1802-31

Son of George Cant 3 (qv). A free burgess voting from 1807. He was married to Rebecca Snell in 1802 (CPL Crisp ML 117). The Poll Book of 1831 records him a Sergeant at Mace.

CAPSTACK EDWARD [146]
Currier and Tanner
fl. 1768-1808

First encountered in 1768 (*IpsJ* 20 February 1768) when, having been earlier apprenticed to Eleanor Onyon (qv) and John Williams, he took over their currier's business on East Hill after Mrs Onyon's death. In 1777 (*IpsJ* 29 March 1777) styling himself a currier and leather dresser, he 'removed to the shop late Mr William Nightingale's (qv), near the Dial Church where shoemakers, saddlers, collarmakers and all others may be served at the most reasonable terms'. This was no. 58 High Street which backed onto Culver Street near St Nicholas churchyard (rated 17 in 1792, when Capstack's personal estate was estimated at £20). One day in 1786 (ERO P/CoR11A, 21 August 1786) William King, a cooper, was walking through St Nicholas churchyard on the common footpath. Suddenly, 'oyl etc.' was thrown on him 'from the window of the workshop of Mr Edward Capstack, currier, damaging his coat'. On looking up he saw William Capstack, Edward's son 'and another' looking down. Capstack had officially taken his son apprentice on 7 September 1785 (no fee). On 7 July 1788 William Taylor was bound apprentice for £52 10s and on 12 May 1794 Capstack's nephew Samuel Lufkin paid the much reduced fee of £5 (ERO D/B 5 Ta1).

C

Capstack was created honorary free burgess on 29 August 1785 and immediately elected Alderman along with six other of Frank Smythies' 1 (qv) supporters, so as to gain a Tory majority on the Corporation. A satirical account of these elections in a letter to the *Ipswich Journal* implied that an occupation in the leather trades made Capstack and fellow honorary free burgess William Swinborne (qv) unworthy of this office; 'Without adverting on the character of these gentlemen, it is evident that the interest of the Borough was particularly consulted in the choice of them' (*IpsJ* 3 September 1785). In an opposition handbill following the 1784 election Capstack had been dubbed 'Ned Leather' amongst the committee to petition for Christopher Potter (qv), the defeated election candidate whom the Smythies group had supported (cf James Green (qv)) .Capstack voted consistently with the Corporation party and served as Mayor in 1787. In 1792 (together with Peter Rogers (qv)) he acted as executor to fellow Alderman, William Swinborne (*IpsJ* 5 May 1792).

On 21 March 1799 (*ChCh* 12 April 1799) Capstack had two hides stolen from his tan yard in St Peters for which one James Costelow was committed to gaol.

Capstack died on 5 November 1808 aged 72 and was buried in a table tomb at St Nicholas, now destroyed. His will (NA PROB 11/1487 Ely 819-874, 23 November 1808) left his St Peters tannery to his son-in-law Benjamin Smith married to daughter Rebecca, and the St Nicholas currying office to another son-in-law Charles White together with an estate in Langham. His daughter Elizabeth, wife of Thomas Wood, Lexden, farmer received the dwelling house in Back Lane St Nicholas, but son William received only 1 guinea per week. A weekly allowance was also made for his nephews Samuel Lufkin, London currier and William Lufkin of Colchester, the sons of his sister Susan, then deceased. The following February (*IpsJ* 29 February 1809) his effects were sold including 'an excellent table clock by Tompion'.

See also: Capstack's son-in-law Benjamin Smith was of Heigham, Norfolk when he married Rebecca, a minor, in 1782

(ERO ML D/ACL 1782). He died 'much regretted, Sunday last' per *IpsJ* 27 January 1810. Also cf. St Nicholas Registers of 21 February 1769, burial of Edward Capstack, 'an old man.'

CAREW THOMAS [147]
Apothecary
fl. 1721-1740

One of the Tory town elite who took over the Corporation on the Whig collapse of 1727-8 occasioned by bankruptcies and depression in the bay trade and the demise of the Dutch Congregation. These reverses were caused by the resumption of French competition with the subsidence of plague across the Channel (*VCH Essex*, Vol. 9, James Boys (qv), Joseph Duffield 1 (qv)).

Carew was also a manufacturer of candied eringo root and at this period Chamberlain's Vouchers show several of his bills for the sweetmeat for presentation by the Corporation to visiting dignitaries. For example he was paid £1 16s in 1721 for 8lbs of eringo together with two presentation wainscott boxes at 2s (ERO D/B 5 Ab1/26).

His will is at NA PROB 11/701, 3 March 1740.

CARLETON CATHERINE [148]
w. 1763/64

The mother of Humphrey Carleton (qv). Her will names her as the widow of Revd John Carlton of Colchester (NA PROB 11/897/133 Simpson, JBB NB Oct-68). It was made 19 February 1763, witnessed Richard Bacon (qv), John Bumstead, barber, proved 9 April 1764.

She desired to be buried with her late husband in a vault at St Marys (at discretion of her executors). Her £725 13s New South Sea Annuities (bought with £800 left her by husband and so placed with her consent by Mr Christopher Carlton) were to be divided as follows:-

C

- £250 to dear daughter Anna Dorothea Smythies (wife of Revd William Smythies 2 (qv)).
- £250 to dear daughter Mary Dunkley.
- £100 each to granddaughters Catherine and Mary Howard via their father Captain Henry Howard.
- Remaining £25 13s to son Humphrey Carleton (qv) sole executor, together with any residue.

There were also legacies of personal items:-

- To daughter Smythies, Red Stone ring set with Diamonds with Aunt Sharp's hair.
- To dear son Humphrey the mourning ring he gave me for his uncle.
- To daughter Dunkley, watch and coffee pot previously given.
- To dear granddaughter and god daughter Catherine Smythies, locket which was her great grandmothers.
- To dear sister Warters mourning ring with my dear Mother's hair.
- To dear sister Gosfright a mourning ring once my sister Carleton's.
- Faithful servant Hannah Hagon 5 gns for 'tender care and great tenderness in my afflictions' and all clothes.

CARLETON HUMPHREY [149]
Gent
fl. 1775-1805

The son of Revd John and Catherine Carleton (qv). He was residuary legatee in his mother's will proved 1764. Through her he was related to the clerical Smythies family and town clerk Frank Smythies 1 (qv). On the occasion of a fracas in the White Hart coffee house caused by a violent and insane outburst from attorney Samuel Wall 1 (qv) (1775) he was one of a number of gentlemen present including William Smythies 3 apothecary (qv), Frank Smythies (qv), and James Blatch (formerly Smythies) (qv) all of whom were related.

In 1806 the 'residence late occupied by Humphrey Carleton Esq., deceased, in the parish of St Mary-at-the-Walls on London Road', was for sale, apply Mr Rudd, High Street. It comprised 2 parlours, one 16½ x 18ft and one 16½ x 15½ft, a breakfast parlour, a large kitchen, brewhouse, pantries and washhouse, a good cellar and convenient detached offices, 3 large bedrooms and attics over the same; a well of water, a garden and large yard: the whole being nearly 3 roods of ground (*IpsJ* 19 July 1806).

CARR SAMUEL [151]
Grocer
1733-1806

The son of John Carr (qv) shopkeeper and composer of music of Boxford and Lucy, *née* Dupont. He was baptised at Boxford on 22 January 1733. In 1756, Carr married Maria, daughter of John and Sarah Richardson (ML D/ACL 1756. cf. John Richardson apothecary (qv)). Their children were baptised at Boxford (JBB NB 84/7:18). A portrait of Maria was at one time thought to be by Thomas Gainsborough, whose sister married Philip Dupont (*ex inf* Hugh Belsey).

Carr was established from at least 1764 at a prestigious bow-fronted house at 11 High Street (rated 16 in 1778 and 5 for warehouse) and owned the next door property occupied by Samuel Smith (qv) (rated 14). He was one of the original subscribers and silver ticket holders for the Colchester Theatre built in 1764. Carr acted as executor to his brother-in-law Richard Newell (qv) in 1766. For a period Carr traded in partnership with Peter Rogers (qv), but the association ended in 1780 (*IpsJ* 30 December 1780) and he continued to do business independently from the High Street premises as a grocer, tea dealer and oilman. On the death of his father, Carr, as main beneficiary and sole executor advertised that he would carry on the business also selling fashionable prints (*IpsJ* 22 May 1784). He may have moved back to Boxford for a period to oversee his father's business as he is described as 'grocer of Boxford' when named in Edward Snell's (qv) will in 1786.

C

Carr himself died on 15 December 1806 (*Ips]* 27 December 1806) aged 72. His will (NA PROB 11/1455, 14 February 1807) leaves 11 High Street and property in Pelhams Lane to his daughter Lucy Richardson Carr (spinster). A leasehold estate at the Hythe and St Botolphs and a share in the brig called *Concord* are left to his son Samuel Puplett Carr. A copyhold estate at Groton is left equally between the siblings charged with various debts and trust monies including the administration of Edward Snell's estate. These legacies were also charged with the payment by the children to their mother of £100 per year for 'so long as it may please God to spare the life of my said wife.' His silver ticket and interest in Colchester theatre was left to his wife, afterwards to his daughter, and all other of his personal estate to his wife. He named his wife, son and daughter as co-executors and requested a simple burial.

See also: *Ips]* 25 April 1789: S. Carr jun. grocer and tea dealer married Miss Oliver, Sudbury; will Richard Pupplett, linen draper, Colchester NA PROB 11/641, 17 December 1730; Samuel Pupplett Carr, grocer, Colchester, NA PROB 11/1671, 9 June 1823; Sarah Carr, widow, Colchester NA PROB 11/1690, 9 September 1824; Revd Samuel Carr, St Peter's Colchester will NA PROB 11/2194, 8 July 1854; John Oliver Carr, grocer, Colchester NA PROB 11/2236, 4 June 1856; Lucy Richardson Carr, spinster Colchester, NA PROB 11/ 2249, 11 April 1857.

CARTER ALEXANDER [994]
Miller
w. 1801

The brother of Stowers Carter (qv) miller.

At one time was in partnership with Thomas Dixon (qv) and John Ram (qv) in the coal trade at the Hythe. The partnership was dissolved in 1791 (*Ips]* 15 October 1791).

Carter's will (NA PROB 11/1354/166) was made 18 June 1800, proved 12 March 1801. He left an annuity to eldest son Alexander and £2,000 bank annuities to daughter Hester. His son John was already placed in business. Son Turpin was left

Drury Farm. His mill and Chiswell Meadow went to son James, subject to £25 p.a. to Alexander Carter. The 'mare which I usually drive to be sold to some person who is likely to prove good master or mistress to her and not suffer her to be abused.' Carter also held farms under Sydenham Rutherford Esq and Ralph Ward Esq.

Elizabeth Carter, widow of Colchester, Essex, (will NA PROB 11/1055, proved 6 July 1779) left her son Alexander Carter the alehouse the Trowel and Hammer at Marks Tey and other lands there, subject to payment to son Stowers Carter (qv) of £200. Small cash legacies were left to the children of her late son John Carter (viz John, Ambrose, Charles, £20 apiece, Samuel £30, Mary £20). Her granddaughter Hester, daughter of Stowers received 'my best teakettle, my biggest looking glass, and my small round table.'

CARTER JAMES [153]
Tailor
fl. 1800-32

Jobbing tailor, autodidact, author and trades unionist. Wrote one of the autobiographical sources for early nineteenth-century Colchester, his *Memoirs of a Working Man* (see below). As a youth he had worked for Alexander Fordyce Miller (qv). Had premises at Priory Street until 1832, when he left Colchester.

For much fuller account see, A. F. J. Brown, *Essex People, 1750-1900, from their Diaries, Memoirs and Letters* (Chelmsford, 1972). The *Memoirs* were published as T. Carter, *Memoirs of a Working Man* (London, 1845).

CARTER STOWERS [995]
Miller
w. 1791

Carter was brother of Alexander Carter (qv). He married Hester, daughter of John Boggis 2 (qv). He received £200 in his mother, Elizabeth's will of 1779 (NA PROB 11/1055, 6 July

C

1779). This was charged on the Trowel and Hammer alehouse at Marks Tey, property which she left to Alexander. Stowers Carter's daughter Hester also received "my best teakettle, my biggest looking glass, and my small round table' in her grandmother's will.

Stowers Carter's own will was proved 12 January 1791 (NA PROB 11/1200, Gentleman of Colchester). Part of the property disposed of was a house in St Mary-at-the-Walls bought of the trustees of Thomas Clamtree's (qv) estate. Carter's executors were his sons-in-law, William May of Upminster Hall, farmer, and John Posford of Layer-de-la-Haye, farmer.

CATCHPOOL RICHARD [155]
Staymaker
1722-1790

A member of the quaker family which included several carpenters and ironmongers. Married Sarah Sparrow of St Peters in 1751. In 1755 their daughter Ann was born and Sarah died. Richard remarried to Lucy Gyant of St Marys in 1767. Ann died in 1770, age 15 (Fitch, *Colchester Quakers*). A free burgess, he voted only occasionally, but consistently for radical candidates.

See also William Catchpool (qv) carpenter.

CATCHPOOL WILLIAM [1220]
Carpenter
1714-1798

A quaker. Had premises in Gutter Lane (St Johns St) at the easterly end of the present (1990) multi-storey bus-park, formerly William Clamtree's, 'but now for many years past' in his own possession (ERO C47, CPL 655, mortgages 1777, 1789). Nevertheless all or part of his premises were advertised in 1768 (*Ips*J 3 December 1768) as a house with new brick front and warehouse Gutter St 'designed for the Bay Trade' to be sold or let, apply Mr Thos Best (qv) on North Hill or Wm Catchpool, carpenter on the premises.

C

Was amongst those Colchester carpenters who jointly advertised work for sawyers in 1765 (*IpsJ* 10 August 1765). The following year, advertised timber for sale (*IpsJ* 30 August 1766). Acted as Overseer of the Poor in 1774 (Holy Trinity Parish Book). In 1789 the Corporation paid him £2 13s 8d for a Bath stove in the Freemen's Chamber (ERO D/B 5 Aa2/1, Borough Chamberlain's Accounts, 16 July 1789).

Although listed in Holden's *Directory* of 1792, he seems to have retired by the 1790s. In 1791 (*IpsJ* 19 March 1791) his son Joseph Catchpool (1749-1835) advertised from Gutter St for from six to eight good carpenters.

William Catchpool was the son of William and Lydia *née* Warner of Boxted. His wife Alice *née* Jeffrey is buried in the Quaker Old Ground, 1786, aged 74. He was buried there 18 November 1798, aged 84 (see Fitch, *Colchester Quakers*). His brief will (ERO D/ABR 29/189, 1799) left everything to sons James and Thomas.

JBB comment: 'Unimportant member of important quaker family.'

CAUTLEY REVD JOHN [157]
Rector, St Runwalds and Messing
fl. 1777-1797

Canvassed unsuccessfully to succeed Palmer Smythies (qv) as Master of the Free School. (Samuel Parr (qv) gained the position). His brief will of 1797 (NA PROB 11/1286, Exeter 141, proved 15 March 1797) made at Messing, made his wife Joanna and friend Richard Dobson Cheveley trustees and mentioned his son John Crispus Cautley.

CHAMBERLAIN THOMAS [159]
Innkeeper, Bear Inn
fl. 1790-5

Per parish rates.

CHEEK JOHN [1120]
Stagecoachman
fl. 1750

Took over the Colchester to Norwich stagecoach from John Porter in 1750 (*IpsJ* 15 December 1750).

See also William Cheek woolcomber, admitted free burgess by right of apprenticeship to John Baker, baymaker (Assembly Book, 1774).

CHIGNALL JOHN [161]
Maltster, Felsted
w. 1771

A baptist, judging from those named in his will, made in 1768 and proved in 1771 (ERO D/AMR 14/65). He left the bulk of his estate to his wife Mary subject to £20 to his sister, Sarah a spinster, £50 to Winnocks charity in Colchester and £10 to Samuel Rootsey (qv) who was named co-executor with his wife.

See also: Chignell family, bakers of St Nicholas (Deeds of 112 High St in ERO C47 CPL 638). Mary Chignell, Lion Walk Registers from 1776 and other Chignells in Lion Walk in 1820s-40s.

CHIGNELL THOMAS 1 [166]
Baker
fl. 1742-59

A free burgess who voted in 1747 for Nassau.

In May 1742 Chignell was occupying 112 High Street (Deeds ERO Acc 46 CPL 638) together with his business partner Thomas Fitch, to whom Chignell's sister Elizabeth advanced capital in the form of a £60 mortgage on the property. In January 1744 Chignell took over the business entirely from Fitch. Elizabeth's financial interest remained until 1749 when, having married a West Bergholt farmer she withdrew and a re-mortgage to Roger Munsey (qv) was arranged. Munsey is named as Chignell's executor in his will made in 1759 (D/ABR 25/142, 1762) which made provision for son Thomas Chignell 2 (qv), failing whom to sister Mary Chignell, the three sons of his brother and one son of his sister Elizabeth.

See also: D'Cruze, *Pleasing Prospect*:84, 89.

CHIGNELL THOMAS 2 [163]
Baker
fl. 1768-75

A free burgess. Voted in 1768 for Fordyce and in 1781 for Potter. Was married in 1768 (CPL Crisp ML104, ERO D/ACL 1768) to Mary Maples of Trinity. Remained at 112 High Street, his late father's property (Deeds ERO C47 CPL 638). Chignell secured mortgages from Nicholas Humphreys (qv) gent and after his death, from Francis Snell (qv) to provide capital. Finally in 1775 the Chignells sold the property to John Banks cordwainer, the bulk of the purchase price of £360 going to Snell to clear the mortgage debt. Was in prison for debt in 1781 (D'Cruze, *Pleasing Prospect*:84, 89)

See also: Holden's *Directory* 1805. Thomas Chignell, son of Thomas and Mary baptised Lion Walk 20 June 1775; Thomas Chignell son of Thomas and Mary Ann bapt. Lion Walk 13 February 1801; cf Census enumerators returns for 1841, 1851, 1881, Free BMD Index Deaths (viewed on ancestry.com) lists a Thomas Chignell dying aged 83 in 1866. D'Cruze, *Pleasing Prospect*:84, 89.

CLAMTREE ISAAC SAMUEL [165]
Attorney
fl. 1777-1823

The son of Thomas Clamtree (qv) and godson of George Wegg 2 (qv). He is recorded as signing three affluent Colchester wills between 1777 and 88, two together with William Bullock (qv). He was a free burgess who voted from 1781-1790, though in 1781 as a resident of Bungay. He tended to support the more

C

respectable candidates. His will is at NA PROB 11/1666, then of Bloomsbury Square, Middlesex, 17 February 1823.

CLAMTREE THOMAS [164]
Customs and Excise
fl. 1741-84

Son of Benjamin Clamtree, carpenter, Thomas Clamtree rose to become one of Colchester's leading civic figures over many years. He was a free burgess voting from 1741 to 1781. A Justice of the Peace for the Borough in 1760-2 and prominent Whig supporter of the agitation to regain the Charter, he was created the first Mayor in the new Charter of 1763. In the general euphoria, King Coel's pump at the top of the High St was repaired and adorned with his name (JBB, *A Friend to his Country*, (unpublished version, 1972), and see also 'A Friend to his Country: William Mayhew and the Recovery of the Colchester Charter, 1763', *Essex Archaeology and History*, 18 (1987), pp. 63-74). Clamtree's continuing importance in the Borough is confirmed by his successive Mayoralties in 1772, 1774, 1776, 1778 and 1780; a record for the eighteenth century. His career was summed up in his obituary in the *IpsJ* of 10 July 1784;

> Tuesday last died Thomas Clamtree Esq, senior Alderman of this Borough. In the year 1763, when our new Charter was obtained, he was appointed by His Majesty the first Mayor; since which time he served that office 4 (*sic*) other years. He was also Surveyor General of the riding officers for this county which office is now annihilated, agreeable to the late Act of Parliament.

He had lived in Queen Street at around mid century (cf. will Sarah Barnard, widow, All Saints, 1760, ERO D/ABR 25/17) but subsequently lived for many years in a mansion in Head Street insured for £3,000 in 1776 (Sun Insurance 369570). The house contents were auctioned by Timothy Walford 1 (qv) on 17-18 August 1784 (*IpsJ* 7 August 1784) and included beds with damask hangings, card tables &c. The house itself was auctioned the following month (*Ips*J 20 August 1784, though the advertisement does not mention Clamtree by name) described as having a hall, three good parlours, a kitchen, brewhouse, three excellent bedrooms with garrets over, cellars and fruit trees in the garden; all in very good repair. Clamtree's widow lived on in St Marys until her death in December 1802 aged 92 (*Ips*J 18 December 1802). She was buried at St Marys.

See also St Marys registers, burial of Thomas Clamtree 24 March 1776.

CLARKE ANN [162]
Innkeeper, Joiner's Arms
fl. 1780

Inherited the inn, per will of her husband John Clarke 2 (qv) in 1780.

CLARKE JOHN 1 [168]
Baymaker
fl. 1734-1767

Died in the autumn of 1767, then holding office as Borough Alderman. His death was formally noted at the next Corporation Assembly on 5 January 1768. He had been appointed Alderman in the new Charter of 1763 and had been a voter from at least 1734 when, as in 1741, he voted Tory in opposition to his Whig-voting father, John snr. In 1747 they both supported the compromise of Gray and Olmius.

Clarke had married Elizabeth Dammant of St Peters at Stanway in 1742 (CPL Crisp ML8, Boyds 1741, ERO ML D/ALL 1742). He had only one sister to survive to adulthood, Elizabeth, who later married Cornelius Curtis. When their father, John snr., a Sabbatarian Baptist, died in 1760 (will ERO D/ABR 25/71, of St Nicholas), Clarke inherited property in Holy Trinity and St Marys and together with his sister, Elizabeth Rutland Curtis, other tenements in Magdalen St, St Runwalds. John snr also left Elizabeth his house in 'St Ellins

Lane' St Nicholas, except for six rooms reserved for the use of his wife, who was also to receive 28s per week.

John junior died intestate in May 1767 and, John snr's wife having predeceased him, leaving his daughter a minor, administration was granted to his sister Elizabeth Rutland Curtis (administration granted November 1768, NA PROB 46: JBB NB Jul 69:39). The property was offered for sale that December, including (*Ips*) 19 December 1767) the late Mr Alderman Clarke's messuage and ½ acre, Maldon Lane, apply Thomas Bayles (qv) attorney.

See also: Robert Clarke, baymaker and Alderman, will NA PROB 11/708 2 April 1741; will Martha Clarke, alias Hendrickx, wife, Colchester, NA PROB 11/504, 18 November 1708; will Judith Clark or Clarke, Colchester, NA PROB 11/709, 2 May 1741; ERO D/ABR 26/258 will of Cornelius Curtis, farmer, Dedham, 1771; ERO D/ABR 30/415 will of Elizabeth Rutland Curtis, widow, Dedham; ERO D/ABR 35/643 will of Elizabeth Rutland Curtis, singlewoman, 1846.

CLARKE JOHN 2 [167]
Victualler, Joiner's Arms
w. 1780

Left the inn and all personal estate to his wife Ann (qv), will John Clarke victualler Holy Trinity 1780, ERO D/ABR 22/190.

CLARKE WILLIAM [169]
Physician
1698-1778

A well known quaker physician and author of medical treatises (*ODNB*). Originally of Lavington, Wiltshire (as was his wife Mary) he practised in Bradford Wiltshire between 1747 and 1772 before coming to Colchester. His publications include *Essay to Discover the Visible Marks of Christ's Church*, 1779, printed in Colchester by William Keymer (qv); *The Province of Midwives*, 1751; *Medical Dissertation Concerning the Effects of the*

Passions on Human Bodies, 1752 (being a translation of his Leiden Doctorate of 1727).

He offered a house in George Lane for sale in 1773 (nfr) and from that date is recorded in St Nicholas rates at 112 High Street rated 10. The George Lane house was described as follows;

> To be Sold and Enter'd upon Immediately in COLCHESTER
>
> A very good convenient DWELLING HOUSE, with sash windows, situate in GEORGE LANE, near the high street and Market, freehold; containing three parlours, a kitchen, wash-house and Garden, four Lodging Rooms and two Garretts, all in good Repair, the Rooms neatly fitted up and hung with Papers, stoved in the chimneys and a Mahogany Beaufet in one of the Parlours.
>
> Enquire of Dr Clarke or Elizabeth Kendall in Colchester.

Clarke died in 1778 at the age of 80 and was buried at the Friends Burial Ground (Fitch, *Colchester Quakers*). His widow Mary continued living in High Street (rates) until her own death in 1787 (also an octogenarian) when the house was again advertised (*IpsJ* 29 September 1787) as a 'very compact, neat brick'd front freehold DWELLING HOUSE in High Street Colchester very near the Market Place' - late occupied by the widow of Dr William Clarke, to be auctioned by Nathaniel Barlow 1 (qv).

CLUBBE JOHN REVD [1181]
Rector, Whatfield, Suffolk
1703-1773

Rector of Whatfield, Suffolk 1735-1773, in succession to his father George. Maintained social and family connections with Colchester. Thomas Spark Seaman (qv), Colchester surgeon, married his sister-in-law Ann Martin at Whatfield 19 December 1745. He apprenticed his son John Clubbe (qv) to Thomas

C

Great (qv) apothecary of Colchester 1755 for 70 gns (NA IR 1/52/134).

Clubbe was a friend of William Mayhew 1 (qv) Colchester attorney, who was lord of the manor of Whatfield Hall. They both had their portraits painted by Gainsborough late in 1757 (JBB, *EAE*:123-142, especially pp. 125-6, 129, 131).

In 1758 he published the *History and Antiquities of Village of Wheatfield, Co. Suffolk*. This was partly a parody of Morant's *Colchester*. His *Physiognomy* (1763) was dedicated to Hogarth.

Morant, *Essex*, Vol 2:183 mentions a farm at Birch, late T. Lufkin's now J. Clubb Clerk, by right of his wife Susan. (ERO Estate map 78 acres in west, centre and east of Birch, 1750 by John Miller of Hadleigh.)

CLUBBE JOHN [170]
Apothecary and Surgeon
fl. 1780

Son of the Revd John Clubbe (qv) of Whatfield, Suffolk, who wrote a pastiche of Morant and other works (d. 1773). Clubbe was a surgeon and writer on venereal disease. He had been apprenticed to Thomas Great, apothecary of Colchester for 70 gns in 1755 (NA IR 1/52/134). He died 2 May 1811 aged 70 (Will NA PROB 11/1523, 6 June 1811).

See also: JBB, *EAE*:123-142, especially 131.

COCK DANIEL [174]
Brewer
fl. 1750s

Occupied large premises in St Botolphs Street which were auctioned in 1754 (*IpsJ* 23 March 1754) and taken over by William and Mary Hickeringill (qv). Cook was a free burgess who voted in 1747 for Gray and Olmius.

See also: vote in 1768 in Borough election for Rebow and Gray by Daniel Cock, surgeon.

COCK HORATIO [173]
Surgeon
fl. 1783-1831

A prosperous and successful surgeon, created free burgess in 1768. Was established in Queen Street by 1783, when there were offered for sale; '... two brick messuages in Queen Street now occupied by Mr Horace Cock, surgeon and Mrs Bradstreet, and further tenements called the White Houses in the same street. Apply Mr Lisle at Copdock (Jordan Harris Lisle (qv)) or Mr Ennew at Colchester (Samuel Ennew (qv))' (*IpsJ* 14 June 1783). All these properties, now demolished, were at the upper end of Queen Street on the west side.

Cock made an advantageous marriage. The *IpsJ* of 27 January 1787 announced that the marriage of H. Cock surgeon to Miss (Susan) Round eldest daughter of James Round Esq (qv) of Birch Hall had taken place on 24th (CPL Crisp ML100, H. Cock, St Nicholas, surgeon and John Fox, surgeon (qv) bound, Horatio (30) to marry Susan Round (26) of Birch; ERO D/ALL 1787).

The Cock household is well documented in the Round family papers (ERO D/DEt/F38). Susan came to inherit East Hill House from George Wegg 2 (qv). The Cocks resided there in later life. In the winter of 1820 the local paper recorded; 'Horatio Cock Esq very humanely distributes weekly potatoes to the necessitous poor' (*Colchester Gazette* 30 December 1820).

In keeping with his social station Horatio Cock was a prominent member of St James vestry and was elected to the select vestry under the new statute 59 Geo III on 16 April 1821 (St Jas Records ERO D/P138/8/1-5).

Cock died in 1831. His will (NA PROB 11/1791, Tebbs 620) was made on 19 July 1831 and proved on 11 November 1831 and demonstrates his affluence. The will specified his desire '...to be buried in a plain wood coffin without cloth covering or ornaments and at a little Expense as may be in any church yard near where I die'. There was to be no hearse, mourning coach or rings.

The will goes on to make complicated provision in respect of a capital messuage he had contracted to buy for £3,000 from Sophia Baskerfield, widow of Thomas Baskerfield Esq, though it was uncertain if she had the right to sell. Cock left lands at Gorleston, Suffolk to his niece Charlotte Matilda, wife of Paul Smith, tea dealer of London; the two freehold houses in Queen Street Colchester (see above) then occupied by John Seex and Charles Coatts; East Hill House; a small piece of land at Ardleigh with a 'trifling building' occupied by Thomas Harris on it, and other property at Clare, Suffolk.

The estate was to be distributed in cash. Susan Cock, his 'dear wife', received the dividends on £6,500 in 7% Bank Annuities for life, to be afterwards divided between Charles Round of Birch Hall (£2,000), George Round of Colchester, banker (£600); Edward Round, brother of the last (£600); Eliza Ann, wife of John Ringler Thompson, his wife's niece (£800).

Cock also left £100 each to John and Ann Kendall's charity, the Colchester and Essex Hospital, the Female Friendly Society, the Lying in Charity, the Society for Promoting the Gospel in Foreign Parts in London, the SPCK, Revd John Dakins, Rector of St James, and to Ruth and Sophia Webb 'our kind and attentive servant maids.' Amongst other legacies to servants was £20 to Samuel Harden 'our gardener'. The document mentions possible inaccuracies in Cock's signature 'owing to (his) sight not being very good.'

COCK JOHN [172]
Innkeeper, Sun
fl. 1784-96

A free burgess voting in 1788-1796 for establishment candidates. Compare John Cock wheelwright voting in 1784 for Potter (April) then Affleck and Potter (July).

COLCHESTER WILLIAM [1182]
Schoolmaster, Dedham
fl. 1730-1773

Ran the Writing School at Dedham (the building later known as Sherman's, Dedham High St), to which many Colchester tradesmen sent their sons (maths and book-keeping were subjects). William Colchester had moved there from Bramford, Suffolk, where he taught mathematics (*IpsJ* 7 and 14 November 1730).

Married twice, to Mary Clarke (Harwich registers, 13 April 1732) and to Susan Skinner (CPL Crisp ML236, 1741) both of Dedham where their children were baptised between 1742 and 1757. He was buried at Dedham 18 July 1773 (died 14 July) and Susannah, his widow, was buried 30 June 1799 aged 85.

The school advertised, in 1751 as an establishment 'where youth are boarded and expeditiously qualified for Trade and Business' (*IpsJ* 12 January 1751). In 1766 appeared a joint advertisement with Susan Scarlin (qv) of the Dedham Ladies' Boarding School and Thomas Grimwood (qv) Dedham Grammar School, notifying the dates of summer vacation (11 June) and the beginning of the following term (7 July) (*IpsJ* 22 February 1766).

Colchester took William Harden apprentice for 10 gns in 1763 (NA IR17/23/210).

An Annual Meeting of former pupils first took place on 22 September 1762 at the Assembly Room Dedham (names to Mr Cutting at the Marlborough Head) (*IpsJ* 11 September 1762). These meetings became established events. Later advertisements give names of stewards at the Dinner, including members of the Colchester Boggis family of baymakers, for example, *IpsJ* 4 October 1766 for the dinner at the White Hart on 17 October, Richard Mudd and John Josselyn stewards; *IpsJ* 3 October 1767 at the White Hart on 7 October, George Death and Thos Boggis (qv) stewards; *IpsJ* 23 October 1771 at the Marlborough Head, James Boggis (qv) and John Brooks stewards; *IpsJ* 15 October 1774 for 26 October at the Sun, John Cook and Wm Marven stewards; *IpsJ* 27

C

September 1780 for 12 October at the Sun, Thomas Boggis Esq (qv) and Mr Robt. Kenningale stewards.

A new Master to succeed Colchester was advertised for in 1773 (*IpsJ* 31 July 1773) and the following year a good penman and Accomptant were required (*IpsJ* 5 November1774).

William Colchester left no will. There is an administration in PROB 11 for 1773.

See also; JBB NB Sep64:39, 83, 85, notes on a visit to Shermans - architectural features and names scratched in bricks including that of William Colchester; JBB NB 78/2:110, notes from Dedham registers, 17 November 1742 baptism of William son of William and Susan Colchester, 7 January 1743, Cyprian, ditto; 4 April 1745 Samuel ditto (died an infant), 22 December 1746 Susanna Colchester who died in 1747; 24 July 1748 Cordelia Colchester; 31 May 1757 Susanna Colchester. Burials: 14 June 1748 Elizabeth Colchester widow, 18 July 1773 Mr William Colchester writing master; 30 June 1799 Susanna widow of William Colchester aged 85.

COLE EDWARD [1196]
Tanner
ob. 1759

Premises at East Bridge. Had a longstanding partnership with William Swinborne (qv).

Monumental Inscriptions at St James (CPL Crisp MIs) include Edward Cole, tanner, died 5 November 1759 aged 55; Elizabeth Cole, relict died 28 March 1787 aged 74; Edward Cole, son, died, 16 September 1784 aged 39.

Cole's will is ERO D/ACR 16/211, 1760 and mentions his children Edward and Elizabeth.

Widow Cole, tanner, advertised at East Bridge in 1762 and 1763 (*IpsJ* 30 October 1762, 14 May 1763).

COLE GEORGE WILLIAM [183]
Wine Merchant
fl. 1773-1807

Son of John Cole snr (qv) and his wife Bridget. Received a reversionary interest in his father's real estate in his will of 1773 (NA PROB 11/849), after that of his elder brother John (qv). This was confirmed in John's will of 1789 (NA PROB 11/1181, 30 July 1789). George William Cole seems to have traded as a wine merchant until 1807 when he announced he was giving up his partnership with Edward Sallows who was to continue in the trade (*IpsJ* 24 October 1807).

COLE JOHN 1 [174]
Coal and Corn Merchant
fl. 1758-1773

Cole was a merchant of St Giles aged 30 in 1758 when he married Bridget Price (25) of St Runwalds, the daughter of Recorder Richard Price (qv) (CPL Crisp ML 278). Was probably the builder of 'Tranent', Crouch Street, in the early 1760s (JBB NB Check:10).

He died early in 1773. On 6 February 1773 (*IpsJ*) Benjamin Page of Fingringhoe and George Bateman 'for many years clerk to the deceased' advertised that they were carrying on the coal and cinder trade of Mr John Cole at the usual place. Debts and claims were to be addressed to Bateman at the deceased's dwelling house, obviously separate from the coal yard. Cole's will (NA PROB 11/985, Stevens 98, proved 5 March 1773, JBB NB Check:10) left his wife Bridget a life interest in his property at Gt. Totham and Colchester as well as the household goods and £500 in lieu of dower, absolutely. The property was then to revert to his eldest son John (qv) then to his second son George William (qv). He also forgave his mother-in-law, Mrs Bridget Price any debts she might owe him and provided she should be maintained and provided with £40 p.a. A final reversionary provision laid down that if all other legatees should fail, the stock etc., valued at around £10,000 should be distributed

C

between various legatees in Colchester and Dedham including Cole's sister Mary, the wife of Francis Pigott MD (qv), and Martin Riddlesdell (qv) whitesmith and blacksmith.

See also: A John Cole voted in 1747 for Nassau but no vote is recorded in 1768. Bridget Cole died in September 1773 (*Ips*] 25 September 1773, JBB NB Check:73), for her will see John Cole 2 (qv). Will of Martha Cole, spinster, Colchester, NA PROB 11/841, proved 28 November 1758. Will Ann Cole, spinster, Wivenhoe, NA PROB 11/1082, proved 26 October 1781.

COLE JOHN 2 [175]
Merchant and Gentleman
fl. 1773-1789

Son of John Cole 1 (qv) and his wife Bridget. As eldest son he inherited the family property in Totham, Goldhanger and a mansion ('Tranent' in Crouch Street) St Mary-at-the-Walls after his mother's death in September 1773 (*Ips*] 25 September 1773, her will is NA PROB 11/991 26 October 1773). Received a mourning ring in the will of James Boggis (qv).

He himself died in 1789 (*Ips*] 18 July 1789). His will (NA PROB 11/1181 30 July 1789) left the real estate to his brother George William (qv), a £10 annuity to his servant Bedford Steer, and made provision for his sister Bridget the wife of Thomas Taylor, gent. of Colchester, of interest on £1,000.

JBB NB Check:10, notes on St Mary-at-the-Walls overseers' rate books, deducing the date of the building of 'Tranent'. There was a Maltings office on the site in 1753 rated £7, in 1762 the building was rated at £8, but in 1764 the property is rated at £17. Thereafter a double house was built on the Odeon site in Crouch Street at about same time by William Smythies 3 (qv) surgeon.

COLE NATHANIEL [1154]
Gunsmith
fl. 1760

St Mary-at-the-Walls rates of 1760 show Cole in occupation of premises on the east side of Head Street near the Fleece and the corner of Back Lane rated 5. After his death the premises were taken over by Thomas Lawrence (qv).

See also: Thomas Lawrence apprenticed to Thomas Cole, Dedham, 1757, £20 (NA IR 1/52/203).

COLE WILLIAM [184]
Composer and Landsurveyor
1737-1824

Full article in JBB, *EAE*:195-206.

CONEY JOSEPH [185]
China Dealer and Cooper
fl. 1768-80

Admitted to Lion Walk Meeting in 1768 and married Mary Lince who was admitted in 1769 (L. Blaxill, *The History of Lion Walk Congregational Church*, Colchester, 1939). A free burgess, who voted from 1768-96 from Colchester and supported radical candidates. However, his business seems to have been wound up in 1780, when on 15 and 16 May was sold (*IpsJ* 13 May 1780):-

> All the ... stock in Trade of MR CONEY, cooper and dealer in china, earthen & turnery wares, in the High Street, Colchester, consisting of 12 dozen of china cups and saucers; teapots, basons &c &c a large quantity of earthenware, 60 malt and flour shovels, twenty scoops, jets, hand tools, pattens, patten-boards, rings and ties, likewise all the household furniture ... an eight day clock &c.... The whole to be sold without reserve.

C

See also settlement order, St Runwalds to St Peters, along with his wife and six children made 12 December 1785, he having failed as a china dealer (St Peters parish records, JBB NB 99/5:24).

COOK FUDGELL [187]
Papper
fl. 1791

Borough Examination Book, ERO P/COR 27 June 1791 and 8 September 1791:

> The several examinations of Edmund Lilley (qv), Benj Smith (qv), Robert Tabor (qv), James Mansfield the younger (qv), Charles Heath (qv), Grange Heard (qv), Peter Devall (qv) all of Colchester aforesaid, baymakers, taken on oath the 3rd day of September, 1791. These Examinants severally speaking for themselves say they suspect that divers quantities of ends and waste have by their several and respective workmen been embezzled and that they severally and respectively suspect that Fudgell Cook, the younger of Colchester aforesaid, Papper, hath purchased the same of their working men respectively.

Cook was convicted and fined £20. Originally accused on 27 June together with Michael Delight and John Field (both qv). Field was convicted and fined £20 on 30 June 1791.

COOK WILLIAM [189]
Merchant
fl. 1786-1795

Partner of Edward Snell (qv) in the Coal Corn and Lime trade at the Hythe. After Snell's death, Cook continued the business in partnership with Snell's trustees and heir Charles Absolon (qv) until the partnership agreement expired in 1794 (24 May 1794 *IpsJ*) and Absolon continued alone. Cook may have moved away from Colchester thereafter as the will of Samuel

Carr (qv) (a Snell trustee) leaves a copyhold estate at Groton in Suffolk occupied by William Cook, maltster. Cook's house at the Hythe was taken over by a Mr Henry Jarvis (qv) until it was sold, freehold in 1802 (13 March 1802 *IpsJ*) when Jarvis moved away.

COOKE SAMUEL [190]
Merchant
fl. 1795-1806

Originally of Sible Hedingham when he married Mary, daughter of Isaac Green (qv) esq of Lexden (ERO ML D/ACL 1788). By 1795 at least he was established as a Hythe merchant. On 28 March 1795 (*IpsJ*), he and George Round succeeded Joseph Green (qv) (brother of Isaac) in the Coal Cinder and Corn Trade establishing the firm of Round and Cooke. They operated from a counting house on St John's Green as well as premises at the Hythe hitherto occupied by Green, advertising 'Bottles, Flagg & Paving stones &c.' Isaac Green (qv) died in 1799 leaving Lexden House, other farms and large cash settlements to Samuel, Mary and their children (Will NA PROB 11/1322, proved 24 April 1799). Cooke himself died in March 1806 (*IpsJ* 22 March 1806) at his house in Rowhedge, which was advertised for sale on 10 May 1806 (*IpsJ*) being 'on the south side of the Colne at Rowhedge, nearly opposite Wivenhoe.' The premises were advertised again on 8 August 1807 (*IpsJ*) and described in great detail as follows:

> To be peremptorily SOLD by AUCTION by LINTON & LAVALLIN.
>
> On Wednesday the 12th day of August 1807 at four o'clock in the afternoon, on the premises (in one or more LOTS as may be determined upon at the place of Sale).
>
> A Desirable Copyhold estate of Inheritance, holden of the Manor of EAST DONYLAND in the County of Essex, Consisting of a Substantial modern brickfronted dwelling house., the late residence of Mr Samuel Cooke, merchant deceased; containing on the ground floor, 3 parlours and

C

2 kitchens; above 4 excellent sleeping rooms and dressing rooms; with brew house, stabling for 3 horses, chaise house, dove house, dairy and cow house, a good paved yard enclosed by a handsome brick wall, a large garden well stocked with fruit trees, containing ¾ acre; & opposite the house (separated only by the street) is a neat flower garden, walled in, which is close to the River Colne, and is particularly well adapted for a coal and timber yard, together with use of the Quay adjoining for lading and unlading all manner of goods without paying any wharfage or any other compensation whatever.... Premises may be viewed by application to the auctioneers.

It seems to be an example of developing domesticity, that the commercially useful area between the road and the river should have been converted to a flower garden, Cooke's business activities apparently taking place from the counting house on St Johns Green or the premises at the Hythe. Cooke also owned a shipyard at Wivenhoe, to which one assumes he commuted by boat. His will (ERO D/ACR 19/455) describing him as an oyster merchant of Rowhedge, distributes his property including the shipyard and numerous cottages, within his family. Edward Auston (qv) is named as executor.

COOPER THOMAS [191]
Fingringhoe and Langenhoe
fl. 1809-1839

Occupied Fingringhoe Hall, which was for sale in 1809 (*IpsJ* 9 September 1809) and owned the Three Cups Hotel in Colchester, which was for sale under his will in 1839 (*Essex County Standard* 6 December, 1839).

COOPER WILLIAM [117]
Clockmaker (and Brasier)
1706-1757

Born 7 September 1706 in East Bergholt, son of Samuel Cooper, yeoman and wife Martha. Apprenticed 24 September 1720 to John Smorthwait (qv) for £20. Admitted free burgess 9 December 1728. Married Magdalen Reynoldson at Aldham, 1729. Smorthwait, an uncle of the bride, stood bond for the marriage licence. The Coopers had seven children between 1730 and 1740, though five died in infancy and childhood. Magdalen Cooper died 16 July 1740, two months before her last child.

Cooper was trading in All Saints from 1729. In 1733 he entered into partnership with Nathaniel Hedge 1 (qv) who had just married Smorthwait's daughter, Sarah. Smorthwait died in 1739, and Hedge took over his business from his widow, leaving William Cooper to continue as a sole trader. Cooper seems to have made fewer clocks after the partnership with Hedge was dissolved, though he also made watches. (*IpsJ* 11 January 1766 advertisement for a watch of his manufacture, lost by its owner). Also may have traded as a brasier; in 1750, took over the Corner Shop off Angel Lane previously occupied by Joseph Weely, brasier, deceased (*IpsJ* 6 January 1749/50).

Cooper swore to the handwriting of Smorthwait's will, which had not been made before witnesses (1736). Cooper was churchwarden at All Saints in 1744 (27 March 1744) and was a fairly frequent attender at vestry meetings. Voted in the Borough poll in 1734, 1741 and 1747. Stood bond for the marriage licences of Edward Covell (1747) and Walter Keeble Marven (1750).

He died 26 April 1767 and is buried in All Saints. He died insolvent, with an estate worth under £40. Letters of Administration were taken out by his principal creditor, William Hickeringill (qv), merchant, on 4 July 1757. Cooper's surviving children Elizabeth and John renounced their interest in the estate.

C

Summarised from B. Mason, *Clock and Watchmaking in Colchester, England*, (Colchester, 1969):268-270.

CORNELL EBENEEZER [193]
Draper
fl. 1775-1790

Son of Ebeneezer Cornell, pastor at Lion Walk Meeting. He occupied premises in St Runwald between Angel Lane and Bear Lane in the High Street from 1770-5 (Rates). In 1780 (*Ips/* 22 January 1780) Cornell took the shop and stock of late Robert Duke (qv) near the White Hart (no. 3 High Street) rated 21 until 1790 (when it was listed as J. Humphreys and W. Younghusband in the rates).

In 1787 he was admitted a member of Lion Walk meeting together with his wife Elizabeth (Blaxill, *Lion Walk*). He was a beneficiary under his mother Margaret's will in 1803 (ERO D/ACR 19/339) together with his sister Margaret and brother-in-law John Rouse, ironmonger (qv), and was co-executor with Rouse.

CORRY JAMES [1167]
Clockmaker
fl. c.1718

Daily Courant 18 December 1718 advertised for a lost watch, made by Corry. Bernard Mason's research on Colchester clockmakers also discovered three long-case clocks signed by Corry. However, he seems to have left no other trace in the local historical sources.

B. Mason, *Clock and Watchmaking in Colchester, England* (Colchester, 1939):250.

CORSELLIS NICHOLAS ESQ [194]
Wivenhoe Hall
1697-1761

A member of the Corsellis gentry dynasty of Wivenhoe and Layer Marney. His parents were Nicholas Corsellis (bur. Layer Marney 1728) and Elizabeth *née* Taylor of Chiswick. He was baptised at Wivenhoe 3 November 1697. He married aged about 30 to Miss Frances Child, 32, sister of Sir Caesar Child bt. of Woodford Bridge at Little Parndon 1740/1 (CPL Crisp ML 240).

He voted in Colchester parliamentary elections in 1734 for the country party (Tory) candidate and in 1741 for Tories, Savage and Gray. He had been created an honorary freeman in 1727. In 1747 as High Sheriff of Essex he presided over the poll without voting. (The town had no Mayor at the time having lost its Charter.)

Corsellis has a monument with the rest of his family at Layer Marney (others recorded there include Nicholas Caesar (qv) 1806, Caesar 1808, Matthew 1835). He died 10 December 1761 aged 64. His wife and brother-in-law are also buried there, the inscription being:-

> In memory of Sir Caesar Child Bart of Woodford Bridge ob. 24 September 1753 *aet.* 51 and of his sister Francis, wife of Nicholas Corsellis of Wivenhoe Hall, Esq, a lady excelled by few in the most amiable accomplishments, so none died more truly lamented, ob. Dec 18th 1759 *aet.* 42.

His will (NA PROB11/872, 6 St Eloy, proved 5 January 1762) was made 7 November 1760 (witnessed Daniel Blyth (qv), John Cotter, Richard Wenham). It leaves the Manor of Wivenhoe and Wivenhoe estate to eldest son Revd Nicholas Corsellis (qv) for life, then in trust to Charles Gray (qv) and John Taylor of Sheene, Surrey (a cousin) for first born, second born etc. sons of Nicholas jun in succession. The Manor of Layer Marney and Layer Tower were similarly left to his second son Nicholas Caesar Corsellis (qv). Out of these legacies, it was stipulated that it would be permitted these sons to allow their wives jointures of £100 p.a. for every £1,200 such wives brought as their portions. John Taylor was appointed Guardian and he, Gray, and Nicholas Corsellis were named executors.

L. C. Sier, 'Nicholas Corsellis', *Essex Review,* Vol 51:135: notes a mortgage on the estate to Sarah Creffield for £1,845 in 1726. Increased to £3,200 by 1738. A private Act of Parliament was necessary for leave to sell a portion to Daniel Harvey. Attorneys were Samuel Ennew (qv) and Francis Smythies (qv) (D/DU457/13 Act for vesting part of estate late Nicholas Corsellis dd. in Trustees passed 1771 II Geo3). There are notes in the writing of Benjamin Strutt (qv) who stated that Samuel Ennew's (qv) and Francis Smythies' (qv) attorney's bill amounted to £275 1s 6d and though Mr Daniel Harvey (qv) was to have paid it all Revd Nicholas Corsellis paid a moiety of £137 10s 9d. See also other references under Revd Nicholas Corsellis (qv).

CORSELLIS NICHOLAS CAESAR [196]
Donyland Hall
ob. 1806

Occupied Donyland Hall from 1775 (for this property see David Gansel (qv), James Ashwell (qv)). Corsellis is listed at the Hall in Chapman and André's map of 1785 though the estate had been purchased by James Ashwell (qv) in 1783. Jeremy Bentham (*Correspondence of Jeremy Bentham,* I. Christie (ed), London, 1968, Vol 1: 243) mentioned in 1775 that Corsellis had taken the place. He, or Nicholas Corsellis had been spending too much money in Paris and retired to the country for economy.

Corsellis also lived for a time at the other family residence (inherited through his mother, cf Nicholas Corsellis (qv)) in Woodford where he was overseer of poor in 1780 and Surveyor of Highways in 1778 (E. J. Erith, *Woodford, Essex 1600-1836: a study of local government in a residential parish,* (Woodford and District Historical Society, 1950)). His residence was 'Gwynne House' Woodford Bridge (by Papworth, largely rebuilt 1816, now (1980s) part of Dr Barnados). He became Collector of

Taxes at Hythe, Colchester on 25 May 1786 after the death of Thomas Wilshire (qv). He voted in Colchester elections from 1781 for the Tory, Affleck, and in July 1784 for Potter. For both polls he was resident at Woodford. In 1790 (Thornton, Tierney) and in 1796 Thornton, Muncaster) he followed his brother Revd Nicholas Corsellis in supporting the radical Tierney and the evangelical Thornton. He was then resident in Wivenhoe.

He married Mary Utterson who died 31 January 1821 aged 74. Corsellis himself was buried at Layer Marney, 24 October 1806 aged 50, having died of an apoplectic fit 'Friday last at Harwood Hill' (*Ips*) 8 November 1806).

His will is at NA PROB 11/1459, Nicholas Caesar Corsellis, Woodbridge Sussex, proved 24 April 1807. See references to other family wills under Revd Nicholas Corsellis (qv).

CORSELLIS REVD NICHOLAS [195]
Rector, Wivenhoe
1744-1828

Rector and squire of Wivenhoe and Layer Marney. Notable for Whig/Radical political opinions in the 1780s which led him to fight a duel with the Ipswich MP:-

> Monday morning a duel was fought at Lexden Heath between the Revd Nicholas Corsellis of Wivenhoe and C. A. Crickitt Esq (qv), member for Ipswich. The cause in dispute originated in some severe language with which the former addressed the latter on Saturday last. Mr Corsellis, after receiving his adversary's shot, fired his pistol in the air; on which Mr Crickitt expressed himself satisfied, and the affair here terminated. S. Tyssen Esq was second to Mr Corsellis and Wm Middleton Esq to Mr Crickitt (*Ips*) 4 July 1789).

Of the seconds William Middleton was MP for Essex and Samuel Tyssen (qv) was of the local radical interest. He had entered Colchester Borough poll in July 1784 at the last minute, collecting 26 votes (including one from Corsellis) not with any hope of election but as a device to allow the outsider

C

candidate, Christopher Potter, to petition. (JBB, *EAE*:92, 148) Corsellis went on to support George Tierney in 1788 and 1790 (together with Thornton) in opposition to the Tory Corporation party. In 1820 he was one of the company who dined at the Three Cups to celebrate the acquittal of Queen Caroline (JBB May 65:47, note from *Essex Review*, Vol 55:7).

Corsellis was the son of Nicholas Corsellis snr (qv) of Wivenhoe Hall (1697-1761) and Frances *née* Child, sister to Sir Caesar Child of Woodford Bridge (CPL Crisp ML 240, at Little Parndon). A generation earlier, a Nicholas Corsellis, grandson of a wealthy India merchant, had been MP for Colchester (1711).

Revd Nicholas continued to live in the family property at Wivenhoe Hall. He maintained a large establishment, keeping 5 manservants in 1780 (NA T47/8 Manservants Tax), at a time when the ratio of female:male domestic servants was in the area of 5:1. He had married Mary daughter of Thomas Goodall in 1762 (nfr) and thus became brother-in-law to Francis Canning (who married Bridget Goodall). The Corsellis' had two sons, Joseph Goodall Corsellis, Rector of Wivenhoe 1826-1835 and Thomas. Thomas became a Colchester free burgess in 1800 and entered the East India Service.

On 12 May 1733 Nicholas Corsellis had taken orders via a Lambeth Degree - one of only three or four a year to be granted, and succeeded to the living at Layer Marney. The advowson and manor had been bought by his great grandfather in 1667 for £7,200. In 1773 (29 May) dispensation was granted for him to hold the living of Wivenhoe, worth £320 p.a., in addition (nfr).

From the early 1780s he became involved in a farm of the Stamp Duty together with Frank Smythies 1 (qv) attorney, town clerk and prime mover behind the Corporation interest in local politics. Corsellis had his fingers badly burned over the partnership to the tune of several hundred pounds. Correspondence survives between Smythies and Benjamin Strutt (qv) (also politically anti-Corporation at the time), acting as agent for Corsellis, as Strutt attempted, largely unsuccessfully, to gain some restitution (ERO D/DHt/E24 1791-6).

Strutt was Corsellis' agent and man of business for his estates at Wivenhoe. Rent books of 1793-1802 included a map of the property. Tenants included Edward Sage Esq (qv). Interleaved in the rent books was left a note from the local Rector Revd Dr. Lind (qv) wishing the Corsellis' a safe journey as they were due to travel abroad and including a pamphlet for their amusement (notes re rent books, JBB NB II Oct 71:32, books then in the possession of L. H. Gant).

Corsellis' brother, Nicholas Caesar also lived locally, at Donyland Hall in 1775 and Woodford in 1780. He became Comptroller of Customs at the Hythe in 1788 (ob. 1806). Corsellis himself died in 1826. His simple will (NA PROB 11/1712, proved 23 May 1826) left all to a second wife Ann (or Hannah). A codicil of April 1826 apportioned £1,000 for repairing the parsonage house at Wivenhoe.

See also: family tree JBB NB 85/5:28-9.

Relevant documents in ERO also include; D/DHt M 180/1 Stewards Accounts, 1786-90, 1801-2; D/DHt A9, Corsellis to Capt. Daniel Harvey 1782-92, also legal expenses 1793; Land Tax assessments 19 June 1794 for Layer Marney, N.C. Corsellis owned, tenant James Sach £40 8s, and another entry for property owned N. C. Corsellis, occupied by Corsellis, £4; owned Revd Mr Corsellis, occupied by Sach £8 8s. Sach is one of the collectors; D/DEt.F2, Lt Nicholas Caesar Corsellis' commission, 1783, as 2nd Lieutenant on the *Triumph*, and in 1801 on the gun boat *Monkey*; D/DHt A9, 10, bills &c; D/DEtL3 of 24 February 1791, copy of settlement and opinion re Trust set up concerning Vine House Farm, Revd Nicholas Corsellis and his daughter Frances, spr.

Corsellis wills: NA PROB 11/851, 29 December 1759, Frances, wife, Wivenhoe Hall; PROB 11/466, 29 October 1702, Martha, widow, Elmstead; PROB 11/695, 30 April 1739, Nicholas of Wivenhoe: PROB 11/872, 5 January 1762, Nicholas, Wivenhoe Hall; PROB 11/1459, 24 April 1807, Nicholas Caesar, Woodbridge Sussex; PROB 11/1738, 19 April 1828, Revd

C

Frederick, clerk, Layer Marney; PROB 11/1639, 22 February 1821, Mary, widow, Colchester.

COURTNEY MRS ESTHER [197]
Muffmaker
fl. 1766

(*Ips*) 18 January 1766):

This is to acquaint the Ladies

THAT Mrs Courtney, near Headgate in Colchester, makes and sells all sorts of MUFFS (made of Foreign Feathers) and English of the most curious colours, Tippets, Hats &c with all sorts of French Trimmings, made in the newest Patterns; also ornamental flowers of all sorts, and Flower-Trees in the most beautiful Manner ... All ladies that please to favour her with their Commands may depend that their Orders shall be punctually obey'd and gratefully acknowledged, by their humble servant,

Esther Courtney

See also: Colchester Borough Examination Books ERO P/CoR/2, 3, 1772, appearances of Thomas Courtney, tailor and Mary his wife; CPL Crisp ML 375, ERO D/ALL 1766, Thomas Harbourne 21, St Mary-le-Bow, Orange merchant married to Elizabeth Courtney, 18, St Mary-at-Walls, at Colchester, 1766; cf Mrs Francis, draper (qv) for possible succession of this property.

COWELL JOHN [1183]
Watchmaker, London
fl. 1761

London career well documented in Clockmakers Company records. Relevant here as having married (1761) Rebecca Green of Lexden, sister of William Green (qv) (CPL Crisp ML 268 John Cowell (23) of St Christopher-le-Stock, London, watchmaker to Rebecca Green (23) of Lexden 1761). William

Mayhew 2 (qv), Recorder, owned a Table Clock by him (codicil to Mayhew's will, 1787). William Phillips (qv) builder (1769) named one of his daughters Rebecca Cowell.

See also: NA IR 1/15/33, Joseph Cowell son of John of Margate, gent, to Thos Deane citizen and clockmaker, £100, 1737; NA IR 1/10/31, John son of Flower Cowell, to Ben Sidey, citizen and clockmaker, £10 10s, 1724.

COWLEY JOHN [198]
Wine Cooper
fl. 1767

Advertised from Headgate (*IpsJ* 25 July 1767).

CRABB ROBINSON HENRY [697]
Scrivener
fl. 1790-1795

The celebrated diarist spent five years between 1790 and 1795 articled as clerk to William Francis, attorney (qv) and his reminiscences contain many pungent observations on Colchester inhabitants.

See also; *ODNB*, Crabb Robinson's papers, still largely unpublished are located in Dr Williams Library, Gordon Square, London, http://www.dwlib.co.uk/dwlib/; JBB, *EAE*: 143-4, 150, 153, 155, 161, 162, 163.

CRACKANTHORP SAMUEL [200]
Merchant
fl. 1776-1799

Was 'of Bocking' when, together with Samuel Tabor, he insured stock at the Hythe worth £1,000 obviously as part of a business partnership. (Sun Insurance 365291). In 1781, having moved to the Hythe he married Catherine Smyth of Trinity, both aged 24 (ERO ML D/ACL 1781). In the 1783 rates his house has a rental of 5, owner occupied and Crackanthorp was also occupier of a

C

malting owned by Francis Freshfield (qv) rated 10. He attended St Leonards Vestry from the year of his marriage.

In 1786 he moved into the town centre (*IpsJ* 16 December 1786); 'Mr Samuel Crakanthorp (sic), importer of foreign wines &c has removed from the Hythe to late Mr George Pickard's (qv) in Head Street … also trading from the London Porter Warehouse at the Hythe.'

The Head Street house was one uphill from the King's Head and during George Pickard's (qv) occupancy had been rated 12 and 9 for the vaults.

Crackanthorp's Hythe property was auctioned on 13 January 1787 (*IpsJ*) together with two cottages fronting the street and a parcel of land belonging to it. He moved again in December 1791 (L/R 23/4 December 1791, Deeds of White House, Balkerne Lane, notes JBB NB June-67 and correspondence with R. Walker, ERO Acc 905, Box 4, Box 10; Land Tax, St Marys 1792-4) when Crackanthorp bought 50 Balkerne lane from Revd Thomas Twining (qv) who was moving into St Mary's rectory. The price was a down payment of £60 plus £300 obtained on mortgage from Frank Smythies 1 (qv) at 4%. Crackanthorp altered the existing coach house into a counting house and added a three-stall stable on the north side. The Balkerne Lane house was somewhat less imposing than the genteel brick-fronted house on Head Street, and the move perhaps marks a discrete retrenchment for earlier that year (*IpsJ* 26 March and 2 April 1791) Crackanthorp declined the wine and spirit trade in favour of Samuel Bawtree (qv) though would continue with the London Porter, Corn and Bottle Trade. If this did mark a turn of Crackanthorp's fortunes, however, there was worse in store for he was declared bankrupt in 1793. The Balkerne Lane house was sold to Thomas Maberley (qv) for £340 and the following year (*IpsJ* 23 August 1794) Crackanthorp's malthouse, brick kilns etc. at the Hythe were auctioned. The matter was obviously not speedily concluded for in 1799 (*ChCh* 14 June 1799) his commissioners in bankruptcy, describing him as 'Maltster, Dealer & Chapman', called a meeting at the Angel for the 9 August next.

CRANE MRS MARY RACHEL [201]
Druggist
ob. 1820

The daughter of Bernard Hugh Pollett (qv) apothecary, and sister to Benjamin Strutt's (qv) wife, Caroline. Married Captain Robert Crane (qv) (CPL, Crisp ML 237, Robert Crane of Kelvedon Esq, Captain of Infantry to Mary Rachel Pollett of St Runwald, 1782). Her mother was 82 dying in 1805, so it is probable the daughter assisted her.

IpsJ 30 September 1809, her stock and utensils at her High Street shop were advertised for sale as she was leaving business, but she evidently changed her mind, since she was still in trade in 1815.

Colchester Gazette, 8 July 1815.

> We are happy to hear that the valuable recipe for CANDIED ERINGO ROOT, for the excellence of which this town has been justly ... celebrated, has been transferred by Mr Charles Great Keymer, the representative of the late Mr Great to Mrs CRANE, druggist.

For further details on candied eringo root, see entries for Samuel Great (qv) and Thomas Great (qv).

Her will (ERO D/ABR 32/44) made 5 November 1819 (still in trade) and proved 17 July 1822 is an admirable document. She had been buried 10 December 1820 with her husband at St Peters, as the will directed.

Mary Rachel Crane, widow, to be buried St Peters with late dear and beloved husband, seven days after departure of soul. To dear only child Robert Prentice Crane, silver 'that was solely mine', her large Bible and other books, china, glass and linen. Messuage in which I now dwell in High St St Peters to be sold with household goods and stock in trade.

£20 to John Prentice Esq of Bath 'who has at sundry times assisted me by pecuniary presents'.

C

£10 each to Robert and Elizabeth Ransome (her executors) (He affirms as a Quaker).

Residue to grandchildren after decease of their mother Jane Crane (who is to have interest of government securities till then.

To grandchild Jane, my Gold Watch (and much silver – described).

To nephew Edward Pollett Strutt my watch in daily use.

To nephew Jacob George Strutt silver sugar tongs.

To niece Sarah the mourning ring I wear for Elizabeth Allen.

To long and valued friends the Misses Gould of Dedham my Straw(work?).

To John Prentice mourning ring with my mother's hair.

To Miss Susan Chapman of Marks Tey, mourning ring I wear for my beloved husband.

Portrait of son Robert Prentice Crane 'I require my executors to preserve for my son, his wife and children.'

For the Goulds see B. Strutt's list of monuments (St Peters) in his *Colchester*, Vol. 2. They lived on North Hill earlier.

CRANE ROBERT [1200]
Army Officer
fl. 1782-1805

He was the son of Revd John Crane of Sturry, Kent and later of Gt. Saling and Saffron Walden (Venn, *Alumn. Cantab.*), who died 5 June 1766.

Robert Crane married Mary Rachel (qv), (daughter of B. H. Pollett (qv), apothecary), 3 September 1782. He was then a Captain of Infantry, of Kelvedon, Esq (CPL Crisp ML 237).

A caricature of him by E.P. Strutt says he was formerly a Captain in the 33rd Regiment of Foot and was at the Battle of Bunker Hill in the American War, 1775 (Colchester and Ipswich Museums). Buried St Peters 31 October 1811 aged 65. Will ERO D/ABR 30/417, made 1805, proved 1811, witnessed Philip

Gretton (qv), William Keymer 2 (qv), Benjamin Strutt (qv) (his brother-in-law). He left his Colchester tenement and shop, and everything else to dear wife Mary Rachel.

CRANFIELD GEORGE [202]
Innkeeper, Golden Cann
fl. 1783

Occupied this small inn near the bottom of East Hill, St James in 1783 when the property was owned by Samuel Tabor (qv) (St James rates).

A George Cranfield acted as executor to George Holder, watchmaker, St Nicholas, 1818 (ERO D/ABR 31/460).

CRANMER JOHN [203]
Innkeeper, Kings Arms, St Peters
w. 1759

Named in Cullingfords Deeds as occupier prior to Revd William Smythies (qv) (Notes, JBB NB Sept 72; Yellow 2:30ff). His will of 1759 (D/ABR 22/554, victualler, St Peter) details many small local properties.

See also: will of Mary Cranmer, widow St Nicholas, D/ABR 26/579, 1776.

CRAVEN CAPTAIN BENJAMIN [204]
Barrack Master
fl. 1787-1802

10 November 1787 (*IpsJ*), Tuesday last was married at St James Church, Colchester, Lieut Craven of the 63rd Regiment to Miss Kersteman of the same place. The Cravens occupied premises in Trinity Street opposite the church (Sun Assurance 68894, 1799, valued at £700 + £500 on household goods, JBB NB Jul 62).

In 1798 *IpsJ* advertised the 8th Colchester Assembly at the White Hart. Undress Ball on Monday August 13th. The officials were B. Craven Esq treasurer, George Round Esq and John Bawtree Esq (qv) stewards (*IpsJ* 21 July 1798). Craven was still treasurer in 1802 when James Boggis Esq (qv) and Philip Havens 2 Esq (qv) were stewards (*IpsJ* 13 March 1802).

Craven gave a £1 10s subscription to the bible society between 1812 and 1821 being late of 22nd Cheshire Regiment and was a member of the Castle Book Society (nfr).

CREFFIELD PETER [1282]
Gent
fl. 1735-1748

One of the prominent Tory family who featured in the political history of early eighteenth-century Colchester. The grandson of Sir Ralph Creffield (qv) and son of Ralph Creffield jun and his wife Sarah whose second marriage was to Charles Gray (qv). Peter Creffield married Thamar Langley and their daughter married James Round (qv), thus placing him in the series of dynastic alliances which resulted in the Round family owning key historic town centre properties, including the Castle, Hollytrees and East Hill House, in the nineteenth century.

Peter Creffield was a fellow commoner at St Johns, Oxford between 1735 and 1736. He succeeded his grandfather to estates at Mersea in 1732 (Foster, *Alumn. Oxon.*).

Accounts from Creffield's household in the 1740s survive in the Round papers (ERO D/DRC/F26), as do detailed correspondence between himself and Byatt Walker 1 (qv) innkeeper, on money and social matters (ERO D/DRC/F17, see transcripts under entry for Byatt Walker).

Creffield died intestate. His administration of 1748 is at ERO D/ABW/b158.

See also: L. C. Sier, 'The Creffields of Colchester, *ER*, Vol. 52 (1943):159ff and Vol. 53:167ff - includes family tree; *VCH Essex*, Vol. 9.

C

CREFFIELD SIR RALPH [205]
Ardleigh
w. 1732

Creffield progressed from the career of a prosperous High Street woollen draper to a knighted gentleman, living out of the town at Ardleigh. He married into the affluent Tayspill family and was prominent in local affairs, acting as Tory Mayor three times. The last was occasioned by Tories decisively re-taking control of the Borough Corporation in the bay trade depression of 1727-9, which had caused many bankruptcies and the collapse of the Dutch monopoly of the trade. As Mayor he had presented an address of thanks from the town to Queen Anne to mark the peace of Utrecht and was consequently knighted by her at Kensington on 19 June 1713.

Together with an ex-apprentice of his, and another Tory town magnate, John Potter, Creffield leased the Corporation fishery from 1700 until 1731, when he sold back his share for 10 gns. Potter had sold out the previous year.

He died where he had lived for 50 years, at Ardleigh in 1732, and was buried at St Nicholas Colchester on 30 June 1732 aged 79. His wife died in October 1734.

His will was made in 1724 (see copy at ERO D/DRC FO, made 31 January 1724, witnessed Nicholas Forster, William Lugar, Samuel Cranfield, Thomas Glascock). He left his estates, messuages and residence, all to his dearly beloved wife Dame Rachel Creffield, sole executrix, 'to be by her disposed of and amongst our children or such other of my heirs expectant of the Name or family of the Creffield at such time and in such manner and proportion and for such estate of Inheritance or Terms of years as my said wife shall think fit.'

He also left his Cousin Hannah Fox, widow, £100 and her sister Rachel Chaplin, £50. 'Cosin Creffield of Stoak by Nayland' received £100. 20s was left to each of his servants at the time of his death.

His house was advertised in the 'Ipswich Gazette' (sic) of 5 July 1735, 'a very good house with coachhouses, stables, granaries, yards, gardens, fish ponds and about 40 acres of arable land.' It later became the inoculation house occupied by John Fox (qv) and John Barnard (qv) (L. C. Sier, 'The Creffields of Colchester, *ER*, Vol. 52 (1943):159ff and Vol. 53:167ff - includes family tree).

Being a part of the Borough's political and social elites the Creffields are well recorded in published sources. See, in particular, *VCH Essex*, Vol. 9, and for Sir Ralph Creffield, entry for Colchester Borough in Romney Sedgwick, *The House of Commons*. Other details noted by JBB include: Morant, *Essex*, Vol 1:209 for the estate at Chapel called Popes which was owned by the Creffields. Poll Book 1768 includes Thomas Creffield, victualler, voting for Fordyce, also Borough Chamberlain's Accounts ERO D/B 5 Aa2/1, 3 April 1779, records Thomas Creffield fined £2 for exercising the trade of a baker without having served 7 years apprenticeship. St Mary-at-the-Walls registers record a number of Creffield marriages and intermarriage with the Coe family in the later eighteenth century. Land Tax, St Mary-at-the-Walls shows Mrs Creffield living next to Revd Thomas Twining (qv) at the White House, Balkerne Lane and the Horse and Groom on the corner of Crouch St in 1783 in property owned by the masters of the Grammar School. Other branches of the family lived in Messing. Morant, *Essex*, Vol. 2:179 records Edward Creffield MA, vicar of Messing, whose will is NA PROB 11/1089/169 of 1782, and for whom see C.F.D. Sperling, *Essex Review* (1895): 122.

CRICKETT PETER [206]
Draper and Tailor
fl. 1768-84

A free burgess who voted from 1768-84 and supported Fordyce and Potter. He advertised from over against the Dial Church (part of 107 High Street, occupied by Mrs Ann Parker (qv)) on 21 April 1770 (*IpsJ*) selling plain suits of best superfine cloth at £4 15s, laced liveries etc. On 28 March 1772 (*IpsJ*) he advertised again from the same premises and also stated that he would undertake made to measure 'Cloaths' within twelve miles of

Colchester and was preparing a ready made stock for the spring trade at fairs in south Suffolk and north east Essex. He became bankrupt in 1773 and his stock was sold for the benefit of creditors on 13 December 1773 (*Ipsj*, JBB Check:61). He remained in the town, however, and in 1783 rented small premises from Hannah Hooker in Back Lane, St Runwald, near Pelhams Lane (rated 5).

See also: 1771 William Bridges apprenticed to Peter Crickett, tailor, £5 (NA IR 1/57/208). William Bridges from London admitted free burgess by right of apprenticeship to Crickett, 1781 (JBB Main Index, ERO C905, Box 1).

CRICKITT C. A. [1145]
High Steward
fl. 1736-1803

MP for Ipswich 1784, Colchester High Steward, Recorder of Ipswich 1787-1803. A Pittite Tory, was positioned alongside Francis Smythies' 1 (qv) Tory Corporation party in Colchester Borough. In 1789 Crickett fought a duel with the politically Whig/Radical Revd Nicholas Corsellis (qv) (fuller details under Corsellis; *IpsJ* 4 July 1789). In 1791 (*IpsJ* 10 September 1791) Crickitt was one of the candidates in heated elections in Ipswich for Bailiffs and other Corporation officials. Frank Smythies was included in the scrutineers. The Tory candidates included William Truelove and J Kerridge. The partnership of Messrs Crickitt Truelove and Kerridge operated the 'Blue' bank in Ipswich.

For a fuller account, see relevant entries in L. Namier and J. Brooke, *The History of Parliament: the House of Commons, 1754-1790* (London, 1964).

CROSS BENJAMIN [208]
Surgeon
w. 1709

Took the oath of supremacy 10 July 1706, described as of St Buttolfs, Colchester, surgeon (ERO D/B 5 R1).

C

Named in his will as a 'Chiruegion' (ERO D/ACR 12/173). The brother of Alice Rolle, wife of Benjamin (qv). As well as providing for his wife and brother, his will leaves considerable property to Alice being various messuages in East Street, including one they occupied, another in St Martins Lane (thereafter to her children) and a farm in Bromley Magna.

There is a stone in St Botolph's churchyard to him, died 23 October 1709, aged 37 (Strutt, *Colchester*, Vol. 2:46, 73).

CROSS EDMUND [207]
Cabinetmaker, Chairmaker and Joiner
1705-1793

A quaker (Fitch, *Colchester Quakers*). Apprenticed in 1723, the son of Edmund Cross of Walton near Felixstowe to Robert Lay of Woodbridge, joiner for £10 (NA IR 1/46/86). Cross married Hannah Hawkins (she d. 1782 aged 73) in 1736. They were established at 108-9 High Street rated 14 by at least 1751. They had twelve children between 1737 and 1752, nine of whom survived infancy. Cross took John Parsey apprentice for £21 on 29 August 1772 (NA IR 1/51/214, where Cross is wrongly described as a surgeon). Parsey married Sarah Norris at St Nicholas in 1765 and was buried there in 1779. The same year Cross sold up the business (*IpsJ* 19 June 1779) and seems to have left the town. He died in 1793 aged 88 and was buried at Helens Lane.

Edmund jun married Mary Mayhew of All Saints in 1770; cf various Cross voters from Sudbury polling in Colchester elections; Cross' business was bought by James Fitch. See will of James Bawtree Fitch (baker, Colchester, 1798, D/ABR 29/113).

CROWE JAMES [210]
Innkeeper, Bear
fl. 1789

Per parish rates.

CUFFLEY PETER [212]
Ironmonger
fl. 1763-5

Had been apprenticed to Jeremiah Loane (nfr). Though not in business in Colchester above eighteen months his bankrupt stock was for sale in 1764 (*Ips*J 27 October 1764) and a further sale (*Ips*J 2 March 1765) shows him to have also been a bricklayer and limeburner. The lime kiln was taken over by by Joseph Green (qv).

CULLUM JAMES [213]
Innkeeper, White Hart
fl. 1786-8

Cullum is listed as occupier in the rates between these years. He was appointed by the 'Society of Gentlemen' who took over the lease of the premises on Christopher Pennywhite's (qv) bankruptcy (see entry for White Hart) and advertised on 13 July 1786 (*Ips*J) that the White Hart was not shut up but was 'being carried on as usual for the benefit of Mr White's (sic) creditors by James Cullum'. His position was obviously subordinate to that of George Reynolds (qv) who was recalled from retirement to run the inn during this period.

CUNNINGTON JOHN and ROBERT [214]
Scriveners
fl. c.1800

These two brothers were apprenticed as clerks to William Mason 2 (qv). Their family originated in Gt. Waltham. In 1801 John compiled a free burgess index for Colchester. He later founded the still (1983) extant firm of solicitors in Braintree where he died, a gent, in 1855. He became author of a collection of reminiscences of Oliver Goldsmith during his stay at Springfield in 1838 (nfr). Robert was a superintendent of

C

excise in Springfield when he married Mary Hare of Witham in 1813 (ML ERO D/AEL 1813).

CUTTER THOMAS [215]
Clerk to the Justices
ob c. 1772
No further details.

D

DAMMANT BARNABY [1168]
Clockmaker
1683-1738

Son of Barnabas Dammant, ironmonger and locksmith, St Peter's parish and his wife Frances. Admitted free burgess 20 December 1700 together with his younger brother William at the comparatively young ages of 17 and 15 respectively. Married Elizabeth Duffield (cf Joseph Duffield 1 (qv)) on 11 November 1713 at St James. Was one of the witnesses to his father-in-law's will on 3 July 1717, which also left £50 to Elizabeth Dammant.

Mason assesses Dammant's work as a clock and watch maker highly. As well as long-case clocks, he made brass lantern and spring-driven mantel clocks. A number of surviving clocks under his signature have ornate lacquered cases (Mason: 249). Dammant took four apprentices; Richard Cooke, son of Richard Cooke, Ipswich, ob., on 8 August 1705, Lawrence Gilson, son of Barnaby Gilson (qv) baker, Colchester on 10 May 1715, £26 10s, Gooday Proctor (qv) in 1720 and William Kilwick, son of William of Harwich on 5 November 1722. As well as making clocks, Dammant continued his father's ironmonger's business and leased lime kilns at the Hythe from the Borough. He frequently supplied All Saint's vestry with 'nails, spades, lime, lead etc.' (Mason:248). After Dammant's death the lime kilns were rented to his widow Elizabeth for £5 p.a. (For the ongoing trading and property interests of Elizabeth's family including at the Hythe, cf Joseph Duffield 2 (qv)).

Voted in Borough elections in 1715 and 1734. Took the Oath of allegiance on 4 November 1723. Was elected a Guardian of the Poor for two year terms in 1722, 1724, 1727 and 1728. Became a Common Councillor and was at the same time promoted to

D

Assistant on 10 December 1727. Served on the committee to administer White's Charity from December that year (11 December 1727). Elected Clavior for Head Ward 1 September 1729 and Borough Treasurer on 7 July 1731. A regular Grand Juryman between 1716 and 1737.

Dammant died on 3 February 1738.

Summarised from Bernard Mason, *Clock and Watchmaking in Colchester*, (Colchester, 1969):244-250.

See also: JBB NB 86/4:21, note from Borough Chamberlain's accounts, 1705, Barnaby Dammant bills for ironing prisoners.

DAMMANT WILLIAM [216]
Surgeon
fl. 1712-1714

Wilhelm Dammant of Colchester surgeon took the oath of supremacy on 10 July 1706 (ERO D/B 5 R1). He is recorded engaging three apprentices; on 15 March 1712, Thomas son of Thomas Nunn of Hadleigh baker for £50 (NA IR 1/42/45 which dates the apprenticeship in 1711), on 1 June, 1714, William son of William Smythies, clerk (qv) for £50 (William Smythies 3 (qv), NA IR 1/43/112), and in 1718, Robert Drury for £60 (NA IR 1/6/48).

See also: Index to Free Burgess Admissions ERO D/B 5 Fb2/2, 1620-1741

DANIEL THOMAS [221]
Attorney
1712-1775

Daniel engaged in a public disagreement with the then owner of Donyland Hall, Gen. David Gansel (qv). Gansel wrote an open letter to Daniel (*Ips*J 12 September 1767) denying the use of cruel man traps.

At this period Daniel lived next door to widow Sarah Purkes. Sarah's late husband had named William Daniel (qv) (Thomas' brother) as executor in his will of 1751 (James Purkes,

Colchester, victualler, ERO D/ABW 97/1/78). Subsequently the relationship between Sarah and Thomas developed and on 6 October 1760 was baptised in St Marys, Thomas, son of Thomas Daniell and Widow Purkas (sic), who had been born on 3 June 1755. Thomas jun. was admitted to the Free School in June 1766. He later married Sarah Johnson, St Botolphs when a gent of that parish in 1778 (ML ERO D/ALL 1778, JBB note, '73 High St').

Thomas snr. was a Whig free burgess voting in 1741 and 1747. He became agent of the Sun Fire Office from 1 July 1758 and continued to act as an attorney, including in the bankruptcy of James Robjent 2 (qv) in 1772. In 1775 he was Stamp Distributor for the County of Essex (*ChCh* 8 December 1775).

He died on 30 November 1775 aged 63, after an operation for the stone in Middlesex Hospital, and was buried in an altar tomb St Peters (not survived). His will (NA PROB 11/1015, 9 Bellas, 23 January 1776) is long and complex, dovetailing with that of his brother William (qv). His personal estate was left in trust to Peter Daniell (qv) and James Buxton (qv) 'for a certain youth now living with me and commonly called and known by the name of Thomas Daniel, natural son of me by Sarah Purkes, wid, deceased' until the lad reached 24, failing which to Thomas' nephew William Barker Daniel. A codicil just before his death left £400 from the personal estate to Mary Holton 'now or late residing in Colchester' and commonly known as Mary Pitt. A reversionary interest was left to Peter Daniell and Robert Harrington, Clerk of Cambridgeshire.

DANIEL WILLIAM [220]
Attorney
1703-1771

Daniel had been much involved in the loss of the Charter (1741). Subsequently, as the campaign to regain the Borough Charter was at its height, Daniel (a Whig voter between 1741 and 1768) had sufficient political standing to offer for the poll in 1761 (together with Sir Thomas Frederick). This seems to have been something of a ploy, however, as he and his partner

D

then stood down allowing Gray and Rebow to be returned unopposed and hence without large expense (*IpsJ* 28 March 1761). He was earlier associated with William Mayhew 1 (qv) (the pro Charter lawyer) through acting as agent for the sale of the White Hart Inn (qv) in 1747/8, (*IpsJ* 9 January 1747/8; JBB NB Aug 65:37) and also in the case concerning the property in 1753.

In 1753 was agent for the sale of Stroud Water Mill in Mersea occupied by Henry Dobby (qv) (*IpsJ* 21 April 1753). Advertised for two servants in 1768, when he was also agent for the sale of a malting office in St Matthews Ipswich (*IpsJ* 7 May 1768).

He married three times, (1) to Bathshua (who died 21 August 1733 aged 23) the only child of Revd John Baker of Hackney, (2) (ERO ML D/ALL, 1743) to Susan Bogard daughter of Cornelius Bogard of Colchester (qv) who died 19 October 1747 aged 39, and (3) (ERO ML D/ALL, 1751) to Dame Deborah Barker. His wives are buried with William and his brother Thomas Daniel (qv) in an altar tomb, St Peters (not survived).

William's will (made 21 January 1771 proved 8 May 1771, NA PROB 11/967, Trevor 202) leaves small cash legacies to nieces and nephews but directs the bulk of the estate to be sold including property in St Peters, St Runwald, Lexden, Stanway, Copford, Ardleigh and the advowsons of south and west Hanningfield in trust for his son William Barker Daniel and heirs, failing whom to brother Thomas Daniel (qv). His debts and funeral expenses were to be met from the felling and sale of the timber in Braiswick wood. His daughter's portions were not to exceed £2,000 and not more than £80 per annum was to be spent on them and his younger sons. His estates outside Colchester were sold off (*IpsJ* 9 March 1771) not long after his death.

1768, Daniel acted as agent for sale of Malting house in Ipswich (JBB Notebook, Check:58); JBB note, William Barker Daniel, author of *Rural Sport* (1801)

DANIELL JEREMIAH 1 [223]
Gent
1670-1742

The son of Jeremiah Daniell, gent, buried St Peters in 1695 and his wife Mary. Had been promoted to Alderman all in one day on 4 August 1719.

This Jeremiah was the Whig Mayor who presided over the scandalous 1741 Borough election when the Tories gained the Borough through improperly creating hordes of honorary free burgesses, then had the result disallowed. In all he served as Mayor in 1720, 1725 and 1740 and voted in 1734 and 1741 (Mayne, Olmius). He was the first trustee of Winsley's charity.

See also: D'Cruze, *Pleasing Prospect*:138-40; *VCH Essex*, Vol. 9:111.

DANIELL JEREMIAH 2 [979]
Gent
1697-1766

Son of Jeremiah Daniell 1. He served on the Borough Corporation, was promoted Assistant 1726 and acted as J.P. during the loss of the Charter (1741). Married three times: in 1721 aged 20 (CPL Crisp ML 330, bound with Jeremiah Daniell snr., at St Leonards) to Ann Lawrence aged 18 of St James (she died 1722 shortly after the birth of a daughter Ann, buried St James); to Hannah Tayspill the mother of the rest of his children, and to Judith Edlyn (they married in 1747 at All Saints, CPL Crisp ML 306, Isaac Boggis (qv) baymaker bound with Daniell) who died shortly before him in 1763.

He left a detailed will (NA PROB 11/916 Tyndal 51-96, 26 February 1766) dividing his estate between his wife and children. The main beneficiary was his second son Peter (qv) who received the substantial house behind All Saints Church (now (1983) 'The Affair') and the next door premises; his father's best Roculo (cloak), a silver tea kettle and lamp as well as any residue which would have included the wife's share of £50 plus her own household goods since she pre-deceased her husband after the will was made. Peter and son-in-law Robert Tabor (qv) also received a messuage in St Peters and two rentaries behind, subject to £90 to eldest son Jeremiah who also received his father's clothes. Three daughters, Hannah Halls, Mary Rudkin and Susannah Tabor received £500 apiece and the eldest daughter Ann Folley was given £250 and her mother's (Ann *née* Lawrence) silver. All the daughters and Peter received the balance of the household goods. Daniell requested to be buried at St Nicholas with his second wife Hannah in a very private funeral with no pall bearers, one hearse and one coach.

JBB note: There were three distinct families of this name in Colchester at this period. ERO holds G. O. Rickwood's exhaustive genealogy. They differ in the spelling of the surname, the nonconformists were 'Daniell', the Anglicans of St Peters were 'Daniel', but those of St Martin's House also used a double 'll'.

DANIELL JEREMIAH 3 [222]
Wine Merchant
fl. 1802

Described as 'lately a wine and brandy merchant' he offered for sale two freehold messuages in St Nicholas (*Ips]* 13 February 1802), one in his own occupation and the other occupied by Mr Diss as tenant (Isaac Diss (qv)). The houses described as a large and a small family house. Daniell married Hester, daughter of John Agnis (qv) gardener and later became an officer in the Customs (per will John Agnis, ERO D/ACR 19/497, 1808).

DANIELL PETER [224]
Attorney
1732-1792

The second son of Jeremiah Daniell 2 (qv) and his second wife Hannah *née* Tayspill. He became the leading nonconformist lawyer in Colchester and a stalwart of Lion Walk Chapel and of the reform cause in the 1780s and 90s despite going bankrupt in 1783.

Born on 12 August 1732 he was admitted to the Free School in March 1744 and became a free burgess voting from 1768 in support of Whig and radical candidates. He was admitted as full member to the Lion Walk congregation in 1755. In 1761 by then an attorney of St Nicholas (25 September 1761, Braintree Registers) he married Margaret Shepherd the daughter of William and his wife Margaret (who was daughter of Thomas Gainsborough the artist and granddaughter of Revd Thomas Shepherd). The witnesses at the wedding were Peter's father, Jeremiah Daniell and Margaret's relations John Gainsborough (father and son, both of Sudbury). Through his sister's marriages Peter Daniell became brother-in-law to other conspicuous Colchester nonconformists including Timothy Walford 1 (qv) and Robert Tabor (qv).

In 1766 he inherited the bulk of his father's estate, not least the family capital messuage at the corner of Culver St and Queen St where he established himself, taking a full part in the duties of All Saints vestry. He is initially found taking a clear political role in the nonconformist interest during the divisive Free School Elections in January 1779 (cf Charles Hewitt (qv) and Revd Duddell (qv)) when he acted for Michael Hills (qv). Hills promoted the unsuccessful opposition candidate, Hewitt, and due to non payment ended by having a serious quarrel with Daniell (D'Cruze, *Pleasing Prospect*:160-5).

In 1784 (*Ips*] 20 March, 21 August 1784; *London Gazette* 22 November 1783, 31 July 1784, 10 September 1785, 2 February 1790) Daniell had the misfortune to become bankrupt and his house and property were auctioned. His position in the community ensured that he would avoid disgrace, however. His house was purchased by his next door neighbour in Queen St who rented it back to Daniell. His brother-in-law Timothy Walford (qv) seems also to have purchased the bulk of the estate and mortgaged it back to him. Certainly Daniell continued to practice successfully in the town, witnessing a considerable number of wills until his death, 'in his 60th year', in 1792 (*Eur. Mag.*, obituary 12 March 1792, *IpsJ* 17 March 1792). He was buried at Lion Walk.

Daniell's will (NA PROB 11/1229, made 14 January 1792, proved 23 March 1793) shows the mortgage to Walford still extant and leaves only his law books and bookcase to his son Samuel (qv) and a 28 acre estate at Layer Marney (probably previously his wife's) to son Thomas Shephard Daniell. Robert and Susannah Tabor (sister and brother-in-law) received mourning rings.

See also his letter to sister Ann Foley, Witham on occasion of her husband's arrest (NA SP36/135/25 et seq, 26 June 1756).

DANIELL RICHARD MD [218]
Physician
ob. 1772

He has a long Latin epitaph on tablet St Martins ob. 1772 aged 72 (cf Strutt, *Colchester*, Vol 2:21). His will is at NA PROB 11/977, 9 May 1772.

DANIELL REVD RICHARD [219]
Rector, Colchester St Martin, Mistley and Bradfield
w. 1778

A keen amateur musician. Received a cremona fiddle and concerto music in the will of George Wegg 2 (qv) of East Hill House, where the local amateur music circle met (P. Holman, 'The Colchester Partbooks', *Early Music*, 28 (2000):577-95).

His will made 5 August 1778 (NA PROB 11/1049/46 Warburton, proved 3 February 1779) requested he should be buried together with his father and mother in the vault of St Martins church at a cost of not more than £15 (or £30 should he die outside Colchester). His dear wife Catherine received farms at Beaumont-cum-Moze and Ardleigh and fields in St Botolphs (occupied John Agnis (qv)) as well as the £500 and the £200 held by the trustees of their marriage settlement (see below) for the benefit of any children of the marriage, since the couple were childless.

Catherine also obtained a life interest in the mansion house St Martins 'where I now dwell' (1983, British Telecom premises, W. Stockwell St), St Cleers Hall St Osyth and farms in Tollesbury, Tolleshunt D'Arcy, Salcott, Marks Tey and Aldham. These last were the subject of their marriage settlement and were consequently left in trust for her to Capt Edmund Affleck (qv) (later MP), Ambrose Godfrey chymist of Covent Garden, James Round (qv) of Birch Hall Esq, and Daniell's brother-in-law Edward Green Esq (qv) of Lawford Hall.

On her death these properties were to revert to any children she may have by a subsequent marriage, failing whom the St Martins mansion was left to her heirs, St Cleer Hall to Thomas Bayles 2 (qv) (attorney) the eldest son of Thomas Bayles 1, gent. ob. (qv), failing whom to his sister Hortensia Bayles for life, then to William Bayles the eldest son of Thos Bayles snr by Mary Dennis his second wife. (JBB note: great aunt Martha Daniel married Christopher Bayles in 1656 he ob. 1665). The rest of these farms and other property would revert equally between Daniell's cousins John Blatch Whaley (qv) and Joseph Blatch (qv).

£20 was left to the poor of St Martins and £40 for the poor of Mistley and Bradfield.

DANIELL SAMUEL 1 [217]
Milliner
ob. 1758

A free burgess. Voted in 1747 and plumped for Nassau. The sale of his stock in trade after his death is advertised in *IpsJ* 10 June 1758. His executor was Mr William Daniel (qv).

D

DANIELL SAMUEL 2 [225]
Attorney
fl. 1792-1828

The second son of Peter Daniell (qv) who survived his father's bankruptcy to continue the extensive attorney's practice established amongst Colchester's nonconformists. He witnessed 29 of the Colchester wills between 1780 and 1828, now deposited in ERO (calculated from survey by SD'C). His first wife was a Miss Hawes of Colchester, whom he married in 1790 (ChCh 5 November 1790). They lived at the Hythe (St Leonards Vestry Minutes, ERO D/P/245, 26 April 1791). She died there soon after, aged 26 (IpsJ 11 June 1791, surname spelt 'Daniel').

He soon moved and attended All Saints Vestry in 1792 in place of his recently deceased father, but established himself finally at Headgate (G.O. Rickwood scrapbook in CPL). He became a full member of Lion Walk congregation in 1799 together with his (second) wife (Blaxill, *Lion Walk*).

DARBY CHARLES [1184]
Bookseller
fl. 1745-1756

Is included among the donors on the bookplates of the Castle Book Society, as 'bookseller' among the other gentry members. He paid rates (12) in St Runwalds from 1748 to at least 1756 and took three known apprentices; 20 August 1745, Mark Duland, £30 (nfr); 1749, NA IR 1/18/217, Thomas son of John Brett, £30; 1752, NA IR17/51/214, Thomas Brand, £10. (£30 is a big fee for a local apprenticeship in this trade).

IpsJ 21 October 1749 the Borough's Petition to the King following the loss of the Charter was at the shop of Mr Charles Darby, stationer. *IpsJ* 7 April 1753, Revd Mr Humphrey

Smythies (qv), *Precepts*, 2s 6d, printed for the author, was advertised for sale at W. Craighton (Ipswich) and C. Darby at Colchester.

See also: JBB NB 90/6, notes on the Darby family of Keddington.

DARE MRS JULIAN [226]
fl. 1765-1785

Occupied premises at 121 High Street, uphill of Samuel Nockolds (qv), rated 13, 1765-1785. She was the sister of Edward Morley 1 (qv) and received £20 in his will of 1763 (proved 1765). She was also connected to the Scalé (qv), Debonnaire (qv) and Letch (qv) families. Her own will (NA PROB 11/1132, proved 19 August 1785) is lengthy and detailed (see notes at the end of this entry identifying some of those named in it):-

IN THE NAME OF GOD AMEN, I Julian Dare of Colchester in the County of Essex being of sound Mind and Memory, do make this my last Will and Testament Revoking all other Wills by me formerly made, and is as Follows, Imprimus,

I give and bequeath to my Nephew All[n] (Allington) Morley (qv) on his paying the sum of two Hundred Pounds of good and lawfull money to my Executors hereinafter mentioned, my House wherein I now live;

I Give to my Niece Ann Debonnaire fifty Pound Bank Stock;

I Give to my Niece Henrietta Scalé (qv) one Hundred Pounds Bank Stock;

I Give to my Brother Edward Morley (qv) Fifty Pounds Bank Stock,

I Give to my Nephew All[n] Morley Fifty Pounds Bank Stock,

I Give to my Nephew Ed[d] Morley Thirty Pounds Bank Stock,

I Give to my Niece Dorothy Harvey Fifty Pounds Bank Stock,

I Give to Mr John Debonnaire Sn[r] Fifty Pounds Bank Stock,

I Give to Ann Debonnaire Jun[r] Thirty Pounds,

D

I Give to my Nephew John Morley Twenty Pounds and my large Bible.

I Give to Mr Peter Bernard Scalé (qv) Twenty Pounds,

I Give to my Nephew John Letch Twenty Pounds,

I Give to Ann Love Twenty Pounds,

I Give to Mrs Carr Ten Pounds,

I Give to Lucy Carr her Daughter Ten Pounds, I also Give the said Lucy Carr my Best Tea Spoons and Tea Tonges, two Dozen of Blue and White China Plates and Six Dishes,

I Give and bequeath to my Niece Henrietta Scalé my Silver Candlesticks, silver Snuffers and Dish,

I Give to my Brother Edward Morley my large Waiter,

I Give to my Nephew All^n Morley my Sauce Boat,

I Give to Ann Debonnaire Junr my Coffee Pot,

I Give to my Nephew Edward Morley my small Waiter,

I Give to my Nephew John Letch my Large Soop-Ladle and my four salt spoons,

I Give to Mr James Boggis (qv) my Punch Ladle,

I Give one Half of my Table Spoons to my Niece Dorothy Harvey and one half to Bernard Scalé,

I Give to Henrietta Ann Scalé my Gold Watch Gold Chain and all the Trinkets Belonging thereto,

I Give to Margaret Sophia Scalé my Diamond Hoop Ring,

I Give to my Niece Ann Debonnaire my suit of Point Lace and apron,

I give to Ann Debonnaire Junr my Best Sack,

Half the rest of my Cloaths and linning, I Give to my Niece Henrietta Scalé, one quarter to Henrietta Ann Scalé and one quarter to my Niece Dorothy Harvey, my Best Suit of Lace^d linning I Give to my niece Henrietta Scalé,

I Give my second Best suit to my Niece Dorothy Harvey and all the remaining Lace and Household linning I Give to Henrietta Ann Scalé,

D

I Give to Henrietta Scalé my Niece my chamber Clock and Half of my Furniture, and I Give to my Niece Dorothy Harvey the other Half, the Kitchen Furniture only Excepted, Which I Give to my Servants Susan Pilborough, Ann Thursby and Robt Wass (cf Bobby Wass (qv), waiter at the Red Lion) to be equally divided between them,

I also give to my said servants twenty Pounds Each and Mourning,

I also Give to my two maids two Common Gowns Each, two Common petticoats Each, two Common aprons Each, a pair of stays to Each, and all my Shoes and stockings to be divided between them,

I also desire them to have the care of my two Cats for Which purpose I Give them a Guinea Each,

I Give to Robt Wass, my sedan Chair and all my old Tubs and Vessels,

I Give to Mrs Isaac Boggis my six Large China Jarrs,

Half of the remaining part of my China I give to my Niece Henrietta Scalé one quarter to Henrietta Ann Scalé and one quarter to Ann Debonnaire jun^r,

I Give to my Brother Edward Morley and the following persons Mourning Rings - to be Bought of Natt Hedge Junr (Nathaniel Hedge 2 (qv)):

Mr and Mrs Scalé, Mr and Mrs Debonnaire, Mr and Mrs Letch, Mr Edward Morley, London, Mrs Harvey, Mr John Morley, Mr H. Morley, Mr A. Morley, Mr and Mrs Great, Mr and Mrs Isaac Boggis, Mr and Mrs Carr, Mr Thos. Boggis, Mr James Boggis, Mr and Mrs Pierse, the Clergyman and Curate of the Parish of Halstead,

And I do desire that no publick Sale be made in my House on any account Whatsoever, and I do Expressly order that My Niece Henrietta Scalé be Immediately sent for on my Decease to take Care of all my things and Give them as I have desired in this my last Will, and I do further desire that I be Carried to Halstead in an Hearse and four attended by two Mourning Coaches and four and laid by my first Husband Mr Bennett,

D

I also desire that Old Dean may have five pounds,

I also Give my Niece Henrietta Scalé twenty pounds for mourning.

All the written legacys I do order to be paid Within two months after my Decease by my Executors hereinafter named.

The Rest and Residue of my Estate and Effects not Bequeathed of this my last Will, after my Debts and Funeral Charges are Paid, shall be equally Divided between my Executors, and I do appoint my Brother Edward Morley, Mr John Debonnaire Sn^r, Mr All^n, Morley and Mrs Henrietta Scalé to be my Executors of this my last Will and Testament Contained in two Sheets of Paper Witness my Hand this Eighteenth June one thousand seven hundred and Eighty Four. Witnessed Nathaniel Hedge 2 (qv), Rose Goodwin, Hugh Miller.

(NA PROB10/2988/21228)

CODICILS dated 20 August 1784:-

- I Do desire that the small Sett of India Creping Boxes be given to Miss Lucy Carr.
- I Give to Mr James Boggis (qv) two of my China Bowls.
- I Do desire that all my China Fruit Baskets be given to my Nephew John Jacob Morley.
- I Do desire that my Pair of China Sauce Boats with the Plates belonging be given to Thomas Boggis Esq (qv).
- I Do request that Mr Edward Snell (qv) may have a Mourning Ring.

The death of Mrs Dare, relict of Mr Wm Bennett a considerable grocer of Colchester and late wife of Mr Dare of London, mercer, was announced by the *IpsJ* 6 August 1785.

Mrs Dare's will associates together a number of middling and gentry families from Colchester and district. The following connections, though for the most part documented under individual entries in the dictionary, are worth underlining here. Edward Morley 2 Esq (qv), will of 16 September 1783, proved 22 April 1785 leaves Mrs Dare, his sister, £20; John Morley Esq of Halstead, will 25 October 1775, proved 27 January 1777, names his sons, Hildebrand, Allington and John Jacob. His

D

daughter is Dorothy, wife of Bridges Harvey; Thomas, Isaac and Jacob Boggis (all qv) were sons of Isaac Boggis 1 (qv) Baymaker, ob. 1762 by his first wife. This Isaac Boggis' second wife, Ann Tenant, wid. was a Morley; her daughter Ann Tenant married John Debonnaire of Bromley near Bow, 15 March 1754; Peter Bernard Scalé (qv) land surveyor, married Henrietta Letch of Dedham in 1765 - she was niece of Edward Morley (qv) - their daughters were Henrietta Ann and Margaret Sophia. Edward Morley jun. ob. 23 April 1786, aged 44, at Bernard Scalé's at Gt Warley - his will leaves Ann Debonnaire £5,000, her daughter Ann £10,000, and many Essex estates and £5,000 to Henrietta Scalé (qv). Edward Snell (qv), not a relative, was Edward Morley's junior business partner to whom he left the business. John Letch was Henrietta's brother. Mrs Carr (*née* Maria Richardson) and her daughter Lucy are not relatives – they are wife and daughter of Samuel Carr, (qv) grocer of 11 High Street. Ann Love is probably related to Edward Love (qv) grocer of St Botolphs Street. Robert Wass is probably Bobby Wass (qv) later the waiter at the Red Lion. Nathaniel Hedge 2 (qv) watchmaker and goldsmith, witnesses and probably writes the will - his premises were a little down the High Street from Mrs Dare. Mr and Mrs Charles Great (qv) apothecary, High Street lived virtually opposite Mrs Dare.

DAVIS GEORGE [229]
Wheelwright
w. 1790

Davis' death was announced on 13 March 1790 (*IpsJ*). His affairs were to be settled by his nephew John Ambrose of Copford and William Francis (qv), his attorney. His estate, after his wife Sarah's death, was to provide for Ambrose and his family, though the wheelwright's business was to be taken over by his 'servant' Jacob Wright (qv) at a fair valuation. A small allowance was also left to his brother William Davis (ERO D/ABR 28/170).

D

DAVIS HENRY 1 [228]
Innkeeper, Horse and Groom
w. 1772

Will mentions wife Rebecca, son Henry (qv), nephew George Davis, wheelwright (qv) (D/ABR 26/336, victualler, St Mary-at-the-Walls).

DAVIS HENRY 2 [230]
Innkeeper, Horse and Groom
fl. 1783-1796

Owner occupier of the inn. His will of 1796 left all his property to his wife Ann (ERO D/ABR 28/606, victualler St Mary-at-the-Walls).

DAVIS SAMUEL [1161]
Man Midwife
fl. 1728

Advertised a course of lectures on midwifery near Headgate 1728 (JBB note ex. inf. L. C. Sier).

DAWES RICHARD [231]
Surgeon
fl. 1742-1776

IpsJ 12 July 1755:

> Whereas it has been industriously reported, that Mr RICHARD DAWES surgeon and apothecary of Colchester, is going to relinquish his Business and leave the said Town, this is to assure the Publick, that the said report is false and groundless, and that he never had any such Design; and therefore hopes for a continuation of the Favour of his Friends &c.

N.B. a Youth suitably qualified for an Apprentice, may, on Application to the said Mr. Dawes, be received on reasonable terms.

Dawes married twice; firstly, when 23, to Christina Mayhew, 24, sister-in-law of William Mayhew 1, attorney (qv) in 1742 (CPL Crisp ML347, ERO D/ALL 1742, names her as 'Christian') and secondly, when a widower of 30 to Mary Firebrace of St Peters, widow, in October 1754 (CPL Crisp ML403, ERO D/ACL 1754; bound with Robert Duke, draper (qv)). Dawes died at Richmond on 6 July 1768 (G. Martin, *The Story of Colchester*) and was buried at St Mary-at-the-Walls Colchester, where he was later joined by his second wife Mary who died on 17 December 1795 aged 68.

See also: Richard Dawes who was Captain in the East Essex militia c.1760-1776 (ERO 1/U 4/10); Richard Dawes buried St Mary-at-the-Walls 25 January 1772 (son of above?); also *IpsJ* 8 April 1809, auction by Henry Hutton of the Marlboro Head, St Botolphs and 5 tenements adjoining, also capital messuage, stables and large garden, Queen Street, now occupied R. Dawes Esq, J. G. Sargeant solicitor acting as agent for sale; CPL Crisp ML108, ERO D/AEL 1750, Richard Firebrace of Southminster and Thomas Sly of Rochford bound Richard (34) to marry Mary Camper (23) of Rochford, 1750; NA IR 1/19/205, 1754, Richard Dawes apprenticed to John Fox (qv), £8.

DAY CATER [233]
Surgeon
fl. 1754-1799

In 1754 Cater Day was apprenticed to Robert Courthorpe Sims, Great Dunmow, surgeon (qv) for £105 (NA IR 1/19/197). Day was a member of the Society of Friends (Fitch, *Colchester Quakers*).

Cater Day, surgeon of Colchester, was declared bankrupt in the *IpsJ* of 26 January 1782. His house in St Nicholas parish was offered for sale in the 8 June issue. He eventually received his discharge in 1786 (*London Gazette* 15 January 1782:7, 16 July 1782:5, 25 March 1786:135, 2 May 1786:196).

He continued in business and billed St Leonard's overseers for medical services in 1783. He also may have worked in association with Robert Sterling (qv) for on 29 December 1787 (*IpsJ*) Day solicited custom from the patients of his recently deceased, worthy friend Mr Robert Sterling (qv). The same paper, however, carried similar advertisements from both Philip Gretton (qv) and Newton Tills (qv) who also presented themselves as heir to Sterling's goodwill.

On 16 April 1799 (*ChCh* 12 April 1799) Day gave evidence which committed Thomas Plowmans, a private soldier in the militia to gaol for rape 'upon the bodies of two infants Judith Ann Maria Nicholls and Susan Hills', both of Colchester, one aged 8 and the other 10.

Day died suddenly. *IpsJ* of 12 October 1799 reports that on Thursday sennight about nine in the evening, Mr Cater Day, surgeon, accidentally fell into the river and drowned. Other JBB notes say he was drowned by driving over the side of Hythe Bridge returning from a drinking party at Wivenhoe (nfr). He was buried in the Friends Burial Ground. His son John died 18 March 1820 (Fitch, *Colchester Quakers*).

DEANE JAMES [1146]
Builder and Architect
1698-1765

See full article in JBB, *EAE*:73-87.

DEBOYS CHARLES [235]
Staymaker
w. 1742

Of St Peters parish. An assistant on the Corporation. His will (NA PROB 11/719/215. Made 15 April 1742, witnessed Samuel Rayner (qv), Robert Potter (qv), Thomas James, proved 26 July 1742) directs that his properties in Norwich, Yarmouth and

Colchester be sold. He left Sarah Angier a tenement in St Osyth and £20. He also mentions Samuel Angier. John Isles, Colchester, carpenter, his kinsman received £130 and his large plain gold ring. His kinsman Charles Deboys Cliters 'who lives with me' received £130. Also mentioned were Richard Cliters (at sea) and Sarah Cliters. Samuel Carter (qv), Gt. Coggeshall, gent. was executor with John Isles.

He has a black memorial stone in St Peters.

DeHORNE JOHN [238]
Hill House, Lexden
fl. 1810

Ips] 19 May 1810; auction by Linton & Lavallin at the Three Cups, 29th May, of 'A Capital and most desirable Freehold DWELLING HOUSE situate opposite the Park, in the beautiful village of Lexden'.

The house had an entrance hall 16ft x 16ft, a breakfast room 17ft x 13ft, a dining room 17ft x 16ft, exclusive of bow, 'with an elegant new built and highly finished drawing room, bow windowed 24ft x 15ft' and eight bed chambers. It was deemed suitable 'for a family of distinction' and was then occupied by DeHorne 'with whose leave the same may be viewed'. DeHorne himself bought the property which was being sold by William Turner, attorney (JBB note: then nearly bankrupt).

DELIGHT MICHAEL [239]
Weaver
fl. 1791

A subscriber to the edition of the 1789 edition of *History and Antiquities of Colchester*. Summoned to Borough sessions in 1791 with Fudgell Cook (qv) on suspicion of receiving embezzled ends and wastes from wool workers.

D

DENNIS PHILIP ESQ [241]
fl. 1782

A Major in the East Essex militia. Married Ann daughter of Francis Pigott MD (qv) by his first marriage (cf Mary Pigott (qv)) on 11 April 1778 at St Martins (JBB note). His furniture and plate was for sale in 1782 (*IpsJ* 21 September 1782).

His widow acquired an interest in the family property in Angel Lane (no. 62) and died August 1832 age 77.

DENNIS WILLIAM [240]
fl. 1773

27 February 1773 *IpsJ*: Brick fronted messuage, occupied William Dennis for sale, Queen St, St Botolphs. Dennis died in Colchester in 1774 (*IpsJ* 27 August 1774) 'formerly a considerable farmer at Tendring.' (cf Morant, *Essex*, re 'Foulshaws', Tendring). His will (NA PROB 11/1001 Bargrave 333, proved 7 September 1774: 'rich but not very interesting' per JBB) mentions a son, Philip. It was witnessed by Samuel Wall 1 (qv), Samuel Wall 2 (qv) and Thos Dye (qv).

DENTON THOMAS 1 [242]
Innkeeper, Goats Head
fl. 1784-1812

Active in St Leonards vestry from 1784. The Dentons seem to have been tenants, at least before 1804 when the inn was sold whilst they were in occupation, along with several other tenements and granaries (*IpsJ* 4 February 1804). Denton's will, made in 1804 and proved in 1812 (ERO D/ABR30/551) left some furniture and a silver watch to his niece Martha Bird who was living with him. His son James benefited by having his debts with a firm of timber merchants at South Moulsham reduced at the discretion of the executors. Denton's grandchildren received an equal share in 'all the crown pieces I am possessed of at the time of my death'. The residuary legatees were his son Thomas jun and daughter Elizabeth

Tayspill (wife of Thomas Tayspill (qv)). The executors were Thomas Denton 2 (qv) and Thomas Tayspill (qv).

DENTON THOMAS 2 [243]
Liquor Merchant, Goats Head
fl. 1793-1813

Active in St Leonards vestry from the 1790s. He died shortly after his father, Thomas Denton 1 (qv). Denton jun's will of 1811, proved in 1813 (D/ABR 31/64, liquor merchant, St Nicholas) leaves his real and personal estate to executors including his brother-in-law Thomas Tayspill for the benefit of his wife and children equally, except a son, Thomas Emery Denton (presumably sickly), who was to receive 20s per week from the executors for 'as long as he stands in need of the money.'

DESBROSSES PETER [244]
Wine Merchant
fl. 1780s

Partner to Charles Whaley (qv), the owner of the White Hart (qv), in a wine merchant's business. Desbrosses was included in James Dunthorne jun's (qv) etching *The Card Party* in 1783, depicting a genteel gathering in the White Hart Assembly Rooms (reproduced in W.G. Benham, 'The Dunthornes of Colchester', *Essex Review*, 10 (1901):27-35). The premises of Messrs Whaley and Desbrosses were in Back Lane and these as well as stock and furniture were sold in 1786 (*IpsJ* 26 August 1786), described as belonging to 'a gentleman leaving the country'. This was presumably Desbrosses, since Whaley snr. had died in 1774 and his son continued in Colchester.

See also John Blatch Whaley (qv) for description of the premises.

D

DEVALL PETER 1 [245]
Weaver
ob. 1767

Devall had operated as an independent weaver before 1767 when two of his apprentices including his own son, took their freedom of the Borough. In the Monday Court, Thomas Smith weaver Colchester (later apprenticed to Peter Devall) admitted free burgess 7 December 1767. In the Thursday Court, Peter Devall son of Peter admitted free burgess 10 December 1767. Devall snr. died that year and has an inscription in St Runwalds; Peter Devall, 'clerk of this parish' died 17 October 1767 age 58, also Elizabeth Devall died 3 June 1771 age 55.

DEVALL PETER 2 [246]
Wool Sorter
fl. 1767-1828

The son of Peter Devall 1 (qv). Took up his Borough freedom by right of apprenticeship in 1767 the year of his father's death (Thursday Court, 7 December 1767). By the 1780s, with the concentration of the bay trade into a few hands, Devall was working directly for Thomas Boggis (qv), one of the larger baymakers. In his working capacity, appeared twice at the local petty sessions.

Borough Examination Book, ERO P/CoR 10A, 7 August 1783: Peter Devall, sorter to Thomas Boggis of Colchester, taketh oath that Edward Philbrooke of Colchester, Weaver has failed to complete his work in the woollen manufactory and gone to work for another master. ERO P/CO R/11, 22 February 1785: Peter Devall servant to Thomas Boggis, taketh oath that John Kemp has failed to weave 42lb yarn into a bay and gone to work for another master.

Devall originally occupied premises near the corner of Queen St and High Street in All Saints. All Saints Land Tax for Queen Street corner in 1783 shows Henry Johnson (qv) (owner occupier) 6; owned Johnson occ. Mrs Williams, 3; Peter Devall (owner occupier) rated 3. Devall bought Henry Johnson's bankrupt premises in 1786 (JBB Note 'Now Watts Factory' CRO C47, CPL 232, 1786).

Devall was mentioned as follows in Boggis' will (NA PROB 11/1193, Bishop 320, made 19 March 1790, proved 16 July 1790):-

> To my faithful servant, Peter Devall, I give the sum of £100 and as a further act and in completion of his services I request he will be aiding and assisting my said brother Isaac Boggis after my decease in the management, ordering or disposing of my business as my brother shall think proper.

Isaac Boggis'2 (qv) letter book (ERO C277 Box 1) shows Devall fulfilling this role and apparently running his own business too.

1 February 1791; to Messrs Wm Browning & Son:

> You can send me a sample of the wool you offer ... My late Master, Mr Thomas Boggis being dead and I having the whole management of his business for his brother.

30 April 1791: To Green & Walford;

> I have only 10 pieces of no. 5 Common which are very white and neat ... you have 6 of my no. 5 on hand, full as good as my master's no. 5, and am confident they are neat and as good colours and any in London.

Arthur Brown, (nfr, but see *Essex at Work 1700-1815*, (Chelmsford 1969)) quotes an advertisement in the *Ipswich Journal* of 1801 for a manager for an extensive Baize manufactory in Colchester – perhaps Devall did not wish to run two businesses after Isaac Boggis' death.

Peter Devall snr. woolsorter died intestate in November 1828 (nfr).

See also: *Essex County Standard* 25 March 1893.

D

DEVALL PETER 3 [247]
Baymaker
fl. 1790s-1834

The son of Peter Devall 2 (qv), and the last of the Colchester baymakers. His main premises were on the corner of Moor Lane and East Hill (see below). He operated in partnership with Robert Tabor (qv) until the latter's death in 1818. (*Colchester Gazette* 27 June 1818; partnership of Robert Tabor and Peter Devall of Colchester, baymaker dissolved by the death of Tabor on 6 February, last. Demands and debts were referred to Peter Devall).

Devall married Mary, daughter of James Taylor 2 (qv) of East Hill, builder. Taylor died in 1806, leaving her 73 High Street, bought from the Boggis estate. One of their children was named Robert Tabor Devall.

In 1893 (25 March 1893) the *Essex County Standard* published an 'Interview with the daughter of the last of the Bay Makers', by its correspondent Mark Downe. A few details can be gleaned from this rather sketchy and sentimental article. The lady was the only surviving member of a family of thirteen children.

> From the fact that Miss Devall was the youngest of the family, probably therefore the pet of the nursery at the time the trade was carried on, she was unable to give many particulars from her own recollections.

All the books, papers and artefacts of the business had by then been lost. She remembered that her father had employed 'chiefly women' who undertook the spinning, altogether between one and two hundred hands. The business made blankets and also wove ' ... quantities of dress pieces called bombazines, beautiful things – worsted and silk.' She remembered '... a dark green one and a very handsome grey.' Of the factory in Moor Lane, she recalled, ' ... the entrance to the private house being on East Hill, where Mr Hale's shop is, and the works extending along the back of the East side of Priory Street. He also held the mill and meadows at Bourne Ponds ...' She did not know where the cloth was sold. 'She only knew that her father used to travel a great deal, but whether he 'went foreign' or not, she did not know.'

The business had been wound up as Devall's son 'did not take to the trade.' A childhood friend of Miss Devall's who had attended school with her at the establishment run by Miss Kemp (probably Miss Keep, of the family who were friends with Jane and Ann Taylor (qv), the authors) reported to Henry Laver a more graphic memory (Henry Laver, 'Last days of baymaking in Colchester', *Trans. Essex. Arch*, x, 1, New Series, 1906). She remembered the two of them running about the warehouse after school and watching the horses driving the mill. She recalled they did not like the greasy preparations for treating the wool.

Laver also recorded memories of past employees of Devall (men whose fathers had fought in the Napoleonic Wars) at Bourne Mill and other premises on the present site of St Mary Magdalene Church, giving detail of the milling, cleaning weaving and roughing processes. In 1833, Peter Devall sold his wool warehouses to George Round, thus bringing to an end the bay trade in Colchester (ERO Acc C47 CPL 233, deed of 8 August 1833).

See also JBB Article, *Essex County Standard*, 22 June 1962, includes photograph showing back door of Devall's house into the wool loft. Will Peter Devall, baymaker, All Saints, Colchester 1845, ERO D/ABR35/438.

DIBDIN CHARLES [248]
Ipswich Composer and Musician
fl. 1764-1787

Dibdin is best remembered for his *Musical Tour* published in 1788 which is an account of a trip around England giving musical concerts, published in the fashionable epistolary form. Letter XXII concerns Colchester;

> To Colchester I posted and being recommended by the ingenious MR MOORE - whose clock and other curiosities the world has seen, and wondered at - to the

D

White Hart. I there received a hearty welcome to - as he said - the land of Oysters, Baize and Eringo from MR REYNOLDS (George Reynolds (qv)), who is known among his superiors by the title of Honest George - by his equals as a kind friend and AGREEABLE COMPANION - and among his inferiors as a generous and liberal benefactor. Indeed, both he and his son, in understanding and demeanour, give you an impression of something considerably above inn-keepers. He shook his head at the idea of a Musical entertainment at COLCHESTER but, as the assembly room was in his house, I resolved to try it. My success turned out neither good nor bad and he and I settled the matter as men should do who mean fairly by each other. One circumstance, however rendered my jaunt to COLCHESTER pleasurable. A gentleman who has everything within himself that can constitute the enjoyments of a country life in the truest and most delectable stile, (sic) laid himself out with the unaffected and hearty kindness of old English hospitality, to charm away every moment of my time ... I shall only say of COLCHESTER - that the applause was excessive the profit scarcely anything.... The White Hart at COLCHESTER is one of the best (inns) in England. It is large, handsome and convenient, and has admirable accommodations. I was witness to MR REYNOLDS' sending out - with some company who had been to pay a visit to Mr RIGBY (Richard Rigby, Mistley Hall (qv)) - two and twenty pair of horses in one morning. I cannot so correctly speak as to the inns of Ipswich for when I was there they were all confusion and it was first come first served. Provision seemed to be very good, and the soles they get from Aldborough are incomparable (letter dated 30 November 1787, C. Dibdin, *The Musical Tour of Mr Dibdin; in which, previous to his embarkation for India, he finished his career as a public character* (Sheffield, 1788), p. 87).

Dibdin described Ipswich and Colchester as 'formerly of consequence, but are now greatly declined. The manufacture of baize as well as most of our staple commerce is going north' (p. 83). Norwich, too, had 'all the heavy stupidity of a city where the manufactory is now on the decline' (p. 89). However at Yarmouth he noticed 'the sprightliness of increasing trade' though the farmers grumbled. He commented 'that Englishmen are never solely in wealth so much as when they complain of the weight of taxes and he impending ruin of the nation'.

Dibdin provided the music for *The Royal Convent* by Mrs Rowe at Ipswich Theatre, given with 'much authentic Saxon detail' in 1784 (*IpsJ* 8 December 1784). His parting concert before he left for the East Indies in 1787 was advertised in great detail. (*IpsJ* 7 July 1787):

> READINGS and MUSIC
>
> FLATTERED with so polite a Reception on Wednesday evening, and strongly solicited by the major part of the elegant audience who then assembled,
>
> On THURSDAY next, July 12th, at the TOWN HALL, Ipswich, will be delivered, for positively the LAST TIME,
>
> READINGS occasionally relieved by MUSIC
>
> In Two Parts, with an Exordium THE whole written, composed, spoken, sung and accompanied,
>
> By Mr DIBDIN
>
> Mr DIBDIN respectfully announces to those ladies and gentlemen resident in and near Ipswich, that being under an indispensable engagement to leave England, in the autumn, for the East Indies, he offers this entertainment to the publick, as a grateful tribute of thanks for a handsome and liberal patronage of Five and Twenty years.
>
> N.B. Price of admittance 3s. To begin exactly at 7 o'clock.

D

DIKES ROSE [250]
Wine Merchant
fl. 1765-1782

She was widow to Thomas Dikes (his will is at NA PROB 11/913, tallowchandler and importer of brandy, Colchester, proved 13 November 1765) and succeeded him in the winemerchant's business at 119-120 High Street in 1776 (rated 14 + 2 for the back lane). According to *Bland's Anecdotes* (Appendix 3) George Pitfield, exciseman, had constant access to her cellar, and was calculated to have drunk 'to his own check at her expense' not less than seven puncheons of rum 'that being his favourite liquor'.

She died in August 1782. Her obituary in the *Chelmsford Chronicle* (6 September 1782) remarked her 'humane and benevolent disposition ... (which) ... endeared her to her friends, who, with the poor lament her loss'. Her long will (NA PROB 11/1096, proved 19 October 1782) names her brother-in-law, Philip Dikes, brandy merchant of Ipswich as main beneficiary and leaves various legacies, including to Morfee Lince (qv). The High Street premises were briefly occupied by Thomas Dikes then the business was sold to Ephraim Shillito 3 (qv) and William Suddell (qv).

DINGLEY MRS [251]
fl. 1815

Colchester Gazette 23 September 1815: Furniture and Prints of Mrs Dingley for sale. She was leaving 71 East Hill (long advertisement not copied).

DINGLEY REVD ROBERT HENRY [252]
Rector, Beaumont-cum-Moze
w. 1792/3

Dingley's will was made on 10 November 1792 during his retirement in Bath, with Memoranda and a Codicil added in 16 March 1793. He died a few days later (20 March 1793) and the will was proved in London (NA PROB 11/1232, 252 Dodwell, 8 May 1793) on the 8th May following.

His wife Elizabeth was named guardian of all children under age though she was to consult the executors regarding the boys' education. She received an immediate £150, a life interest in the plate, household goods, china, carriages and horses (thereafter to eldest son Robert Henry Dingley or eldest surviving son), and absolute possession of the contents of the cellar and personal property at Beaumont, except the books, which were directed to whichever son should first be admitted to a degree at either university. Her income was secured from the interest on £5,000 worth of Bank 3% annuities to be purchased by the executors Stephen Martin Leake of Harpur Street, London and Charles Edward Lewis of Powis Place, Middlesex. She was to loose this income if she remarried (per Codicil). After her death £2,000 worth of these annuities was directed to his eldest son (who also received a further £2,000 in his own right at 21), the reversion falling in turn to Dingley's other sons in order, being William Augustus, Francis Fitzalleyne and Frederick. The remaining £3,000 was to be divided between all sons equally, failing whom to any female children on their marriage.

The executors were also to purchase a further £2,000 worth of Bank annuities to pay the income for her life to Dingley's sister Susannah Cecilia Hoare. After her death this sum would fall into the residue of the estate which was to be divided between all children equally at age 21. He directed that an £18 annuity to Francis Bawling should be continued.

The Memoranda dealt with matters less central to the testator, but if anything more interesting to the historian. To his niece, Sophia Elizabeth, the wife of Hon. William Grimston, Dingley left his best 'onyx ... (ring) ... engraved with an urn set round with Brilliants, which I had made in memory of her dear Father.' A shirt pin of enamel inscribed 'Vale' in brilliants and surrounded with rubies was left to Mrs Webb;

> ... in Memory of that ever Blessed angel her first born sister ... humbly hoping they will thence derive some

D

> estimation for them not altogether unmixed with affection for the Testator.

To the Hon. William Grimston and Nathaniel Webb Esq he made;

> A most ardent and respectful request that they will shew some patronage and protection towards my dear children, hoping they will reward them with the same affection as I have had for their wives, whom since their father's death I have regarded with the tenderest solicitude and attachment of a parent.

Regarding his executors,

> ... who on all occasions have been my kindest and firmest friends and advisers, unable to make them any adequate recompense I will not wound their generous feelings with the mean pittance of pecuniary bequests as is consistent with my situation and the claims of my family, well assured they will be repaid by the sentiments of their generous Hearts and by the Almighty Rewarder of good Actions.

Consequently he left Leake a satin wood dressing case containing shaving apparatus and Lewis an agate onyx ring.

A good friend, Miss Everard received a 5 gn. ring, and a Miss Gibson his copper plate *Prayer Book* with silver corners and a book of manuscript prayers transcribed by Mrs Skeate.

His friend Edward Bogges, with acknowledgment of his professional assistance was left two fowling pieces. Further; 'I beg that the small account subsisting between us (if as I apprehend the balance is in my favour) may be never further thought of.'

> I beg my friend Mr Leake may be requested to accept the Survey I had made of the Parish of Beaumont-cum-Moze which he is at perfect Liberty to present to my successor in the living or otherwise to dispose of as he thinks fit.

(JBB note: This survey was made by Chapman.)

D

Donations of 3 or 5 guineas were left to Sarah Walsh, Thomas Harvey, Elizabeth Bennett, and Mr Evans, Mr Crooks assistant. Dorothy Meggott received 5 gns '... as an additional reward for the care of the child during our absence and other loving Services.'

£10 was left to Hannah, Mrs Hoare's housemaid 'for kindness during my long illness'. This last was however later scored through.

He also noted that he owed £5 5s to Harrison the horse dealer at Colchester. A second memorandum detailed that Mr George Reynolds (qv) had an account of Sundry Articles expended by him which he desired Mr Leake to settle. Half the value of a picture, which Leake's late father and himself had purchased at Mr Mayhew's sale (William Mayhew 2 (qv)), which was in the custody of George Reynolds, was the property of Leake.

Dingley had, he stated, fixed a plan by Mr Reynolds' assistance and under Mr Lewis' sanction for the receipt of the Trinity pension for Nurse Paine, which he had written to Mr Reynolds in his last letter. Reynolds seems to have managed Dingley's Colchester affairs.

Mr Parker, painter of Colchester, had;

> with much exact^n and some impertinence, presented a bill for painting my Carriage and work done at Beaumont. I paid him 2 gns on account and since he has had ten pounds or gns of Mr Leake by the hand of Mr Watkins (qv) of the King's Head Colchester. What the acc^t exceeds the sum paid I do not accurately recollect. I have keep (sic) him in suspence by reason of his extort^n and insolence. I doubt whether he is not already recompensed <u>all</u> his Charge of £9 9s for the Chaise. On enquiry of the first Coachmaker here Mr Kilyert (?) at Bath is full 1 gn. and ½ over charged and I think the work done at Beaumont <u>full in the same proportion in his acc^t</u>. However (it) should be finally settled with or without some reduction as shall seem just with some consideration had of the time he has been kept unpaid.

217

D

> Be it further remembered that there remains a claim unsettled (w^t Astle Hills) ... (cf will of Michael Robert Hills (qv)) respecting a Miniature of my Grandfather something relative to Jewels, Plate etc.

> If my decease takes place at Bath I beg my old and truly beloved Friend Edward Whitwell Esq ... (to look after Dingley's widow &c and settle with Doctors) ... and that Mr Whitwell will through my dear friend Stephens procure me to be deposited at Camerton to save his dear sister trouble.

£200 or his house in Wood St., Bath was left to his dear sister who had looked after him so tenderly. A Memento Ring of the late Mr George Reynolds was to be presented to Reynolds jun (qv), '..requesting him to wear it as a joint Testimony of his Regard and a memento of his late Father.'

A note later erased mentioned he was endebted (sic) to the Revd J Cook, Rector of Tendring for a Banbury cheese sent him to Bath.

> I wish to be considered whether the old Chaise Horse (Folly) should not be offered to Mr Crowder who presented him to me for his reacceptance. ... As the little Black mare (Dobby) will probably be useless to my dear Boys I wish her to be presented to the little Grimstones and the Bay in the same Acc^t to to Mrs Webb.

Also;

> Mr F. Smythies (qv) of Colch', atty, has an Acc^t ags^t me to what amount I can form no conjecture.

A bundle of letters among his papers would help ascertain Smythies' claim which for years Dingley had (he said) been asking Smythies to allow him to settle.

> A box of Surveying Instruments which is at the bottom of my bookcase I wish to have presented to my good friend Mr T. Ranes of Lt. Bromley Hall as a token of his regard.

The memoranda were witnessed by William Falconer MD and Edward Whitwell who appeared personally at the probate hearing to testify to the authenticity of these documents. Edward Whitwell had known Dingley 20 years.

DISS ISAAC [253]
Scrivener
1740-1814

Baptised at Bocking 22 August 1740, son of Isaac, wool comber and apprenticed to Richard Shoobridge, cabinet-maker, Braintree for £20 in 1755 (NA IR/17 20/64). Diss first came to Colchester as a married man in 1762. He had married Susannah Hills at Braintree on 3 December 1761 (*IGI*, which lists no children). His father had lived in St James parish, Colchester for the previous ten years (Settlement Examination, ERO P/CoR 4, 9 April 1773).

From at least 1763 Diss jun. lived in a small house in Queen Street, All Saints, rated 3, next door to Robert Tabor (qv). It is likely he was already a nonconformist and he received the support of Tabor and other leading Lion Walk members. By 1770 he was acting as clerk to the nonconformist lawyer Peter Daniell (qv) and witnessed the will of the presbyterian silversmith James Thorn 1 (qv).

Diss was an amateur auricula grower and was steward at the Auricula Feast held in 1772 (*IpsJ* 25 April 1772). By at least 1775 he was active at Lion Walk and sufficiently well placed to be one of the signatories of the letter appointing the new minister Giles Hobbes (qv). The following year he became a full member and was later elected Deacon. He seems to have founded the Sunday School in 1782 (Blaxill, *Lion Walk*:36).

His career as a scrivener was also progressing. For many years All Saints parish records are kept in his careful hand. Diss was in charge of prosecutions when heavy fines were levied for assault on the Water-bailiff's assistants. Prosecutors were Anthony Tabor (qv) of Brightlingsea and others (6 October 1783, William Mason's Borough Chamberlain's Accounts, ERO

D

D/B 5 Aa2/1). Interestingly, given the political differences between the nonconformist group in Colchester and the Tory Corporation party, in 1787 Diss was used by Frank Smythies (qv) to replace him temporarily as town clerk while Smythies was Recorder. Diss never made the political use of the office that Smythies had, however, and was succeeded in the job only two years later (13 July 1789) by Thomas Harden.

Between 1780 and his death in 1814, 43 Colchester wills mention Isaac Diss. He worked with William Mason 2 (qv) attorney in the 1790s (e.g. will of John Ram (qv) 1793), but from 1800 seems to have been working independently. In most cases he acted as witness having drawn up the document for signature but in eight cases he was named executor - always of a nonconformist will - and received small legacies of under £25 in six of these wills. 21 of the 43 wills overall are made by nonconformists or evangelicals.

When Diss died in 1814 his funeral was attended by 250 scholars and teachers from the Lion Walk Sunday School. His obituary in the *Ipswich Journal* of 27 August 1814 describes him thus:-

> Tuesday morning last died much regretted, Mr Isaac Diss of this town in the 75th year of his age. Prudent and sincere, he was highly esteemed by the religious community of which he was, for many years a member; his benevolence made him a zealous and indefatigable promoter of the Sunday and Lancastrian Schools, children of which were wont to look up to him as a fostering father; his charity constituted him a warm friend to the poor; his zeal urged him gratuitously to execute the office of Secretary to the Essex Union Society for the Spread of the Gospel, and his kindness qualified and made him a useful member of society in general. His piety did not partake either of the gloom of the cloister or the bigotry of a party; but he was the offspring of cheerful Christianity by which he cordially embraced all who loved the Lord Jesus Christ in sincerity. His religion enabled him to meet death with composure and even in

the pangs of dissolving nature, to triumph in his Redeemer.

The chamber where the good man meets his fate
Is privileg'd beyond the common walk
Of virtuous life, quite on the verge of heaven.

The *Colchester Gazette* published its own obituary on 27 August 1814, in which Diss is described as 'the useful Man', who 'lived for others.' His will (NA PROB 11/1561, Bridport 560, made 1812, proved 17 October 1814) is lengthy and leaves numerous legacies of between £20 and £100 to relatives and about twenty four others. It also mentions a silver spoon given him by the Prince of Wales in 1797.

See also, re Diss's apprenticeship; *ChCh* 31 July 1778 'Sunday died Mr Richard Shoobridge, cabinetmaker of this town. He was a strenuous asserter of public liberty, an ingenious artist well versed in the circle of the sciences; and from a peculiar turn of mind, quickness of apprehension, and social disposition, highly respected by a very numerous acquaintance.' Another apprentice of Shoobridge was Thos. Wood, 1761, £20 (NA IR 1/22/186). Wood's will ERO D/ABR 27/180, 1780, makes no reference to Diss.

DIXON THOMAS [254]
Merchant
fl. 1761-1809

Dixon married (CPL Crisp ML378, ERO D/ALL 1761, St Leonard registers 17 May 1761) in 1761, a corn and porter merchant of St Leonards aged 27 to Jane Ballard (25). She died in 1786 aged 31. A second marriage is recorded in 1788 (CPL Crisp ML381, ERO D/ACL 1788, Boxted Registers per *IGI*, 13 July 1788) between Thomas Dixon, St Leonard merchant and Mary Munson of Boxted, though this may well have been that of Dixon's son. Dixon père married his last wife on 15 May 1802 at All Saints (registers, CPL Crisp ML 383). She was Mrs Sarah Campling, widow, who had earlier had an illegitimate daughter by William Mayhew 2 (qv). Dixon lived in a small house at the Hythe rated 3 in 1783. It had a summer house (cf *IpsJ* 11 April 1795) and a greengage tree in the garden. Dixon finally requested in his will to be buried under this tree in a lead coffin with a 6ft deep brick grave topped with flat stones.

Dixon regularly attended St Leonards vestry. He acted as overseer in 1780 and 1790 and was churchwarden from 1785 to 1791. In business he had entered the coal trade in partnership with John Ram (qv) and Alexander Carter. The agreement was finally dissolved in October 1791 (*IpsJ* 15 October 1791) although both Ram and Dixon continued separately, Dixon at his yard near the Horseshoes at the Hythe. Dixon's nephew, William Dixon (qv) was also in business at the Hythe, and the interlinking of family property is demonstrated in that when William was bankrupt in 1795 Thomas' house was offered for auction (*IpsJ* 15 April 1795). It was apparently not sold, however, since it was later mentioned in his will. On 21 May 1808 the *IpsJ* reported the death 'of a decline' of Miss Dixon only daughter of Mr Thomas Dixon Colchester corn merchant.

Dixon himself died in 1810 (D/ACR 19/558, merchant of Colchester) leaving his wife, Sarah an interest for life in his house and all household goods etc. Nephew William received a reversionary interest in the house as well as the proceeds of selling the coal, corn seeds, vessels and barges after settlement of debts, expenses and an outstanding mortgage on the house.

St Leonards vestry minutes record a Thomas Dixon junior attending meetings from 1789 as well as Dixon senior. If this is Dixon's son he must have predeceased his father.

DIXON WILLIAM [255]
Merchant
fl. 1795-1810

Nephew of Thomas Dixon (qv). His bankruptcy in 1795 involved the offer for sale of Thomas Dixon's house as well as the vessels *Twin Brothers* (71 tons) and *Friends Goodwill* (72 tons) (*IpsJ* 15 April 1795).

DOBBY HENRY [256]
Woollen Draper and Tailor
fl. 1768-1786

Dobby was admitted free burgess on 14 March 1768 by right of apprenticeship to Thomas Shaw (qv). He voted from 1768 to 1784, favouring Fordyce and Smyth (the radical candidates). He occupied a house on the east side of Headgate from at least 1773-1783 (rated 8) and was married in 1765 aged 30 to Elizabeth Shaw, also 30, both of St Mary-at-the-Walls. Elizabeth died in 1771 and shares an altar tomb in St Marys with her husband who died on 13 December 1786 aged 56. His will (NA PROB 11/1141 Norfolk 209-261, 6 April 1786, draft of 16 February 1782 in ERO, nfr) directs the sale of the house at St Marys and land at Peldon and leaves cash legacies to charities and many friends.

See also: 1747 Poll Book records a voter, Henry Dobby.

DOBSON ROBERT [257]
Cheesemonger, Tea Dealer and Grocer
fl. 1768-87

The son of Robert (d. 24 March 1760) and Mary (d. 28 March 1783). He married Mary Cook of Thorrington in 1768 (CPL Crisp ML317, ERO D/ACL 1768). He occupied premises on the north side of the High Street near the Lamb, rated 14, until in 1770 he moved to an extensive shop on the uphill corner of High Street and Pelhams Lane rated 40. His wife Mary died on 14 August 1776 aged 32 and he himself on 30 March 1787 aged 47 (altar tomb, St James naming many family members). His will (NA PROB 11/1153, 7 May 1787) left £3,000 apiece in Navy annuities and an estate in St Osyth to his daughters Mary and Margaret at 21, the residue to his sons James and Robert. His executors were Dr Robert Sterling (qv), Revd Mr Talman Rector of Birch, and Thomas Wood (qv). Wood continued the grocery business until Robert jun took over in 1792 (IpsJ 23 June 1792).

D

DOWNS NATHANIEL [261]
Staymaker
fl. 1777-1784

Not among the most eminent Colchester tradesmen, Downs occupied small premises at the bottom of Angel Lane between at least 1777 and 1783 (St Martins Rates 1783, occ. premises owned B. Foakes with Burgis and Gasnel, rental 7). His advertisement on 22 February 1777 (*IpsJ*) denied that he had left off business and said he would be at Mr Appleton's at the White Hart Kelvedon every Monday during the summer season.

He was a free burgess voting in the 1780s and changed support from Smyth to Potter between 1780 and 1781.

DRAKE REVD RICHARD [262]
Rector of Gt. Oakley and Hadleigh
w. 1737/8

Drake's will (ERO D/AAW 2/235, 1738, clerk, Gt. Oakley) leaves his successor, his nephew Revd Thomas Grimwood:

> the large Map of Essex, adorned with the arms of the Subscribers and another Map of the whole world the Crown Head, the Founder of Both Universities and the cupboard on which are the effigies of Dr Nicholas Morgan ... (LLB, ob. 1532) ... first founder of My Parsonage.

His daughter Susanna was the wife of George Elliston of Gt. Oakley (D/ALL 1730) and his sister Ann the wife of James Hamilton of Norwich, weaver (nfr).

DRAPER MARK [1005]
Clockmaker
1729-1776

Of Dunmow, when he married in 1723 (CPL Crisp ML367, Mark Draper, Dunmow, clockmaker and John Read Stratford shoemaker bind Mark (22) to Mary Lumpkin (23) of Stratford, 1723). Sworn a Colchester free burgess on 24 February 1729 (ERO D/B 5 R1, Borough Oath Book:30). Mason considers he may have been apprenticed to Barnaby Dammant (qv), however there is also an apprenticeship recorded to John Fordham of Great Dunmow (NA IR 17/5/17, son of Margaret widow, apprenticed to John Fordham of Gt Dunmow, clockmaker, £12). He lived in Witham but voted in Colchester from 1729. A vote in that name is also recorded in 1781.

See also Bernard Mason, *Clock and Watchmaking in Colchester* (1969):407-10 for Draper and his apprentices.

DRAWBRIDGE JOSEPH [263]
Exciseman
fl. 1787

Married Sarah Hurrell of West Bergholt in 1787 (ERO ML D/ACL 1787).

DUDDELL REVD [264]
Coggeshall School
fl. 1768-79

Ran a successful school at the Vicarage in Coggeshall where on 30 July, 1768 (*IpsJ*) he offered to take six young gentlemen to board and educate.

In 1779 he became the Low Church candidate in the elections for the vacant mastership of Colchester Free School which became a heated issue in Borough politics and occasioned much scandal (for which see Charles Hewitt (qv), Francis Smythies (qv), D'Cruze, *Pleasing Prospect:160-5*).

D

DUFFIELD JOSEPH 1 [265]
Cardboardmaker
fl. 1710 -1717

With his wife Sarah, was left a house in the will of Philip Stowers (qv) cardboard maker, subject to £5 p.a. to Stowers' wife, thereafter to Duffield's daughter-in-law, Sarah the wife of George Kelly distiller of Colchester, £5 each to Duffield's children, Joseph 2 (qv), Thomas, Elizabeth and Mary, and 40s to the testator's nephew Thomas Stowers. Duffield was co-executor with Sarah Pryor, Stowers' daughter and residuary legatee (ERO D/ACR/12/176, 1710).

Duffield's own will was made on 3 July 1717 (witnessed by Ephraim Shillito 1 (qv), Barnaby Dammant (qv) and Deborah Barker - all his neighbours in All Saints). It was proved on 1 October 1717 (ERO D/ACR 8/13). He left:-

- To son Joseph (qv), Horsepits Farm West Bergholt, house occ. Joseph Moor in All Saints, tenement Hog Lane Wivenhoe. Also the residue.
- To wife Sarah, £20 p.a. to be paid by Joseph, also £50 she can leave in her will as she pleased.
- To daughter Elizabeth Dammant, £50
- To daughter Mary Duffield, £250
- To daughter Sarah Kellie, £50.

Joseph and his wife Sarah were named co-executors.

DUFFIELD JOSEPH 2 [266]
Cardboardmaker
fl. 1717-1747

The son of Joseph Duffield 1 (qv) and his wife Sarah. From his father's will of 1717 he inherited a farm, Horsepits, in West Bergholt and tenements in All Saints and Wivenhoe, as well as the residue of the estate. He was joint executor together with his mother.

In 1719 he was trading in partnership with Richard Bowler (qv) when they advertised old wool cards 'at a reasonable price'

D

either at Colchester or 'at their warehouse at Richard Fidswell's in Old Swan Lane, Thames Street, London' (*Essex Review*, Vol. 45: 248, advertisement of 19 October 1719). In 1722 Duffield took John West (qv) (son of Robert West, cordwainer) apprentice for £10 (NA IR 1/48/40).

In 1724 (ERO D/DU 518/5, 15 June 1724) a lease from the Corporation was assigned to Duffield from Robert Chignell, merchant on the Coal Yard at the 'Old Hithe,' St Leonards, late occupied Mr Benjamin Cock (cf Thomas and Mary Duffield (qv)).

In 1728 (Assembly Book, 27 January 1728), following the demise of the Dutch monopoly of the Colchester baytrade, he and Isaac Boggis 1 (qv) became Hall Keepers of the woolmarket for a year with a first refusal of a lease thereof. Duffield was an Alderman from at least 1730 when he served as Mayor, an office he also held in 1734 and 1738. He was at the centre of the group of Tory Aldermen who were in control of the Borough during the 1730s and whose struggle for a Corporation majority with the local Whig party led to the loss of the Borough Charter in 1741 (*VCH Essex*, Vol. 9; D'Cruze, *Pleasing Prospect*:138-9). He voted Tory in the Borough polls of 1734 (Houblon) and 1741 (Savill and Gray).

His premises were in All Saints, rated 6, opposite the Seahorse (cf James Green (qv)), now 122 High Street. After his death in 1747 his widow continued there until 1766. He was a subscriber to Morant's *Colchester* in 1748.

His will (1747, ERO D/ACR 15/255, merchant, Colchester) made on 10 March 1746 when he was weak and infirm, was witnessed i.a. by his partner Richard Bowler (qv). It was proved on 28 September 1747. He directed that his real estate; the Three Cups Inn (qv) St Peter occupied by Robert Walker (qv), messuages in All Saints occupied himself, John Edwards and Elizabeth Dammant should be sold to pay his debts and the following legacies.

- To loving brother Thomas Duffield, a farm call'd Horsepitts, West Bergholt occ. Bracken Brett, subject to his discharging a mortgage of £600 to William Round

D

Esq (see under James Round (qv)) on The Three Cups. Thomas was also given £100 towards the cost of so doing.
- To loving sister Elizabeth Dammant, £700.
- To daughter Mary Duffield £900.
- To his executors £500 to discharge a bond given to Mr John Cook of London as a further part of the marriage portion with Ann his wife if she or her children are living.
- To two other daughters of his brother Thomas, Mary and Elizabeth, £200 each.
- To three daughters of his late sister Kellie; Sarah Raynham wid., Elizabeth Kellie and Susannah the wife of George Witherley, £100 each, less £5 to Susannah which was spent on her marriage.
- To Robert Hawn, an infant son to Mary one of the daughters of his late sister Kellie, £100 when 21, part of which to be laid out on his apprenticeship and interest for his support and maintenance meantime.
- To Mary Wheely 'one of my present maid servants for her long and faithful service to buy her mourning', £15.

The residue was to be divided equally between the executors who were his brother Thomas Duffield and sisters Elizabeth Dammant and Mary Duffield.

DUFFIELD THOMAS and MARY [267]
Lime and Coal Merchants
fl. 1717-1750

Two of the children of Sarah and Joseph Duffield 1 (qv). They were siblings of Joseph Duffield 2 (qv) one of the Tory Mayors of the 1730s who sold freedoms of the Borough in order to raise revenue. Thomas was one of the free burgesses hastily created for the election of 1741 whose votes were later discounted. In 1741 he voted dutifully for the Tories Savage and Gray and for Gray and Olmius in 1747.

D

Joseph Duffield 2's (qv) will of 1746/7 left Thomas a farm 'Horsepits' in West Bergholt subject to a mortgage of £600 to William Round Esq of the Three Cups, also £100 to offset part of the cost of redeeming this debt, and £900 to Mary. (Another sister, Elizabeth Dammant received £700). All the three siblings acted as executors.

By 1750 Thomas and Mary who had been trading as Lime and Coal merchants at the Hythe, declined the trade in favour of William Hickeringill (qv) (see his entry for further details).

DUKE ROBERT [1019]
Draper
fl. 1750-1780

Not a Colchester free burgess. Duke advertised (*IpsJ* 17 March 1750 NS) that he had taken the shop of Mrs Ann Harrington. Together with a Mr Brook of Halstead, particulars were to be obtained from Duke of a house for sale on the Colchester to Ipswich Road in 1761 (*IpsJ*, JBB NB Apr 71:33, nfr). By 1762 (*IpsJ* 27 February 1762) he was also acting as agent for the Original Essex Militia Insurance Office. In 1766 he came into conflict with the Master Tailors who protested at his intention to expand his drapery business into tailoring. (*IpsJ* 15 and 23 March 1766). It seems likely that Duke tried to resolve this problem by entering into partnership with tailor Francis Snell (qv). They advertised from the Eagle and Child, opposite the Fish Market, late the shop of Robert Smith (qv) throughout November 1766 (*IpsJ*). However, this partnership was short lived and Samuel Phillips (qv) advertised from this address on 30 May 1767 (*IpsJ*).

Duke took a number of apprentices: 1755, William Lawrence, £100, NA IR 1/52/93; 1763, Samuel Hassell, £100, NA IR 1/23/185; 176? (per original source), Stephen Boston, £15 15s, NA IR 1/56/75; 1770 Thomas Hammond, £60, NA IR 1/57/69; 1773, John Woodward, NA IR 1/58/175.

Duke traded for many years at 3 High St near White Hart, rated 21, and was for a long time churchwarden at St Peter's

D

(G. O. Rickwood Scrapbook, CPL). He retired in 1778 (*ChCh* 6 March 1778), selling off the remaining stock but Miss Duke continued to trade until 1784 (*IpsJ* 16 October 1784, Miss Duke, milliner, selling off stock in Head Street).

Duke died in 1780. His furniture, and a farm at Copford was for auction early that year. The shop was taken in 1780 by Ebeneezer Cornell (qv) (*IpsJ* 22 January 1780). He seems to have died insolvent. His bankrupt estate was assigned to John Sebborn (qv) the following March (*IpsJ* 11 March 1780).

Duke had married Jemima Joseph of Feering in 1750. She died and was buried in St Peters, 1761 (nfr). Her mother's sister had married Sir Richard Bacon (qv) hence Jemima was co-heiress to the barony Fitzwalter (in abeyance). Robert's son Joseph (baptised St Martin 5 May 1756) claimed the succession in July 1784, but in trouble over a bastardy case when an ensign at Coxheath, emigrated to America. When in 1844 the Committee of Privileges decided that Jemima Duke's descendants, if any, had a claim, all trace of them had been lost. (Further detail in G. O. Rickwood scrapbooks.)

DUNKLEY THOMAS [270]
Surgeon
fl. 1754-1767

In 1754 Thos Dunkley, 22, of St Marys, Colchester, apothecary, married Mary Carlton, 26, of the same parish (CPL Crisp ML 379, ERO D/ALL 1754).

> THOMAS DUNKLEY
>
> Apothecary, Surgeon and Man-Midwife BEGS leave to acquaint All Gentlemen and Ladies that the Partnership between him and Mr Wm. SMYTHIES of Colchester is dissolved; that he hath taken a House near the Dial Church, and hath fitted up his Shop with a fresh Stock of Drugs. ...' (*IpsJ* 18 October 1755, William Smythies 3 (qv)).

D

There then follows a long passage, printed in italics where the printer denies that 'Drops' for 'Drugs' in the advertisement previously published was his error and not Mr Dunkley's slip of the pen.

Dunkley was living in Earls Colne in 1757 when he advertised; 'To be Sold at Earl's Colne the SHELL of an Apothecary's Shop, viz a Counter, Drawers, Shelves, Pots and Glasses, and some Drugs. Enquire of Mr Thomas Dunkley, surgeon in the same town' (*IpsJ* 30 April 1757).

IpsJ 16 May 1767 announced the death of Thomas Dunkley, late of Earls Colne, surgeon. His executor was Mr Humphrey Carlton (qv) of Colchester. His will is at NA PROB 11/927, proved 16 April 1767.

See also NA PROB 11/941, proved 10 August 1768, will of Joseph Dunkley, gent of Maldon, Essex.

DUNNINGHAM JOSEPH [271]
Cardmaker and Innkeeper
1695-1771

Dunningham was a substantial and long-lived tradesman. He was created Assistant in 1763 and later Alderman. In 1740 he was running the Three Crowns and Star (qv) at the north west end of High Street, named in rivalry to the Old Three Crowns in Head Street. In 1743 he leased the (nearby) Wool Hall (IpsJ 1 October 1743). He offered the Three Crowns and Star, an adjoining tenement and the Three White Naggs (qv) for sale on several occasions in 1755, 1756 when he retired from trade (G. O. Rickwood, *ECS*, 23 March 1935) and again in 1761:-

> To be sold
>
> A Freehold Estate in the Parish of St Peter, Colchester, consisting of a large Dwellinghouse, three Story (sic) high, six Rooms on a Floor, besides closets; a kitchen, good wine vaults and cellar, having a Brick Front handsomely sashed, and was new-built in a substantial Manner a few years ago; Likewise two Houses adjoining thereunto, with Stable-Room for 24 Horses; the whole

D

well tenanted, in good Repair, and now lett at upwards of Forty Pounds a Year.

Enquire of Mr Dunningham in Colchester (IpsJ 17 September 1761).

His will (ERO D/ABR 26/220, 1771, gent of St Peter) names John Pilborough (qv) as executor. Dunningham was buried in an altar tomb in St Martins.

See also: Abraham Dunningham attends St Leonards vestry from 1776; Thomas and William, farmers of Ardleigh, named in a bastardy bond of 1774 (Borough Sessions, nfr); IpsJ 11 December 1790 auction of farming stock Joseph Dunningham at Gt Bromley, under Sheriff's execution, and at Colchester various items of household furniture – origin not specified (removed for conveniency of sale); also IpsJ 22 January 1791.

DUNTHORNE JAMES 1 [1185]
Limner
1730-1815

James Dunthorne 1 was born in 1730, the son of John (qv), Baptist minister from 1739-56. A John Dunthorne is mentioned in All Saints vestry book 1731-51, but may have been his grandfather, as he was said to be 84 when he died in 1756.

As son of John, James Dunthorne was apprenticed to Joshua Kirby, 'limner etc.' Ipswich in 1745 (NA IR 1/17/151, £25). On 3 October 1752 he married Elizabeth Hubbard at St James (registers). (She was buried St Nicholas 8 September 1812.) Several of his children baptised at Lion Walk in 1760 do not include his son James Dunthorne 2 (qv).

Parish rates between 1754 and 1788 show James Dunthorne in Pelham's Lane, St Runwalds rated 8 and close by in 1770 rated 10 (no. 12 High Street). *IpsJ* 20 August 1768 indicates he had moved since his premises near Buttermarket were taken by John Brock (qv) saddler. G. O. Rickwood also identifies his premises in late life as 104 High St., on the boundary of St Nicholas with All Saints.

D

In 1760 was paid £1 17s by All Saints churchwardens (Churchwarden's Accounts) as part of expenses occurred to mark the death of George II. Dunthorne advertised for an apprentice in 1762 (*IpsJ* 3 July 1762) and the following year (*IpsJ* 10 September 1763) advertised the print of a mosaic pavement at Mr John Barnard's, price 1s 6d coloured. (This was John Barnard (qv) surgeon. The Roman mosaic was at his then house, the Old Queen's Head, in the High Street. For this house see Thomas Bayles (qv).)

A joint advertisement with William Cole (qv) for land-surveying appeared in the *IpsJ* 3 September 1766. 'N.B. Perspective views of particular places will be inserted at the Head of the Plans if desired'. Stuart Mason (*Essex on the Map*, (ERO, 1990):112 ff.) finds no evidence that this partnership lasted. Only a map and drawing of Copford Place 1810, is signed by both. A little later, drawings of St Osyth and Birch Hall in the *Gentleman's History of Essex*, have his style (1769-72). Between 1765-7 he was paid £9 15s 6d for work at the Octagon Chapel (Lion Walk), then being built (ERO ERO D/NC 52/5/2). In *IpsJ* 28 March 1767 he advertised a coach for sale (perhaps painted by himself). He made the brass stamp design for the Castle Book Society in 1794 and in 1796 was paid 12 gns by the Corporation for (painting) the King's Arms (Chamberlain's Accounts, ERO D/B 5 Aa3/1, 23 September 1796).

Dunthorne was well enough connected in Colchester to be left a guinea mourning ring by George Wegg Esq (qv) (will 1775/6).

He died late in 1815 (*IpsJ* 30 December 1815) aged 85, 'a celebrated painter much respected.' A sale of his 'Relics' included 'inimitable Deceptions in Oil-Colour' (presumably *trompe-l'oeil*) (*Colchester Gazette*, 14 August 1816) but none of his paintings have been identified, though JBB queried whether the unattributed doll-like portrait of Charles Gray (qv) or that of Mayor John King (qv) (now in Tymperleys museum) might be his work.

He was buried St Nicholas 'from St Mary's' aged 85, 1 January 1816. His will is at ERO D/ACR 19/679, 1816.

See also W. G. Benham, 'The Dunthornes of Colchester,' *Essex Review*, Vol. 10 (1901):29, the source for this information unless otherwise referenced, also for sketch portrait probably by E.P. Strutt captioned 'Let me take your Portrait, Dear'; D'Cruze, *Pleasing Prospect*:103, 121-2; JBB, *EAE*:196, 198. Signatures of both father and son James Dunthorne 2 (qv) may be compared on a Winsley's Bond for Luke Hubbard, gardener, 1782 (ERO D/Q 30/4/9). High Street addresses *ex inf* Bruce Neville. Borough Petty Sessions ERO P/CoR 8 Aug 1779 includes the settlement examination of James Ratcliff glazier and painter, then in the common gaol. Ratcliff stated that about 13 or 14 years ago he had been apprenticed to James Dunthorne, St Runwald, for 7 years and served his time.

DUNTHORNE JAMES 2 [1110]
Limner and Musician
c.1758-1794

Born c.1758, the son of James Dunthorne 1 (qv), painter of St Runwald. Dunthorne junior married Elizabeth Shillito (qv) at All Saints on 7 December 1779. They had three children baptised at St Nicholas; Edward in 1782, Charlotte 1784 and Louisa in 1789.

Dunthorne had musical and artistic ability, but was unable to convert this into a properly remunerative career. Above all he was unable to establish much of a reputation in London although a number of his designs were engraved by Rowlandson and some were shown at the Royal Academy in most years between 1783 and 1792. He made a living chiefly through keeping a print shop at the more fashionable uphill end of Colchester High Street, on the downhill side of Samuel Carr (qv) the grocer, (no. 12) and after 1779 at no. 104.

His *forte* at this period were pictures of fashionable Colchester social events, including *The Card Party* (reproduced in W. G. Benham, 'The Dunthorne Family', reference below), *A Musical*

D

Entertainment (viewable at www.bridgeman.fr, Image number DEC 84530, wrongly attributed to John Dunthorne of Dedham) and *The Tea Room at a Colchester Ball* (reproduced D'Cruze, *Pleasing Prospect*:123*)*. These included pen sketches of local residents, for example in *The Card Party* set in the assembly rooms of the White Hart inn, Miss Mary Keeling (later Mrs George Round), Dr Moses Griffiths (qv), Mrs Whaley the White Hart proprietor's wife and his partner, Peter Desbrosses (qv) the wine merchant have been identified.

Elizabeth Dunthorne, his wife, was sister to Charles Shillito (qv) the author of (i.a.) *A Country Book Club* (1788), for which Dunthorne designed the frontispiece. *The Monthly Review* (July 1789) thought this 'not destitute of humour'. It was etched by Thomas Rowlandson. Dunthorne also selected some more melancholy subjects. *Death Preaches to a Careless Audience* (1785) includes a thin-faced officer who judging by comparison with the central figure in the frontispiece of the *Country Book Club* may be Charles, his brother-in-law. *Ague and Fever* and *The Hypochondriac* (1788) are medical studies. Under the latter appear the following verses:

> This Mind distemper'd - say 'what potent charm
> Can Fancy's spectre - breeding rage disarm?
> Physic's prescriptive art assaults in vain
> The dreadful phantoms floating 'cross the brain!
> Until with Esculapian skill the sage M.D.
> Finds out at length by self-taught palmistry
> The hopeless case - in the reluctant fee:
> Then, not in torture such a wretch to keep
> One pitying bolus lays him sound asleep.

Although the verse does not specify how terminal was the sleep that Dunthorne advocates, his own subsequent 'long affliction' may be prefigured here. Earlier he was outgoing enough to send up a 6ft air balloon from the Castle which traveled as far as Purleigh near Maldon (*IpsJ* 3 and 10 January 1783).

He was a violin player as well as an artist, and was part of the musical circle who met under the aegis of wealthy lawyer

D

George Wegg 2 (qv) at East Hill House. As such he came to the notice of the Rector of All Saints, Dr Nathaniel Forster (qv) and Revd Thomas Twining (qv) of St Mary-at-the-Walls. Both these were well-connected scholars and Twining was himself an amateur musician of some ability. Each of them made separate applications to their contacts to find some better opportunity for Dunthorne, who was unable to make a successful career in Colchester.

On 1 March 1782 (BL Add Mss 11277), Dr Nathaniel Forster (qv) wrote to his cousin Peter Forster, Rector of Hedenham, Norfolk, to describe how for Dunthorne's benefit 10 concerts had been arranged with 30 subscribers at half-a-guinea. 'Two acts in each concert, five pieces in each ancient and modern. The performers are Twining, Hankey, Jones, Smith and Brockwell, divines, with young Dunthorne and 5 others. Vast collection of music. Twining always enchanting. All Jones' young men are subscribers.' Jones was Revd William Jones (qv), perpetual curate of Nayland (from 1776) and another musical enthusiast and author. In 1784 Dunthorne subscribed to Jones' *Art of Music* (published in Colchester by William Keymer (qv)) and may have engraved the scores.

Also in 1784, on 12 November, Twining wrote to a famous friend, the musicologist Charles Burney (see *ODNB*), asking for his aid:

> I want your opinion and advice about a young man of this place who is interesting to me. He is a painter, a sensible, modest, quiet man – I won't say he has a genius for his profession; that is a word that is not to be prodigally bestowed: but has talents; seems (so far as I am able to judge) to draw correctly, and has really considerable ingenuity in the invention of subjects of the ludicrous kind, some of which were in the two last years' (Royal Academy) exhibitions. ... He is a married man; his wife is a milliner, but her business has not answered, and his cannot in such a place as this; he has a few scholars, sells prints, and now and then paints a Portrait: but all this is scarcely bread and cheese, and

moreover he is here out of the way of improvement. He wishes much to be *établi* in London if he cou'd get employment there as a drawing Master ... if it should perchance be in your power to suggest anything, you will give me great pleasure. At the same time, I am aware of difficulties: I know (at least I am told so) that London is overstocked with artists and ingenious men who want employment.

Twining continues that he would be personally sorry if Dunthorne left Colchester.

He has true Musical feelings, and relishes Em. Bach, Haydn &:c., tho' as a fiddler he is shambling and incorrect. He loves humour, and has that modest quietness, and unpushingness (a pretty vocable!) about him, that never did anything but harm to its possessors since the world stood (Walker (ed), *Thomas Twining*, Letter 89 to Burney 12 November 1784:265-6; Letter 90 30 December 1784:268 sends 'Thanks as to the Painter &c'.)

There were, however potentially other opinions as to Dunthorne's character. Benjamin Strutt (qv), himself an artist, antiquarian and later Borough Chamberlain (JBB, *EAE*:143-61) writing of a circle of young, artistic and literary contemporaries in Colchester in the late 1770s was jocularly unflattering about several friends including Dunthorne who he characterized as 'a Mimic' and 'faithless and insincere.'

H. D. Bland, whose rather malicious *Anecdotes* of that era survive in manuscript is even more damning:-

James Dunthorne, limner and musician, was on excellent terms with himself. He was insufferably vain and self-conceited. He was playing at a concert where he thought himself the first fiddle, and honest Joe Manning ... (apparently the only professional musician in the group) ... was stationed at the same music stand, which gave great umbrage to Dunthorne, and he contemptuously desired Joe to stand farther off, at the same time saying that men of his talent could not well brook the

D

encroachment of their inferiors. Joe felt nettled at the observation, and retorted aloud 'you an artist, Jim?' A pretty artist surely as, clever a fellow as you think yourself, you are not artist enough to --- without ----ing' which raised a laugh at Dunthorne's expense (Appendix 3, *Bland's Anecdotes*: 83-4).

Bland always framed his anecdotes to make the better story and was not likely to have been a direct witness. He was most likely retailing a story heard second or third hand or fitting the crude joke to a plausible candidate. What the story suggests, perhaps, is that what Twining read as 'unpushingness' might also be perceived as a certain over preciousness.

Dunthorne was clearly ailing in the 1790s, and a further benefit concert was held for him on 30 July 1793, his wife publishing her gratitude to supporters after the event. His Drawings, Prints, Music etc. were sold on 16 August 1794 (*IpsJ*) so the family's financial difficulties seem to have been acute. He succumbed to a 'long affliction' soon after and was buried at St Nicholas on 11 October 1794. His widow, carrying on in business. She is listed as a perfumer in the High Street in Holden's *Directory* of 1805. Elizabeth died on 10 March 1807 (*IpsJ* 21 March 1807).

James Dunthorne 2 adopted a different artistic persona than did his father, James Dunthorne 1, who painted coaches as well as portraits and took work engraving maps and surveys. Thomas Twining's assessment seems accurate. As a 'limner' of talent if not of genius, Dunthorne found it difficult to make his way without breaking into the London market. Whether or not Dunthorne amounted to a 'Colchester Hogarth' his history exemplifies not only the opportunities but also the vicissitudes of the career of a minor artist in a Georgian provincial town. His artistic legacy, if nothing else, provides the historian with rare visualisations of the polite society of eighteenth-century Colchester.

Adapted with additions from D'Cruze, *Pleasing Prospect*:122-6 and JBB, *EAE*:109-11.

See also W. Gurney Benham, 'The Dunthornes of Colchester, *Essex Review*, 10 (1901), 27-35 and 116, which also specifies that the two John Dunthornes of Dedham are different people; *ODNB*, entry for John Dunthorne, snr and jun refers to James Dunthorne junior as 'the Colchester Hogarth'; For the musical circle at East Hill house and Dunthorne's *Musical Entertainment*, see Peter Holman, 'The Colchester Part Books', *Early Music*, November 2000:577-595, also here, George Wegg 2 (qv); house numbers *ex inf* Bruce Neville.

DUNTHORNE REVD JOHN [272]
Baptist Minister
fl. 1733

Minister at Eld Lane Baptist chapel until his death in 1756 (4 April). Had previously been the minister at a baptist congregation at East Bay (St James) which had separated from the Eld Lane chapel in 1721 (Spurrier, *Eld Lane*).

Published *Hymns, or, Spiritual Songs, composed on Several Subjects for the Benefit of the Godly. To which is added A Hymn from the Chamber to the Grave: At the Request of his Friend S____ B____, The Third Addition* (sic) *with Additions*, published in Colchester, printed for the author by John Pilborough. 6º, 1733, 47 pp.

DUNTHORNE RICHARD [273]
Attorney
fl. 1765-c.1845

The son of James Dunthorne 1 (qv) and Elizabeth *née* Hubbard and hence brother to the caricaturist (James Dunthorne 2 (qv)). Was baptised at Lion Walk in 1765. He was trained by William Mason 2 (qv) and signed his first will with Mason and his clerk Thomas Beswick in 1778. Crabb Robinson (qv) found him 'a poor creature who tried in vain to be something' (JBB Notes on Crabb Robinson, *Material Reminiscences in Old Age*, ms in Dr Williams Library, JBB NB May 69:108ff). Dunthorne continued in Colchester and retired to one of the Winsleys Charity

D

Houses (no. 18) on 19 March 1832, where he remained until 1845.

DUPRÉ Mr [275]
Dancing Master
fl. 1761-67

Taught in north east Essex in the 1760s (*IpsJ* 1 August 1761).

> Dedham 22nd July, 1761
>
> MR DUPRÉ nephew and Pupil of Mr LABBÉ, late Dancing Master to the Court, begs leave to inform the Publick that he has met with great Encouragement at Several Places in the County of Essex viz at Colchester, Witham, Tolleshunt D'Arcy, and other places, and is at present Dancing Master of Dedham and Felstead Schools; he has likewise lately opened a school at Bocking, Braintree; where, and in all other places, he shall make it his study to recommend himself to the favours of those who are so kind as to employ him in his Profession.

See also *IpsJ* 17 January 1761.

He had died by 1767 (*IpsJ* 6 June 1767) when his widow sold his 'Instruments and Books of Music' at her house in Kelvedon.

DURRELL ROBERT [997]
Brandy Merchant
fl. 1750

Advertised from the bottom of Queen Street near Botolphs Gate in 1750 (*IpsJ* 8 September 1750).

DYE THOMAS [276]
Scrivener
fl. 1747-76

Clerk to Samuel Wall 1 (qv). He signed 19 wills between 1747 and 1775, 11 together with Wall. After Wall was declared insane

D

he also worked with Thomas Bayles (qv) and William Suddell (qv). His own will (NA PROB 11/1021 23 July 1776, scrivener of St Marys) witnessed by Wall and his son was made on 21 December 1768 and proved on 23 July 1776. It left all his estate to his loving wife Ann who was named as sole executrix. Her will is at NA PROB 11/1072 23 January 1781.

DYER BENJAMIN [278]
Clothier
fl. 1734-52

One of the first Winsleys Trustees and a trustee and supporter of Lion Walk meeting (20 November 1726, ERO D/NC 52/5/1, 10), though according to Blaxill's sources (Blaxill, *Lion Walk*) he himself was an anglican. His sister married Arthur Winsley (qv) baymaker and benefactor, and his daughter Mary married Revd John Collins (qv) of Lion Walk (their daughter Hannah later married Robert Tabor (qv)).

Dyer was admitted free burgess in 1694 and voted Whig until 1747. His will made in 1744, proved 1752 (NA PROB 11/11794, 28 May 1752) leaves all his real and personal estate to his wife Rebecca for life (*née* Coveney. They married at Berechurch in 1704 in ML index, ERO, but without reference number) then to his two daughters Mary Collins and Hannah Dyer (spr), the executrixes. Shortly after his death some of his tenements on the north side of Magdalene Street St Botolphs together with another part brick tenement in Duck Lane were offered for sale (*IpsJ* 15 August 1752).

See also NA PROB 11/736, 8 December 1744, will of William Dyer, gent, Colchester.

DYER REVD MR [277]
Clergy
fl. 1767

IpsJ 12 December 1767 records an auction by Henry Lodge (qv) of various properties including a dwelling and malting office in the pleasantest part of St Leonard, now occupied by Revd

D

Mr Dyer. It is typical of the auctioneer to emphasise that the rector's dwelling was in the 'pleasantest part' of what was probably Colchester's most industrial parish.

E

EARDLEY JOHN [279]
Surgeon and Apothecary
fl. 1764-1787

J. Eardley of St Nicholas, Colchester, surgeon aged 30 married Sarah Cock aged 23 in 1764 (CPL Crisp ML469, ERO D/ACL 1764). From at least 1769 they lived in All Saints parish at the house now (c. 1985) Markhams.

Bland (Appendix 3, below) records that;

> Mr Ardley, an apothecary and surgeon, lived near the Sea Horse, used to drink every day 5 or 6 glasses (small) of Hollands and water.

In 1783 he billed All Saints Vestry £10 for medical attendance.

On 26 April 1787, 'died Mr Eardley, surgeon and apothecary in Colchester' (*IpsJ* 28 April 1787). The *Chelmsford Chronicle* (4 May 1787) adds that on the Sunday following his son died, a youth aged about 17 'after a lingering illness.' Eardley's effects, including 3,000 red bricks were advertised on 18 May 1787 (*ChCh*) and his furniture etc. on 26 May 1787 (*IpsJ*). His wife Sarah was regularly relieved by the Essex & Hertfordshire Medical Benevolent Society, their first petitioner (JBB Note nfr).

EDGAR CAPTAIN [280]
fl. 1779

IpsJ 5 June 1779: Furniture for sale at late dwelling house of Captain Edgar, on East Hill by Henry Lodge (qv).

See also: NA PROB 11/1048, Hay 26, 2 December 1778, will of Robert Edgar Esq, Ipswich.

E

EDWARDS JOHN [282]
Surgeon
fl. 1736-1756

Had an extensive and scholarly library which was sold off after his death. On 3 December 1757 (*IpsJ*) Timothy Taft, bookseller of Chelmsford advertised 1,000 volumes in Greek, Latin, French, Italian and Spanish etc. which included Edwards' collection. He had died the previous winter and his will (ERO D/ACR 16/107 proved 3 December 1756) left the bulk of his estate to his wife, Sarah except for small cash legacies to Revd Mr Henry Chambers, vicar of Colne, Mr Joseph Jekyll of Russell St, Covent Garden and three others. He desired to be buried in the parish church of Kirby with a marble stone laid over the grave bearing his name and age.

Had been established as a surgeon in Colchester from at least 1736 when he stood bond for the marriage of John Blatch, grocer (qv) (CPL Crisp ML480). His premises were at the top of North Hill (JBB note, nfr). His wife was Sarah Blatch. They married 26 October 1736. Her sister Elizabeth married William Smythies 3 (qv) surgeon and in 1770 left her nephew James (qv) £2,000 if he changed his name to Blatch (cf James Blatch (qv)).

See also the will of John Blatch, merchant, Colchester NA PROB 11/728, Boycott, proved 25 August 1743.

EISDELL THOMAS [283]
Baptist Minister, Colchester
fl. 1758-1772

His will (ERO D/ABR 26/283, 1772) gives his residence as Holy Trinity parish. It names his three sons, Thomas, Joseph and Richard and daughter Elizabeth, all minors. The executors were his brother-in-law Jesse Ward, Gt. Wigborough and friend Mr William Munsey (qv), Colchester, Grocer and Linnen Draper.

The will was made on 1 August 1771 (witnessed Martha King, Isaac Diss (qv)) and proved on 6 September 1772.

E

See also Spurrier, *Eld Lane*.

ELDRED JOHN [284]
Gent
fl. 1782

Of an old Suffolk family which came to Colchester in the seventeenth century (JBB note, nfr). His house, 'Olivers' at Stanway was advertised to let, late John Eldred Esq, brick'd and sash'd, wainscotted dining room 30 x 20 (21 September 1782 *IpsJ*).

See also will of Dulcibella Eldred, ERO D/ABR 21/375, 1736; will of Mary Eldred, ERO D/ABR 21/185, St Marys, spinster, 1736.

ELLINGTON LEONARD [285]
Bayfactor
fl. 1766

The Borough Servants and Apprentices Book (ERO D/B 5 Ta1) records Leonard Ellington the younger apprenticed to his father, Ellington senior of Old Broad Street, without fee on 20 November 1766. The Ellingtons were London residents but free burgesses of Colchester Borough.

JBB note, nfr - Gave the Mayor's chain.

ELLIOTT Adm GEORGE [286]
Gent
w. 1795

Had a house in Trinity St and another in Copford.

IpsJ 10 September 1796: Admiral Elliott's furniture in Copford was for sale, including very fine coaches etc. and 40 dozen bottles of Champagne. His will (NA PROB 11/1267, Newcastle 630) was made on 31 December 1790 when he was resident at Copford (witnessed Robert Yates (qv), Samuel Ennew (qv), Thomas Beswick (qv)) and proved 10 November 1795 by

Thomasine Ann Elliott spr. It leaves mansion house Copford and properties in West Ham, 'Greyes' and Birchington in Kent (both part of his wife's marriage settlement) and also in Barbados.

Amongst those mentioned are his friend John Graves Simcol, Governor of N. Canada, sister Catherine Hayward wid., sons John Elliott, Luther Graves Elliott, daughter Thomasine Ann and wife Susan. No mention of why the family are all buried in Holy Trinity, where the monument survives.

ELLIS THOMAS [1100]
Exciseman
fl. 1739-1784

Was 22, an exciseman of Dedham when he married Susannah Mixer (21) also of Dedham in 1739 (bound together with Charles King, hatter of Dedham, CPL Crisp ML 457).

John Wall (qv), in his will of 1781 (proved 1783) expressly forbade his nephew Samuel Wall 2 (qv) to marry or cohabit with any daughter of Thomas Ellis.

Ellis also acted as 'distributor' for the servants tax in 1784, Mary Rebow's accounts note a payment to him for £5 10s 5d for five menservants (ERO C47, Rebow Box 3, JBB NB Dec 65: 44).

ENNEW SAMUEL [287]
Attorney and Clerk of the Peace for Essex
1717-1795

Ennew was born in 1717, the son of Thomas Ennew, clothier of Colchester (Thomas' will NA PROB 11/693, 11 December 1738). In 1733 he was apprenticed for 7 years to Samuel Carter, jun. attorney of Great Coggeshall for the large fee of £55 (NA IR 1/13/195). Carter was then a fairly young man having himself been apprenticed to Thomas Mayhew of Colchester (see William Mayhew 1 (qv)) in 1710 for £100 (NA IR 1/41/28, the son of Mary Carter, Braintree widow). From the time he emerged from his apprenticeship (1740) until 1784, Ennew was steward to the Rebow family, especially Isaac Martin Rebow (qv) (MP for Colchester 1755-81 and Recorder from 1763). Ennew was appointed Deputy Clerk of the Peace for the County on 2 October 1759 and on 2 October 1770 was promoted to be Clerk of the Peace. The records were carefully kept during his term of office. In 1768 he had negotiated the Gaol Act by which the new county gaol was built at Moulsham, Chelmsford (by William Hillyer, county surveyor, and William Staines, contractor and later Lord Mayor of London).

Ennew was a Whig free burgess who voted from 1741 at least. He was no radical, however, and was a supporter of the Rebow/Gray compromise in the 1760s to 1780s. He had been appointed Town Clerk 1763 (31 October) by Rebow. In 1764 (Ass Bk 1 September 1764) he was elected an Alderman of the Corporation, avoiding the intermediate stages of Common Councillor and Assistant. He was elected Mayor on 29 September 1767 and then gave up the Town Clerk's job to his late apprentice Frank Smythies 1 (qv).

Ennew's position as Clerk of the Peace led him to play an important and clearly profitable role as a political agent within the county (Namier and Brooke, *The House of Commons*). He had a regular correspondence with Lord Hardwicke (BL Add Ms 36,349-36,278; JBB NB 73/1). He clearly expected to be able to leave his interest in the Borough in the safe hands of his protégé, Smythies. On the occasion of the 1772 food riot, for example, during which Ennew was in Bath, it was Smythies who answered Lord Rochford's letter enquiring into the situation. Smythies, however, was too ambitious to simply remain as Ennew's shadow and was able to generate his own Tory interest in the Borough after the ending of the Compromise. From the mid 1780s Ennew largely withdrew (in high dudgeon, it seems) from the arena of Borough politics. In the period of disarray following the 1781 election, and the subsequent petitioning, Ennew was among seven prominent Whig members of the Corporation who tendered their

E

resignations, though these were not accepted (Assembly Book, 29 August 1782).

When the Whig MP, Sir Robert Smyth (qv) refused the Mayoralty in late 1784, Ennew was called upon and served a second term as Mayor during 1785. This year saw the agitation of the party around Smythies in the petitioning following the two 1784 elections and the mass elevation of Smythies' supporters to the Alderman's bench. After this fracas of October 1785 Ennew ceased attendance at Borough Assemblies, returning only once in 1787 to see Smythies again triumph at the Recordership election. Ennew, however, retained his seat on the Alderman's bench until 1792 (resigned 20 October 1792, Assembly Book). Ennew expressed poor opinions of Smythies in letters to Lord Hardwicke and seems finally to have considered Borough politics not worthy of his attention. He did not vote in the Borough after 1784.

Ennew lived at the corner of Head Street and Sir Isaacs Walk in the house built as the Rebow's town house before the family moved to the estate at Wivenhoe Park. The property was rented from the Rebows and rated at 14 (St. Mary's rates, 1787).

The relative political calm of the Compromise period had made Ennew a leading figure in Borough affairs through his connection with Isaac Martin Rebow. Ennew's family connections also formed part of his local interest. On 17 June 1760 he became godfather to Isaac Samuel Clamtree (qv) (bapt. Holy Trinity 13 February 1760) the son of Thomas Clamtree (qv) who was later named as the first (Whig) Mayor on the new Corporation of 1763. Clamtree, jun. was later also to become an attorney with connections to another of Ennew's associates, William Bullock (qv). Bullock later succeeded Ennew as Clerk of the Peace on 5 April 1785.

In 1771 Ennew was named as trustee with Richard Rigby (qv) to his brother-in-law's estate. Isaac Bevan had been Rigby's Steward. Ennew's first wife, Sarah, was the daughter of Henry Bevan (qv) of Lexden. She died on 18 June 1766. The following year Ennew was left £100 by Henry Ennew Bevan, her nephew. (NA PROB 11/1029, 29 March 1777, of Lexden. This was the will which, according to *Bland's Anecdotes* (Appendix 3), Smythies was caught out trying to alter to his benefit). Ennew was also witness to the will of Charles Gray (qv) made on 20 February 1781 (proved 1782).

In May 1784 (*IpsJ* 8 May 1784, 'in London') Ennew married Mrs Ann Parker, the daughter of John Vernon Esq of Southampton Buildings (another connection in the legal profession). He finally died on 14 December 1795 aged 78, and was buried with his first wife in Lexden churchyard.

His will made on 14 December 1795 (NA PROB 11/1268, Newcastle 683, 31 December 1795), left his 'now dear wife Ann' £300 per annum being the interest on £10,000 in the funds for life, thereafter to her three sisters. A property was left to her brother, John Vernon. Other north Essex properties were left to William Bullock (qv), Isaac Samuel Clamtree (qv) and William Mason (qv), 'having no relations of my own but such as are very remote and with whom I have little or no connection....' A further £500 in cash legacies went to friends and distant relatives including £40 to his clerk, Thomas Beswick (qv), £10 to George Salmon (qv), carpenter, and £200 to Mrs Elizabeth Harvey, the widow of his late old and much respected friend Daniel Harvey (qv). His wife Ann was residuary legatee and her brother John Vernon, with William Bullock, were executors.

See also Robert Mayhew apprenticed to Samuel Ennew £30, 1748 (NA IR 1/15/70); Thomas Younge apprenticed to Samuel Ennew, 12 April 1772, no fee, scrivener (Borough Servants and Apprentices Book, ERO D/B 5 Ta1); *IpsJ* 17 December 1791 on the occasion of an anonymous letter to Mrs Rebow giving information of a plan to rob her house that winter. Mrs Rebow advertised a £30 reward for further information. Apply her or Mr Ennew.

ENNIFER JOHN [288]
Innkeeper, Golden Lion St Peter
fl. 1754

Ennifer advertised on 21 December 1754 (*IpsJ*):-

E

This is to Aquaint all Gentlemen and others, That JOHN ENNIFER, Huntsman to the Subscription Pack of Hounds belonging to the Town of Colchester in the county of Essex, has recently taken the GOLDEN LYON INN in the High Street of Colchester aforesaid where all who please to favour him with their custom, shall meet with such Accommodations as become a creditable Inn, and their Favours gratefully acknowledged by their obedient humble servant, JOHN ENNIFER.

ESSEX JOHN [291]
Gardener
fl. 1799-1812

Son and main heir of Thomas Essex (qv). Inherited his father's lands and business which he continued until he died in 1812 (25 April 1812, registers St James). His estates were then sold (*Ips]* 27 June 1812).

Ref: ERO D/DC 33/21, 27 June 1803, Essex under notice to quit Chapel Lands, cf Thomas Essex (qv).

ESSEX THOMAS [290]
Gardener
w. 1796/9

Ran an extensive business with a large amount of garden ground both near Priory Street, St Botolphs and on St Ann's Chapel lands. Essex owned the Priory Street ground and rented the Chapel Lands together with the chapel and yard (situated between the Ipswich and Harwich roads) on a 21 year lease from 13 February 1782 at £10 p.a. (ERO D/DC 33/21, 27 June 1803, John Essex (qv) under notice to quit on expiry of lease).

Essex is recorded in John Inman's diary of 2 March 1770 (J. B. Harvey Scrap Book, Colchester Public Library) as planting the cherry trees in Childwell field (St Botolphs). In 1795 he advertised seeds at 2s 6d per packet of the new and valuable

'American Sprout... which may be had in great perfection from December till March' and is 'equal to flavour to asparagus' (*Ips*] 14 February 1795).

Essex died in 1799 aged 83. His tombstone in St James, shared with Ann his wife, is decorated with reliefs of a rose, an auricula and a pineapple plant. His detailed will of 1796/9 (NA PROB 11/1324, 6 May 1799) gives an extensive listing of his real estate including his house and garden ground in St James and St Giles, two tenements in Magdalen Street. These are left to his son John (qv), main beneficiary and residuary legatee, subject to payment of £1,000 to son George Essex (with interest at 5% p.a.). The leasehold land, gardening stock, plants, tools etc. were also left to John. A grandson, Joseph Essex (son of Thomas Essex deceased) received the interest on £250. Executors were son William and grandson also William, both curriers of London who received 5 gns each for mourning, being 'already well provided for.'

See also will of George Essex, gardener, Colchester NA PROB 11/1639, 3 February 1821.

EVANS REVD TRISTRAM [292]
Rector, Beaumont-cum-Moze
fl. 1723-1777

Became Rector of Beaumont-cum-Moze on 11 June 1723 (Morant, *Essex*, Vol 1:487).

Evans made a second marriage to Penelope Gardiner of Braintree on 13 December 1766. He is the recipient of the builders note book, now deposited in ERO D/Dre.Z.27 (which he 'borrowed in 60s when Samuel Frost (qv) was building cottages &c on Guy's Hospital land' at Beaumont. JBB Note).

His will was made in 1776. (ERO D/ACR 13/ 18, 1777):-

> In the Name of God Amen, I Tristram Evans, Rector of Beaumont with Mose having lost or mislay'd my last will and Testament do declare them null and void, and do make this present will to prevent mistakes. 1st if my son Kirkham be living I bequeath him Thirty pounds as

before also dividable among his Children if he left any. Also I give ... (the rest of my estate) ... to my daughter-in-law Ann with this Condition that she shall distribute among her Children at proper ages some small portion according to her discretion and ability. And do hereby make her the sole Executrix of this my last Will and testament. In Witness whereof I have hereunto set my hand and seal this 23rd day of April 1776.

Tristram Evans.

P.S. Let Miss Ingram have my watch for I was only Tenant for life of it.

Witnessed: Robert Canham, Thos. Woodthorpe, Francis Bowling. Proved 18 October 1777 by Ann Evans, widow and daughter-in-law.

He was buried at St James Colchester.

EVATT ROBERT [293]
Surgeon
c.1709-1755

Was a surgeon of Dedham in his late twenties when he married Sarah Grimwood (21) in 1737 (CPL Crisp ML473, ERO D/ALL 1737 bound by Thomas Goodall of Abberton, gent). He moved to Colchester within two years and stood bond for the marriage of Henry Evatt, surgeon of Dedham to Sarah Warren, Little Bentley (CPL Crisp ML45, 1739, both 21, marriage to take place at Elmstead or St James Colchester).

Robert Evatt died in 1755. He merited a lengthy and glowing obituary in the *Ipswich Journal* from Robert Sterling (qv) his assistant of nine years and successor, who would refer to him as 'Uncle' (JBB note, nfr).

To the PUBLISHERS of the IPSWICH JOURNAL

SIR,

October 2, 1755

If you are as much a Friend to Virtue as I believe you to be, you will not refuse inserting the following; it is drawn up in Haste, and incorrect, but it comes from the Heart. I am, yours &c.

But all our Praises who should Lords engross?
Rise, honest Muse, and sing the Man of Ross
POPE

Yesterday died at Colchester, Mr Robert Evat, Surgeon and Man Midwife. He had strong natural Sense, and great Sagacity and Judgement, which, with much Experience, render'd him eminently successful in his Practice, and equal to any thing he undertook. He never caluminated, nor lessed'd (sic) others; but acquired an high Reputation by his Assiduity and Readiness to attend upon his Patients, for whose Relief he was ready to go at any Hour, and neglected his own Health to a blameable Degree. In some extraordinary Cases, when he had been call'd, and the Friends of the Patients, diffident of the Abilities of a Country Surgeon, had sent for the Top of the Profession from London; the Methods he had used were so approv'd of that the perfecting the Cures was left entirely to him, and he gain'd Esteem of those who were sent for; which a short Acquaintance with his many amiable Qualities soon heighten'd into a sincere and lasting Friendship. Ever ready to attend the Poor as well as the Rich, and assist them with his Purse as well as Medicines; He possessed that natural Politeness which flows from good Sense and a benevolent Soul; and was belov'd of all Parties, because a Friend to the Good and to the Distressed of all. No Man could take more Delight, or was more indefatiguable in doing Good. When he had conferr'd a great Obligation, his Behaviour was always as respectfully kind to the Persons he had oblig'd, as if they had been his Benefactors. The Business he was in, gave him more Opportunity of doing Good, that with a much larger Fortune he could otherwise have done; and he lost none of them. He was a most affectionate Husband and

E

Parent; and tho' he so bountifully scatter'd, by the Blessing of Providence, he still encreased, and left a handsome Provision to his Family. - When thus he liv'd, need it be added, that he died lamented?' (*IpsJ* 11 October 1755.)

See also: Free School Registers (ERO T/B 217/1), Henry son of Henry Evatt of Hartest Suffolk, ob., admitted 16 June 1729 age 11; will of Henry Evatt, surgeon of Manningtree, 1748, ERO D/ACR 15/269.

EYRE JOSEPH [297]
Musician and Composer
ob. 1789

Composer of *Eight Sonatas in Three Parts*, c.1765. This publication had 469 subscribers, including many prominent Colchester people.

IpsJ 30 May 1789 advertised all the household furniture and effects of Mr Joseph Eyre deceased, at his late dwelling house in East Bergholt (the house near the church) including a fine toned harpsichord, bass viol and other musical instruments. Particulars were obtainable from Mr William Eyre or Richard Everitt, both of Hadleigh. (Everitt was the auctioneer). The sale took place on 17 June and the two following days.

Eyre's will is at NA PROB 11/1178/196 made 8 November 1780, proved 7 April 1789.

F

FALYARD WILLIAM [1300]
Gent
w. 1784

His will, gentleman of Colchester, Essex, is at NA PROB 11/1114, proved 4 March 1784.

FANE RODNEY [1275]
Counsellor at law
ob. 1733

Not fully researched. Lived in All Saints (Arthur Weddell, 'All Saints Colchester', *Trans EAS,* Vol. 12, pt. 4, (1912):335). A Suffolk County voter through ownership of property in Ipswich (Poll Book 1727). Married Mrs Hannah Moor, All Saints 1 May 1727. Deceased 2 October 1733 'in commission of the peace for Middlesex,' worth £25,000 (*Gents. Mag.* (1733): 550).

FARRAN JOSEPH [298]
Gardener
d. 1791

IpsJ 20 August 1791, reported Farran's death from drowning having been seized by cramp whilst bathing in the river. He left a wife and five children.

FAUNCE COLONEL [299]
fl. 1815

> Most Desirable
> FREEHOLD ESTATES
> EAST HILL, COLCHESTER

F

To be sold by AUCTION
by W. JACKSON
on Monday, the 6th March, 1815
At the WHITE HART INN, Colchester
At Three O'Clock in the Afternoon

IN THREE LOTS

LOT 1: A comfortable MANSION, pleasantly situated in East Hill, now in the occupation of Col. Faunce, and consists of 3 good parlours, 4 bed chambers, fitted up with closets and fire places, 2 dressing rooms, 3 servants bedrooms, and a large lumber room, an excellent cellar, butlers pantry, large kitchen, wash house, scullery, and coalhouse, with a stone yard, flower garden, good kitchen garden, and drying ground, with pumps of hard and soft water. The whole in good repair, and early possession may be had.

LOT 2: A good Dwelling house and a Front Shop, now in the occupation of Mr Hunniball, coachmaker, under a lease which expires at Christmas 1819, and adjoins to Lot 1, Consisting of a good residence for a family with a shop in front, and a spacious room to show carriages for sale; a large workshop above, and every convenience attached for carrying on the coachmaking or any branch of trade.

LOT 3: Three stables and a coachhouse contiguous to Lot 1, being situated down Land Lane, East Hill, were adapted for the standing of 7 horses and a carriage with good lofts over, and a paved receptacle for muck.

Further particulars and conditions of sale may be had of Peter Firmin Esq Dedham, and of the auctioneers, Colchester. (18 and 25 February 1815, *IpsJ*).

FENNING JOHN 1 [301]
Gent
fl. 1806

(*IpsJ* 20 September 1806): Substantial Brick dwelling recently built of Mr John Fenning in the Lexden Road, parish St Mary's (ob.); 2 parlours, 2 kitchens, brew house, cellar &c. Apply Mr A. F. Miller (Alexander Fordyce Miller (qv)) and Mr Daniel Fenning.

An earlier advertisement of 15 March 1806 (*IpsJ*) offered the property for auction at Kings Arms and added the house had 56 ft front, recently built.

FENNING JOHN 2 [1301]
Blacksmith
w. 1736

His will is at ERO D/ACR 14/ 476, 1736, leaving all to his wife Mary.

FENNING JOHN 3 [302]
Coachsmith
fl. 1783-90

Occupied a tenement behind St Runwald in the High Street in 1783 rated 2 for the dwelling house and 3 for the shop. John Mannall (qv) was at this address September 1788 (JBB NB Blue 2:80, parish rates D/P 178/11/2-3). In 1790 (*IpsJ* 3 April 1790) Fenning advertised from near the Horse and Groom in St Marys offering 'axel trees etc.' compare John Fenning 2, Blacksmith.

FENNING SAMUEL [1002]
Butcher
bkt. 1798

His bankruptcy was notified in 1798 (*Eur. Mag.*, 24 July 1798).

F

FENNO JOHN [1015]
Stationer, Printer, Bookseller
fl. 1777-1790

Married Hannah Shearcroft, widow, in 1777 (CPL Crisp ML52, ERO D/ACL 1777). Advertised from premises in the Fishmarket, selling a printed sermon by Revd Storry (qv) of St Peters (*ChCh* 21 December 1782) and also that year selling theatre tickets (*IpsJ* 1782, JBB Bird 3:29, nfr). He moved to a shop opposite the Red Lion in 1784 (*IpsJ* 7 August 1784) and the same year (*IpsJ* 1 November 1784) printed V. L. Bernard's (qv) second sermon to the Ipswich Freemasons (Bernard was Rector of Frinton). In 1786 he was agent for the auction of a brick-fronted dwelling, together with Timothy Walford 1 (qv) (*IpsJ* 2 September 1786) and placed a general advertisement for printing and book-binding later that year (*IpsJ* 11 November 1786, Feb 72:5, JBB note, A.B. Doncaster, Castle Bookshop c. 1980 has had bindings marked 'J. Fenno' on spine). In 1789 advertised the publication of the first ten numbers, 3p each *The History & Antiquities of Colchester selected from the most approved authors* (*frontis.* by Wm. Betts, engraved J. Reading) (*IpsJ* 14 February 1789). This publication attracted around 200 subscribers, all from Colchester or neighbourhood.

Fenno was rated 12 in St Nicholas opposite the George (56 High St) between 1788 and 1796. Advertising from these premises in 1790, he announced he had opened a shop in Bocking. He had recently published Martin Carter's *A True Relation of the Siege of Colchester*. This volume had about 160 subscribers, all Colchester save for 33 in the neighbourhood (first edition published by John Pilborough (qv)). He also operated a circulating Library in Bocking (*ChCh* 26 February 1790). Later in 1790 he advertised on behalf of the owner of a 'paroquat or small parrot' which had escaped from a servant's arm (*IpsJ* 22 October 1790).

See also ERO ML D/ALL 1815, John Fenno Shearcroft, printer of Bocking, to Rebecca Bateman; Pigott's *Directory*, 1832, includes Thomas Shearcroft, Bank St Braintree, Bookseller, Stationer, Printer and Binder; will John Fenno, St Stephen,

Coleman Street, City of London, NA PROB 11/1342, Adderley, proved 12 May 1800.

FENWICK ROGER [303]
Mariner
fl. 1737-1747

Was appointed mate of the *Wivenhoe* smack in Colchester port on 7 February 1737/8 (NA Calendar of Treasury Books & Papers 1737/8:625, JBB NB 84/1:11). He died in 1747 leaving all his goods to his wife under the supervision of his Captain, Robert Martin (qv), and after her death to his daughter Mary Rust. ERO D/ACR 15/256, mariner East Donyland. See also will of Sarah Fenwick, Wivenhoe, 1756, ERO D/ACR 16/97.

FIELD JOHN 1 [304]
Gunsmith
fl. 1784

> GUNSMITHS WORK. Performed in all its various Branches by JOHN FIELD, who hath taken the shop, late William Lawrences' snr (qv) at the Bottom of Gutter Street; where Gentlemen may be assured of having their commands duly executed, as well and as expeditious as in London; therefore hopes, by his assiduity and due attention to merit their favours (*IpsJ* 24 April 1784).

FIELD JOHN 2 [305]
Weaver
fl. 1791

Convicted and fined £20 together with Fudgell Cook (qv) for receiving embezzled ends and wastes from wool workers.

F

FIRMIN JOHN [306]
Surgeon
fl. 1676

Took oath of succession 15 November 1676. Surgeon of Colchester (ERO D/B 5 R1, Borough Oath Book).

FISIN JAMES [309]
Musician
1750-1847

See full article in JBB, *EAE*:207-220.

FISKE JOHN [310]
Surgeon and Apothecary
fl. 1763-1773

Ips] 27 August 1768 was advertised:

> A Freehold Messuage or Dwelling House, with Kitchen, Brewhouse, Pump and large Stable to the same belonging, situate in the parish of ALL SAINTS in Colchester in the occupation of John Fiske. surgeon and apothecary. Enquire Thomas Daniel, attorney (qv).
>
> N.B. There is a Back-way or Passage for Chaises and Horses to and from the Stable.

This was no. 73 High Street next Thomas Boggis (qv) (Minories) and Boggis then bought the property (from the wife of a Head Street gunsmith) which he required in order to complete extensions and alterations to his own house. Fiske moved to 28 High St. Both Fiske and Boggis were members of Colchester Corporation. Fiske was Chamberlain of Colchester 1763-1772 and had been named Assistant in the 1763 Charter, voting for Rebow and Gray in 1768 (cf. Robert Fiske voting Whig in 1741). He was elected Alderman on 20 August 1771 in opposition to his neighbour, Boggis. Fiske received 55 votes to Boggis' 10. Boggis came last of 4 candidates, and though later twice serving as Mayor there are signs he was unpopular at this time.

Fiske moved in 1772 to the 'old accustomed Apothecary's shop' (cf Jordan Lisle (qv) who had the shop from at least 1748) at 28 High Street, St Runwald (Rated 20, Lisle occ., in 1770, Widow Fiske in 1775 and Robert Harris in 1780).

John Fiske also diversified into inoculation. In partnership with (Cater?) Day he took over John Franklyn's (qv) inoculating house at Mile End in 1767 (*IpsJ* 27 June 1767). On 28 March 1771 (*IpsJ*) he advertised inoculations in a house pleasantly situated, charging 2-3 gns. On 20 March 1773 he claimed to have inoculated 99 persons that year with no ill effects and good pustules. (14 of Ardleigh, 11 Berechurch, 19 Langham etc., only 6 of Colchester.)

He married Mary Agnis the daughter of Robert Agnis gardener (qv). He took two apprentices, John Alefounder for £45 in 1767 (JBB NB Aug 69, nfr) and William Frost (qv) later of Kelvedon for £20 in 1763 (NA IR 1/54/178).

He died on 26 September 1773 (*IpsJ* 2 October 1773) 'Surgeon and Alderman of Colchester'. His will (made 25 September 1773, proved 7 October 1773, ERO D/ACR 17/242) left all his properties in Lawford and Colchester in trust to Revd Thomas Stanton DD (qv) of Colchester (the nonconformist minister at Stockwell Chapel) and his father-in-law Robert Agnis, to pay the rents to his 'dear and well deserving wife, Mary' while she remained a widow, for the maintenance of herself and their children, the monies to be divided equally between the children after her death. Stanton and Agnis were named executors and guardians of the children.

On 6 November 1773 (*IpsJ*) Mary Fiske advertised her intention to carry on his business as surgeon, apothecary and man midwife 'by the Assistance of a Gentleman well skilled in the above branches of business' (apparently William Frost (qv) who then returned from Kelvedon).

H. C. Robinson (qv) knew Mary Fiske in the 1790s. His *Material Reminiscences* of 1794 mentions her 'numerous family scattered in the world except a single daughter'. She lived with her sister

F

Mrs Wright who was 'in rather better circumstances. They managed to live on the profits of a small druggists shop and on a small annuity possessed by Mrs Wright. They had a brother named Agnes (John Agnis (qv)) who occupied a nursery ground near Moor Lane - with these worthy people I spent more time than with anyone else. I was at ease and and home ... They attended Mr Harris' Meeting (Rees Harris (qv) of St Helens Lane Meeting) – and were old fashioned Presbyterians' (*Material Reminiscences*, unpublished ms, Dr Williams Library, p. 46, JBB NB May 69:108ff).

FITCH JAMES [1236]
Glazier
fl. 1768

Voted in the 1768 election. His son was a baker, James Fitch, glazier, of St Nicholas, who married Susanna Jones, a minor, of All Saints, Sudbury there, 2 February 1768 (registers). The other is a baker rated in All Saints, Colchester on Queen Street corner, 1763-1776. Was buried 10 September 1794 aged 75 (CPL Crisp MI). There are extended genealogical links between the Fitch, Bawtree, Bevan, Thorn, Vince, Hodges families (cf Albertus Bevan (qv) carpenter).

See also ERO D/ACR 15/177, will, Jacob Fitch the elder, reedmaker, 1745.

FLACKE HORATIO [311]
Sea Bathing Proprietor, Wivenhoe
fl. 1734-1754

IpsJ 7 April 1753

> Whereas the use of BATHING in SEA WATER has been found so universally serviceable in many Diseases, and the Want of a private and convenient Place has prevented many Persons from making use of so advantageous a Remedy; This is to inform the Publick, that the BATH at WIVENHOE, near Colchester in Essex, is now much

more commodious, by being inlarged, and other Additions lately made; where proper Attendance of a Guide, with Dresses, will be provided, by applying to Mr HORACE FLACKE at Wivenhoe aforesaid. Subscribers to pay One Guinea, upon Entrance, for the Season; other Persons TWO Shillings every Bathing.

Horace Flacke, surgeon, was made a free burgess on 24 July 1729. He voted Whig between 1734 and 1747. He had married in 1722 (CPL Crisp ML85, ERO D/ABL, 1722, Horatius Flacke and John Hunt of Wivenhoe bound, Horace to Mary King of the same). He took John Rayner (son of Mary, wid) apprentice in 1730 for £50 (NA IR 1/12/18). Further advertisements for his sea water baths at Wivenhoe and Harwich appeared on 11 May 1754 (*Ips*J). The business at Wivenhoe was later continued by Thomas Tunmer (qv) (W. Radcliffe, 'Thomas Tunmer and a Forgotten Spa', *The Practitioner*, 193 (1964): 363-7).

FOAKES THOMAS and SARAH [315]
Coastal Trade
fl. 1746-1788

The family who befriended John Oathwaite (qv) mariner when he first came to Colchester (*Bland's Anecdotes*, Appendix 3). Sarah Foakes was a member of the Lion Walk meeting, and a Sarah Foakes died on 13 April 1833 at the Gift Houses aged 89 (probably a daughter of this family). She is described in Lion Walk records as 'an eminent christian. For several years she was totally deaf but continued to the last to edify all by her heavenly and animating discourse.' One branch of the family was obviously poor and receiving parish assistance in the 1780s. However, Thomas Foakes was paid a constables' bill in 1788 and Captain Foakes (probably the same) was paid the same year for escorting a girl to London (St Leonards Overseers Accounts D/P 245/12/6).

FORDYCE ALEXANDER [316]
Banker
fl. 1768-1780

Stood as a radical candidate in the 1768 and 1780 parliamentary elections in Colchester. In 1768, though he came third in the polls behind Charles Gray (qv) and Isaac Martin Rebow (qv), he attracted a considerable amount of support (G: 874, R: 855, F: 831 votes; *Ips]* 27 February 1768). The honeymoon period due to the new Borough Charter was over. The fact that the debts as well as the privileges of the old Corporation were to be revived doubtless disinclined many voters to the Compromise MPs (Gray and Rebow) who had ushered in the Charter. This election was contemporary with the Wilkite tumults and though Colchester shows no clear or direct support for Wilkes, the issues of 'rights' and 'liberties' were clearly invoked.

The election was hotly contested and two nonconformist baymakers published letters assuring workers that, unlike other baymakers, they would not turn off weavers who voted against their employer's preference. The degree of enthusiasm of Fordyce's supporters is demonstrated by the numbers of children named in his honour (e.g. Alexander Fordyce Miller (qv), tailor; Alexander Fordyce Cook, infant bur. St Botolphs 10 August 1769).

He was created an honorary Colchester free burgess in 1771 (ERO Colchester Borough Oath Book, 21 October 1771, free burgess entry on a 2s stamp of 10 July 1780, JBB NB 86/6:45).

Fordyce was the youngest son of Provost Fordyce of Aberdeen (*ODNB*). He had three celebrated brothers, David a philosopher and professor at Aberdeen, James a presbyterian divine and poet and William (later Sir William) a physician. Alexander Fordyce sought his career in the south and became a partner in Neale, James, Fordyce and Down the London bankers. The firm speculated freely and made large gains through acting on early intelligence, a process in which Fordyce was clearly involved and benefited financially. He

F

bought a fine house in Roehampton and is said to have spent near £14,000 on the Colchester election.

In 1770 he married Lady Mary Lindsay of Balcarnas, the second daughter of Earl Balcarnas.

Fordyce lost money heavily due to speculating too deeply amidst market fluctuations in 1771 with insufficient distinction between his own funds and those of the banking house. He absconded from his creditors in 1772. He was declared bankrupt for £100,000 in the city panic of that year. His examination at the Guildhall became a celebrated occasion; 'It was with difficulty he passed through an immense crowd assembled to see him. When he sat down at the tables, he discovered in his looks the highest sensibility, but in a few minutes he became quite composed' (*Gents. Mag.*, 1772:434, Saturday 12 September 1772). He said he would reappear when desired, 'should his attendance be ever so hazardous to his own person' (*ODNB*; *Gents. Mag.*, 1765: 274, 1770: 344, 1772: 311, 339, 436, 596, 310-11, 434).

The sale of Mr Alexander Fordyce's house in Bear Lane, Colchester was advertised. Enquirers were directed to William Seaber (qv), Fordyce's political agent in Colchester (*Ips*) 29 May 1772 and 19 September 1772 for a fuller description). The house was again to let in 1783 (*Ips*) 22 February 1783: To be let or sold, capital mansion House formerly of Alexander Fordyce, full text see under Francis Ram (qv)).

Fordyce made a second and notably unsuccessful attempt to enter Colchester politics by offering himself at the somewhat confused contest of 1780. By then, however, he was clearly 'yesterday's man' and Whig and radical support went to Sir Robert Smyth (qv). Fordyce died in 1789.

Colchester babies named for Fordyce in 1768 included;

Alexander Fordyce Cook, bur. St Bots 10 August 1769, cf Richard Cook, mariner, Greenwich, voted for Rebow and Fordyce in 1768; Fordyce Sherman, schoolmaster (voted in 1796), cf. John Sherman cooper, plumped for Fordyce in 1768; Alexander Fordyce Sangster, whitesmith (voted 1807), cf in 1768 William Sangster, whitesmith, plumped for Fordyce, next in the list to John Sherman above, as if voting together (Poll Book); Alexander Fordyce Miller (qv) tailor, well known in Napoleonic Colchester was bapt. 31 March 1768; John Fordyce Maples (qv) Capt. R.N. whose father John Maples (qv) carpenter, voted for Gray and Rebow, but whose uncle William Maples (qv), gardener, supported Gray and Fordyce; Alexander Fordyce Hedge, butcher (Borough Examination book, ERO P/CoR/16, 1 March 1792).

See also: *ODNB*, relevant entries in Namier and Brooke, *The House of Commons*; J. Hoppit, 'Financial Crises in Eighteenth-Century England', *Economic History Review*, 2nd ser., 39 (1986): 39-58.

FORSTER REVD DR NATHANIEL [1115]
Rector, All Saints
1726-1790

Rector of All Saints, Colchester from 1762, having been presented to the living by Balliol College, Oxford. A writer on political economy and politics and well as theological matters. A friend of Jeremy Bentham. Perhaps the most intellectually gifted of Colchester's later-eighteenth-century clergy, and active in local affairs, in the better management of the Port (1781) or Charity Schools (1780s), petitioning against the Slave Trade (1788) or helping to found Sunday Schools (1786), for which he drew up the very humane rules (Nathaniel Forster, *A Discourse on the Utility of Sunday Schools, being the Substance of Two Sermons preached in the Parish Church of All Saints, Colchester* (Colchester, 1786)). As a classical scholar he was friend and aid of the Revd Thomas Twining (qv), translator of Aristotle's *Poetics*. He acted as patron to the local poet Charles Shillito (qv) and was friend to the Lind family including the insolvent clergyman Charles Lind (qv), his son John (qv) and his two daughters Laetitia and Mary Lind (qv). Politically, he was a Whig, a supporter of Sir Robert Smyth MP (qv) in the 1780s. The impression that emerges from local sources and correspondence is of an urbane and likeable personality. He died 12 April 1790 and is buried at All Saints. His will (NA

PROB 11/1195, made 29 August 1789, proved 20 August 1790) left £2,500 to his son Edward at the age of 23 together with all his books and papers. The residue went to his beloved wife Rhoda, his executor. She died Witney, Oxford, aged 75 in November 1805.

See the full entry for Forster in *ODNB*; his correspondence at BL Add Mss 11277; references in the Bentham correspondence, J. Bentham, *Correspondence of Jeremy Bentham*, I. Christie, (ed.), Vol II, (London, 1968) and in that of Thomas Twining, especially the accounts of Forster's last illness and death, R. S. Walker (ed.) *Thomas Twining*; All Saints Parish records, ERO D/P/200; JBB, *EAE*:3, 89, 92, 95, 99, 103, 110, 146, 169, 172, 177, 215; D'Cruze, *Pleasing Prospect*:11, 66, 67, 68-9, 71, 117, 124, 132; sale of his property *IpsJ* 4 September 1790.

FOWE ELIZABETH [319]
Innkeeper, Angel
fl. 1773-6

Widow of William Fowe (qv). The Auricula Feast of 1773 (1 May 1773 *IpsJ*) was held 'at Mrs Fowe's'. She ran the inn alone until she married Thomas Woods (qv) in 1776 when he joined her as proprietor.

FOWE WILLIAM [318]
Innkeeper, Angel
fl. 1766-74

Before becoming innkeeper at the Angel, Fowe had worked for George Pickard (qv) wine merchant. He took the Angel 'in the Fish Market' on 22 March 1766 (*IpsJ*). In 1769 (29 April 1769 *IpsJ*) and in 1770 (5 May 1770 *IpsJ*) he hosted the annual Auricula Feast previously held at the Castle near North Bridge. He died shortly afterwards, before the feast of 1773.

FOWLER REVD CHAPPELL [320]
Rector of Frating
1704-1781

Son of a mercer of Southwell, where he married Millicent Thornton 29 November 1746, and had properties later left in his will.

Fellow of St John's Cambridge 1727-1747, and Rector of college livings at Frating and Thorrington 1745-1781 (Venn, *Alumn. Cantab.*), which were amalgamated (according to a board in the church at Thorrington) in 1763. According to Morant (to whose *History of Colchester* he was a subscriber 1748) he greatly improved the Parsonage at Frating, and his children were baptised there. He died 24 December 1781 in St Martins parish, and was 'of Colchester' when he made his will (NA PROB 11/1086/17, made 15 January 1779, proved 31 January 1782, witnesses being Dr Moses Griffith (qv) and Griffith's son-in-law John Yeldham).

His third son, Whaley Thornton Fowler, was 'of Frating, clerk' when he married Ann Cook Powell in 1784 (nfr).

FOX JOHN [321]
Surgeon and Apothecary, Dedham
fl. 1730-1747

IpsJ 10 October 1747:

> Lost; a surgeon's Pocket Case of Instruments between Ipswich and Colchester, Half-a-guinea reward from Mr Fox, Dedham, or Mr Thomas Moore, watchmaker at Ipswich.

Fox (as apothecary) had married Alice Norman of Boxted in 1730 (CPL, Crisp ML85, ERO D/ACL 1730) when John Franklyn (qv) the inoculator, stood bond. On March 11 March 1758 (*IpsJ*) Fox advertised for an apprentice.

In 1767 (*IpsJ* 7 March 1767) Mr John Fox snr. Surgeon at Dedham and Mr John Barnard, surgeon in Colchester were fitting up a large house at Ardleigh, (late the seat of Sir Ralph

Creffield) for Inoculation, They charged 5 and 4 gns for separate rooms; 3 gns for servants; ½ gn board for Friend or Servant accompanying patients.

See also CPL Crisp ML123, ERO D/ACL 1719, William Fox of Dedham, surgeon and Timothy Peacock of Dedham bound, William (29) to marry Mrs Hannah Cresfield (sic), 19 November 1719.

FRANCIS GEORGE [1231]
Plumber and Glazier
ob. 1788

Born about 1726, son of a perukemaker, Thomas, who had been admitted free burgess in 1721. This was the Thomas Francis tried for sodomy alongside George Gray (qv) in 1739-40.

Alderman George Gray (qv) (father of Charles) left George Francis the plumbing and glazing side of his Head Street business, plus £500, (NA PROB 11/755/181, 29 July 1747). Gray's nephew Theophilus Hall (qv) had the wine and iron business and Red Lion estate, much more important. Both his executors.

IpsJ 25 June 1757, advertises for a journeyman painter and glazier, but by 26 November (*IpsJ*) he was bankrupt. Assignees were John Bartholomew (qv) and Joseph Dunningham (qv). Remainder of lease of his shop in High Street opposite White Naggs was for sale 6 May 1758 (*IpsJ*).

Buried Lion Walk 2 December 1788 aged 62, and his wife Mary 18 December 1796 aged 73; 'Her trials were many borne with patience' (CPL Crisp MI). She was born Mary Ougham, daughter of a Maldon carpenter, and had married him in 1749 (ERO D/ACL 1749).

Their children more interesting:-

William Francis (qv) the attorney (c.1759-1816).

James, miller (of Kelvedon and Gt. Coggeshall) (1762-1836) - this became a prominent family in Colchester later in the nineteenth century.

F

Thomas, apprenticed to Ephraim Shillito 1 (qv) cardmaker, later of Dursley, Glos. born around 1753, created free burgess 1781.

George was admitted free burgess 1768, voting for Rebow and Fordyce, and again in 1780 for Potter, in 1781, and for Smyth at both elections in 1784.

See also full family tree etc. in correspondence between JBB and Mr David Francis of Kyneton, Victoria, Australia, 1989, ERO Acc 905, Box 9.

FRANCIS JAMES [325]
Clerk
fl. 1780-1836

A relation (nephew?) to William Francis (qv) to whom he acted as clerk during the 1780s-1800s. He married, when a gent of St Mary-at-the-Walls to Mary Hunt of that parish (ERO ML D/ALL 1790). He died on 4 July 1836 aged 74 and is buried at Lion Walk Chapel together with his wife Mary who died 1 February 1843 aged 73.

FRANCIS MRS [323]
Draper
fl. 1790s

IpsJ of 20 February 1796 announces the sale of 'a very desirable business situation comprising a substantial house and shop in full trade, in the millinery and drapery line, in a pleasant and constant place of traffic, near Headgate, now and for many years past, occupied Mrs Francis'.

See also Martha Enoc (sic) apprenticed to Ann Francis, milliner, 3 years, £6, 1761 (NA IR 1/54/70).

FRANCIS WILLIAM [324]
Attorney
fl. 1770-1816

Son of George Francis, glazier (free burgess voting in 1768) and baptised in Distillery Pond (Eld Lane Chapel) on 28 October 1780. Was apprenticed to William Cole, schoolmaster (qv) for £5 in 1773 (NA IR 1/58/175). Thereafter became clerk to Peter Daniell (qv), and later with the Daniell family and Isaac Diss (qv) became one of the main nonconformist lawyers in Colchester. Henry Crabb Robinson (qv) who was articled to Francis between 1790-5 remembers him as a pious dissenter; 'a very inferior man of low birth who was good natured but ignorant and married well, twice.' (Henry Crabb Robinson, MS, *Material Reminiscences in Old Age*:35, Dr. Williams Library).

Francis' first wife was Susanna née Rootsey (daughter of Samuel (qv), IpsJ 13 July 1782 for wedding announcement) who died soon after in about 1785 (will ERO D/ABW 110/2/29, 1782/8) leaving her £500 marriage settlement to her husband. With the proceeds of this he apparently purchased the freehold of Tymperleys, Trinity Street (IpsJ 24 December, 1785)) which he already rented from the Maples family (cf Cole and Hale survey of 1818 when the property is occupied by his son William W. Francis).

In April 1788 he proved his first wife's will. The following June, then about 25, he married Sarah Wallace of St Peters (St Peters Registers 18 June 1788). She was daughter of the prosperous grocer John Wallis (qv). Both Francis' wives were from the Eld Lane Baptist Chapel.

Following the logic of his non-conformist convictions Francis was a consistent pro reform voter between 1780 and 1812 when he supported D.W. Harvey (cf *ChCh* 14 December 1787 where he is identified as a supporter of Robert Smyth's party on the Corporation). He maintained an extensive attorney's practice (later together with his son William W. Francis) making more than 47 Colchester wills (of those now deposited in ERO) from 1780. Was also agent for the British Tontine in 1792 (*IpsJ* 18 February 1792).

He died on 8 May 1816 aged 57 and was commemorated with a wall tablet in the Baptist Chapel together with his second wife Sarah who died on 3 March 1825 aged 62. His will is at NA PROB 11/1585, 6 November 1816.

FRANKLYN JOHN [326]
Surgeon
fl. 1730-1767

Ips] 28 March 1767; J Franklyn, Surgeon offered inoculation at Mile End. This business was later taken over by the partnership of Fiske and Day (cf John Fiske (qv)).

In 1730 Franklyn had stood bond at the wedding of John Fox, apothecary of Dedham (qv) and Alice Norman of Boxted (CPL Crisp ML85, ERO D/ACL 1730).

FREEMAN RICHARD [328]
Attorney
fl. 1742-1780

Freeman was the son of Thomas Freeman and his wife Diana *née* Stuteville. He was apprenticed to William Mayhew 1 (qv) in 1742 for the large amount of £150 (NA IR 1/50/142). He seems to have acted very much as a junior partner and Mayhew maintained a lively correspondence with him during the campaign to regain the Charter. He was a member of the Castle Book Club in 1752.

Freeman seems to have maintained a business interest in Chelmsford through family connections. In 1780 (22 April 1780, nfr) he witnessed the marriage in Chelmsford of his relative Sarah Scrutton (identified as receiving a mourning ring from Freeman's father, Thomas). In 1786 (ERO D/DGe132) when based in Chancery Lane, he acted as agent for the sale of Chelmsford property.

FRESHFIELD FRANCIS 1 [331]
Salt Merchant
1711-1773

Son of Richard 1 (qv) and wife Elizabeth. A quaker (Fitch, *Colchester Quakers*). Francis Freshfield and his wife Elizabeth had three children, Elizabeth who married Robert Seaman a woolcomber from Norfolk, John and Francis 2 (qv). As well as continuing the family salt business, Francis 1 increased the Freshfield holding of local inns, having presumably inherited the nucleus from his brother Richard 2 (see Richard 1 (qv)). His will of 1770/3 (NA PROB 11/988, 5 June 1773) left the following collection to his son John; Plough, late Black Bull, St Botolphs; Colchester Paquet in Magdalen Street; Faulcon, west side North Hill St Peters; Cock & Blackbirds North Street; Whale Fishery and the Goat and Boot East St, St James; Mariners, Magdalen Green; King's Head, Lexden; Brick & Tile Copford; £90 in lieu of the Cock & Pye, Wyre St, lately sold: as well as £1,000 cash. He had also at one time been owner of the Bear, St Nicholas which he had sold to Thomas Great (qv) (per Great's will of 1760) Most of these properties were later sold off in 1780 (*IpsJ* 4 November 1780).

The salt making business including the salt shop St Runwalds, the hoy *Hopewell* (40 tons), the barge *Rebecca*, the lighter *The Chance* and the family house St Leonards, were left to Francis 2 (qv) together with all household goods etc. Freshfield's daughter Elizabeth received £1,670 and a silver coffee pot as well as the interest on £4,000. A small annuity was left to a servant Sarah Watson 'who resides in the Salt Shop' and similar provision was made for two other servants.

See also wills of Susanna Freshfield, widow, Colchester, NA PROB 11/517, 9 August 1710; Francis Freshfield, mariner, Colchester NA PROB 11/472, 18 October 1703; sentence of Francis Freshfield, Colchester, NA PROB 11/524, 6 November 1711; will of Robert Seaman, surgeon, Harwich, NA PROB 11/427, 27 August 1695.

FRESHFIELD FRANCIS 2 [333]
Salt Merchant
fl. 1773-1808

Son of Francis Freshfield 1 (qv). During the tenure of Francis 2 sufficient parish rates and other sources become available to be able to assess the size of the Freshfield family's property holding. The family house in St Leonards, owner occupied was rated 9 in 1783, their malting, then occupied by Samuel Crackanthorp (qv) rated 10, a deal yard and house rated 9 (owner occupied), various tenements, the Salt Office rated 11, the Swan inn (8). The High Street shop extended into St Nicholas as well as St Runwald rated 4 in St Nicholas and 2 in St Runwald, both owner occupied until 1785 when the St Nicholas shop was rented to Philip Buckingham. Comparing this list with the will of Richard Freshfield 1 (qv) of 1756 it is clear that the holding had remained very substantially intact. However, it was Francis 2, not uncommon for the third generation of a trading family, who began to dismantle it, taking advantage of rising property prices and wisely wary of the uncertainties of business in the 1790s he sold the concern in 1797 to John Eglonton Wallis (qv) and James Wallis Ashwell (qv). They ran the salt works and shop until 1802 when they reaped the whirlwind in J. E. Wallis' cataclysmic bankruptcy.

Freshfield lived on until 1808 when he died at St Mary's parish aged 66 (*Ips]* 22 October 1808) his goods being sold the following November 26th. His will, (NA PROB 11/1488, 16 November 1808) which mentions no specific property, made large charitable bequests. He had apparently remained a conscientious quaker having been led by his principles to be examined in Borough petty sessions on 11 March 1782 (ERO P/CoR/10) for a refusal to pay rates for the repair of St Leonards church for the previous 3 years.

FRESHFIELD RICHARD 1 [330]
Salt Merchant
1688-1756

One of the Quaker family of Colchester and owner of the salt works at the Hythe. It stood at the foot of Hythe Hill, partly on piles projecting out onto the river (Shown in prospect of the Hythe, reprinted in D. Stephenson, *The Book of Colchester* (1978): 93). Local seawater was mixed with rough black salt made at South Shields and later with rock salt mined at Cheshire and evaporated and refined in saltpans and ovens. The business also owned one or more hoys engaged in fetching the salt water as well as premises in Middle Row in the High Street for retailing the produce. Richard Freshfield married twice. By his first wife Elizabeth he had two sons Francis 1 (qv) and Richard 2. In 1724 he remarried to Priscilla Havens, sister of Philip Havens 1 (qv) baymaker. His will of 1753/5 (NA PROB 11/815, 10 May 1755) shows how much wider his business concerns were than the salt works. To his son Francis he left his house, granary and deal yard; the Swan Inn St Leonard, the salt works and equipment, a hoy the *Endeavour* of 30 tons, a ship or brigantine the *Elizabeth*, and the salt shop and Butchers Stall and Chamber adjoining in St Runwalds. Richard 2 received a brewhouse St Botolphs, the Mariners and the Goat and Boot inns in Colchester,* the Brick and Tile inn, Copford and all brewing stock and equipment, plus various tenements attached to these inns. £200 each went to niece Sarah and nephew Richard Young and items of family plate to his sister Elizabeth Fish (Middlesex) and Ann Havens his sister-in-law.

*Two of a string of inns sold 4 November 1780 (*IpsJ*)

FREWEN DR EDWARD [13]
Rector of Frating
fl. 1744-1831

Revd Chappell Fowler's (qv) successor at Frating and Thorrington from 1778. However one of Fowler's sons seems to have been curate till Frewen arrived in 1789. Frewen officiated

F

till 1793, then disappeared from the locality until 1812, after which he is recorded as resident at Frating.

At St John's College Cambridge he rose to be senior Dean, and only left after marriage with Sally daughter of Richard Moreton, of Little Moreton Hall, Cheshire in June 1789. He was vicar of W. Firle, Sussex and died 19 March 1797 aged 75 (handsome tablet at Frating).

Frewen's stay in Colchester has elements of comedy in it, as seen in the letters of Thomas Twining (Ralph S. Walker (ed), *Thomas Twining*):

14 November 1789 (p. 325) Twining had heard of Frewen through Mr Cowper Vicar of Harwich. Revd Nath. Forster also liked him. 'I will certainly call, Monday or Tuesday'.

5 December 1789 (p. 328) 'Mr Frewen I find after only two talks with him is a very absent man.'

15 March 1790 (p. 337) '... another strange piece of news. Mr Frewen after giving £1,000 for a house here, furnishing it handsomely, and coming to settle here in all the forms, is actually going to sell his house and quit the country.... I am sorry to lose a sensible man where they are not quite as common as oysters.'

The house was Michael Hills' mansion in Queen St (in the 1980s the Police Station) rated 30 in 1791-1793. From October 1793-1795 it is listed as occupied by a Mrs Shepherd. In July 1796 John Bawtree of Wivenhoe, brewer paid £1,200, and it remained in that family.

However Frewen's departure from Colchester was not quite so precipitate. On 14 June 1791, his father died at the family estate at Northiam (*Gents. Mag.*:583). Between 10 September and 10 October his sister and mother came on a visit (*E. Anglian Notes & Queries* (1901/2) 9:277-8) being entertained and accompanied by Mr Brook Hurlock and sister round Colchester and going to Dedham to see them (JBB note: WHY they visited Brook Hurlock has not been not discovered - he was Rector of Lamarsh since 1761 and later a friend of Constable).

F

A further reference from the Twining correspondence (p. 400) is dated 17 March 1792. 'Mr Frewen has been at Cambridge and is returned <u>Doctor</u> Frewen. He is, I believe, the first Doctor with crop hair and uncovered ears.' (This change of fashion was completed 1795 by Pitt's hairpowder tax. Peruke-makers became known henceforth as hairdressers).

A letter from Twining of 27 November 1792 records Nathaniel Barlow's 1 (qv) Mayor-making when Dr Frewin drew up loyal declarations against corresponding societies. Twining still had belief that the revolution would suceed in reforming France, and in sum it seems that Frewen did not finally live up to Twining's expectations of him. He never became a member of the Castle Book Society and disappeared from the local record until 1812, when he appeared to settle in Frating.

Frewen died at Frating, 18 December 1831 aged 87 and has a tablet there by Luffkin.

The family estate was at Northiam, Sussex founded by Accepted Frewen, Archbishop of York (d. 1664). Revd Thankful Frewen (1669-1749) was there. His son Thomas (1704-1791), M.D. 1755, is in *ODNB* as early pioneer of inoculation at Rye. Married Philadelphia Tucker there. A son Thomas d. 1773 and a daughter, Philadelphia, was born 1750 but died unmarried.

FROST M. [334]
Mantua Maker
fl. 1780-1

Occupied premises near All Saints church in 1780 (*IpsJ* 6 May 1780) having returned from London. In 1781 (*IpsJ* 8 May 1781) she advertised from rooms near the Three Cups where she made up dresses.

FROST SAMUEL 1 and 2 [1271]
Carpenters, Beaumont
ob. 1781, 1789

Father and son, carpenters at Beaumont.

F

A man of this name worked for Isaac Green (qv) 1749/50.

Father's first wife died 5 September 1754. Of several children baptised at Beaumont, his son is bapt 13 November 1752, daughter Martha 26 March 1749. Second wife Mary Mashland, widow of Beaumont, 1754.

Ips] 14 September 1765, advertised for a foreman to a Brick kiln to make 300,000 bricks and 100,000 tiles next season, and shortly afterwards (*Ips]* 14 December 1765) that he had lost a black letter-case containing estimates of carpenters' work. He advertised for two sawyers the following year (*Ips]* 15 February 1766).

His will is at NA PROB 11/1085/588, made 13 October 1780, proved 8 December 1781. It leaves much property:-

- To son Samuel, copyhold messuage and nine acres held of manor Shughaugh, Great Oakley, also land and premises held of Guy's Hospital, also messuage I now dwell in (in Beaumont) and all working tools.
- To daughter Martha, copyholds of manors of Newhall and Oldhall in Beaumont and £200.
- To daughter Hannah wife of John Quilter, cottages in Great Oakley and Mose, and Quilter is forgiven debt of £323 on condition he mortgages the premises concerned to son Samuel for £100 instead.
- To daughter Sarah, wife of Leonard Nunn (miller of Bradfield, married in 1779), tmt newly erected on land of the manor of Shughaugh, and another on waste of rectory of Bradfield.
- To wife tenement holden of manor of Mose (occ wid of Philip Cook) for life, then to Sarah. Also interest of £900 3% stock.
- To executors son Samuel and Leonard Nunn, £300 in trust to place out at interest for son Benjamin (bn. Jan 1747/8, app. John Pilborough of Ramsey, tailor, 1761, £10) and Mary his wife, then to be divided between their children. And £50 for the education of their son Benjamin now 9.

Residue in fifths to same legatees (complicated).

The will of Samuel 2 (timber merchant, Beaumont) is at NA PROB 11/1185, proved 24 November 1789.

On 10 January 1784 Martha (dtr) of St Mary-at-the-Walls spinster married William Redmore Bigg (qv), limner of Covent Garden. He is admitted to the Beaumont copyholds that year. She is buried Lexden 4 June 1836 aged 89. He is buried St Giles in the Fields 6 February 1828 aged 74.

IpsJ 5 October 1789, Samuel 2 advertised for 2 or 3 journeymen.

IpsJ 3 February 1810, Dwellings in Beaumont and Great Oakley for sale, Samuel 2 being deceased. Detailed listing.

It may be noted that Martha Bigg was six or seven years older than her husband. They both shared an admiration for cottage life and diet, which shocked John Constable, though he was a loyal friend to old Bigg (JBB, *EAE* :181, 191-4).

Frost's copyhold buildings should be investigated for rateable value, occupants etc. They are on Guy's Hospital estates so John Yeldham, steward is relevant (JBB note: were the 300,000 bricks in 1765 for Guy's?).

NB very fine survey of Guy's Hospital lands in Beaumont and Oakley, 1780 is at ERO D/DBm 13.

It is worth wondering if Charles Gray's (qv) loan of James Deane's (qv) builders' book of 1730 to Tristram Evans (qv) Rector of Beaumont had to do with Frost's many building projects in 1765 (ERO D/DRc Z/27).

FROST WILLIAM [332]
Surgeon and Apothecary, Kelvedon and Colchester
fl. 1763-1773

Apprenticed to John Fiske (qv) in 1763 for £20 (NA IR 1/54/178). When Fiske died in 1773 Frost sold up in Kelvedon and moved back to Colchester to assist his late master's widow. His new built brick messuage in Kelvedon was for sale on 16 October 1773 (*IpsJ*), with its handsome Entrance and Staircase,

F

Parlour on each side etc., as he was moving to Colchester, opposite the Town Hall.

FULLER MAJOR [335]
fl. 1807

25 July 1807 *IpsJ*:-

> COLCHESTER
> A handsome & substantial Brick-built
> FREEHOLD DWELLING HOUSE and PREMISES
> with immediate possession
> To be SOLD by AUCTION
> by BUNNELL and JACKSON
> At Mr Raltons, the Three Cups Inn, Colchester
> On Wednesday at August 5th, 1807, precisely at 12 o'clock

The above Estate is situated opposite that beautiful new built Bridge, called East Bridge, in the parish of St James, and now in the occupation of Major Fuller the proprietor, commanding a delightful prospect of the fields, meadows and woodlands, truly picturesque, comprising lofty and well proportioned rooms, a parlour, drawing room, 4 bedrooms, dressing rooms, servants rooms, kitchen, excellent cellars and convenient offices; a neat garden well fenced in and planted with choice fruit trees also a kitchen garden detached, with a large piece of ground lately fenced in, fronting the house held in a long lease from the Corporation at a small rent.

The premises are well supplied with water, low in the rates and taxes an in substantial repair having been built but a few years upon the most approved plan.

N.B. This estate may be purchased by Private contract prior to the 30th inst. If sold notice will be given.

Conditions at the place of sale.

G

GALE ABRAHAM [336]
Innkeeper, Sailor and Ball
fl. 1768-73

A free burgess voting in 1768 for Rebow and Gray. In 1781 two of that name both voted for Potter.

Was succeeded at the Sailor and Ball by Alice Gale (1783-1793, alehouse recognisances).

See also: Abraham Gale, illiterate, Navy Volunteer 7 December 1796. Paid £29 6s bounty and expenses in All Saints churchwardens accounts; Abraham Gale, wheelwright voted in April 1784. Alice Gale was innkeeper at the 'Sailor and Bail' between 1783 and 1793.

GANSEL DAVID ESQ [338]
Architect
fl. 1730-1770

Ips] 12 September 1767 published an open letter from Maj. General Gansel to Mr Thomas Daniel (qv) of Colchester dated from Donyland Hall, 4 September in which Gansel absolutely denied having a setting dog or setting net, nor had he seen any partridges for six or seven years past, it being alleged he discharged a whole covey of 127 without sparing one.

> P.S. As I do not recollect an Instance of refusing a Hare to anyone of my Neighbours who desired it, but immediately direct the Gamekeeper to kill one for them; so I flatter myself every neighbour wishes to oblige me in endeavouring to preserve the Game. And I am sure no Sportsman of a qualified Gentleman who knows the circumstances of extensive and strong cover, together with the large Quantity of Paling, which renders Donyland as the Asylum for Game, and thence to spread

to the surrounding Manor would wish (even if not desired to the contrary) to destroy the Nursery from which their sport must have Origin.

Gansel originally lived at Leyton Grange which he designed and built in 1720 (see Catalogue of *Visual Arts in Essex* exhibition at Ingatestone Hall (n.d.) fig. 33). He appears in Colvin's *Biographical Dictionary of English Architects* and his portrait is in *Essex Review*, Vol. 55 (1945):50.

He moved to Donyland in 1730 and became a JP for Colchester in the 1740s. Morant, *Essex*, Vol. 1:86 says 'he made a park and greatly improved the house and gardens' at Donyland Hall. Therefore perhaps he built the pavilions. For full description of the property see James Wallis Ashwell (qv) – description for a sale of 1802.

Gansel's will (NA PROB 11/799, 455 Searle, proved 13 February 1753 - not noted in full) leaves the estate to his wife for life then to son William who became a General and died in Fleet Prison for debt in 1774 (G.O. Rickwood in *E.R.*, Vol. 53: 81-5).

GARDENER LT COL HON W. H. [339]
Commander Royal Artillery in Colchester
fl. 1816

Colchester Gazette 30 November 1816

An eligible and compact Family Residence with Offices, Garden and Land adjoining at present occupied as an Hospital for the Royal Artillery, ...near the Barracks, Frontage on road leading to the Hythe. To lett. Apply Lt. Col. Gardener Commanding the Royal Artillery, at the Barracks.

This was Hill House, Hythe. On 21 December 1816 (*Colchester Gazette*) the Ordnance Ground was similarly to let.

GARLAND JOHN [340]
Innkeeper, Colchester Paquet
fl. 1780-7

Garland was listed as innkeeper when the inn was advertised for sale on 4 November 1780 (*IpsJ*) with a number of others. In 1787 he was living in Moor Lane (10 August 1787 *ChCh*) in another property for auction. Garland was witness to the will of Jacob Hendrick, woolcomber, made 24 December 1780 (ERO D/ACR 18/212).

GARLAND THOMAS [1134]
Scrivener
fl. 1709-c.1749

Witnessed numbers of Colchester wills, particularly in the 1730s (JBB NB 77/5:16). The earliest mention of him found in local sources is in a set of deeds, dated 4 June 1709, where he is named as the son of Margaret Decleur wid (ERO D/DHt T72/61).

Thomas Garland from Colchester was buried at Chelmsford 11 March 1745. There is another burial in the same name at St Botolphs, Colchester for 21 March 1749 (registers).

GARNETT THOMAS [1219]
Bricklayer
ob. 1769

Strutt's *Colchester*, Vol. 2:27 records a table-tomb, of which only the top remained when Crisp's MSS for Holy Trinity MIs were made (in CPL). In church porch and trod over so only first named person was legible. Commemorates:-

- Rose, late wife of Thomas Garneet dd. 27 September 1754, aged 61.
- Thomas, son of Thos and Rose Garneet dd. 11 June 1755, aged 30.
- Thomas Garneet senior dd. 8 July 1769, aged 71.

G

Thomas's will (ERO D/ACR 17/341) made 8 June 1769, proved 12 July 1769, leaves his property in trust to Peter Daniell (qv), William Smith and Manasseh Powell to pay son Stephen (who has his working tools) £20 annually in quarterly installments, and after him to daughter Rebecca, wife of Thomas Munnings of Wivenhoe.

He mentions messuage in Black Boy Lane occ. Michael Delight (qv) and his own house in All Saints leased from Trustees of Mr Reading's Charity School (see Barnet Reading (qv)). The property, three tenements, was for sale *IpsJ* 12 August 1769.

This son Stephen was a bad lot. He married his first wife Susan Nightingale of St Botolph's when he was 20 and she 23, in 1756 (ERO ML D/ACL 2756), but 31 December 1757 she had run away from him (*IpsJ*). He is frequently in Quarter Sessions minutes charged with violent behaviour towards all and sundry, threatening his father etc. (ERO P/CoR/2-5, 3 June, 26 June 1771, 7 November 1774, 13 September 1775). On 15 July 1765 had to give surety of £40 accused of assault by John Brown, bricklayer (ERO D/B 5 Sb5/5). Later, *IpsJ* 25 July 1787, his (second) wife Mary died, 'of ill-usage.'

I have not found any mention of work by Garnett, but an Abstract of Title of February 1800 (ERO D/DSb T16) concerns a 'Messuage or Tenement and Premises called Masys or Massies in the parish of St Martins, formerly the estate of Thomas Garnett deceased' and described in 1784 when conveyed to John Worts, baker, as 'two messuages, two cottages two gardens and one orchard' and is a strip of land between East and West Stockwell St, north of the lane between the two, just by St Martin's church. It was acquired 19/20 June 1744 by Garnett and Nathaniel Barnes (qv) of Colchester victualler, with other properties for £203, and these were divided 28 May 1746, this property being held in trust for Thos Garnett the younger, bricklayer (not yet 21). The occupants in February 1800 are Thomas Sebborn and Samuel Moore, the purchaser Mrs Magdalen Shorey (qv).

See also ERO P/CoR/11A, settlement examination of 22 January 1787, Stephen Garnett, St Botolphs, bricklayer. 20 years ago had been apprenticed to Anthony Whiting, St Nicholas, cardmaker deceased, for 7 years. 16 years ago had occupied premises in All Saints and paid rates.

GARRARD JOSEPH [341]
Carrier
fl. 1791

IpsJ 22 October 1791. Garrard operated carriers' wagons from a warehouse in Colchester, whence one Joseph Green stole a parcel containing haberdashery and twenty county banknotes (property of Henry Makin, Bildestone).

GIBBON REVD CHRISTOPHER [343]
Curate All Saints Colchester, Tollesbury
fl. 1733-1760

Chiefly notable for having married Mary Gainsborough, sister to the artist.

He entered Emmanuel College, Cambridge in 1733 and was Master of Cavendish School in 1741 (Venn, *Alumn. Cantab.*) After his marriage, the Gibbons lived at Colchester, where Mary traded as a milliner (cf. Mary Gibbon (qv)). Gibbon's will made 27 November 1759 (ERO D/ABR 25/144, clerk, St Peters, 1762) when they were residing in St Peters parish made Mary the sole executrix and main legatee except for £1 to their son John for mourning. The will was proved on 19 February 1762. Gibbon has a ledger in St Peters, recording his death on 9 April 1760.

GIBBON ELEANOR and SARA [1102]
Boarding School
fl. 1764

IpsJ 2 and 9 June 1764 carried an advertisement by Eleanor and Sara Gibbon:-

> Mrs Gibbon, Governess of the Boarding School at Colchester and late one of the French Teachers at Mrs Castlefranks at Clapham, takes this opportunity to acquaint the Publick, that she has taken the Boarding School at Chelmsford in Essex; where young Ladies will be boarded and carefully educated with proper assistants.

The school charged 14 gns a year and 1 gn entrance for board, English and Needlework, day scholars 7s a quarter. Other accomplishments offered were French, half a guinea entrance and ditto a quarter; Music 1 gn entrance and 1 gn per quarter; Dancing 1 gn and 22s 6d; Writing and Arithmetic 7s a quarter. School began on 2 July.

Compare Mary Gibbon (qv) milliner.

GIBBON MARY [344]
Milliner
fl. 1753-62

Sister to Thomas Gainsborough, the artist, married to Revd Christopher Gibbon (qv). She took Tryphosa Smith as apprentice in her milliners' business in 1753 (NA IR 1/51/200), Mary Wood in 1754 for £25 (NA IR 1/51/280) and Sarah Wood in 1760 for £21 (NA IR 1/53/211) as well as several others up to the end of 1761 (see JBB, *Gainsborough in his Twenties*, ERO C905, Box 5), all for between 20 and 30 gns and mostly for three year terms. She left Colchester for Bath in 1762 and the following appeared in the *IpsJ* of 16 April 1762 (JBB viewed the *IpsJ* in the original. Two weeks are missing from the microfilm version at this date).

> Mrs Mary Gibbon, late of Colchester, milliner, now removed to Bath, begs the favour of such persons who stand indebted to her, to pay those debts to Mr Wm. Mayhew (1 (qv)) of Colchester, on or before 30th April instant, who is empowered to receive and give discharges for the same by, Mary Gibbon.

See also JBB, *EAE*:132-3; *IpsJ* 24 April 1784, household furniture of Mrs Mary Gibbon of Sudbury for auction.

GIBBS SAMUEL [980]
Bookseller
1730-1816

Baptised St Nicholas 4 May 1730, second son of Joseph Gibbs (qv) later organist in Ipswich and Mary his wife. Mary was buried at All Saints, Colchester 30 October 1766, aged 65. Her grave also commemorates four children who predeceased her.

In 1761 Gibbs was teaching music at Dyer's Boarding School for young gentlemen at Tolleshunt D'Arcy (*IpsJ* 17 January 1761). His lessons were advertised at 'a Guinea Entrance and Half a Crown at each time of Teaching.' (Dancing lessons at the school were given by Mr Dupré (qv).) He seemed to have combined this with a bookseller's, stationer's and bookbinder's business opposite the Blue Posts in Witham (*IpsJ* 28 March 1761), where his wife also traded as a milliner. She advertised for an apprentice on 15 August 1761 (*IpsJ*) whilst in the same advertisement Gibbs offered a great variety of Paper-hangings, and exceeding good Roman Strings for Violins or Basses, as cheap as in London. The following year he advertised part-songs by Luigi Senzanome (*IpsJ* 2 December 1762).

A few years later he moved to Colchester and advertised on 12 September 1767 (*IpsJ*);

> Book-seller, stationer and book-binder at the Stationer's Arms in the Head Street near North Hill, Colchester. SELLS Books in all Faculties; also Bibles, Common-Prayers, Testaments, and all other School-Books; all sorts of mourning gilt, and plain Writing-Papers; red and black Ink, Quills, Pens, Wax, Wafers and all other Stationary (sic) Wares. Binds Books neatly in all sorts of Binding, and makes and sells all sorts of Merchants, and Tradesmen's Accompt Books rul'd to any Pattern.
>
> N.B. Gentlemen, &c may be regularly furnished with any of the Monthly Magazines, and all other Books published by Subscription; also Medicinal Preparations from the

G

original Warehouses, and every other Article usually sold by Booksellers.

William Keymer (qv), the established Colchester bookseller, placed rival advertisements at this time (*IpsJ* 29 August, 12 September, 3 October 1767). Keymer's reaction is understandable, since Gibbs seems to have moved into premises next door to him. Gibbs was rated 20 in St Runwald's rates of 1788 (opposite the Town Hall, between Keymer and James Thorn 2 (qv) silversmith). These premises were later taken by next-door neighbour James Thorn and Gibbs moved downhill to St Nicholas, and was located three doors below the Red Lion, rated 10 in 1792 (Land Tax assessments, leased from William Brockway). Gibbs was listed in Bailey's *British Directory* for 1784 (Bookseller, Stamp Office, and Agent for the Insurance Office, High St) and a similar entry occurs in the *Universal Directory*, 1791. Not listed after 1800. Ann Taylor (qv) recalled in her later autobiography seeing her earliest published material in Darton and Harvey's *Minor's Pocket-Book* displayed in the window of 'old Mr Gibbs' the bookseller' in 1799 (J. Gilbert (ed), *The Autobiography and Other Memorials of Mrs Gilbert*, 2nd edn (1876)).

Gibbs was one of those local tradesmen to receive a one-guinea mourning ring in the will of George Wegg Esq 2 (qv) (1775/7) and so was probably part of the literary and musical circle which Wegg assembled at East Hill House and was listed amongst the Colchester subscribers for the Defence of the Country at the beginning of the French Wars (*IpsJ* 31 March 1798, gave 2 gns).

Gibbs seems to have married twice, though his first marriage has not been traced. No children of this marriage were mentioned in his will (see below). He later married Hannah (see Susannah Gibbs (qv)) Hopkins, spinster, milliner opposite Dial Church (St Nicholas). Her marriage settlement 6/7 April 1770 made the Revd Nathaniel Forster (qv) of All Saints trustee of her property in Elmstead occ. Edward Avery, and the stock and profits of her business as milliner. Ephraim Shillito 1 (qv) and his daughter Elizabeth Shillito (qv) were witnesses at her

G

wedding and also of her will, made 27 December 1771 (ERO D/ABR 26/380, proved 1772) which cites the marriage settlement. Samuel Gibbs was named sole executor and beneficiary (except for £20 left to her sister, the wife of Mr Samuel Anderson). She was buried at St Nicholas, 21 January 1772.

(Maliciously?) on the title-page of a book in the Castle Library (Dr William King's *Discourse on the Inventions of Men in the Service of God* (1694) (viewed by JBB when in the ESAH collection at Hollytrees) someone has written the names of Samuel Gibbs and Elizabeth Shillito, united by a line of x's (kisses?) (JBB NB Oct64). Elizabeth Shillito (qv) had been apprenticed to Mrs Gibbs and in February 1771 set up in business at her parents' house in All Saints.

Gibbs died at Kelvedon aged 85, 10 January 1816. He is buried where a flat stone read(s) 'Samuel Gibbs, son of Joseph Gibbs, organist of the Tower Church, Ipswich, who died Aged 85 Years'.

His will is at NA PROB 11/1577, 76 Wynne, of Kelvedon, gent, proved 26 February 1816. Executors, nephew Joseph Bullen, sister Sarah Gibbs, spinster. Mentions great nephew Thos Henry Bullen of Kennet near Newmarket, clerk, and niece Elizabeth Alexander, wife of John Alexander of Earls Colne. Made no mention of Colchester.

His sister Ann married John Bullen of Kennet at Ipswich St Nicholas, 10 October 1757. His sister Sarah was buried aged 81 at St Mary Tower, 10 October 1818 'from Kelvedon.'

See also: Borough Examination Books (ERO P/CoR/5, end of 1774 or early 1775, nfr), settlement examination of George Hewett bookbinder who let himself to Samuel Gibbs in St Marys for £12 p.a. 7 years ago and served a year; will of Ann Gibbs widow, Colchester made 1756, proved 14 February 1766, NA PROB 11/916.

G

GIBSON GOLDEN LEE [985]
Tailor
fl. 1803-1805

In 1803 leased a shop and house on the High Street, St Peters, near the Foundry Yard, for £25 per year from the trustees of Winnocks' Charity. The property fronted the High Street and stood on the corner of the passageway into the Foundry Yard. It included a parlour behind the shop, 'with one closet on the right of the stone passage.' Two staircases divided the shop and the parlour (necessary because of the complicated layout of rooms upstairs) with a 'closet, passage, coal place and cupboard' fitted underneath. The kitchen was at the back. Upstairs was a dining room over the shop, and there were three bedrooms, one over the parlour, a second over the next door shop (downhill) and a third over the passageway into the Foundry Yard. A third storey had garret rooms over the bedrooms. There was also a workshop across the passageway from the rest of the property. (Winnocks Leases, ERO D/Q 31/1/2, 8 July 1803 - Lease and counterpart thereto, to Mr Golden Lee Gibson, Taylor, Colchester for 14 years from midsummer 1803, 8 July 1803. For the Foundry see Joseph Wallis (qv)).

His business was not successful, however, and his bankruptcy was notified two years later (*Univ. Mag.*, 25 February 1805).

GIBSON JOHN [345]
Tailor
d. 1796

A free burgess and consistent Tory voter, he was elected Common Councillor on 27 August 1778, Assistant on 8 July 1788 and Alderman on 31 July 1789. His support of the Corporation party that emerged in the late 1780s gained him the Mayoralty in 1792. Revd Thomas Twining's (qv) correspondence contains an account of his Mayoral feast (R. S. Walker (ed) *Thomas Twining*, Vol. 2:388-9, October 1791). Gibson had been an active attender at All Saints vestry meetings in the

1780s but by 1791 John Gibson & Co occupied premises in St Runwald rated 24.

GIFFORD HOPE [347]
Gent
fl. 1685-1719

Is mentioned in Colchester Oath Book:261 as having signed the Declaration of Allegiance and against the Solemn League and Covenant, 5 January 1685 (ERO D/B 5 R1).

Notable for having made two wills, both of which were proved. The first (ERO D/ABR 18/167; JBB NB Blue Lion 77) was made on 7 June 1717 (witnessed by Kary Dobie, Elizabeth Dare, Mary Robinson) and proved by Gifford's widow Martha on 4 July 1721. It is a relatively simple will. It specifies that the funeral is to be attended by no more than 20 persons who are to have gold rings 'but no scarfes or hatband.' £10 was left to Colchester Charity School and 40s to the poor of Holy Trinity. The residue was left to his dear and loving wife Martha, sole executrix.

The second will made in 1719, has no signature but was attested by John Essington Esq of Ironmonger Lane, St Martins, London as being in Gifford's writing and proved two days after the first on 6 July 1721. By contrast it is long and very interesting. It details that Gifford is infirm and to be privately buried. It leaves £10 to the Charity School and £3 to the poor of Holy Trinity to be laid out in bread. Then it directs:

- To: William Grange and Elizabeth his wife £10 to be paid out of the first years rent of the lands and tenements he holds of me (see below)
- To: Elizabeth, now wife of James Haggar, watchmaker, over against the Pewter Pot Inn in Leadenhall Street, London, £100.
- To: her sister, Diana Bowden, spinster, £100.

Gifford's son-in-law Sir Anthony Thomas Abdy bart. is left a whole series of properties in Colchester which comprise the

G

Castle Lands etc. and the buildings erected by Thomas Norfolk (see *VCH Essex*, Vol. 9). These are:

- Middle Mill, Colchester, the Mill acre, 5a Meadow in Kings Meadow occ. Joseph Chiswick, miller in All Saints and Mile End parishes.
- Castle Bailey and Sheepshead field + messuages thereon + gardens therewith in All Saints or East Donyland, occ. Wm Granger.
- Adjacent messuage and garden now occ. Thomas Went.
- And all the several messuages in All Saints or other parts of the town occupied by Joseph Duffield (qv), - Spurgeon wid., Mr Crickett, Wm. Bottle, Mrs Harden wid., Mr Kelly, Joseph Fitch, Thomas Unwyn, Mrs Nevill, wid.
- And all parcels of land or pasturage called Gt and Lt Shetland (sic) (Sholand), the Shale and Broomfield (cf J F Round papers), 34 acres in St Mary-at-the-Walls and Lexden late occ. William Cole.
- Land called Castle Grove 12 acres Mile End occ. Wm. Boys and wood and woodland called Blayd Wood 30 acres plus 12 acres adjoining the same wood on the Colchester to Elmstead road in the parish of Wivenhoe occ. John Snelling.
- The hundred of Tendring and the Bayliwick of it and the hundred court.
- And all fees, leets, views of Frankpledge, wastegrounds, waifs and strays and the goods of fugitives and felons, and all felo-de-sees and all timber trees in this Bailiwick or which belong to the Castle and the Castle Acre in Tendring and the Castle land 4 score acres or more and the Castle land meadow 20 acres and the 2 acres meadow adjoining the castle - all late occupied Mr Thomas Reynolds.
- And all the reversions and remainders of these lands occupied by Thomas Reynolds expectant on the death of Dorothy Blower of Wighton near Walsingham,

Norfolk, formerly the widow of Robert Norfolk, late of Romford Esq And all the Tythes arising from these lands belonging to the Castle and certain pastures in the parishes of St James, All Saints, St Mary-at-the-Walls, Mile End, Greenstead, Lexden and E. Donyland, and all other messuages he holds in these parishes.

To have and to hold to the said Sir Anthony Thomas Abdy bart., on condition that he pay annually in quarterly payments to 'my loving friend James Deane (qv) of Colchester' for life £40 at the Moot Hall.

Judging by Morant's discussion of Tendring Hundred (Morant, *Essex*, Vol. 1: 730), the first will seems the operative one. He gives the owners of the Castle lands after Hope Gifford as Miss Gifford, the heiress who sold to Revd Francis Powell, who then sold to Henry Biggs, who sold to Charles Gray (qv) in 1750.

GILSON BENJAMIN [1296]
Baker
fl. 1734-1786

Benjamin Gilson, brother of Daniel (qv) died 9 August 1786 aged 81. Named as a baker in the Poll Book of 1734; a gent in later poll books. Made Channel Commissioner 1750 and again in 1780. Voted for Smyth in 1784.

His will is at NA PROB 11/1146, 515 Norfolk, made 1783, proved 12 August 1786, and leaves:-

To niece Mary Poyner (qv) spinster, farm at Stanway occupied by Daniel Rudkin.

To nephew John, apothecary in the City of London £300 and £100 each to his seven children.

Similar sums of £300 and £200 to several cousins and nephews.

To Thomas Sacret (qv) of Colchester, yeoman, £200 and piece of garden ground, with Summer house erected on it, in St Botolphs or adjoining same parish, now in own occupation and adjoining that of Thomas Sacret's garden. Later increased to £250.

G

To executors nephew Robert (London woollen-draper), John Gilson son of nephew John, niece Mary Poyner (qv) he left the shop and baking office in All Saints (Rated 1 in 776, Gilson 5, Bridges 8; In 1795 Bridges 6, Stephen Betts (qv) 8. 63/63a High St., now (c. 1985) Markhams) now occupied by William Bridges (father of Theophilus Bridges (qv)) with messuage adjoining now in my own occupation, on trust to renew the lease to William Bridges for seven years before offering it for sale, he to have preference of buying. This sale to produce money for the following legacies:

- £20 Mr (Rees) Harris (qv) minister at St Helen's Lane and £50 at interest for benefit of ministry 'where I usually attend.' (Gilson was the first signatory of the memorandum sent by a group of nonconformists to Winsley's Trustees, 1772, cf James Thorn 1 (qv)).
- Sarah Taylor £20 at 21, daughter of now wife of Thomas Sacret (qv).
- Sarah Bridges £10 at 21, daughter of William.
- Maidservant Martha Smith £20, later increased to £100.

To Mary Poyner, the two adjoining messuages in St Mary-at-the-Walls one in her own occupation, the other lately occupied by Revd (William) Shillito (qv) (37 Crouch St). (cf Francis Merry (qv) bricklayer, another signatory of the Winsley's memo).

A memo adds £50 at 21 to George Rusher, son of Mary and George of the Height (Hythe) with lawful interest.

'The Burow in the Bow Window Room is to be given to the widow of Wm. Gilson.' He was a baker and later customs officer, dd. 1781. His daughter married in 1782 (nfr).

Mary Poyner died 18 Jun 1810 aged 83.

GILSON CHARLES [1295]
Baymaker
ob. 1770

Brother of Benjamin Gilson (qv) and Daniel Gilson (qv) gent. Was named Channel Commissioner in the list of 1750. Is buried in the family table tomb at Lion Walk, died 3 April 1770 aged 69.

GILSON REVD DANIEL [1272]
Minister
fl. 1691-1738

The first minister of St Helens Lane chapel. His will is ERO D/ACR 15/1, proved 1738.

JBB note: Gilson family members were free burgesses by right of birth from mid seventeenth century, and continue to vote when they settle elsewhere; eg. Samuel, free 1656, is ancestor of numerous Samuels, glaziers in Gt. Coggeshall up to 1788. Nathaniel, free 1713, baker, was the parent of the branch of the family in Whitechapel and Spitalfields. From Jeremiah, free 1710, descends a family in Needham Market including papermakers at Creeting St Mary. The father of Samuel above was Barnaby, son of Barnaby, a baker, and this is the most frequent family trade. Colchester Poll Book 1734/5 lists 16 Gilson burgesses in all from Colchester, Coggeshall, Halstead and London. Colchester Gilsons were mostly nonconformists associated with Lion Walk (see other entries here).

GILSON DANIEL 2 [1273]
Gent
ob. 1769

Son of Nathaniel Gilson, baker. Was apprenticed to Henry Fleming, citizen of London and cloth-worker, 1718, £36 15s (NA IR 1/6/101). His will is at NA PROB 11/950, 244 Bogg, made 1768, proved 10 July 1769. It named his brothers Charles and Benjamin executors; niece Mary Poyner (qv) was left his

G

diamond ring (see CPL Crisp ML 250, 1722, Francis Poyner married Sarah Gilson). Is buried in the family table tomb at Lion Walk (died 12 January 1769 aged 66) as is his wife Elizabeth (died 7 November 1768, aged 54, JBB Note, nfr - *née* Whiting, a second wife married in 1762), brother Charles (qv), sister Elizabeth (died 4 February 1783 aged 75), and brother Benjamin (qv).

GILSON THOMAS 1 [1297]
Baker
1727-1768

Created free burgess 1727 (nfr). His will, Thomas Gilson, baker, Colchester, is at NA PROB 11/938, proved 16 April 1768.

GILSON THOMAS 2 [1298]
Baker
w. 1804

Thomas Gilson, baker, Colchester, NA PROB 11/1404, proved 28 February 1804.

See also Poll Book 1812, vote of Thomas, son of Thomas Gilson, baker; Thomas (baker) and John Walter (brother of Thomas) were made free burgesses in 1816.

JBB Note (JBB NB Mar72, notes on Deeds of Thoroughgoods): One bakery, in the Gilson family for many years, is 21 Head St till recently Thoroughgoods. A deed of 1844 has plan with huge oven at back of premises. After the Head St fire of Dec. 1834, which badly damaged Mr Gilson's, a plaque was put up in the gable with town arms and dates 1689 and 1835. 22 June 1844 premises were sold by trustees of Thomas Gilson, baker decd. and were purchased by John Walter Gilson for £350 following auction at Fleece 10 April last. Lot 2 in this auction was perhaps part of premises up Church Street.

GLANDFIELD WILLIAM [1244]
Plumber and Glazier
ob. 1798

15 September 1776 married Rachel Green at Little Horkesley (by banns, ERO D/P 307/1/2).

1 August 1778 advertised in *IpsJ* as plumber glazier and painter (late journeyman to Mr Unwin) 'near the gate on East Hill.' He was rated 6, as was Unwin in All Saints from 17881-97.

Will ERO D/ACR 19/131, made 14 June 1797, proved 8 February 1798. Exors 'brother' John Green of Gt. Horkesley, farmer John Salmon, Aldham carpenter and wife.

Left all to widow as long as she remains so. If not to be divided between children; sons Edward and John Green to be apprenticed in what trades they choose. Son William to assist mother in carrying on the business, till she thinks proper to resign it to him (she was still in business there in 1809). 5s to invalid son James.

GLIDE THOMAS 1 and 2 [1201]
Pot Makers, Thorpe
fl. 1750s

Father and son at Thorpe le Soken

Marriages and Deaths: Thos Glide married Mary Usher at Thorpe 3 June 1712, buried 13 January 1749/50; Thos Glide married Mary How 1735 (nfr), buried (spelt Glyde) 22 November 1760.

Thomas 2 advertised *IpsJ* 5 January 1750/1: Pot-maker at the White Lyon, Thorpe, carrying on business of late father, wanted an apprentice. Earthen pipes that last 40 years underground at 1s 6d a yard etc. and will carry a large current. Follows similar advertisement of 29 December 1750 (*IpsJ*) announcing that he had moved from the Anchor where he had no stable room to better premises with stables.

IpsJ 8 October 1757 Afflicted with Gout. Offered 'a large Sortiment of extream good EARTHENWARE well-leaded and the best of the kind that has been exposed for sale for many years past... All Country Gardeners that want any Auricula-pots, or Jot-pots ... may have any Quantity of extraordinary good Flower-pots on the shortest Notice'. He also makes Earthen Pipes for underground Drains and 'Welms for Gateways'. Fire crack'd Ware, well mended with White Lead and Oil half-price. A Journeyman 'may depend on good Encouragement. and constant Work either by the Week or Hundred.'

See also: CPL, Crisp ML271, ERO D/AML, 1778, William Glyde of Colchester cabinet-maker and John Day bind William to Lucy Sturgeon of Holy Trinity; ERO will Elizabeth Glide ERO D/ACR 14/470.

GODFREY JOHN [350]
Surgeon, Coggeshall
fl. 1767

IpsJ 11 July 1767:

COGGESHALL July 8

Lately was performed by Mr John Godfrey Surgeon in this Place an Operation in Surgery which claims a Place in your Paper, that Persons unhappily in a similar Situation may not totally despair of Relief. Mr John Jolly, Steward to the Hon. Gen. Honeywood having his upper Arm carious in the joint, (a case which never yields to the common Methods in Surgery, but continually emaciates the Patient without any Prospect of a Cure) was happily released from his miserable Situation by losing his Arm at the upper Joint which Mr Godfrey performed with great Success as Mr Jolly can testify being in as good a state of Health as ever he was in his Life. This operation prevents Mr Jolly from lingering out his Days by a constant Discharge & does great Merit to the Operator.

GONNER JOHN [356]
Seed Merchant
fl. 1774-1799

On 10 June, 1774 (*IpsJ* 18 June 1774) Gonner, then a captain in the Holland trade, was married in London to Miss Sebborn of Colchester, daughter of John Sebborn (qv). Gonner continued as a mariner until John Sebborn jun. was accidentally drowned in 1786, when Gonner took over his late father-in-law's business. He advertised from the premises adjoining the White Hart and begged leave, 'to inform his friends, and the Public in general that the business will be carried on in all its branches, at the said shop of his predecessor, on the lowest terms, and hopes for a continuance of their favours' (*IpsJ* 8 April 1786). Gonner was a free burgess who voted in 1781, April 1784, 1788, 1790 and 1796 in support of the Corporation party. He was elected Common Councillor in 1787 and Assistant in 1790. On 31 October 1795 (*IpsJ*) one of his daughters was married and on 12 January 1799 (*IpsJ*) his daughter Ann married Mr Woodcock jun of the local watchmaking family (see William Woodcock (qv)).

GONNER THOMAS [355]
Chairmaker
1705-1788

At age 24 married Elizabeth Eats, 21 of Brightlingsea (CPL Crisp ML221, ERO D/ABL 1730) in 1730. In 1731 was admitted free burgess by right of apprenticeship to John Agnis (qv) and voted in 1768, 1780, 1781 and 1784. Was parish clerk of St Peters for 53 years. On 5 October 1773 was one of Thomas Boggis's (qv) nominees in elections for Sergeant at Mace, and was Clerk of the Market in 1780 (Poll Book). Lived on North Hill, rated 2.

G

GOODAY SAMUEL [1238]
Carpenter
w. 1692

Occupied the carpenters' yard in All Saints, opposite the Church and next door east of the Castle Inn, which remained in this trade for around 100 years. A rate list preserved by Morant (ERO D/DRO, Vol. 5, no 48) shows him here in 1689 rated 2d a week.

His will of 1692 (ERO D/ACR 11/26) directs that property in St Peters Sudbury, and St Mary's 'without the gate there called Headgate' and woods at Stanway are to be sold for children John, Samuel, Susan and Mary. Residue to son John Gooday. Witnesses James Wilder, Daniel Pilston, Ady Mott.

The will of William Talcott stapler (at the present Minories), NA PROB 11/444, 52 Lort, made 1697, proved 15 February 1698, left legacies to the above as 'cozens,' i.e. to John, carpenter £15 and acquits him of a debt of £5, Samuel £11, Susanna £12, Mary £25.

Two freedoms by apprenticeship in Colchester Oath Book (ERO D/B 5 R1): 17 February 1697 Philip Gray apprenticed to Samuel Gooday; 11 May 1699 John Toller apprenticed to John Gooday. (The Tollers were of Stanway and Copford, nfr).

GOODWIN THOMAS AND WILLIAM [359]
Boot and Shoemakers
fl. 1760s-80s

William came from Nayland in 1785 to take over the premises at 101 High Street that his brother Thomas had occupied since 1766. Thomas himself had succeeded his old master, John Paine (*IpsJ* 17 September 1785, ERO C905, Box 1, Index 1983).

See also: Thomas Goodwin apprenticed to John Paine 1761, £7 7s, NA IR 1/54/104); John Paine apprenticed to Thomas Goodwin, butcher, of St James Westminster, 1741, £20 (NA IR 1/16/93).

GOOSE NAPTHALI [360]
Chymist and Druggist
fl. 1806-1826

Married Sarah Walford, daughter of Timothy Walford 1 (qv) cabinetmaker in 1806 (CPL, Crisp ML164, ERO D/ALL, 1806). In June of that year he advertised the opening of his shop in the High Street (*IpsJ* 14 June 1806). He became Treasurer of the Colchester Philosophical Society 'for the Promotion of Scientific and Literary Pursuits', formed on 3 May 1820 (Cromwell, *Colchester*, Vol. 2). He participated in attacks and counter attacks in the *Colchester Gazette* later that year (*Colchester Gazette* 9 December 1820). Though named as trustee and executor of both his brother-in-law and father-in-law's wills (cf Timothy Walford 1 and 2 (qv)) he was unable to act as he pre-deceased them both, dying in 1826 aged 43, a 'great loss', due to his 'highly cultivated mind and urbanity of manners' (nfr).

GOSLIN JOHN 1 [1270]
Carpenter
fl. 1749-1757

In 1749, when of St Botolphs, married Ann Walker (22) at St Martin, bound by Byatt Walker 1 (qv) St Peters, innkeeper (CPL Crisp ML144, ERO D/ALL 1749). Seems to have died by 1757 when the yard was for sale, along with five other tenements, St Botolphs, enquire Widow Goslin or Augustin Wayland (qv) carpenter in the same street.

See also: Assembly Book 10 March 1768, William Goslin created free burgess, 'of Brooks Market, Holborn.' He voted from London in 1781, 'Great St Helens,' and from Bishopsgate in 1788.

John Gosling of Lexden Hostler and Jacob Brunning of St Botolphs, carpenter bound, John to marry Elisabeth Ward of the same 1795 (CPL Crisp ML136, ERO D/ACL 1795).

The *British Directory* of 1791 lists John Goslin, carpenter. John Gosnall, died Angel Lane, 14 December 1809 aged 67 (*IpsJ*), his

G

will is at ERO D/ACR 19/549. Byatt Goslin, late of Colchester, now of London, cabinetmaker, is mentioned in the 1809 will of Thomas Dixon (qv). These Goslins also vote from London, see Poll Books of 1812, 1820.

GOSLIN JOHN 2 [364]
Innkeeper, Bear
fl. 1782-8

Occupied the Bear between 1782 and 1788 as tenant to Abraham Stradling (qv). He was a free burgess voting between 1780-4. He supported Potter in 1781 and in April 1784 but abandoned him for Smyth in July 1784. 'Wid. Gosling' was said to occupy the Bear in Stradling's will of 1811.

See also will of John Gosling, victualler, ERO D/ACR 15/418, made 1730, proved 1736.

GOSLIN JOHN 3 [361]
Glover and Breechesmaker
fl. 1785

In *IpsJ* of 16 July 1785, advertised from the 'Original Porter Shop where he now lives.'

GOSLIN JOHN 4 [366]
Gent, Beverley Lodge
fl. 1813

IpsJ 1 May 1813: Beverley Lodge, a white fronted cottage residence slated and with 20 acres was for sale (Winstanley & Son London). This was followed by subsequent advertisements. *IpsJ* 26 June 1813: Beverley Lodge for Auction by William Linton (qv) with the adjacent land in small lots. Also for sale was the furniture of Mr John Goslin, removed to his residence in London. The *IpsJ* of 7 August 1813 offered Beverley Lodge plus 10 acres.

G

The land was clearly being sold off for building in the new suburban development along Lexden Road. This was a property which frequently changed hands (22 May 1819 *Colchester Gazette*: again for sale. Long description not noted; *IpsJ* 19 June 1824: again for sale. No owner. Good description not noted).

See also: entry for Thomas Anderson (qv) who built Beverley Lodge; Auction of household furniture and farming stock Mr James Goslin, deceased, Gt Horkesley, *IpsJ* 17 and 24 September 1791.

GOSLIN STEPHEN [363]
Innkeeper, Goat and Boot
fl. 1768-1783

A free burgess who voted for Rebow and Gray in 1768. A Stephen Goslin, is listed as owner occupier of the Goat and Boot in 1783 (may be a son).

See also Stephen Goslin, yeoman voted in 1780 (for Smyth) and Stephen Goslin haydealer voted in 1781 (Affleck) and 1784 (for Affleck in April and Potter in July); Stephen Goslin, maltster, will ERO D/ACR 14/463, 1736; Stephen Goslin, fellmonger, will ERO D/ACR 15/140, 1743.

GOUDE ANTHONY and SARAH [365]
Wagon and Horses
fl. 1751

Sarah, described as sister and heir to Nicholas Lues (qv) (despite her non appearance in his will ERO D/ABR 24/54, 1751) and her husband bought out George Wegg jun's (qv) interest in the Wagon and Horses for £260 and accrued interest, thereby redeeming Lues' mortgages (Deeds of Wagon and Horses, ERO D/DHt T337/12).

G

GRAY CHARLES ESQ [423]
MP
1696-1782

See full article in JBB, *EAE*: 61-72

GRAY GEORGE [1299]
Glazier
w. 1747

Born 1677/8 of a Nayland family. His wife Elizabeth is buried at Holy Trinity Colchester, 17 October 1727. The father of Charles Gray (qv) MP (L. C. Sier, 'The ancestry of Charles Gray', *ER*, lxi:92).

Alderman, also Borough Chamberlain between 1719 and 1725. Was also part of the committee appointed in 1713 to sell freedoms to finance the Corporation's legal expenses. Politically a Whig, in contrast to his son, Charles. A Whig Alderman at the time of the Tory ascendancy on the Corporation in the 1730s, and as such fell foul of the Tories' attempts to secure a Corporation majority by removing their political opponents. In the autumn of 1739 was indicted for sodomy together with Thomas Francis and for a similar assault on John Blatch, and when the offences were found was removed from the Alderman's bench. For a discussion of this case, referencing of primary sources, and its implications in local politics see D'Cruze, *Pleasing Prospect*:148-152; for an overview of local politics of the period see *VCH Essex*, Vol. 9.

Perhaps unsurprisingly there is no mention of his son in George Gray's will of 1747 (NA PROB 11/755/181, made 2 July 1747, proved 2 September 1747). He left:

- To sister Susan Hall of Nayland Suffolk, £50 annuity to be paid quarterly, charged on the Red Lyon estate in St Nicholas Colchester (The Red Lion inn).
- To Henry Hall, nephew, apothecary in the City of London, £500.

G

- To niece Sara, wife of Thomas Smith, Nayland, maltster, £500.
- To maidservant Susan Everett, £50.
- To George Francis (qv) Colchester, Glazier, all that part of the messuages etc now in my own occupation except the Iron Warehouse and Wine Cellar and Vaults in parish of St Mary-at-the-Walls plus the stock of lead and glass with the tools and utensils belonging to the Glazing and Plumbing Trade of which I shall die possessed and debts concerning same, also £500.
- To nephew Theophilus Hall (qv), the Red Lyon estate occupied by Adam ?Hurd, Robert Paris, Thomas Francis, ? Murrels and a tenement late occupied by John Blumfield and now empty. Also a messuage occupied by Mr John Lenham and cellar and wine vaults under same in my own occupation in St Mary-at-the-Walls and the residue of the estate.

Theophilus Hall and George Francis were executors. George Francis was Gray's godson and the son of the Thomas Francis who had been Gray's co-defendant in the sodomy case.

Gray asked to be buried in the Chancel at Nayland in a Vault to be made for that purpose in or as near as may be to the same place where my late Grandmother was buried.

GRAY T. [1163]
Baker
bkt. 1804

Was declared bankrupt in 1804 (*Universal Magazine* 17 November 1804).

GREAT CHARLES [369]
Grocer
fl. 1762-1797

The son of Thomas Great, apothecary (qv) who, though trading as a grocer rather than in his father's trade, continued to make

G

and sell the family speciality of candied eringo root. He married Mary Edwards of Langham in 1751 (nfr).

This Charles Great was amongst early donors to the Castle Book Society. His gift included anatomy books etc, perhaps inherited from the earlier apothecaries in the family.

In flight from French revolutionary invasion, the Prince of Orange and suite came to Colchester from Harwich in 1795.

> The Prince of Orange attended divine service at St Peter's Church on Sunday morning. On Monday his Serene Highness viewed the collection of pictures in the possession of Mr Great, by whom he was presented with a box of Eringo Root which was graciously received (31 January 1795 *IpsJ*).

Great died in 1797 and was buried with his family in St Nicholas (see MI under Thomas Great (qv)). He had requested to be buried simply with no hearse, by daylight before 5 p.m., decently and privately near his brother's grave. His will (NA PROB 11/1290, Exeter 320, 9 May 1797) left the family house where he had lived and 'also the Toft in the High Street opposite my dwelling aforesaid' to his wife Mary.

After her death, her nephews Charles Great Keymer (qv) and William Keymer the Younger (William Keymer 2 (qv)) became trustees to sell the estate and pay the interest from £500 to his sister-in-law Mrs Ann Keymer, then to her husband William Keymer 1 (qv) bookseller. Then the principal was to be divided between their children, the two above trustees and their sister Ann Keymer equally.

£500 was left to Mrs Mary Folkes 'who takes care of my said wife in her present unhappy affliction'; £200 to their servant Rose Goodwin after his wife's decease, £20 each was left to the other servants, Samuel Muffatt, Phillis Ives and Elizabeth Hailes, provided they were living with his wife at the time of her death.

The children of his brother-in-law, John Pooley Edwards, now or late merchant in Jamaica, received £500 each after his wife's death, the legacies to lapse if not claimed within two years thereof. The residue of the estate was to be divided between Charles Great Keymer, William Keymer jun and Ann Keymer. His wife and nephews were named as executors. He added that if his wife did not recover from her affliction she was to be cared for tenderly and not removed to any public or private madhouse.

Mrs Mary Great died 'after a long affliction' the following year (*Ips*) 14 April 1798). Her will is at NA PROB 11/1306, 26 May 1798. The property was then offered for sale;

> EXTENSIVE FREEHOLD PREMISES
> In the HIGH STREET COLCHESTER
> To be SOLD by PRIVATE CONTRACT
> And entered upon at Michaelmas or sooner if required,
>
> All the Capital Premises, late in the occupation of Mr CHARLES GREAT, deceased; comprising on the ground floor, a shop, containing in front 39 feet, in which the grocery and tea businesses &c have been carried on for many years; 2 good parlours, a kitchen and scullery, very large cellars; on the second storey, a large dining room, and a smaller one in front, with five bedrooms backwards; on the upper storey, 2 large bedrooms and garrets. A large yard and neat gardens well planted with choice fruit trees and a good pump in the same: two terras Cisterns, brew office, chaise house, stabling &c. the breadth of the premises backwards contained above 60 feet.
>
> For further particulars enquire of Mr Charles Great Keymer, woollen draper or of Mr Wm. Keymer jun., bookseller, Colchester.
>
> N.B. The ERINGO ROOT continues to be candied and sold at the above shop as usual (*Ips*) 5 May 1798).

On 5 May, 2 June, 22 September 1798 (*Ips*) the house was again advertised together with '... the genuine collection of PAINTINGS of the said Mr Charles Great in which is included the two capital Portraits of Sir John Jacques and his Lady' (see under Samuel Great (qv)).

GREAT SAMUEL [367]
Apothecary
ob. 1706

The Great or Groot family of apothecaries were of Dutch origin. They had premises in High Street, two doors below the Red Lion, with a sign 'at the Twisted Posts and Pots' where they continued until the death of Charles Great (qv) in 1797.

Their collection of pictures, reputedly by Van Dyke, was an attraction in the locality. These were finally offered to the National Gallery by William Keymer, heir to the Great family (cf Charles Great Keymer (qv)) in 1854 – and refused. G. O. Rickwood records this on 26 April 1854 as a 'Day of Humiliation' (CPL G. O. Rickwood Scrapbook - from Crozier's Diary, also Charles Great (qv)).

Samuel Great (ob. 1706) was first in the family to make candied Eringo Root, originally sold in Colchester by Robert Buxton apothecary (qv) also Mayor (ob. 1655) to whom Samuel Great had been apprenticed.

Great's wall tablet, formerly in St Nicholas, now in All Saints, states:-

In Memory of
Mr Samuel Great, Apothecary
died 9th May, 1706 aged 80
and Susan his wife
died 14th June 1722, aged 83
She was daughter of Mr Nicholas Jacques
Merchant (Brother to Sir John Jacques Baronet)
they had issue, 8 sons and 4 daughters.

See also will NA PROB 11/768 Anna Maria Great, widow, Colchester, proved 8 March 1749.

G

GREAT THOMAS [368]
Apothecary
fl. 1747-1762

This Thomas Great was grandson of Samuel Great (qv). Hollytrees Museum has a bottle and eringo box with label, made by Thomas Great. As well as the apothecary's shop, at one time, the family also owned the Red Lion. A rainwater head in the yard with a red lion brandishing a post with fleur de lys head also bears the initials TG for Thomas Great (father of this individual).

Ips] 5 September 1747:-

> PYRMONT WATER (in large sized Bottles)
>
> Just arrived and sold by Thomas Great, Apothecary in Colchester; of whom may be had other sorts of MINERAL WATERS at the cheapest rates.

Colchester Corporation frequently made gifts of eringo root to visiting dignitaries. In 1721 Thomas Great charged the Corporation £1 16s for 8lbs gilt eringo and 2s for two 'wainscot boxes' to present it in (ERO D/B 5 Aa1/32; compare 16s for 4lbs paid Mr Buxton and 6d for a box in 1620, ERO D/B 5 Aa1/4).

Great was a free burgess who voted in 1741 for Savage and Gray and in 1747 for Gray and Olmius. In 1747 John, son of John Sparrow, was apprenticed to Great for £63 (NA IR 1/18/33) and in 1755 he took John Clubbe (qv) of Whatfield, son of Revd John Clubbe (qv), apprentice for £73 10s (NA IR 1/52/134). Great was an associate of Austin Stapley (qv) surgeon of Ford Street, Aldham. He stood bond for Stapley's wedding in 1750 (CPL Crisp ML45) and is named as a creditor in his will of 1773 (ERO D/ABR 26/298).

Thomas Great died in 1762 and his house was advertised (*Ips]* 20 March 1762, JBB NB 76/5: 21) though the property was evidently not sold:-

> To be sold by auction by Henry Lodge (qv) at the Red Lion, The Late Dwelling House of Mr Thomas Great,

G

apothecary, deceased, being an entire new Building, within two years, fronted with Brick and sash'd with a good accustomed Shop ... the Rooms being all new floor'd, wainscotted and hung with good papers.... Marble slabs, chimney pieces and Jambs (?) ... also adjoining (? opposite) Public house, the Bear occupied by James Unwin (qv) ... also Barbers shop adjoining occupied Daniel Adkinson.... All freehold in High Street, St Nicholas Parish.

The fashionable household goods were also advertised. Prospective purchasers should enquire of Mrs Great, widow and executrix or Thomas Bayles, attorney (qv).

His will (NA PROB/11874, 109 St Eley, made 30 May 1760, proved 30 March 1762) asked that he be buried with his ancestors in St Nicholas. He left property at Peldon (cf Austin Stapley (qv) above) to pay his liabilities as executor of Charles Saunders, farmer (qv). He left the St Nicholas properties later advertised (above) to his wife, Elizabeth (the last two of which had been purchased of Francis Freshfield 2 (qv)). Elizabeth also received all the household goods, china &c. Great was buried, as he requested in St Nicholas, where a flat slate ledger records:-

Thomas Great
son of Samuel Great
died May 14th 1731
also
three sons of the said
Thomas Great.
viz
Demetrius Great
died 1750
Thomas Great
died January 10th 1762
and
Charles Great
died April 28th 1797
aged 73

G

>Mary Great
> wife of the above
> Charles Great
> died
> April 8th 1798
> aged 70

GREEN EDWARD ESQ [373]
Sudbury and Lawford Hall, Essex
w. 1814

His will (NA PROB 11/1560) was made 29 May 1814 (wits. Elizabeth Hubbard, Coffee House Sudbury; Mary Rayner daughter of Mr Hubbard, R. Frost, solicitor of Sudbury) and proved on 23 September 1814. He left to his daughters Elizabeth, the wife of Revd Robert Hill and Mary Green Pochin, £1500 of stock apiece. The residue was left to his wife Elisa, the sole executor.

GREEN ISAAC [1207]
Master Carpenter
1721-1799

Isaac Green was by far the wealthiest Colchester builder of his period and obviously well-regarded. Son of Daniel Green who bought Wegg's Land (Magazine Farm, ERO D/DEl T383, 1724-1822) in 1724, and Elizabeth his wife.

Freeman by right of service to Henry Bevan (qv) who dd. 13 August 1767.

A bill from him for £102, in 1752 among Rebow vouchers mentions his workmen: 1749 Leppingwell, 1750 Shimmen, Burnham, Nutman, Frost, Deeks, 1751 Goss, Daw junior and senior (ERO C47, Box 2. cf Dorr in an account from Henry Bevan (qv) of 1744).

His writing is much better than Bevan's but spelling is erratic; 'Emidately' in letters (ERO D/DU 161/362) to Philip Roberts Esq of East Bergholt, 1770-1771, when a Mrs Bridget Grimston

G

was dying at 'Tendering.' He mentions a Fever and not being able to get a Boot on his foot, and as for Mr 'Ben. Boggas" farm, 'I think I never saw worse yards in my life.'

Took apprentices; 1752 Robert Marne £21 (NA IR 1/51/214), 1755 William Phillips (qv) £21 (NA IR 1/52/93); 1755 William Lay (qv) 20 gns (NA IR 1/53/139). Isaac Green's apprentices were unusual in that they did not claim the freedoms of the Borough to which they would normally be entitled. Richard Marne (1752) disappears without trace from local records.

Bills for work at The Cups for Samuel Martin Esq of Alresford Hall, accompanying similar bills for Francis Merry (qv) bricklayer, are £54 10s in 1764, £34 12s in 1768, £22 in 1772, and small payments to William Lay (qv) 1770-3, but £21 again with Merry in 1775. This suggests that Green gave up building about then. He calls himself 'gent' in 1777 (ERO, Rebow papers D/Dht Bl, Small Account Book no. 4, 4 March 1766); Isaac Green, 'Balance' for a bill for Carpenter's work to Xmas 1764, £100 2s 8d. This is at Wivenhoe Park.

Assistant in Charter of 1763, Alderman 1772, resigning 11 July 1782. Seems to have worked as an election agent for Rebow; a Rebow voucher of 1780 for £2 0s 6d is for cash spent on some voters for Isaaac Martin Rebow (qv) and Sir Robert Smyth (qv) (ERO C47, Box 2). Paid to him by Samuel Ennew (qv). One of the signatories to a letter to Sir Robert Smyth re Channel duties (14 February 1781). Was appointed a Harbour Commissioner (Act of 1780).

Lexden Manor Court, (ERO D/DEl M163-174) Occupied tannery (where Bevan's 'Cherry Orchard' was) admitted 25 October 1753, surrendered 9 April 1790. This business may have been his chief concern. Lexden House at the top of the hill is not on Chapman and André's map, 1775/7, but marked with an avenue to it on Plume's survey of Green's estates (1797, ERO C/T523). This brick box much enlarged since had remains of eighteenth-century detail in 1963, and a hip roof survives. Admitted to this property 13 September 1764, heriots discharged 5 July 1785.

G

Was appointed executor in a number of local wills; 1763, John Alefounder 1 (qv) carpenter (apprentice to Henry Bevan 1 (qv)); 1777, Henry Ennew Bevan (see under Samuel Ennew (qv)); 1787, Dr Francis Pigott (qv) (Angel Lane); 1793, Dr Pigott's widow (qv), daughter of John Cole (qv) the merchant who built the big box 'Tranent' in Crouch St., 1762-4; 1790, Mrs Elizabeth Potter Bevan, named as her 'good friend' and residuary legatee.

Ips] 16 December 1780, Trustee with the Revd Dr Nath. Forster (qv) and William Townshend (qv) (attorney) for the creditors of Revd John Bree (qv) late of Marks Tey.

Married Mary Duffield, 1753, who had Cooke in-laws. Their daughter Mary married Samuel Cooke of Sible Hedingham in 1788 with a dowry of £4,000. Mary Green, his wife died 25 November 1795 and he 'after a lingering illness' on 24 March 1799, aged 78 (MI Lexden).

His will (NA PROB 11/1322) was made by William Mason 2 (qv) 16 April 1796 proved 24 April 1799. He left:-

- His Lexden house and a farm at Mile End to grandson, Samuel Green Cooke (qv) subject to annuity to sister Hester Thorn – she had married James Thorn 1 (qv) as his second wife in 1753, and survived him by 44 years.
- Farms at Easthorpe, Copford and Marks Tey to grandson Joseph Cooke.
- Farms at Tolleshunt Beckingham to Samuel Cooke (qv) (son-in-law).
- Marriage settlement of loving daughter Mary confirmed, £4,000.
- £3,000 3% stock to grand-daughter Ann Cooke at 21 (interest for her upbringing).
- £2,000 to daughter Mary for her sole and separate use and all his household goods.
- £100 to brother Joseph Green (qv) as token of affection (a merchant who later left Olivers, Stanway to Mary).

G

- £10 to a number of nieces and godsons. (one is Isaac Green, son of John of Fordham Hall, farmer - the Greens originated from there).

See also other MIs Lexden: Eleanor Marion Cooke wife of Samuel Green Cooke of St John's Green, died 19 November 1822 *aet.* 23; Samuel Cooke of St Johns Green died 23 August 1825, *aet.* 73 and wife Mary, died 27 February 1831 *aet.* 75; Samuel Green Cooke, died 25 March 1868 *aet.* 76; Emily Jane Cooke, died 17 December 1866, *aet.* 72; Joseph Cook, died 4 April 1864, *aet.* 68 (JBB NB Apr 63:36).

GREEN JAMES [374]
Innkeeper, Seahorse
fl. 1763-1789

A free burgess voting from 1768 to 1788. He supported Affleck in 1781 and Affleck and Smyth in April 1784 but then switched to Potter in July 1784 and Jackson in 1788. His role within the emerging Corporation party is confirmed by a satirical newspaper advertisement lampooning Potter's supporters in February 1785 (*IpsJ* 26 February 1785) meeting in the house of 'Neptunes Nag' owned by 'Shining Jemmy'. In 1788 his sureties for the alehouse recognisances were Richard Weatherley (qv) and Ephraim Shillito 3 (qv), Brandy Merchant. Green was always active in All Saints Vestry and was overseer in 1782, 1785 and was elected for 1789. His will (ERO D/ACR 18/324) left all his personal estate as well as a life interest in the Seahorse to his wife Sarah (qv), which would thereafter revert to his son John.

GREEN JOHN 1 [377]
Woolcomber
fl. 1783-1815

Was apprenticed in 1758 to Samuel Johnson (qv) beater for £5 (NA IR 1/53/95).

Green published a public apology in the *IpsJ* of 2 March 1793 for 'having raised and spread ... scandalous reports of James

Triggs (qv)' late innkeeper of the Red Lion and then assistant to Benjamin Hall (qv) baymaker. The Red Lion had been the base for the supporters of the radical candidate George Tierney (qv) in the elections of 1788 and 90 and Triggs had left the inn soon after Tierney's defeat in 1790. Green was a free burgess who supported Tierney in 1788 but switched to the rival candidates in 1790. His earlier voting pattern from 1768 to 1784 shows that he had previously been in the habit of supporting radical and 'outsider' candidates. His change of political allegiances may have been related to his dispute with Triggs.

Green lived in a small house in Trinity Street from at least 1783. His will of 1810/15 (of Holy Trinity, ERO D/ABR 31/201) leaves it to his wife Mary and children, who were still resident at the time of the Cole and Hale survey of 1819.

GREEN JOHN 2 [371]
Coach harness maker
fl. 1771

Was apprenticed to John Cage (qv) collarmaker in 1754 for £15 (NA IR/15 52/7). Himself, took Benjamin Jackson apprentice for £10 10s in 1771 (NA IR 1/51/208).

A copy of his will is at ERO C47, CPL790.

See also Mrs Green (qv) saddler, Headgate.

GREEN JOSEPH [375]
Merchant and Lime Kiln Proprietor
fl. 1765-1808

Green took over the lime kiln at the Hythe in April 1765 (*IpsJ* 6 April 1765) and by 1776 he owned barns, granaries, wines, beers etc in St Giles and St Leonards valued for insurance at £1,300 (Sun Insurance 363665). In 1795 he declined the coal, cinder and corn trade in favour of his niece's husband Samuel Cooke (qv) and George Round (qv) (*IpsJ* 28 March 1795) and recommended the new firm of Cooke and Round to his customers. This was not a complete retirement, for in 1796 he acted as assignee in the bankruptcy of John Ram (qv) together with John Collins Tabor (qv). Joseph Green was brother to Isaac Green (qv) of Lexden and received £100 (a token remembrance in relation to the wealth of the family) in Isaac's will of 1796/9 (NA PROB 11/1322, 24 April 1799). Joseph Green himself died in 1808 and was buried with his family at Lexden on 25 December 1808 aged 75. The *IpsJ* published an obituary on 31 December 1808 (giving his age as 85) and described him as 'an eminent merchant, universally respected'. On 4 February 1809 (*IpsJ*) his furniture and books were advertised for sale. His will made on 10 January 1801 and with codicils of 1802 and 1805 was finally proved on 18 April 1809 (NA PROB 11/1495). He left the bulk of his real estate to various of the children of Samuel and Mary Cooke with cash legacies of between £50 and £200 each to nine other friends and relations including his sister Hester Thorn, William Philips (qv) carpenter and his wife Dorcas (*née* Taylor of Lexden).

GREEN MRS [372]
Saddler
fl. 1794

Had premises in Headgate where she was succeeded by Thomas Barns (qv) on 12 April 1794 (*IpsJ*).

See also John Green 2 (qv), harness maker.

GREEN SARAH [376]
Innkeeper, Seahorse
fl. 1789-1801

Inherited a life interest in the Seahorse from her husband James Green (qv). She left (ERO D/ACR 19/256, 1801) the inn to her eldest son James, subject to a mortgage of £206 incurred by her husband, to be reduced to £100 from her personal estate, the residue of which was to be left to her son William.

See also *Essex Review* 53:125, William Green of the Seahorse, drawing by Dunthorne; will of William Green, gent, 1819, ERO D/ABR 31/488, legacies to Greens of St Peters.

GREEN WILLIAM [370]
Draper
fl. 1760s

Ran a linen drapery business at Lexden which was sold up in 1766 (*Ips*J 8 November 1766, JBB NB Blue 1:106).

GRETTON REVD CHARLES [379]
Rector, Springfield
w. 1779/1783

The second of three generations of Grettons to hold the living at Springfield. Revd Philip Gretton died 16 February 1745 and Henry Gretton (bapt. 3 October 1751; bur. 28 April 1795) succeeded his father.

Charles was also the father of Philip Gretton (qv) surgeon and apothecary. His will (ERO D/ABR 27/417, 1783, Springfield) mentions other sons Charles (bapt. 15 April 1755), John (bapt. 21 December 1753), Mark (bapt. 26 February 1764) and daughters Sarah (bapt. 10 March 1758, later married Revd John Dennison, White Notley - per will Philip Gretton (qv)), Catherine (bapt. 3 October 1759) and Maria (bapt. 29 September 1750). By his marriage settlement with his late wife (Elizabeth, bur. 14 April 1776 age 52), he held a farm at Wisbech which he advised son Henry to sell.

Gretton died on 4 October 1783, aged 69.

See Transcript Springfield Registers in ERO T/203/61, 73 and Mons ERO T/Z215/112 for these and other family entries.

GRETTON Philip [378]
Surgeon and Man Midwife
fl. 1786-1834

*Ips*J 15 April 1786: Advertisement for Philip Gretton, midwifery and surgery at East Bergholt. Was one of the doctors who attended Jacob Pattison (qv), the stabbed apprentice. Was also

G

a friend of the young Benjamin Strutt (qv) (see JBB, *EAE*:115, 147, 155, 160, 219).

In 1787, Gretton, having moved to the late dwelling house of his deceased friend Mr Sterling (Robert Sterling (qv)) solicited the future custom of Sterling's patients (*IpsJ* 29 December 1787). Newton Tills (qv) and Cater Day (qv) also advertised themselves as Sterling's successors.

Became a member of the Castle Book Society in 1794 (ERO Acc C905 Box 2, 'Boggis IV' notes from original records including Minute Books, Book of Laws and Orders 1790–1813, Book of Clubs including Treasurers' Accounts from 1792).

Gretton died in 1834. His will (NA PROB 11/1829, proved 23 July 1835) left his property to his wife Susan Margaret, then to his brother Major Charles Gretton of Springfield (who in the event predeceased him, so a codicil names a nephew Philip Dennis of Alnwick, Northumberland, surgeon, the son of his 'surviving sister' Sarah, the wife of the Revd John Dennis, Vicar of White Notley). Gretton's sisters Sarah and Elizabeth are also mentioned. He left the distribution of mourning rings and other tokens to the discretion of his wife.

GRIFFITH COL EDWARD [383]
4th Regt Dragoons
ob. 1781

Griffith died on 6 March 1781 aged 60 (Mon. St Peters). His death was announced in *IpsJ* of 10 March 1781 as having taken place at his house in Colchester (North Hill) on Thursday night. His will (NA PROB 11/1077, Webster) made 8 January 1776 (witnessed Edmund Affleck (qv), John Affleck) left all to his wife Elizabeth. It was proved on 5 April 1781. His furniture was advertised for sale on 31 March 1781 (*IpsJ*).

GRIFFITH MOSES MD [381]
Physician
1698-1785

See full article at JBB, *EAE*:20-50.

GRIGSON THOMAS [386]
Ironmonger
ob. 1762

Traded from 57 High Street where he was rated 12 in 1757. Was a churchwarden at St Nicholas alongside Henry Lodge (qv). Died in 1762, buried St Nicholas 7 May 1762. Sale advertised *IpsJ* 12 February 1763 disposed of his stock in trade near St Nicholas church.

GRIMWOOD JOHN MATTHEW [388]
Barrister, Recorder and High Steward
fl. 1787–1832

The son of Thomas Grimwood (qv) of Dedham and Elizabeth *née* Lechmere. The Lechmere family resided at the property at the top of East Hill known as Winsleys (See *IGI*, Maria Sophia Lechmere (qv), D'Cruze, *Pleasing Prospect*: 34-5, 58-9).

Grimwood was practicing at Grays Inn when he was appointed Deputy Recorder and thus heir apparent by the then Steward and Recorder for the Borough, the dying William Mayhew 2 (qv). Grimwood was challenged for the office by Frank Smythies 1 (qv) the Town Clerk against whom he brought a legal action. This was settled in 1790 securing Grimwood the Recordership which he retained till his death. He was later created High Steward (1803-7).

Grimwood received a mourning ring from Samuel Ennew (qv) in 1795. He died on 2 December 1832 (*ECS* 8 December 1832) aged 78 'at his residence in Bloomsbury Place'. His country residence, Boxted House, 'a Genteel Villa Residence ... erected within 15 years' was offered for sale in 1833 (*ECS* 18 May 1833). He was buried at Boxted where a wall tablet records he was also Lord Treasurer's Remembrancer of the Court of Exchequer and the Registrar of the Corporation of the Sons of the Clergy. The tablet also commemorated his wife Elizabeth, daughter of the Revd Robert Cooke the vicar of Boxted parish. She died 14 November 1825 aged 68.

GRIMWOOD THOMAS [387]
Dedham Grammar School
fl. 1750-66

Ips] 22 February 1766 under Susan Scarlin (qv), advertisement for his and other schools in Dedham. Grimwood had vouched for the character of a new mistress at the Ladies School in 1750 (*Ips]* 27 January 1749/50).

In 1736 he had married Elizabeth Carolina, the daughter of Richard and Rebecca Lechmere (cf, her sister Maria Sophia Lechmere (qv); www.familysearchinternational.org, Compact Disc #72, Pin #171033). They had seven children including the barrister and later Colchester Borough Recorder, John Matthew Grimwood (qv).

GROVES [389]
Gunsmith
fl. 1813

Advertised the sale of his bankrupt stock near the Plough in Magdalen Street (*Ips]* 17 July 1813).

GUSTERSON HENRY 1 [1257]
Carpenter
1739-1803

Married three times (nfr); (1) to Sarah Cruswell, St Peters, 1765, (2) to Jane Aldridge, All Saints 1769 (she bur. St Nicholas 16 February 1789) and, (3) to Sarah Gosard, wid, Lexden, 1791.

In 1778 was paid £14 16s 0½d for work as a joiner at Wivenhoe Park (Rebow Accounts, ERO C47, Box 2).

His will, ERO D/ABR 29/590, left tmt. St Helen's Lane to wife Sarah for life, then to three children Henry, Sarah wife of Henry Gale, and Hannah. Also tmt. next door to where he dwells, occ. widow Bland. Stephen Candler (qv) and Isaac Diss (qv) attest his writing of codicil giving 'chest o'drawers' to Hannah.

(JBB note: address suggests he was one of Stephen Candler's (qv) workmen.)

See also William Salmon (qv) of Lexden, who married Elizabeth Gusterson (a sister?), 1744.

GUSTERSON HENRY 2 [391]
Innkeeper, Golden Lion St Mary
fl. 1780-1803

Was innkeeper at the Bell in St Botolphs in 1780-1, but had moved to the Golden Lion by 1783. Might be the same person as Henry Gusterson 1 (qv).

H

HADLEY JOHN [392]
Gent
fl. 1774-1814

The son of John Hadley the inventor (*ODNB*). He lived at West Bergholt Hall and in Holy Trinity, Colchester.

Earlier he had lived at Copford where part of his household furniture was offered for sale in 1774 (*Ips*J 28 September 1774). West Bergholt Hall was offered for sale by private contract in 1792 and 93 (*Ips*J 19 May 1792, 20 April 1793) described as 'a good farm house with additional building in front, late the residence of the proprietor' also three farms (apply Mr Alston, attorney at Nayland). The *Chelmsford Chronicle* of 23 July 1814 advertised the Capital Mansion House, Holy Trinity parish occupied by John Hadley Esq for auction. There were 2 gardens, one large, a large entrance and hall etc, 7 bedchambers. The furniture was for sale, Culver Street on 24 September 1814. (This is the house long since demolished east of Trinity Church on Culver Street, previously occupied by the Creffield family, then Revd John Halls (qv); JBB NB Apr72:149, ex. inf. Geoffrey Martin and ERO T/M268).

He died at West Bergholt in 1816 (*Ips*J 16 February 1816) and is buried there (Mon in churchyard; JBB NB Jul 63:17).

HAGON JOHN [33]
Gingerbread Baker
w. 1784

Of St Mary-at-the-Walls. Father-in-law of John Mannall (qv) gingerbread baker. His will of 1784 is at ERO D/ABR 27/450.

H

HAINES HEZEKIAH [394]
Copford Hall
w. 1763

Left a legacy to improve the library of the Castle Book Society.

> Hezekiah Haines Esq, late of Copford Hall in Essex dec'd by his last Will dated 25th Feb[ry], did give and bequeath to Samuel Ennew (qv) of Colchester in the said County, gent, the sum of Nine hundred Pounds, then standing in the said Testators Name in the Fund call'd New South Sea Annuities, upon Trust to pay the several Legacies therein mentioned, [which include] ... To Charles Gray (qv) of Colchester aforesaid Esquire the sum of One Hundred Pounds to be by him applied for the Improvement of the Library and the Benefit of the Book Club there, in such manner as he shall think fit.

The will (NA PROB 11/894) was proved in PCC in 5 December 1763. A list of volumes purchased by Gray for the Castle Book Club follows. These include dictionaries, maps, atlases, books of history, geography and genealogy, reference books on antiquarian coins and medals, the works of John Locke, Boyle, Lord Bacon, Newton, Addison, Swift, Montesque, Shakespeare, Bishop Warburton, Lord Littleton, Hurd, D'Alembert and Voltaire, commentaries on poetry and music, The *Illiad* and *Odyssey* and its translation by Pope, as well as volumes of parliamentary debates, *The Spectator*, *The Tatler* and *The Guardian*.

HALL BENJAMIN [396]
Merchant and Baymaker
bankrupt 1795

Related to Theophilus Hall (qv) winemerchant and owner of the Red Lion. He traded in partnership with John Thurstan (qv) merchant who was bankrupted with him in 1795. Thurstan's wife, Mary was cousin to Theophilus Hall and received a legacy in his will. After James Triggs (qv) left the Red Lion in 1790, following the Borough election defeat of

George Tierney (qv) (whose supporters met at the Lion), he (Triggs) became Hall's assistant until at least 1793 (cf John Green woolcomber (qv) who had slandered Triggs). Hall had bought the large mansion on East Hill late John Blatch Whaley's (qv) after Whaley's death in 1788 (*IpsJ* 16 August 1788). This 'fine house and furniture' were again for sale after Hall's bankruptcy (*The Star* 3 January 1795, *IpsJ* 3 January and 18 April 1795). Hall seems to have come to something of a sticky end. He had failed to satisfy the bankruptcy commissioners that he had given a sufficient account of his estate and was confined to Newgate prison in London. The commissioners offered a 5% reward for the discovery of any undisclosed property (*IpsJ* 24 January 1795).

HALL THEOPHILUS [397]
Wine Merchant
fl. 1747-1772

Was apprenticed to Abraham Brown, Baymaker for £28 in 1723 (NA IR 1/48/40). A free burgess who voted in 1747 and 1768 and supported Rebow's election petition in 1755 (JBB, *A Friend to His Country*: 26).

He owned the Red Lion and adjacent tenements. He lived in Head Street (nos. 15-17) one door uphill from St Mary's Lane, rated 11, also owning the corner house, between at least 1747 and his death in 1772. Hall was nephew and executor to Charles Gray's (qv) father George (qv).

Hall's will of 1772 (NA PROB 11/978, 26 June 1772) disposes of more than £9,000 in annuities to nieces and nephews in London and Nayland. The Red Lion and the Headgate property was inherited by his nephew, Thomas Smith (qv), son of Hall's sister Sarah of Nayland. He left small legacies to Revd John Crisp (qv) and Revd Thomas Stanton (qv) both dissenting ministers, and appointed two prominent Colchester dissenters Samuel Rootsey (qv) and John Wallis (qv) as trustees.

See also Blaxill, *Lion Walk*.

H

HALLEY REVD THOMAS [398]
Vicar, St Peters
fl. 1739-1759

For twenty years, vicar of St Peters Colchester. Witnessed the will of William Seaber 1 (qv) in 1746 (ERO D/ACR 15/216) and the administration of Peter Creffield (qv) in 1748 (ERO D/ABWb158). That year he was one of a number of local clerics, doctors etc. to sign a public notice declaring the town free of smallpox (*IpsJ* 6 August 1748).

His own will of 1759 (NA PROB 11/851, Artan 402, 22 December 1759) mentions his wife Elizabeth (*née* Seaber – they had married in 1757) and brother-in-law the Revd Richard Boys (qv) Rector of West Bergholt, (who had married Elizabeth's sister, Mary Seaber in 1754) and deals with property at Boreham.

Halley was buried at St Peters in 1759 and shares his tomb with his late wife Elizabeth, who died in 1784, by that time the widow of Samuel Chapman, M.D. of Sudbury (Strutt, *Colchester*, Vol. 2:15).

HALLS JAMES [401]
Fishmonger
fl. 1765-1784

One of a numerous family of fishmongers and fishermen including several free burgesses of varying party. In 1765 (*IpsJ* October 12 and 19) a squabble over the price of oysters was publicly continued between Halls and Daniel Manning (qv) of the King's Head. Halls accused the innkeepers of selling at 4s 4d per barrel and offered his own at 3s 6d. On 12 November 1768 the *IpsJ* reported 'James Halls oyster packer, Dealer in Fish, Rabbets, Lemons &c who lately lived near the 3 Cups' had taken a shop at the east end of St Runwalds Church in the Fishmarket, 'where gentlemen may be served with the best Colchester Oysters &c'. Halls traded from 148 High Street from at least 1764-68.

In 1774 there was a row in the shop. Catherine Bryner, a sailor's wife swore at Petty Sessions that Halls and his wife Sarah assaulted her. Catherine Rayner (sic) also charged Halls with 'striking her several times in the face with a cloth' (ERO, Examination Book, P/CoR/5, 28 November 1774).

HALLS JAMES ESQ [400]
c. 1753-1847

The father of John James Halls the painter (*ODNB*). Probably the son, by a first marriage, of James Halls Esq (the brother of Revd John Halls (qv)) who was a widower of about 38 when he married Hannah Daniell in 1755 (CPL Crisp ML443).

Was notable in Colchester in the late eighteenth century for his political radicalism at a time when such opinions were unpopular. His son was apparently named after Jean Jacques Rousseau. A report by the local postmistress to the Home Office on potential subversives includes detailed reference to Halls:-

> ... the Known Leading Disaffected Men in this Town are Mr James Halls a man of large property (left him by an uncle the late Rev'd Mr Halls who was a very good man) who I heard and I believe I may say it is a Truth, to Capt Mason (William Mason 2 (qv) attorney) of the Colchester Loyal Volunteers, that he despised them all, He Hated the Government and Constitution, and look'd on them as a set of Government Spies, with a great deal more Abusive Language - and this very Mr Halls has let a House and Furniture and pays Great attention to 3 French Emigrants to this town - who when they first came lived in a Little room very obscurely, they are called Count Sebville & Berenger, the third I don't know the name of, Mr Halls called on them on Monday Even' and advised Sebville to go to London on Tuesday morning, by all means, which he did, but I know not the purport of their business ... (NA HO 42/13, April 1798).

H

Henry Crabb Robinson (qv) was impressed by Halls. He wrote:-

> There was living in the town a private gentleman of reputed talents and elegant manner with the shyness of a scholar, whom I used to see at Keymer's (William Keymer (qv)) the bookseller's shop. This was Mr James Hall(s) and proud I was when I could get into talk with him. But he never flattered me as Strutt (Benjamin Strutt (qv)) did by appearing to think I was worth talking to.

Writing fifty years later Robinson adds: 'This Mr Halls was probably an unmanageable man — still is?' He also recalled one particular occasion when Halls spoke in public:-

> I recollect that on one occasion there was a meeting at the Castle on I forget what public business [and he finds a note that it was in March 1792, on account of the danger to the community of the number of dogs in town]. The ordinary motion of thanks to the Mayor for presiding being made, Halls moved an amendment in studiously obscure language. In his speech I recollect was the allusion to Pope's line: 'The merit of Vespasian ought not to be given to Titus'. And it concluded with an amendment 'That the thanks of this meeting be given to F (rancis) Smythies 1 Esq (qv) for graciously permitting the Mayor to hold the meeting'. A tumult of hisses and applause followed. The low party must have been very strong to allow such an assault on the hero of the majority (H. C. Robinson, *Material Reminiscences*, unpublished ms, Dr Williams Library, JBB NB May 69:108ff. In fact the meeting was in the Castle, not the Moot Hall, and was organised by the Revd Yorick Smythies (qv); see also *IpsJ* 25 February, 24 March 1792).

A few years later Halls spoke at a public meeting in favour of ending the war with revolutionary France. In February 1795 (*IpsJ* 2 February 1795; CPL Rickwood Annual Register) Halls and Robert Tabor (qv) proposed a motion for a Declaration of Peace. The motion was opposed by Frank Smythies 1 (qv),

Town Clerk and his brother-in-law Revd Thomas Twining (qv). The motion was lost by 36 to 105 votes.

Halls lived originally in Crouch Street then in St Nicholas. In 1797 (*IpsJ* 8 April 1797) his commodious freehold dwelling behind St Nicholas Church; late the residence of James Halls Esq was for auction on the premises (by Timothy Walford 1 (qv)). This probably marks his move to Greyfriars, earlier the home of his uncle and aunt. He remained there until the death of his wife Amelia *née* Garnett daughter of the Bishop of Clogher (ob. 29 January 1813 aged 57), when The Priory, formerly part of Greyfriars monastery, property of James Halls Esq was to be auctioned (*IpsJ* 24 July, 7 and 21 August 1813).

COLCHESTER, ESSEX
To be SOLD by AUCTION
by Mr ROBINS
At Garraways, London on Tuesday, August 26th
at Twelve in ONE LOT

THE PRIORY, formerly part of the GREYFRIARS MONASTERY, a very eligible FREEHOLD ESTATE and immemorially tithe free, land-tax redeemed, a capital and spacious Family Mansion, situate on a fine commanding eminence, the top of East Hill, the most preferable part of Colchester, the residence and property of JAMES HALLS Esq. The House is a substantial brick edifice, with a double bowed front, and contains, on the ground storey, a neat entrance hall, library, drawing room, breakfast room, capital dining parlours, store room, roomy closets, water closets &c; 7 airy bed chambers on the first story, with store room, closets &c, 4 good chambers on the upper story, with store rooms, closets &c. The offices comprise excellent kitchen, store closets, servants hall, bake house and scullery, pantries, larders, dairy, and roomy cellars in the basement, paved yard, with gates to the Street, double coach house, with a very extensive store chamber over it, and two three stall stables, brewhouse, and various outbuildings all of the most substantial brick, and in perfect repair, lawns and pleasure grounds, fish pond, a capital kitchen garden, partly walled and well stocked with fruit trees, another garden completely walled round, dry gravel walks, productive orchard, farmyard, and outbuildings, enclosed by walls, the whole occupying a frontage of about 170 yards, and rich pasture field walled round, also lying compact, and containing about 11 acres; a most desirable Residence for a Gentleman's Family, commanding extensive views of a beautifully rich country; the buildings and grounds are in the most complete order, and immediate possession may be had.

May be viewed by applying at the Premises, where particulars may be had; and at the Three Cups Inn, White Horse Ipswich, Black Boy Chelmsford; White Hart, Romford; of Mr Halls 24 Old Buildings, Lincolns Inn, at Garraways, of Messrs Hope and Broughton, solicitors, 432 Gt Marlborough Street, and of Mr Robins, Warwick Street, Golden Square, London.

HALLS REVD JOHN [399]
Rector of Easthorpe
1708-1795

Resident at Greyfriars, the mansion he built (1755) on the old priory site at the top of East Hill St James. Held the living of Easthorpe from 1735-1795.

The son of Robert Halls (qv) attorney, was entered pensioner at St Johns, Cambridge on 30 November 1725, after an education at Bury Grammar School. He matriculated in 1727 and obtained his LLB in 1731 (Venn, *Alumn. Cantab.*:291). He married Elizabeth Selly (daughter of the brewer Elizabeth Selly (qv)) in 1747, bound by Charles Lind (qv) (Rector of East Mersea and resident in All Saints). His bride's age is given as 35 to his 36. (CPL Crisp ML 485, not in ERO index). They originally lived in Holy Trinity before their removal to Greyfriars.

In 1754 (*Ips]* 30 November 1754) there was:-

To be LETT and Entered upon at Christmas next. A DWELLING HOUSE late Sir Ralph Creffield's (qv) in COLCHESTER, now occupied Revd Mr Halls, with good stables, coach house, and other offices and a large Garden.

Enquire further of Mr William Lisle (qv).

This property near Trinity Church was empty when re-advertised on 30 August 1755 (*IpsJ*) (cf. John Hadley (qv)).

Halls also owned an estate called Porters in Fordham (Morant, *Essex*, Vol 1. 2:229), which was indicated in the deed naming him trustee of Elizabeth Burkin's Colchester estates ERO D/DU/445/7). The Burkins were relations of his wife's family. Through his mother-in-law, he also obtained St Mary's Cottage (next the church) which she left to her daughter Elizabeth in 1769.

Elizabeth Halls died aged 76 and was buried in St James on 15 February 1788 together with two infants John (aged 5) and Elizabeth (4). Her will is at NA PROB 11/1162, 29 February 1788. Halls himself died aged 87 in October 1795. His obituary (*IpsJ* 17 October 1795) recorded him as 'a most benevolent and universally respected character' who had been 60 years Rector of Easthorpe. His will is at NA PROB 11/1267, 10 November 1795. No children survived him and his will left his property to his nephew James Halls (qv) (father to John James Halls (qv) the artist; cf *ER*, Vol. 24).

HAMILTON JAMES [402]
Coachmaster, New King's Head, Innkeeper White Hart, formerly Draper
fl. 1764–1803

Hamilton is first encountered in 1764 parish rates established as a draper at 16-17 High Street. He abandoned the trade in 1766 (*IpsJ* 26 July 1766). Although Hamilton is first recorded at the White Hart in 1766 he was trading in 1765 (*IpsJ* 6 April 1765, viewed in original this issue missing on microfilm) when the Colchester Machine from the White Hart to London was

H

advertised (fare 12s) together with the Harwich Machine which stopped there. Hamilton remained there until 1773 when the inn was 'to Lett' on 31 July 1773 (*IpsJ*) and he transferred to the New King's Head at the top of North Hill from which he ran a coaching business (see Charles Whaley's (qv) will made 11 January, proved 18 November 1774, which lists the property as still occupied by James Hamilton and William Griggs, contradicting the parish rates).

Bland (*Bland's Anecdotes*, Appendix 3) has much to say about Hamilton, nicknamed 'Duke', in his opinion a dissolute character constantly in financial difficulties. He was cousin to Earl Abercorn which helped his credit. 'He frequently absented himself from home and generally returned with the means to satisfy his creditors'. He called the inn a 'hotel' which, says Bland, meant it became known as 'Hamilton's Hot-Hell'. He was very attached to his son and grieved greatly at the boy's early death, locking himself away during his illness and cursing God when his prayers to save the child were unanswered. He also figured in the story of Frank Smythies' 1 (qv) scandalous and opportunist will making. Hamilton supported the outsider parliamentary candidate, Christopher Potter (qv) in the early 1780s, and when Richard Rigby (qv) (then the Paymaster General) rode into town in support of Admiral Affleck (qv), Hamilton rode up brandishing a whip and cried '… the coachmaster against the paymaster; we'll beat you for a thousand'.

In 1782 Hamilton was running both the Post and Stage coach;

> Colchester Stage Coach; 8 o'clock every Monday, Wednesday & Friday from the King's Head Colchester to the Spread Eagle, Gracechurch Street, returning at the same hour every Wednesday, Tuesday, Thursday and Saturday, each inside 11s, outside 6s 6d. Colchester Post Coach; 10 o'clock each Tuesday, Thursday & Saturday from the Three Cups returning Wednesday, Friday & Monday at 8 from the Spread Eagle. Each inside 15s, 7s 6d outside (*IpsJ* 19 January 1782).

H

The following year Hamilton entered into partnership with Thomas Hedge (qv) which brought new capital into the business. In 1784 (16 September) he sued Thomas Taylor, sheriff's officer in the Thursday Court for £10, the price of a mare (ERO D/B 5 Cb2/38).

Hamilton sold up the King's Head in the summer of 1790. The furniture and effects included the coaches, many beds etc (*IpsJ* 8 May 1790, *ChCh* 7 May 1790). He won a case in the Court of Common Pleas (*IpsJ* 5 March 1791) the following year against Boys of the Spread Eagle, Gracechurch Street where his coaches terminated, gathering £40 damages for illegally distraining goods. It may be that the dispute with Boys helped speed Hamilton into retirement. His wife died in April 1791 (*IpsJ* 23 April 1791, 'Thursday last') and Hamilton himself was at the Spreadeagle in Witham when he died on 31 May, 1803 (*IpsJ* 4 June 1803).

HAMILTON WILLIAM [404]
Hardwood Turner
fl. 1778-9

The examination books reveal Hamilton as somewhat disorderly. On 19 October 1778 he was accused of assault by Daniel Jackson (qv) gunsmith. On 6 January 1779 his settlement examination records that he had been apprenticed to Miss Fauntleroy of St George's in East Middlesex twenty one years ago (ERO P/Co R8). This examination was taken the day after Martha Sansum (widow) had appeared at the Sessions in an affiliation case; she was expecting his illegitimate child. He married her that year (ERO D/ACL 1779).

HARBOTTLE LUCKIN [406]
Messing
ob. 1766

Harbottle's residence, Messing Hall, was pulled down and the materials sold after his death (*IpsJ* 1 November 1766). The

H

contents were auctioned by the Colchester appraiser Henry Lodge (qv).

Eight months later the demolition was well underway:

> To be sold at Messing Hall near Kelvedon Essex; Bricks, Tiles & Timbers, Doors and Sashes and Sash frames; a very good Wainscott Staircase, a large Quantity of Wainscot, a very good Bow Window, a large Quantity of painted Glass which is very Curious and a great Quantity of Lead and Iron.... To be sold by Robert Kemp, Bricklayer in Kelvedon Essex who attends the same place every Monday' (*IpsJ* 15 August 1767).

HARRIS REES [407]
Minister, St Helen's Lane Chapel
fl. 1782-1795

The minister of St Helen's Lane Independent Chapel preceding Isaac Taylor (qv). He was also agent for the Phoenix Assurance (advertisements include *ChCh* 26 March 1790, 14 January 1795).

HARRIS ROBERT [1277]
Apothecary
fl. 1780-1788

Occupied 28 High St, that had been an apothecary's shop since the 1760s (cf Jordan Harris Lisle (qv)). Rated 20 as Robert Harris in 1780, as R. Harris & Co. in 1785 and as Harris and Rowe in 1788. (JBB note; cf 'Trumpeter Rowe' who died 1791, nfr.)

HARRIS STEPHEN [999]
Miller
1788

IpsJ 5 July 1788, mill for sale, apply Stephen Harris on the premises.

HARRISON Family [410]
Surgeons

Various MIs at St Leonards (Strutt, *Colchester*, Vol 2:64-5).

JBB Note: Relations of William Mayhew 1 (qv).

HARRISON WILLIAM [408]
Innkeeper, King's Head
fl. 1753

On 13 October 1753 (*IpsJ*) the King's Head Charter Club published its views in an address from 'Philo Burgi'.

See also Mary daughter of William and Mary Harrison buried St Peters, 5 May 1771; NA PROB 11/860, will of William Harrison, gent, Colchester, proved 29 November 1760.

HARVEY CAPT DANIEL [411]
Customs
fl. 1778-1795

Owner of a series of revenue ships, all named the *Repulse*. One was captured by the French after running aground through chasing a smuggling cutter too close to the shore at Calais. It was finally recaptured by the English in 1779 but only after the crew had spent thirteen months in a French gaol (A. F. J. Brown, *Essex People*:202, Harvey Benham, *Once upon a Tide*: 156-60, 185, 173, 166). Harvey lived at Wivenhoe and the family were one of the social circle of the Rebows at Wivenhoe Park (Brown:65-9). Daniel Harvey died in February 1794 (*IpsJ* 1 March 1794), his furniture being sold off thereafter (*IpsJ* 3 January 1795).

His daughter Harriett benefited under the will of Revd Joseph Brockwell (qv), by which time she had married Mr Parrey, Alderman of Bury St Edmunds.

H

HASSELLS WILLIAM [412]
China Dealer
fl. 1759-61

Advertised (*IpsJ*) on 28 April 1759, JBB NB Aug 69:138).

> WILLIAM HASSELLS, POTMAKER ... just returned from his Pot House in Staffordshire, and has brought a large Assortment of all Sorts of Stone and Earthenware of the newest Patterns, viz white stone blue and white ditto, Agate, Tortoiseshell, cream colour and black, both gilt painted and enamelled ... is (trading) at Bury ... and (at the) warehouse in Wyer Street, Colchester (Saturdays and Monday only).

After Hassell's death Richard Hassells and John Keeling (qv) took over the business (*IpsJ* 2 May 1761) at the same premises and offered a fresh assortment of 'Delft and glassware of all sorts'.

HATTON JOHN [413]
Gardener
ob. 1756

IpsJ 29 May 1756:-

> Now on show, at the house of John Hatton of Colchester, deceased, and to be sold, as follows: Eleven TULIPS call'd Brulantes, or Fires in Snow, at 3s each Price; 23 call'd Prosperpines at ditto; five dozen of high Rigaux, well broke & steady, but not named, at 12 guineas, and so in Proportion.

> N.B. The above Sorts were brought from Holland by the late Proprietor in 1749, and encreased ever since in his own yard. Also a small punch HORSE, seven years old.

HAVENS PHILIP 1 [414]
Baymaker
1692-1769

One of the dynasty of Quaker baymakers of this name (Fitch, *Colchester Quakers*). This Philip Havens played a part in the campaign to regain Colchester's Borough Charter, as a prominent member of the 'Charter Cookery Club' in opposition to William Mayhew's 1 (qv) party (JBB, *A Friend to his Country*). Clearly wealthy, he is recorded standing recognisance at Borough Sessions with John Cole merchant (qv) and Samuel Wall attorney and gent. (qv), for John Shimmon, carpenter called on suspicion of felony (ERO Quarter Sessions file D/B 5 Sr207, 7 October 1765). The case was not found.

Havens was son of Robert, a baymaker (his will NA PROB 11/874, 29 March 1762) and his wife Elizabeth *née* Talcot. He himself married Ann Lowe (1702-1769) in 1721 (Fitch, *Colchester Quakers*). He was a Borough voter, supporting Brooksbank in 1754, Whigs in 1741, Gray and Olmius in 1747 and Rebow and Gray in 1768.

He died at Tottenham in the spring of 1769 (*ChCh* 19 May 1769) a 'very considerable manufacturer of baize'. The details of his will disclose how considerable (NA PROB 11/949, 209 Bogg, made 17 June 1767, proved 16 June 1769). From the marriage settlement of his late wife, Ann *née* Lowe, involving property both freehold and copyhold in Gt. Wigborough, Salcott, Virleigh and Much Bromley, the executor (his son Philip 2 (qv)) was to pay £1,000 shared equally between himself and Philip 1's daughter, Ann the wife of John Kendall (qv). The real estate involved was to be left to Philip 2 who also received; 'all that capital messuage or tenement wherein I now dwell with all that workshop, millhouse &c' thereunto belonging, also tenements to the north and south of said dwelling (4 occupiers listed) in the parish of St Giles; also a farm in Greenstead occupied by Bezaliel Angier 1 (qv). Philip was also left two farms and a messuage in Suffolk (Capel and Lt. Wenham) for life, entailed to his male heirs thereafter (trustees being Joseph Burnham (qv) Colchester, woollen draper and Samuel Rootsey

H

(qv) oylmiller), but subject to Philip being entitled to settle 10% of the value on his first wife if he marry.

John and Ann Kendall were left two farms in Ardleigh, entailed to their children, as well as the interest on £2,000 capital stock (4% Consols) to be raised from the personal estate, to John Kendall for life. Cousins in Tottenham and Manchester received £30 each and John Griffith of Chelmsford, linen draper, as well as the two trustees, received £21 apiece. Havens' servants James Triggs (qv), Ann Andrews and Rachael Polly were left 5 gns each. Plumstead Havens, a Colchester weaver (and free burgess) received 4gns p.a. The residue went to Philip 2.

HAVENS PHILIP 2 [415]
Baymaker
1732-1782

Followed his father Philip Havens 1 (qv) as one of Colchester's leading quaker merchants and traders. Was called upon to stand recognisance of £250 for Robert Kendall (qv) draper (Havens' brother-in-law) together with one Peter Dawson of St Giles in the Fields, London, in the celebrated Pattison Case (Borough Sessions Book, ERO D/B 5 Sb5/4, 7 April 1777). Had inherited the bulk of his father's considerable estate in 1769.

He married Lucy Alefounder (cf Lucy Baas (qv)) in 1768. After his death she advertised a good dwelling house to let on St John's Green (*IpsJ* 8 May 1779). St Giles Land Tax of 1786 gives Mrs Havens as owner occupier of a house rated 26 together with mills rated 2 and tenements occupied by Christopher Orrin (4) and John Frostick (5). She married Capt. Robert Baas in 1789.

IpsJ 2 June 1792 announced the death in London 'a few days since' of Miss Lucy Havens, second daughter of the late Philip Havens.

HAVENS PHILIP 3 [416]
Baymaker and Gentleman
fl. 1768-1796

Achieved gentry status in 1794 when he bought Donyland Hall from James Ashwell's (qv) executors; typically for the third generation a prosperous trading family and indicative of the decline of the bay trade. He married Mary Ann Sage, daughter of Edward, grocer of Wivenhoe (ERO D/ACL 1796).

HAWES MRS LYDIA [41]
ob. 1813

IpsJ 30 October 1813: Mrs Hawes ob. Substantial brick mansion in middle of Queen Street with 111ft frontage for sale, including former surgery and apothecary's shop.

Her will is at ERO D/ACR 19/621, made 1794, proved 1814.

HAWKE HON MARTIN [418]
fl. 1804

A later occupier of the house earlier occupied by William Mayhew 1 and 2 (qv) in St Leonards. It was for sale in 1804 (*IpsJ* 9 June 1804) together with other estates in the parish, described as having a pleasant view from the back, a large garden and two acres of pasture.

HAWKINS WILLIAM [1246]
Timber and Deal Merchant
c.1757-1812

Probably the Colchester tradesman who benefited most from the building of the Barracks, and as founder of a family very notable in Victorian times (see Andrew Phillips, *Ten Men and Colchester*, E.R.O. 1985).

Parents not traced. Not a free-burgess though several Hawkins were (cordwainers etc.).

H

Two wives, maiden names not found. MI's at Hythe 1) Lucy dd. 2 October 1802 aged 41 and 2) Martha dd. 30 May 1807 aged 39 (CPL Crisp).

First mention. *IpsJ* 16 August 1788. Creditors of Mrs Ann Dowson, late sacking manufactory near St Johns Green to apply Mr Wm. Hawkins, sawyer or Mr James Waynman (qv) attorney.

IpsJ 16 March 1799, Auction at Three Cups in 26 lots, newly erected brick dwellings, property of Francis Smythies 1 (qv) Esq decd and Mr Hawkins timber merchant of Colchester. These were: York buildings, Magdalen St, near Barracks; Public house, the Evening Gun; Adjoining shop; 27 other adjoining properties. And on the second day: lease of New Quay, Hythe (expires at death of Mr John Ram (qv), worth £50 p.a.); more properties near Barracks; Duke of York Inn opposite Barracks; Plough Farm, Bentley, near the Green.

William Hawkins' own will (ERO D/ACR 19/595, 1812) leaves to his son William Hawkins the younger and son-in-law William Miller Parker:-

- Parcel of land ... near the Barracks now occ. Thomas and Henry Page.
- Dwelling house and shop occ. said Thos Page and adjoining premises occ. Messrs Heath (Charles Heath (qv)), Verlander and others 'and by them used as a Magazine' in par. St Botolphs, 'part of the hereditaments purchased by me of the Corporation of Colchester'.
- Messuage occ. - Finch, shopkeeper, adjoining a messuage occ. John Gray baker.

UPON TRUST to pay an Annuity of £10 out of the rents and profits to my granddaughter Charlotte Hawkins, the natural child of my daughter Lucy the wife of the said Thomas Page.

Also to Charlotte, mess. and Bake office in par. St Bots. abutting north on the back way to the Duke of York and west upon Water Lane, late occ. John Gray, baker. If Charlotte dies, this is left to son Wm. Hawkins and daughter Elizabeth, wife of Wm. Miller Parker, and daughter Sarah Hawkins as tenants in common.

Thomas and Henry Page were gardeners. Thomas married Lucy Hawkins in 1803 (ERO ML D/ALL 1803) and both are buried with her father at the Hythe, she in 1839 aged 76, Thomas 1849 aged 79, will ERO D/ABR 26/348.

Heath (Charles Heath (qv)) and Verlander were principal bakers to the garrison. Hence Hawkins had a close hold on the local trade.

The will continues, giving:-

- £1,600 to Elizabeth Parker.
- £1,600 to Sarah (£800 at 21, £800 at 24, and £100 p.a. till she is 21, chargeable on the 'Messuage or tenement lately erected and built by me, with the timber yard, garden, land etc. now in my own occupation' with outhouses, stables &c. 'the Fee simple and Inheritance of which I purchased of James Wallis Ashwell' (qv) which he leaves to his son William.
- Son William, residue of estate.

Son William, and son-in-law Wm. Miller Parker executors.

Made 16 October 1812. wits. Wm. Sparling jun., F.P. Keeling, clerk to Mr Sparling, Henry Hyland, of Colchester carpenter. (Hyland not met with elsewhere.) Proved 25 December 1812.

His pedestal tomb at the Hythe says he died 12 December 1812, aged 55.

His house first appears in St Bots. rates, May 1805 as 'a deal yard and new Building not finished' and rated 10 in August. It was advertised, a modern white brick dwelling 32 ft in front with large walled garden, in 1808 (*Ips]* 10 December 1808). The elegant stationmaster's house of 1866 perhaps replaces it, or it was thereabouts. James Wallis Ashwell's (qv) mansion was later Hawkins' (date acquired not found, but rated 28 with other properties before Ashwell's bankruptcy, 1811). It later became the Board room of the Tendring Railway (A. Phillips, *Ten Men*:48).

24 June 1809 *IpsJ*: 'Thirteen timber carriages, laden with oak trees of large dimensions, part of a quantity lately felled in Rushbrooke Park, near Bury, arrived at Mr Hawkins' timber yard last Saturday, one of which contained 10 loads. They were decorated with green oaken bows, ribbons &c. forming a gratifying spectacle to the beholders, who seemed to view them with admiration, and in the pleasant anticipation of their being converted into the safeguards of our Isle.'

For Rushbrooke Hall see Burke and Savill's guide. The 3rd Davers Baronet dd. 1806 and the mansion passed by 'amicable arrangement' to Col. Robert Rushbrooke, who was evidently asset stripping patriotically.

28 October 1809 *IpsJ*: Hawkins roasted an ox in his timber yard at the Hythe for 200 workmen, their wives and friends - to celebrate the Jubilee of George III (cf. Alexander Fordyce Miller's (qv) party on same occasion).

Hawkins' father dying aged 55, son William was not very old (26) when he succeeded to the business and bought the Hythe yards from J. Collins Tabor (qv). 29 April 1815, marriage at All Saints to Mary Ann Warwick. Mon. in St Botolphs. He died 18 February 1843 aged 57, she 19 November 1834 aged 39. The big marble monument, with Hope and Anchor by Joseph Edwards (1814-1883) is signed 1854 (Unveiled in July. R. Gunnis, *Dictionary of British Sculptors*, 1951). Edwards a very notable Victorian.

HAYWARD HENRY [1210]
Builder and Architect
1754-1829

Family background not established.

19 November 1776, married by banns St Mary-at-the-Wall to Maria Sophia Pollard (who died 25 January 1817).

1788: Lexden Court books (ERO D/DEP Court Book A:33) Buys broken down cottage on Bergholt Road, 27 June 1788.

1784: Birth of Henry Hammond Hayward (qv), bapt. not found.

H

15 October 1790; Homage in Lexden Manor Court, following Isaac Green (qv) and William Phillips (qv) lease (ERO D/DEP Court Book A, no page noted).

7 November 1800; buys King's Head, copyhold on north side of Lexden Street for 14 years, £10 p.a., already occupier, renewed for another 10 years at £35 p.a. on 2 August 1815 and 5 June 1824. Now (c. 1990) the Crown Inn.

1792, listed as a carpenter in the *Universal Directory*.

Subscribed 10s 6d for Defence of the Country during the French Wars (*IpsJ* 31 March 1798).

ERO C47 CPL 744, lease 14 years from Michaelmas 1800 dated 7 November 1800, Mrs Ann Rawstorn Lexden spr. to Henry Hayward carpenter, 10 gns p.a. messuage or tenement, north side of Lexden Street formerly occ. Wm Wright. See also ERO C47 CPL 729 of August 1815 and a further lease of 1824 at CPL 866.

23 July 1802, Borough Chamberlain's Accounts (ERO D/B 5 Aa2/5), £3 14s 'for attending going the bounds, fixing posts etc.'

30 April 1803 (*IpsJ*), freehold estate for auction Stanway. Apply Mr Hayward, builder, Lexden (see also the sale of furniture of Mrs Hammond, *IpsJ* 21 May 1802).

1804, Samuel Winnock's (qv) will mentions his house in Lexden parish; 'held under Henry Hayward.'

30 December 1829 *Suffolk Chronicle*. Died after long affliction, 19 years churchwarden of Lexden Church 'He lived beloved and died regretted.'

Will, NA PROB 11/1768, 176 Beard, made by attorney William Mason 3 (qv) 25 April 1826, proved 20 March 1830 by son, Henry Hammond Hayward (not otherwise mentioned in the will) and daughter Elizabeth Steel Hayward, spinster. It is very long.

To second wife Mary *née* Carter, her life interest in her settlement of 1 August 1818, farm in Elmstead etc, then to daughter Maria Sophia, wife of Robert Hale. (He is buried at St Mary's 1851 aged 75, she with the Haywards at Lexden.)

H

Also to wife, new built messuage in Crouch St, now occ. Mrs Daniells and her daughters, 'being one of the houses recently (built) by me on the estate which I recently purchased of Mrs Alice Cracknell', then to daughter Elizabeth Steel Hayward for life, then to grandson Robert Hayward Hale, son of daughter Maria Sophia.

Also to Elizabeth Steel H., new built messuage in Crouch St now occ. Mr Shugar (W. R. Shugar Esq) 'being the other of the houses lately erected by me on Mrs Alice Cracknell's estate', for life, then to grandson William Henry Coleman, son of daughter Harriet and James William Coleman (whitesmith. married in April 1815).

These are 12-14 Crouch St with big round-headed windows (staircases?) seen from back - red brick.

Further properties are: a tenement on East Hill occ. Mr Barrett, the Vine Inn and cottage adjoining at Nayland, properties in Lodder Lane and elsewhere in St Giles in multiple occs., a farm at Wigborough bought of devisees of Samuel Lufkin decd., meadow at Wormingford and West Bergholt, an acre 1 rood and 36 perches allotted to him as part of Lexden Heath common land, and he and others are owed money as a bond due 1823 for rebuilding Lexden Church (1820-1).

See also 28 May 1808 *IpsJ*, death of Mr Henry Hayward senior, aged 69 at Thorndon, Sfk. His will is NA PROB 11/1479, proved 14 May 1808

Essex County Standard 2 December 1868 for later sale of West Terrace, Lexden Road now The Avenue.

HAYWARD HENRY HAMMOND [1211]
Builder and Architect
fl. 1812-1862

> St Mary's Terrace Hayward built
> So strong and well and without gilt.

(doggerel poem of reminiscences of post-Napoleonic times, nfr.)

H

4 April 1812 (*IpsJ*): John Bridge (qv) builder in Lion Walk advertises slates with a woodcut of a house with slate roof, as if a novelty here. And it does introduce what Henry Hammond Hayward excelled in – very plain good proportioned houses, sash-windowed, white brick fronts (sometimes red on garden side) and above all, slate roofs, low pitched with white eaves and lead copings.

These are quite different from the eighteenth-century tiled M-roof containing attics, but concealed behind parapets. But note also elegance of mansard roofs providing good attics in smaller buildings in the c18th.

This work really falls outside an eighteenth-century Dictionary, but is too fine not to include, and internally it carries on the excellence of the c18th joiners, in particular, had attained, most notably in their staircases.

Son of Henry and Maria Sophia (*née* Pollard), bapt. 25 April 1784.

He's Henry Hayward the younger in 1816 when leasing the former White Hart Inn from the widow of C. A. Crickitt (qv) banker for £125 p.a. (part still occupied by the bank). His offices in Bank Passage, and timber yard on the stables-site in Culver Street (still so when his son Henry Winnock Hayward mortgages them in 1857 and 1864, ERO C47, CPL 559).

Henry Hammond Hayward purchases the premises from Mrs Crickitt's assignees in 1830, 30 April for £1700 (his father has a Culver St address as well in 1827, so they worked together, though the son was architect as well as builder).

Main commissioned works:-

1820, Essex and Suffolk Fire Office (Laing architect).

1835, Head St, north of Church St after Marsden's Bazaar fire. White brick now mostly painted over.

1845, Corn Exchange, next to Fire Office, Raphael Brandon architect).

1846, Wivenhoe Park (alterations by Hopper).

1853, Grammar School, Lexden Road (Tudor).

His own investment:-

H

St Mary's Terrace, East and West (21-31 and 33-53), Lexden Road. Elaborately divided between his children in his will made 19 January 1859, proved 15 March 1862 (ERO C47, CPL 543).

Buried Lexden (registers). Died at Lexden Cottage 11 January 1862 aged 78. Buried with wife, Charlotte Elizabeth died 16 April 1853, aged 70 and Eliza youngest daughter, died 8 October 1865 aged 43. Successor son Henry Winnock Hayward ARIBA 1825-1893, built the Avenue etc. was not in his father's class.

HEARD GRANGE 1 [419]
Woolcomber and Baymaker
c. 1731-1815

Not one of the foremost baymakers of the town, but sufficiently prosperous to acquire the freehold of his own property and be elected Common Councillor on 6 August 1789. He voted in Borough elections from 1768 to at least 1796, generally supporting whichever candidate would give a one Whig/one Tory representation. He was also an auricula grower and was steward at the Auricula Feast at the Angel in 1781 (*IpsJ* 21 April 1781, spelt as 'Grainge' Heard).

He had been admitted free burgess on 10 August 1767 by right of apprenticeship to Short Peartree and at about this time must have married Elizabeth since their son, Grange Heard was born on 24 October 1767 and baptised 21 February 1768. This child died on 11 April 1768 but a second son, also named after his father was born and baptised at St Peters 6 August 1769.

Grange and Elizabeth Heard lived on North Hill, St Peters in premises on the west side rated 5. When the owner of the adjoining Green Yard, James Robjent 2 (qv) went bankrupt in 1778, Heard was able to buy up the property from the assignees for £109 10s; described as:-

> All those two messuages or tenements in St Peters parish now occupied himself and Henry Downs the elder ... (being) ... all that messuage or tenement called Buttons

Garden, with the garden inclosed, containing in length south to north 49 ft and width east to west 37 ft and abuts on the yard of Edward Brown carpenter towards the south, on a piece of ground belonging to a messuage occupied Henry Downs the elder and, hereinafter mentioned, to the North, and on a field called Green Yard towards the west, and a piece of ground now or lately belonging to Francis Freshfield 2 (qv) to the East; which said messuage formerly occupied by John Pike and John Baker (qv) now occupied Grange Heard. ...(also)... all that messuage parcel of Buttons Gardens now occupied by Henry Downs abutting on the garden of the messuage aforesaid of Grange Heard to the south, on Green Yard to the west, on ground of Francis Freshfield to the East and on apiece of garden now used and belonging to messuage late occupied by Fudgell Jay and now James Green the younger to the North. Containing at the west end, south to north 24 ft and at the east end 25ft and in breadth 34ft with... (a) ... passage to and from the same with use of the common yard and necessary and spring water at the cistern adjoining a certain street called North Street in parish, St Peters (ERO C47 CPL494).

Grange Heard died in 1815 (*IpsJ* 16 December 1815) in his 84th year and having retained his position on the Common Council.

See also will of William Grange (yeoman, Colchester, 1741, ERO D/ACR 19/103) names kinsmen John and Wm Heard of Bradwell and Pattiswick.

HEARD GRANGE 2 [420]
Baymaker
fl. 1769-1812

The son of Grange Heard 1 and wife Elizabeth, baptised at St Peters on 6 August, 1769. He was admitted free burgess on 4 February 1790 by right of descent and voted with his father in 1790 and 1796 for one candidate of each party.

H

On 22 April 1794 he married Mary Howe at St Peters where he was later buried on 27 February 1805.

See also vote of Grange Heard, gent. for Davis 1812 (either father or son); St Peters burials, Susan Heard 21 August 1781.

HEARSUM JEREMIAH [1258]
Carpenter
fl. 1734-c.1780

Free burgess 1734, apprenticeship to Joseph Todd. Regular voter up to 1784. Son John, free 1768, gaoled for stealing lead from John Unwin (qv) 1780. Son Jeremiah is a mariner (nfr).

Chamberlain's Accompts (ERO D/B 5 Aa1/35):
- 1767 (51) Hersom and Shade for surveying, £5 10s; Hersom's bill, £5 11s 6d.
- 1768 (48) Mr Hersom's bill, £2 19s.

His own bills in Chamberlain's vouchers, show very illiterate handwriting. For example, 4 November 1774, for 'Est Broace', £57 5s 5½d; 1770, for work on Buttermarket ('planck', 'lowance', 'breadge', 'middel').

HEATH CHARLES [422]
Baymaker, Baker and Army Contractor
1754-1828

A baptist who prospered as an army baking contractor during the Napoleonic wars. During the fears of invasion in October 1803, numbers of troops were stationed in Colchester and Heath was 'commanded to bake 25,000 loaves of 6 lb each, every fourth day.' (J. Gilbert, *Memorials... of Mrs Gilbert*, 1874, Vol 1:174). Holdens 1805 *Directory* lists Heath & Verlander, army bakers. The 1791 directory had listed Heath as a baymaker, however, and he is known to have issued ½d trade tokens 'payable at Charles Heath, Baymaker Colchester' in the 1790s. (Matthias, *English Trade Tokens*, NY 1962:46-7). In 1791 Heath was amongst leading baymakers giving evidence against Fudgell Cook jun (qv), being prosecuted for receiving ends and waste embezzled by wool workers (ERO Borough Sessions Book D/B 5 Sb5/6).

He had been apprenticed to Joseph Baines baker (qv) for £7 on 29 October 1767 (NA IR 1/56/115) and was admitted free burgess by right of that apprenticeship on 8 February 1776. In 1783 Heath served as overseer in St James and in 1787 stood for election as Common Councillor, but was unsuccessful, this being a period of Tory ascendancy on the Corporation. He voted from 1784 to 1820, supporting Whig, radical and reforming candidates though preferred the evangelical Thornton to the radical Tierney in 1790.

He married Sarah, the daughter of James Mansfield 2 (qv) (she dd. 1827; cf. draft will of James Mansfield snr. ERO DHt 72/77, made 15 January 1789). Heath's premises were on East Hill, near the bottom on the right hand side descending, near Mansfield's house. They married at St James on 27 July 1775 and moved to St James (Settlement Examination ERO P/COR 12 May 1775). The Heaths had five children baptised in St Helen's chapel between 1787 and 1796 (registers are missing before 1784), including Elizabeth (11 May 1790), Mary Ann (22 May 1796) and Samuel (2 February 1789).

Heath died in 1828 aged 74, and was buried at the Baptist Churchyard in Stanwell St, remembered as 'a sinner saved by Grace'. His will (ERO D/ACR 20/373) made 13 December 1825 and proved 11 February 1829 leaves 5s per week and £20 worth of goods to his wife Sarah (who in the event had predeceased him - see above) leaving the residue of the estate to his daughters Elizabeth and Mary Ann whom he enjoined to contribute to the maintenance and comfort of their mother.

See also Samuel Heath admitted free burgess 8 November 1810 and voted in 1820; CPL Crisp ML272, ERO D/ACL 1844, William Grace, Southampton m. Mary Ann Heath, 1844; CPL Crisp ML40, ERO D/ACL 1831, Wm Candler, Wivenhoe m. Elizabeth Heath 1831; JBB note – a Mary Heath witnessed Charles Shillito's (qv) wedding in Bath (1780), not traced.

H

HEATHFIELD JOHN [424]
Tinman
fl. 1735-1757

Heathfield (son of James) was apprenticed in 1735 to Charles Towson, tinplateman of London for £12 (NA IR/17 14/55). In 1746, then of St Nicholas, Colchester and aged 28 he married Martha Spink (30) (ERO D/ACL 1746). It appears there was a family connection with the town for in 1736 (CPL Crisp ML280, ERO D/ALL 1756) a John Heathfield, then a widower of 30 married Amy Whiskin, 30 of St Marys. Heathfield appears to have traded in London for some years, returning to Colchester in 1757 (*IpsJ* 18 June 1757) when he set up in All Saints over against the Sea Horse, offering brooms and brushes among many other items. At the same time he advertised for an apprentice.

HEDGE CHARLES [431]
Silversmith
fl. 1773-1808

The son of Nathaniel Hedge 2 (qv), baptised at All Saints 11 February 1773. Apprenticed to his father and subsequently spent a year's further training with Messrs Love, jewellers of Bond Street. On returning to Colchester traded from the premises at 18 High Street, next door to his father's clockmaking business at no. 19 (Mason: 346).

A free burgess (25 May 1796) who voted first in 1796 for Thornton and Muncaster. He was a Lieutenant of the Loyal Colchester Volunteers in the late 1790s and subscribed 5 gns for the Defence of the Country in 1798 (*IpsJ* 13 March 1798). He was elected Common Councillor on 7 September 1805 after a four year period as Coroner between 1800 and 1804. He married on 8 May 1807 in Hanover Square to Miss Frances Dubois. The following year, trading in Colchester he purposed 'attending the Public Breakfast on 9th inst. with a select assortment...' of goods (*IpsJ* 5 November 1808). He died very shortly afterwards and his father took the jewellery and goldsmith's business into his own hands. (*Ips]* 26 January 1809).

Summarised from B. Mason, *Clock and Watchmaking in Colchester,* (1969): 323-4, 346-8.

HEDGE JACOB [430]
Watchmaker
fl. 1769-1794/8

Son of Thomas Hedge (qv), baptised at All Saints 29 July 1770. He married on 17 August 1789 to Sarah Bridges (17) of All Saints and near to the Hedge family premises of 97 High Street. The relationship seems to have been stormy since Hedge was bound over for £20 and two sureties of £10 apiece at the Borough Sessions to keep the peace towards his wife on 4 October 1790 (cf. also Borough Sessions 10 January 1791 and 2 May 1791). Jacob was created free burgess on 3 June 1790 and supported Jackson in the election that year. He died soon after between 1794 when he is last recorded in the parish rates and 1798 when his widow married Sgt. Maj. William Gough of St Runwald.

Summarised from B. Mason, *Clock and Watchmaking in Colchester,* (1969): 322-3.

HEDGE JOHN [477]
Watch and Clockmaker
1737-1778

The eldest son of Nathaniel Hedge 1 (qv). John Hedge was created free burgess on 19 January 1764 but voted only once, in 1768 for Rebow and Gray. In 1764 he stood surety for Byatt Walker's 2 (qv) marriage licence. Hedge himself may have married twice. A marriage licence of 1767 (ERO D/ALL 1767) records the marriage of John Hedge to Sarah Love, wid. Mason also records a marriage in 1771 to Ann Gosling of St Botolphs when he was 34 and she 17. The couple occupied a house at 94 High Street (next door to the Castle Inn). They moved to the Hedge family business premises in 1772, which Nathaniel snr

H

(qv) had vacated to move a few doors away (to no. 103) when he made his second marriage. John traded in partnership with his brother Thomas (qv) (e.g. *IpsJ* 16 July 1774, 1 May 1776, 19 August 1776; Thomas and John Hedge appointed to receive and exchange deficient gold coinage).

With his marriage and his father's retirement from the business, John Hedge took on other responsibilities of a head of household. He served on the Grand Jury for the east ward on 7 April 1772 and was elected Common Councillor on 31 August 1772. The same year he began attendance at All Saints vestry meetings. He later served as overseer in 1776 with his brother Thomas (qv) (All Saints vestry minutes 16 April 1776).

Hedge's wife Ann died on 16 September 1775 aged 22 and was buried at All Saints on 20th. John Hedge made his will when 'sick in body' on 3 February 1778, leaving £20 to his father and the residue to his brothers and executors Nathaniel 2 (qv) and Thomas (qv), subject to annuities of £30 to his father and £10 to his mother when a widow. His mother-in-law also received 5 gns and 5s per week. Hedge died 2 March following.

Summarised from B. Mason, *Clock and Watchmaking in Colchester* (1969):313-5, 337-8.

HEDGE MARTHA [429]
Milliner
fl. 1765-75

Née Gibson, she married Nathaniel Hedge 2 (qv) on 1 February 1765 (nfr), She advertised on 4 May 1765 (*IpsJ*), her advertisement in the paper following one from Nathaniel, acquainting her friends that she had just bought from London 'an assortment of the most genteel and fashionable goods'. B. Mason (*Clock and Watchmaking in Colchester*, (1969):308 ff) believes she continued in trade till 1775.

See also Judith Burridge apprenticed to Martha Hedge, milliner £25, 1767 (NA IR 1/56/115).

HEDGE NATHANIEL 1 [425]
Clockmaker
1710-1795

The second son of a family of weavers living in St Mary Magdalen. Was apprenticed to John Smorthwait (qv), clockmaker on 1 May 1728 for £10, who at the same time purchased the freehold of a tenement in St Mary Magdalen from Hedge's father (this property was later left by Smorthwait to his brother and purchased back by Hedge in 1753). Two years before the formal end of his period of apprenticeship, on 2 October 1733, this Nathaniel Hedge was married to Sarah Smorthwait, daughter of John. The Hedge's first child (Sarah, bapt. All Saints 19 February 1734, ob. 1735) was born three months later. There is no conclusive evidence to support Bernard Mason's interpretation, that Smorthwait 'turned them out of the house, and from that moment he ceased to have a daughter', (Mason:304) though it may be indicative that even though both resident in All Saints parish, they married in the village of Alresford, outside Colchester. Hedge then set up in business in All Saints in partnership with another of Smorthwait's ex apprentices, William Cooper (qv), until, when his old master died in 1739 he took over the stock etc of that business, including an apprentice Samuel Downum (on 22 March 1739) and commenced trading alone. Hedge's business prospered largely by making comparatively cheaper kinds of clock. At first (and probably using parts bought along with the Smorthwait stock in trade) he made a number of brass lantern and hooded wall-bracket clocks. He also made many 30-hour, one-handed, long-case clocks, apparently by batch production from around 1750, and comparatively fewer of the more expensive and up-to-date eight-day clocks. He also seems to have produced a good number of watches. (Mason: 331, 332, 336).

Hedge was a regular attender at All Saints vestry and on the Law Inquest (petty jury) at Borough Sessions. He was churchwarden in All Saints in 1744 (27 March 1744) and served as Overseer five times between 1751 and 1769. Acted as executor to the carpenter and house builder James Deane (qv) in 1765 (*Ips]* 26 October 1765). He was sworn a free burgess on 24 April 1734 and though his early votes show a preference for balanced representation (one Whig, one Tory), from 1784 he supported the Tory Corporation party. By 1768 he was also a county voter. He was Assistant on the Corporation from 31 October 1763 to 5 September 1785 and a Grand Juror at Borough Sessions in 1764.

The Hedge premises were at 97 High Street, opposite the Sea Horse rated 12. Hedge also owned 103 High Street rated 6 (1787 Land Tax) whence he moved at the time of his second marriage (1772) leaving his eldest son to operate the workshop at no. 97. Sarah Hedge had died on 1 May 1770 aged 62 and was buried at All Saints. In November 1772 Hedge married Elizabeth Mead, a widow of All Saints. Hedge died on 14 March 1795. His will (ERO D/ACW 36/4/17, made in 1787, proved 1795) made provision for his wife of 8s per week plus her clothes, linen and £15 worth of household goods. The vast residue of the estate was left to Hedge's sons Nathaniel 2 (qv) and Thomas (qv), the eldest son already being established at 97 High St

Summarised from B. Mason, *Clock and Watchmaking in Colchester*, (1969): 301 ff. Mason refers to this individual as Nathaniel Hedge (3). For his seventeenth century antecedents see Mason: 299-300.

HEDGE NATHANIEL 2 [426]
Clockmaker and Jeweller
1735-1821

Son of Nathaniel 1 (qv) and Sarah Hedge. He married Martha Gibson of St Nicholas on 1 February 1765 and they soon took a shop in the High Street (no. 19) whence they advertised their respective trades, cf. Martha Hedge (qv) milliner;

> Nathaniel Hedge jun watchmaker and goldsmith - takes this Method of acquainting his Friends that he has taken a shop near the Obelisk in Colchester and as well as all

sorts of watches and Clocks, Plate, Plain Gold Funeral Rings, Jewellery, Japann'd and Plated Goods etc.

Ladies and Gentlemen and others that please to honour him with their Commands may depend upon being served on the lowest Terms, and the favours gratefully acknowledged by their obedient humble servant.

N. Hedge jun.

Jobs done ... in the neatest manner.

M. Hedge Milliner, is pleased to acquaint her Friends that she has just bought from London an Assortment of the most genteel and fashionable Goods and hopes for the continuance of their favours, which will be gratefully acknowledged (*IpsJ* 4 May 1765).

Between 1766 and 1767 he made the movement for the clock of St Nicholas (the Dial church). Rather than compete with the batch production of cheaper 30-hour clocks which were a feature of his father's business, Hedge jun seems to have concentrated on the manufacture of eight-day clocks in more expensive cases (Mason: 340, 342). In 1801 he was commissioned to produce a new turret clock for the refurbishment of the Old Bay Hall (Mason: 348, 352). For some time traded in association with his son Charles (qv), silversmith (ob. 1809) and between 1807 and 1813 operated the clockmaking trade in partnership with Joseph Banister (qv), previously his journeyman (Mason: 348-353). Banister thereafter took over the clock-making side of the business, leaving the 'jewellery, gold and silver business' to Hedge (*IpsJ* 20 January 1814). For a while at least after Charles Hedge's death, his father ran the jewellery business in partnership with ex-apprentice, George Lewis (Mason: 350, *IpsJ* 2 July 1812).

Hedge was admitted free burgess on 19 January 1764 (once the Borough Charter had been restored). Though he supported the Whig Smyth in 1780, from 1788 he voted for Corporation party candidates. He was elected Common Councillor in 1765 and Assistant in 31 August 1772. He was a frequent Grand Juror between 1767 and 1791. In 1784 (4 October 1784) stood surety

H

in Borough Sessions for his journeyman, William Lane, summoned for an order to be made for support of an illegitimate child.

In 1770 the Hedges moved further up the High Street to St Runwalds and in 1775 moved again to 19 High Street (cf Joseph Banister (qv)). Hedge was churchwarden at St Peters from 1779 to 1811. He subscribed 5 gns to the fund in Defence of the Country during the French Wars in March 1798. He also became auditor of the Essex Equitable Assurance in 1804 and a Town Director between 1814 and 1816.

Hedge made his will on 29 April 1816 (NA PROB 11/1654, proved 18 March 1822) leaving all to his wife Martha thereafter to his daughter Mary Ann (the Hedges' sons had all died young). Martha died only 8 days after the will was made (*IpsJ* 11 May 1816) and was given a lengthy and pious obituary in the local newspaper. Mary Ann went on to write some 36 books for children. Nathaniel Hedge retired from business in 1818 (*Colchester Gazette* 21 March 1818) in favour of his then partner Joseph Banister (qv). He died in 1821 aged 86, 'universally beloved and esteemed'. The inscription on the family vault reads; 'The hoary head is a crown of glory / If it is found in the way of Righteousness. Blessed are the pure/ in heart for they shall see God.'

Summarised from B. Mason, *Clock and Watchmaking in Colchester*, (1969):308 ff, 340 ff. This is the individual referred to by Mason as Nathaniel Hedge (4).

HEDGE THOMAS [428]
Clockmaker and Coachmaster
1744–1814

Born to Nathaniel (qv) and Sarah Hedge and baptised at All Saints on 30 May 1744. Traded in partnership with his brother John (qv) in the family clockmaking business (e.g. *IpsJ* 16 July 1774, Thomas and John Hedge appointed to receive and exchange deficient gold coinage) until he diversified into operating a coaching concern (see below).

H

He married Sarah Gosling (18) of Little Bentley and moved a few doors down from the family house to 93 High Street next the Castle Inn. They had two sons, Jacob born 1768 and Thomas in 1770. The marriage proved unsuccessful and Sarah was required to find two sureties of £10 (Jacob Brown, Lt Bentley and John Gosling of Ramsey) and bound over to keep the peace to her husband at Quarter Sessions on 27 April 1778, a month after the couple had moved back to 97 High Street, the family premises, on the death of Thomas' elder brother John (7 March 1778). The matter recurred at subsequent Quarter Sessions (13 July 1778) and the sureties were increased to £50, until in April 1783 when Sarah refused to supply sureties she was gaoled in the castle for 12 months (discharged 19 April 1784). In the late 1790s Hedge remarried Judith Ann (ob. 25 July 1807) and they had a son John Thomas in 1801. Hedge's use of the courts to solve his marital difficulties was but one aspect of a generally litigious character and he also prosecuted two cases of theft (ERO D/B 5 SB5/4, 7 April 1766 and Mason: 337, 11 April 1774) and one of assault (14 April 1777).

He was admitted a free burgess on 29 August 1765. Hedge voted from 1780 (for Rebow and Smyth) and was a firm supporter of Potter and the Corporation party thereafter. He was active in All Saints vestry and on the Grand Jury for East Ward from the 1770s. He was created Common Councillor on 31 July 1775, Assistant on 30 August 1784 and Alderman on 27 August 1790. He served as Coroner between 1788-1796 and was Mayor four times from 1796. During his second Mayoralty In 1801 his 'Friends' presented him with a silver cup (now in Hollytrees Museum) and a purse of gold for his 'exemplary and effectual exertions in bringing to public justice a band of robbers'. Interestingly, though the presentation was made on 30 June 1801, it was not reported in the *Ipswich Journal* until 14 November 1801.

His political career was buoyed up by an increasing commercial success. He diversified his occupation after the death of his brother (and partner) John Hedge (qv), advertising for journeymen clockmakers to support the original business, which he seems to have disposed of altogether in the late 1790s

(Mason: 338-9). In 1783 he had entered into partnership with James Hamilton (qv) in the post coach from London to Colchester, then on to Woodbridge and Ipswich, acquiring property at Ingatestone and Ipswich, as well as Colchester, for stabling and as post houses. The partnership also ran the Hambro Mail coach from 1798 to carry foreign mails via Yarmouth. On 20 October 1798 Hedge also became commissioner for the Land Tax, a commissioner for taking Bails on 22 January 1802, and in 1804, now a leading citizen, he became a director of the Essex Equitable Insurance. His public stature was increased by his captaincy of the Volunteer Corp of Infantry (referenced to *IpsJ* 19 August 1803, per Mason:320, however not traced on microfilm) and his appointment as Master Extraordinary in the High Court in Chancery (*IpsJ* 16 February 1808).

He died on 16 July 1814, 'universally esteemed and respected' (*Colchester Gazette* 23 July 1814). His long entailing will, made on 7 August 1811 (NA PROB 11/1560, proved 10 August 1814) secured the bulk of his fortune to the son of his second marriage.

Summarised from B. Mason, *Clock and Watchmaking in Colchester*, (1969):315ff, 337-8.

HEMSTED STEVEN [433]
Surgeon and Apothecary, Haverhill
fl. 1784

Author of a *Description of a Pulverising Mill lately invented for the use of Apothecaries* (Brit Mus 117, m47). He married Ann daughter of Solomon Smith baymaker (qv). He died and his effects were offered for sale in 1784 (*IpsJ* 7 February 1784). His widow died at Colchester the following year (*IpsJ* 17 September 1785).

H

HEWES BYAM [1000]
Miller
w. 1793

Miller at Mile End Mill East (Farries, *Essex Windmills*, Vol. 3:94). His will is at ERO D/ABR 28/452 of 1793.

See also the will of Byam Hewes jun. made 1821, not proved (ERO D/DU/491/41).

HEWES JOHN [432]
Baker
fl. 1754

IpsJ of 27 July 1754, advertised the sale of Hewes' convenient dwelling house and bakery in East Street near the Rose and Crown. John Alefounder 1 (qv) acted as agent.

HEWES ROBERT [1169]
Clockmaker
1711-1769

Born in 1711, the son of Robert Hewes, a cornchandler. Married Mary Dearsley at St James 24 March 1732. The Hewes' had two sons (John bapt. 18 June 1733, Robert bapt. 9 November 1743). Traded next door to the White Hart, and also in the 1730s had a shop in Chelmsford (*IpsJ* 3 March 1739, when his Chelmsford shop moved premises). According to Mason, a maker of more expensive clocks.

Admitted free burgess 11 March 1735 and voted in the Borough poll in 1734, 1741, 1747. Took Thomas Bones apprentice in November 1760.

See also B. Mason, Clock and Watchmaking in Colchester, (1969):281-86; ERO wills D/ABW 95/2/8, Roger Haws (sic), St Peter, Blacksmith, m. 1738, p. 1745/1746; will D/ABW 95/3/60, Benjamin Hewes, Colchester, cornchandler, 1747; will D/ACW 32/3/34, Robert Hewes, aged 14, of Colchester, 1767; free burgess admission 1788, R. Hewes by right of apprenticeship to Jeremiah Howgego, fisherman, Harwich (JBB NB AssBk1).

HEWITT REVD CHARLES [435]
Master of the Free School and Rector St James and Greenstead
fl. 1779-1840

A Cambridge classics scholar, Hewitt was the successful pro-Corporation candidate in the election for the Mastership of the Free School in January 1779 following Samuel Parr's (qv) move to Norwich. He was opposed by Revd Duddell (qv) and the Seaber political faction in the Borough (cf Wm Seaber 2 (qv)). The opposition in town politics was largely nonconformist or low church in sympathy. It had mobilised on the occasion of the 1768 general election and the agitation of 1779 included many of the same names such as Peter Daniell attorney (qv), Michael Hills baymaker (qv), John Rogers, quaker and chinaman (qv).

The circumstances are reported in a letter from Revd Thomas Twining (qv) to Parr. The election was staged with all the sound and fury – '.. the blackguardism of electioneering..' as Twining put it - of a parliamentary poll (R. Walker (ed), *Thomas Twining*, letter 52, pp. 160-2). Duddell conceded when, with the voting standing at 487 to 470 in favour of Hewitt, word arrived that ..'there were then upon the road 100 votes more in Mr Hewitt's favour.' (*IpsJ* 23, 29 January 1779). Apparently Charles Gray (Tory MP) (qv) had been guilty of some wavering from the Corporation cause and victorious Hewitt supporters paraded around the town halting and hallooing outside his door. Seaber was similarly treated to a haranguing from Frank Smythies 1 the town clerk (qv) and rising leader of the Corporation party.

Hewitt ended his days less contentiously. He was Rector of St James between 1783 and 1798, and of Greenstead from 1799, where he finally died on 4 February 1840 aged 97. His wall tablet there commemorates the 52 years of his incumbency. He left £165 in trust to the minister and churchwardens for the poor of the parish. This was devoted to day and boarding schools.

See also D'Cruze, *Pleasing Prospect*:160-5.

HICKERINGILL REVD EDMUND [437]
Rector, All Saints, resident Pond Hall, Wix
w. 1708/1709

Known as the author of numerous vitriolic published sermons and pamphlets. His will (NA PROB 11/509, proved 27 June 1709) is a characteristic document. He named his dear daughter Sarah, wife of Henry Burdox as sole executrix. His son Thomas;

> To whom I have given a great estate... (is left) ...£40 and my best coach and two of my best coach horses or mares on condition nevertheless that he give no disturbance to my executrix and ... if he be troublesome therein he shall not have the said £40, coach, nor horses nor any part thereof.

Another son, Mathias, received £40. An estate in St Saviours, Southwark was left in trust to Thomas and Elizabeth Knollys of Manningtree for the use of son Thomas. An estate at Nayland went to son-in-law Henry Burdox. An estate in 'Much Clacton' was left to daughter Mary for 1000 years. His grandchildren Ann and Sarah Burdox received the great and small tithes of Wix, those of Fingringhoe being mortgaged. A daughter, Frances, was warned to behave herself, but his 'dear daughters Ann and Sarah' were left the residue. He continued;

> ... and I would have them bury my Corps decently but frugally in the Church or Chancell of Wicks aforesaid if it may be convenient and with the service of the Church but no fawning funeral Harangue. But let poor and rich, young and old which happen to be at my funerall have gloves at least but no body, not so much as my children, gold rings which are useless to all but the Goldsmiths, for

the greatest service men alive can do for the dead is to forget them.

The will was witnessed by Nathaniel Ennew, John Flanner and Edward Firmin and proved at PCC on 27 June 1709.

A stone was raised to Hickeringill in All Saints church recording such a hyperbole of self praise that at the behest of the Bishop of London, sections were removed in 1716. All Saints Churchwardens rates (ERO D/P200/8/1, 3 April 1716) records payments of 1s each to 'Joseph Manning for going to Brightlingsea to Mrs Burdox for her consent to raze and obliterate part of ye inscription of Mr Hickeringill's gravestone,' and to Thomas Brown the stone cutter. Morant, (*Essex*, Vol. 1, Appendix:21) commenting that 'The fulsom and Fals stuff printed in italics, hath been chisel'd out ...' records both this circumstance and the full inscription thus;

> Sub hoc marmore jacet *Reverendus admodum Dominus Edmundus Hickeringill, tam Marte quam Mercurio clarus, quippe qui terra mariq; militavit non fine gloria, Ingeniiq, vires scriptis multiplice argumento insignitis* demonstravit: Sacris tandem Ordinibus initiatus, huijuse Parochiae 46 annos Rector; vitam, spe meliore fretus; intrepide reliquit Novemb 30 anno D'ni 1708, aetatis vero Suae 78, sub eodam hoc tumulo recumbunt Anna uxor p'dilecta pia, prudens, pudica; denata Apr 6 1708 aetat 67 atq Edmundus utriusq; filius natu quartus diem obiens Mar 25, 1705 aetat 59. Longaevos parentes moerore pio adhus superstites prosequuntur Thomas, Mathias, Anna, Sarah, Maria et Francisca.

HICKERINGILL THOMAS [436]
Pond Hall, Wix
w. 1771/1794

The son of Edmund Hickeringill (qv) and a beneficiary in his entertaining will. The younger Hickeringill adopted the life of a country gentleman at Pond Hall, Wix. His own will (ERO D/ACR 19/31) was made on 17 May 1771 (witnessed Samuel

Alston, William Sudell jun (qv), and James Alston - the lawyer and his clerks). It provides an annuity for his daughter Deborah Hickeringill, leaving the residue to his son Edmund who proved the will on 12 March 1794.

See also: wills of Mathias Hickeringill, gent, Colchester, NA PROB 11/730, proved 17 November 1743; Thomas Hickeringill, Pond Hall, NA PROB 11/760, proved 3 March 1748, Elizabeth Deborah Hickeringill, spinster, Pond Hall, NA PROB 11/1434, proved 10 December 1805.

HICKERINGILL WILLIAM AND MARY [438]
Brewers, Lime and Coal Merchants
fl. 1750-1775

William Hickeringill announced on 12 May 1750 (*IpsJ*) that:-

> Mr Thomas Duffield and his sister, having left off merchandising in LIME & COALS, and assigned all their kiln and yard to Mr William Hickeringill, Merchant, at the Hithe aforesaid, he takes this public opportunity of informing such Persons as used to trade with the said Mr Duffield and sister in those Articles and all other Persons, that they may be supplied with Lime and Coals at those Places as usual, and that he will take particular care they shall be served there-with at a reasonable price, and as good as can be procured, and that their orders shall be punctually observed; for which he shall acknowledge himself their most obliged humble servant.
>
> William Hickeringill.

He was created Alderman in the 1763 Corporation and his death was announced on 28 August 1766 (*IpsJ*) in Colchester 'an eminent brewer in that town'. His will, made in 1753 (NA PROB 11/922, proved 3 September 1766) concerns only a half share in the advowson of Fingringhoe and a tenement and 26 acres being part of his marriage settlement dated 27 April 1749 which he left to his son William at age 21. Administration was granted to Mary Hickeringill, as no executor nor residuary legatee was named. She continued in trade until 1775 (*IpsJ* 2

H

September 1775) when the brewery in St Botolphs St (formerly occupied by Daniel Cock (qv)) was advertised to let.

See also Thomas and Mary Duffield (qv)

HICKS GEORGE [440]
Innkeeper, Three Cups
fl. 1753-1763

The Cups housed the local Post Office in the early 1750s but this moved to the Three Crowns when George Hicks took over the Cups in 1753 (Edward Robinson (qv)). On 29 December 1753 Hicks advertised; 'CLOSE POST CHAISES, to lett hung with Steel Springs (very safe and easy) with able Horses, to any Part of England, by GEORGE HICKS at the THREE CUPS INN in Colchester, late the Post Office'. Hicks and his wife remained at the inn until 1763 when he was bankrupted (*London Gazette* 23 April, 23 July, 29 October 1763, 18 April 1764).

Once he received his discharge in 1764 the Hicks' announced a change of business:-

> G. and M. HICKS, who lately kept the THREE CUPS Inn in COLCHESTER, have taken the Shop late Mr R. Alefounder's (qv), near the Cups, and laid in a genteel Assortment in the MILLINERY Way, also China, Glass and Earthen-ware; he likewise sells, wholesale and retail, Wines, Brandy, Rum and Holland Geneva, neat as imported. They take this Opportunity of returning Thanks to all their Friends, for all Favours received; and their future Favours shall be gratefully acknowledged, by their obedient humble Servants, G. and M. HICKS (*IpsJ* 28 April 1764).

See also: *IpsJ* 24 March 1792, Mr Geo Hicks Salem, maltster, married Miss Elizabeth Powell, of Birch at the Quakers Meeting, Colchester.

HICKS WILLIAM [441]
Maltster and Coal Merchant
fl. 1798-1808

Attended St Leonard's vestry from 1798. Hicks sold up his 'very extensive Malting Office, Coal Yard &c' at the Hythe together with new built tenements 'at the foot of Hythe Bridge' in 1808 as he was 'going into another line of business' (*IpsJ* 30 July 1808).

HILLS ABIGAIL [444]
w. 1788

Aunt of Michael Robert Hills (qv), her sole executor, to whom she left all her estate in her will of 1788 (NA PROB 11/1169, made 16 June 1788, witnessed Philip Verhorslet of Colchester gardiner and James Wainman, proved 12 September 1788) except for:

- £800 Consolidated 4% stock to Elizabeth Dingley.
- £50 each for grand nieces Celia and Fanny (qv), wards in Chancery to their Guardian appointed by Court of Chancery.
- 2s a week for Sarah, now wife of John Manning, Colchester, woolcomber.

HILLS CHARLES [443]
Baymaker
fl. 1768-1780

Lived in East Lodge, All Saints, next door to Charles Gray MP (qv) with whom his relations seem at times to have been difficult. A letter from him survives in Gray's correspondence (ERO D/DRg4/41).

> Sir,
>
> My Brother informs me he has had some conversation with you concerning my Summer-House. With respect to having a Bow-Window, I never entertain'd the least

thought of such a thing. I only mentioned that it would be a great Addition to the Place. I already think myself greatly obliged to your very kind indulgence in granting me the Liberty to carry it out a few Inches further, but, if, on consideration, you find that even such Alteration will be disagreeable to you in the least, I shall be happy to have it remain in its present state.

I am,

Sir, your most obed[t] Humb Serv[t]

Charles Hills

Charles Hills was younger son to Michael Hills, baymaker (qv). His elder brother Michael Robert Hills (qv) appears to have shown no interest in the business and so Charles succeeded his father in the trade. On that account, Jeremy Bentham, a family friend, felt that Charles was the favourite of the two sons (J. Bentham, *Correspondence of Jeremy Bentham*, I. Christie (ed), Vol. 1, (London, 1971):284-5, Letter of 6 October 1775).

Charles Hills was a free burgess voting for Rebow and Gray in 1768 and Rebow in 1780. He married Sarah, only daughter of James Buxton (qv) at St Mary-at-the-Walls on 26th April 1774 (Parish registers, *ChCh* 30 April 1774). They had two daughters, Celia Susannah and Frances (qv). Charles Hills died early in the autumn of 1780 (*IpsJ* 25 November 1780). His residence in All Saints with 'large lofty warehouses and chambers over the same, lately used in the manufacture of baize' were for sale by his father, Michael Hills on 10 February 1781 (*IpsJ*). Charles Hills had died intestate and administration was granted (ERO D/ACA c8 21) in March 1781 to his father Michael who was also made guardian of the two daughters, Sarah Hills having renounced the right of guardianship. The estate was valued at under £300.

Sarah Hills, Charles' widow lived until 22 March 1788 and was buried in a large altar tomb at St Mary-at-the-Walls.

H

HILLS FRANCES and CELIA [1283]
fl. 1788-1830s

Frances Hills was the second daughter of Charles Hills (qv) baymaker and his wife Sarah, the daughter of James Buxton (qv) grocer. She and her sister Celia Susannah therefore grew up at East Lodge, All Saints next door to Charles Gray (qv) MP at Hollytrees, part of the affluent society that gathered in that parish. Charles Hills died in 1780 as a comparatively young man. He was son of Michael Hills (qv) baymaker and younger brother to Michael Robert Hills (qv) who was able to live on the family capital as a gentleman at Colne Engaine. Charles Hills died intestate with an estate valued at under £300, and his father Michael was made guardian of Frances (Fanny) and Cecilia. Their mother died in 1788 (aged only 36) two years after their grandfather. The sisters received the interest on £2,000 in their grandfather's will, to be administered by their uncle Michael Robert Hills but he, too, died the year following (1789). It seems that as well as experiencing the deaths of most of their close kin over a few years, Frances and her sister also became entangled in a serious family row over money – including their own inheritance. Their uncle, Michael Robert Hills had quarreled with his sister – the girls' aunt Elizabeth – over the disposal of their mother's estate. She was the wife of Revd Robert Dingley (qv) and the Dingley's initiated an unsuccessful court case in Chancery in the names of Elizabeth Dingley and Celia and Frances Hills (NA C 12/615/3). As a result, Frances and Celia had become wards of court by 1788, when another aunt, Abigail Hills (qv) left them £50 apiece. Their maternal grandfather (James Buxton (qv)) also left them a share in his estate in 1795. Although affluent, it does not seem likely that Frances or Celia had much direct control over their property.

Frances married Lieutenant John Matthews of the Royal Horse Artillery at St Marys in 1801 (*Ips]* 7 August 1801 and St Mary-at-the-Walls registers 3 August 1801). Celia was a witness to her marriage as was James William Buxton, (presumably) son of James Buxton. A few months later, Celia married the physician R. D. Mackintosh (qv) (CPL Crisp ML798, St Mary-at-the-Walls registers 5 October 1801). Witnesses at Celia's wedding included Frances' husband John Matthews, Caroline and James Buxton and Mira Stapleton. The Stapletons were particular friends of Jane and Ann Taylor (qv) the writers, and Ann Taylor clearly knew Celia and Frances Hills well. In her autobiography, Ann Taylor mentions how unhappy Frances' marriage turned out to be. Apparently Matthews had swept Frances off her feet, and proved to be a wretch later, having a mistress and making Fanny drudge for them (J. Gilbert, *Memorials of Mrs Gilbert*, Vol. 1, (1874):112-113). She had much more pleasant memories of Celia's husband. She recalled R. D. Mackintosh as 'an admirable physician,' who cured Cecilia of some early eccentricity, and they were 'truly valuable Christian friends' much later (139, 111). Celia had died by 1836, when Mackintosh married for a second time.

HILLS MICHAEL [446]
Baymaker
fl. 1731-1786

One of the small group of prominent baymakers who controlled the Colchester trade during its decline. Hills was a friend of Jeremy Bentham and family. Bentham reported in his correspondence (6 October 1775) that, '... the Old Gentleman himself dresses plain, sees nobody, goes nowhere, but confines himself wholly to the business' (J. Bentham, *Correspondence of Jeremy Bentham*, I. Christie (ed), Vol. 1, (London, 1971):284-5, Letter of 6 October 1775).

This was in marked contrast to his eldest son, Michael Robert Hills (qv), who was at the time building himself a country mansion at Earls Colne. Michael Hills occupied a capital dwelling in Queen Street (plan at ERO C/T/478/41, reproduced in D'Cruze, *Pleasing Prospect*:32, the building housed Colchester Police Station in the 1980s).

Extracts from Hills' accounts (ERO D/DOM 222, proceedings between Philip Astle Hills and Revd R. H. Dingley (qv) - a later court case over family property, cf M. R. Hills (qv)) show something of the concerns and business of a substantial clothier at the time;

Rec'd of Philip Sansom (cardmaker (qv)) for 1 dozen and a half of old cards	10s 6d
For 2 Hill Horses	£14 0s 0d
Of Mr Eley of Dedham for Tazil (teasel)	£25 6s 4d
Note of Hand 1774, from Revd Valentine Lumley Bernard (qv) 'who is very poor - and the note is out of date'	£5 5s 0d
pd Samuel Gibbs (bookseller and agent for *IpsJ* (qv)) for advertisements, 1787	£1 4s 0d
pd Judith Mayhew for wages	£5 0s 0d
pd Mrs Strutt (presumably Caroline, wife of Benjamin Strutt (qv)) for teaching of Miss' Hills (Cecilia and Fanny (qv), daughters of his son Charles (qv))	£15 10s 0d
pd Wm Keymer 1 (qv) for funeral of Mrs Curtis (Hills' sister ob. 1786)	£96 11s 9d
cost of funeral of son Charles (qv)	£34 0s 0d
Dr Wood (Loftus Wood (qv)) physician)	£6 0s 0d

Hills' father was Thomas Hills. He was apprenticed to William Daws, baymaker for £21 in 1731 (NA IR/1/13/12). He was a free burgess voting from 1741 when he supported the Tories (Gray and Olmius in 1747; Rebow and Gray in 1768 and Affleck in 1781 - all respectable and substantial candidates). He was churchwarden at St Botolphs from 1780.

He died in the late 1780s. His house was offered to let in 1788 (*IpsJ* 1 November 1788) This capital mansion had an '...exceedingly good hall, handsome staircase, a drawing room, 3 good parlours, 4 good bedrooms, attics, spacious garden &c'.

A later sale advertisement for the property (*IpsJ* 13 August 1791) emphasised the 'eating parlour and library and drawing room each 24ft x 18ft' as well as the servants hall and 3 pumps, 1/4 acre of ground. It also remarked that, 'Colchester is a pleasant and healthy town abounding in genteel company and has a market well supplied with fish &c.'

Hills had made his will on 28 January 1785 (NA PROB 11/1147, Norfolk 569, proved 2 November 1786) naming his 'dear beloved wife' and son Michael Robert Hills as executors. His wife received a life interest in all the real estate which then reverted to M. R. Hills who also received £3,000 and 'my chambers in the Temple, purchased in his name on account of his being a better Life now confirmed to him, also my property in the Colchester Theatre'. Hills junior was appointed trustee of £2,000 for granddaughters Celia and Fanny (qv) (daughters of son Charles (qv)), to be invested in an annuity. Hills' wife received the residue of the estate after a further £3,000 had been left to my 'daughter Dingley' (wife of Revd R. H. Dingley (qv)).

See also *IpsJ* 8 May 1790 two bay rowing mills etc property of late Michael Hills for sale.

HILLS MICHAEL ROBERT [445]
Colne Park
dd. 1789

The eldest son of Michael Hills (qv) baymaker who had established his son as a gentlemen on the profits of his trade. This kind of intergenerational mobility amongst the prosperous eighteenth-century middling sort was not uncommon.

Judging by the opinion of a famous family friend, Jeremy Bentham, Hills seems to have been a solitary character despite his social advantages;

> Micay Hills is absolutely turned Hermit. He shuts himself up ... among his well-bound books and Cockle shells and exercises the most *strenua inertia*. His house must certainly be a magnificent one; the old gentleman I understand from Mrs Townsend gave him Carte Blanche with regard to the expence (sic); and it is to be absolutely his own, with the estate around it. Yet I have all along

that this son was not at all in favour with the father; but that the younger who is in the business was the favorite. Everybody supposes the young man will marry, when the house is finished, but nobody pretends to know the person. All this while, the Old Gentleman himself dresses plain, sees nobody, goes no where but confined himself wholly to the business' (J. Bentham, *Correspondence of Jeremy Bentham*, I. Christie (ed), Vol. 1, (London, 1971): 284-5, Letter of 6 October 1775).

Hills had not always been so withdrawn. He travelled for several years, completing his education after Colchester Free School (entered October 1752 aged 9, ERO T/B 271/1), Trinity College Cambridge 1762, and Lincolns Inn 1766, by undertaking the traditional 'Grand Tour'. Earlier he had played a lively role in the Colchester Free School Election where his father was a leading partisan. This was reported in the correspondence of local clergyman Thomas Twining (qv) to Samuel Parr (qv) ex Master of the Free School in January 1779:

> Keymer (William Keymer 1 (qv) bookseller) has this minute told me, that H(ills) has said he would give £1,000 never to have engaged in this affair. 'My friends (said he) have deserted me', 'No, Sir (he was well answered) you have deserted your friends…

> Young Michael has got into several scrapes by putting himself in the way, and impudently tempting people to affront him. A pretty girl laid him fairly on his back, a daughter of Rogers the Quaker who was Hewitt's (Charles Hewitt (qv), rival candidate in the election) friend. She was standing at Keymer's door, and happened to cry Hewitt, at the instant Mr H was passing. He put his hand round her waist and said 'Does the spirit move thee, pretty Quaker?', 'Yes it does, Mr Michaell. Thou art very vulgar. Thy father is more so'. Let me just tell you that the counsel, who came down on Hills side desired the postboy, who drove him to Witham, to let Mr Hills know that he never wished to have any connection with him again and was heartily ashamed of him and his

> cause. They say H absolutely refused to pay him what he had bargained to pay him. H and Peter Daniell ((qv), attorney) have already had a violent quarrel' (John Johnson (ed), *Works of Samuel Parr LLD* Vol. 1, (London, Longman, 1828)).

Despite Bentham's speculations, Hills never married, and lived in splendid isolation in his mansion, Colne Park, Colne Engaine. He died there on 28 September 1789, aged 47. He received glowing obituary in the *Gentleman's Magazine*, Vol. 2, (1789):957-8, obit. 28 September) which firstly recited his educational achievements, then continued;

> Some years afterwards he visited several parts of the Continent, where he improved his taste for the polite arts, and enriched his collection of curiosities. After having spent about two years abroad he returned to his native country, and formed the design of settling in one of his estates near Earls Colne where he erected a mansion house and laid out his park and grounds with true taste and judgement.

> Hills bequeathed the greatest part of his real and personal estates to Philip the second son of Thomas Astle Esq of Battersea Rise, Co. Surrey who has taken the name and bears the arms of Hills - Mr Hills only sister married the Revd Mr Robert Dingley (qv), Rector of Shobury, Essex.

Michael Robert Hills left a long and complex will (witnesses William Cole, Thomas Philips, John Pitchingford, made 29 October 1787, NA PROB 11/1184, Macham 498, proved 13 October 1789) whose prime purpose was to ensure that his sister, Elizabeth Dingley received no share of his fortune. The enmity had arisen out of a quarrel over the disposal of their mother's estate. The Dingleys took the matter unsuccessfully to Chancery (in the names of Elizabeth Dingley and the Misses Hills, the children of Michael Hills' younger brother Charles), leaving the named heir Philip Astle (qv) (who changed his name to Hills in order to inherit) in possession (NA C 12/615/3).

H

Hills began his will by leaving his poor Soul to Almighty God asking forgiveness for all the Sins he had committed in this 'vain and transitory life.'

He left a good suit of mourning to all Tenants who attend his funeral, which was 'to be conducted in like style to his father's funeral' at St James, Colchester (the bequest of suits was later revoked). His servants received 2 years wages.

All his lands and house in Colne Engaine, Earls Colne, White Colne, Bures, Lamarsh, St Botolphs and St James, Colchester, Little Holland, Frinton, Fordham, West Bergholt were left to trustees Charles Matthews (qv) of Colchester Esq., Thos Sewell of Colne Engaine Esq and Revd Thomas Carwardine of Colne Priory, on Trust for William Dean, son of Anthony Dean of East Bergholt, in default of whom to my much esteemed friend Philip Astle, son of Thomas Astle of Battersea Rise, Surrey Esq., in default of whom to the second son of Nicholas Caesar Corsellis (qv) of Woodford Bridge Essex, and to take the name of Hills.

Hills ordered that a 70ft Column to be erected in his Park to his memory and be kept like the Park in good order.

The trustees also had charge of £2,000, the interest to be divided between his two nieces Celia Hills and Fanny Hills, daughters of my late brother Charles Hills ob. (qv), share and share alike.

To: Celia Hills he also left 'the use of the two portrait paintings of my late father and mother' which were to be placed in Colne Park mansion after her death.

To: friend Jones Panton, son of Paul Panton of Plas Gwyn, Anglesea, £2,000 and my best Diamond Ring (later revoked this bequest, leaving Panton £1,000 only).

To: Jones Panton's elder brother Paul Paton 5 gns for a ring.

To: aunt Mrs Abigail Hills (qv) widow of Colchester £100 plus a ring.

To: Mr Francis Hills of Colchester, officer of excise £20.

To: Mrs Mary Sweeting, Colchester widow, £10.

H

To: Sarah Manning now wife of John Manning of Colchester, rower £50 (cf. will of Abigail Hills (qv)).

To: Mrs Ann Richardson (if still living with me at my death) £50 and a ring (bequest later revoked leaving her £10 only).

To: Mrs Mary Massey of Earls Colne spinster £200.

To: Miss Chapman daughter of late Colonel Chapman of Saffron Walden £20.

To: Charles Cooper of Gt. St Helens, St Mary Axe, Packer, £100 and £50 each to his children at 21.

To: Trustees a further £300 the interest on which was to be divided between Henry, Ann and Honoria Carwardine, three children of Thomas Carwardine, at marriage or at 21. Similarly the interest on £100 was left for the education of James Blyth Waynman, son of James Waynman, (qv) Colchester gent.

To: William Carwardine another son of Revd Thomas Carwardine, my 'cabinet of curiosities at 21 (bequest later revoked and given to Astle).

To: Martha Mayhew widow, 'late of Colchester shopkeeper but now residing in London' £20 and to her daughter Judith Mayhew 'who many years lived in my family,' £200.

To: John Hawks and Lambert Tettrell, late servants to my father and mother £10 each.

To: John Barrow of Wakes Colne carpenter 'as a mark of approbation of his Sobriety and Industry,' £20.

To: the Industrious Poor of Colne Engaine not taking collection £50, and the like to the poor of St James, Colchester - to be paid by the respective Ministers.

To: Esteemed friend Colchester, Edward Ayre (Eyre) of HM train of Artillery, £50 for mourning and ring.

To: William Cecil, Norfolk St Strand, Esq., and his sisters Harriett and Sophia, £10 each for mourning and a ring.

To: Mrs Mary Boyd of Colchester, Samuel Crowley Esq of Argyll Street, Westminster, Revd Nicholas Corsellis (qv) of Wivenhoe Park and wife, Caesar Corsellis (qv) and his wife,

H

Thomas Boggis (qv) of Colchester Esq, Weaton Hollys of Newton Park, Cornwall; 5gns each for a ring.

To: Samuel Crawley a diamond shirt pin.

Mourning rings of 1gn each were left to 'Several gentlemen who shall be members of the Gosfield Club and of the Halstead Book Club and of the Book Club at Colchester (of which several Clubs I am a member) (this bequest later revoked).

Mourning rings of similar value were also left to: Lord Nugent of Gosfield Hall, Sir James Marriott of Twinstead Hall, Robert Weskett of Tower Hill Esq and wife, Revd Harvey Ducane of Coggeshall and wife (bequest revoked), Capt John Harrison of Coptford Essex and wife (bequest revoked), Henry Sperling of Dines Hall Esq and wife (bequest revoked) and John and Harry Sperling their sons (bequest revoked), - Buxton Earls Colne and wife (bequest revoked), Mrs Younges of Earls Colne, Mr Rainbird and his wife, Capt Henry Brown and wife, Earls Colne, John Morley and Allington Morley (both (qv)) of Bluebridge House Esq., Mr and Mrs Hill of Wakes Colne, Capt - Marriott and his wife of Sible Hedingham, John Round (qv) of Colchester Esq and his wife, Revd John Halls (qv) and his wife, Ann Bumstead (qv) wid., Ann the wife of Capt Wm Sharp, Mrs Powsey, Mrs Wegg, Mr Gray (Charles Gray (qv)), Mrs Powell (Susannah Powell (qv)), Revd Shaw King (qv).

1s each was bequeathed to Revd R. H. Dingley 'and that unfeeling woman his wife', because of her unkindness to him after his mother's death.

A later Codicil made the revocations indicated above and left £600 to Abel Ward the son of Seth Ward Bishopsgate Street at 21, £20 each to Thomas Fowell Buxton and wife, £10 and good suit of clothes to Thomas Fenton servant (cf. will James Boggis (qv)).

See also will of Philip Hills, Colne Engaine, NA PROB 11/1771, proved 24 May 1830.

HILLS THOMAS [442]
Carrier
fl. 1754

Of East Hill, Colchester. Advertised weekly wagons to London on 9 November 1754 (*IpsJ*).

HITCHCOCK WILLIAM [1245]
Carpenter
c.1721-1792

Of a Dedham family. Named as son of William when apprenticed in 1736 to Thomas Semen of Dedham, carpenter, £5 (NA IR 1/14/157).

Of Dedham, carpenter, aged 27, when married to Mary Warner, aged 26, of Ardleigh, at Holy Trinity, 12 April 1748 (CPL Crisp ML310).

1749 - 1787 much employed by Winsley's Trustees, whose properties include farms at Elmstead and on Mersea Island, as well as Brick Farm by the twelve Gift Houses, and Winsley's own house opposite the Minories, referred to as 'Lechmeres' after the ladies who were tenants 1754-85 (see Maria Sophia Lechmere (qv), ERO D/Q/30; JBB report to Winsley's Trustees, ERO Acc 905, Box 7). Hitchcock's bills sometimes consolidate work at several places. The first for railings 1749, £7 15s; Mersea 1750 and 1751, £32 18s and 9 gns; Lechmeres 1761 £20 18s; 1764 £3 4s 6d; 1769 £5 7s 11d (no location); 1771 9 gns; 1773 at dwellings £8 15s; 1778-9 £47 2s 6d including £15 7s ¼d for Lechmeres; 1780-3. 'By work and stuff at Mrs Lechmere's' £10 12s ½d and 'at Powell's' £27 6s 10d; 1787, last mention £14 7s 6d.

For Octagon Chapel (Lion Walk Independent, ERO D/NC 52/5/2, Maples and Hitchcock) 1765-7, £400.

1780 New house rated 12 on east side of Queen St (about where now (c. 1990) there is the entry to the Bus Park) in his occupation till taken by Revd Yorick Smythies (qv) in 1790.

H

All Saints Parish Surveyor 1781-3; Bill for repairs 1782, £5 6s 1½d.

ERO D/ACL 1786, CPL Crisp ML 409, married again. Of All Saints, carpenter, to Elizabeth Smith, widow, of St Botolph's.

His signatures are poor, but bills often written for him in better hand. In 1756 he signs himself 'Hitchacock'.

IpsJ 10 August 1765, he is one of the group of carpenters advertising work for sawyers.

His son William set up as a carpenter in Rochford, and *IpsJ* 31 July 1773 advertised for 3-4 journeymen carpenters at 12s a week and beer.

His widow remarried by 1788 (CPL Crisp ML123) to William Wade of Rochford, widower, carpenter, a freeman of Colchester who voted previously in 1788 and 1784 from Southminster. Wade had been 24 in 1773 when he married Margaret Stonard of Paglesham (CPL Crisp ML434). They had 4 children William, Joseph, Sarah and Mary who benefit from their grandfather's will (see below).

Hitchcock's will ERO D/ACR 18/396, made 28 July 1790 (witnessed M. Peter and Samuel Daniell) proved 4 February 1792. Executors William Wade of Rochford, carpenter and William Cole (qv) of Colchester, landsurveyor, are friends, to whom he leaves in Trust all his Messuages and tenements in par. St Giles, some in Stanwell St, near St John's Green and another in Magdalen St now or late occ. John Beeson, Richard Munson, John Blackwell, Thomas Byford and Isaac Howard, 'and all other freehold estate whatsoever', and a one acre copyhold on Dedham Heath occ. Joseph Heyes. To sell and divide equally between the four grandchildren above at age 21.

To his now wife Elizabeth, late Smith all her own goods, furniture etc. before marriage, plus £10 'to be accepted in full of all claims of dower.'

Other plate and china between granddaughters at 21 or marriage, £20 to grandson William at 21 (interest to be paid him meantime), £5 each to executors plus reasonable expenses.

H

Stock in trade to be sold to meet debts, and residue to be divided between said children at 21. No other legacies.

IpsJ 7 April 1792, Auction of his furniture, and unexpired lease (5 years) of his house (no address). The rent of his tenements on St John's Green, £8 (John Beeson) and Magdalen St, £2 12s (Isaac Howard). Also tenement at Dedham. George Dodson, auctioneer. 17 December 1792 (*IpsJ*), advertisement for Debtors and Creditors. To be addressed to Wade, Cole, or Samuel Daniell (qv) attorney.

HOBBS GILES [1155]
Minister, Lion Walk
1775-1808

For a full account of his activities in Colchester, see Blaxill, *Lion Walk*. ERO D/NC 52/5/2 includes correspondence in 1773-4 regarding the disagreements within the Lion Walk congregation over Hobbs' appointment, his invitation to preach for an initial six months and his agreement as well as several sermons. His will is at NA PROB 11/1481, proved 3 June 1808.

HOLBOROUGH THOMAS [1170]
Clockmaker
1676-1727

Admitted free burgess in 1697 and traded in St Runwald as a watchmaker and silversmith from 1698. Took Tobias Searson apprentice (Monday Court 29 August 1698). Married Jane Bateson in 1699, their daughter Hannah was baptised at St Runwald's 12 December 1701. Mason mentions five appearances as creditor in actions brought at the Thursday Court between 1700 and 1706 when he moved to Ipswich. Died there in 1727, where he was succeeded by his son, also Thomas.

Summarised from B. Mason, *Clock and Watchmaking in Colchester*, (1969):242-3

HOLME JOHN [447]
Landsurveyor
ob. 1813

His effects were for sale at the Hythe after his decease including 'very excellent and modern furniture' (19 June1813 *Ips*).

HOLMSTED JOHN [448]
Surgeon
fl. 1706

Surgeon of St Mary's Colchester. He swore the Oath of Succession in 1706 contemporary with William Rowght surgeon (qv) (Colchester Oath Book, ERO D/B 5 R1).

HOLTON BARKER [449]
Innkeeper, Angel and Carpenter
1695-1778

Baptised on 9 June 1707 at Stoke-by-Nayland. His parents were Edward Holton and wife Mary *née* Barker, married on 22 July 1695, both of Nayland. Holton was apprenticed to Edward Bartholomew (qv), carpenter, for £8 in 1722 (NA IR 1/47/128) and admitted free burgess by right of apprenticeship in 1734 (Monday Court). Holton voted in 1741, 1747 and 1768 for the better established candidates. He was created Common Councillor in 1763 and promoted to Assistant on 10 August 1767. A bill survives from him in the Chamberlain's Vouchers of 1737-8 (ERO D/B 5 Ab1/34) and in 1762-3 he was paid 50 gns by Charles Gray (qv) for repairing a breach at Middle Mill according to contract (ERO D/DR B1).

Took William Smith (son of William) apprentice in 1744 for a fee of £10 (JBB NB Oct63, nfr). He was one of a number of Colchester carpenters who advertised jointly on 10 August 1765 offering work for sawyers (*Ips*). He was also witness at the marriage of John Butcher, carpenter at St Peters on 28 July 1765. In his settlement examination of 1787 John Halenter,

H

reported that he had served Barker Holton for two years for 3 gns and 2 years for 4 gns (ERO Examination Book P/Co R11A, nfr).

Holton was an active member of the Lodge of Freemasons at the Angel. He was Master of the Lodge seven times between 1750 and 1768 and so can probably be established at the Angel from as early as mid century though no rate books survive before 1766. On 21 November 1761 (*IpsJ*) the freemasons were requested to meet at Brother Holton's at the Angel prior to a visit to a theatrical performance.

Holton seems to have married three times. In 1735 he married Frances Starr (24) of St Peters at Greenstead (ERO ML D/ALL 1735). The will of Susan Simpson (made 1752, proved 1770, ERO D/ACR 17/150) leaves the bulk of her property to Barker Holton and his second wife Elizabeth who had died by the time the will was proved in 1770. In 1762 he married Sarah Wright a widow of Wivenhoe (ERO ML D/ALL 1762). He died on 17 August 1778, 'advanced in years' and was buried at Stoke-by-Nayland on 23 August.

His will (PCC PROB 11/1048, proved 7 December 1778) leaves his personal estate to widow Sarah then cash legacies of £30 to his sister Mary Chapman of Ipswich and £50 to Elizabeth Holton otherwise Starr, Colchester, spinster (apparently a daughter of his first wife). The value of his real estate was to be divided between the trustees, James Chaplin, ironmonger of London and nephew George Holton of Nayland, butcher, for the benefit of two brothers of James and two sisters of George as well as Elizabeth Holton. One John Goff the elder of Stoke was to be paid 4s weekly in the church porch at Nayland at 11 a.m. each Monday morning, and then to his son after him.

See also Sarah Holton's (Wright's) will of 5 June 1784, proved 20 February 1785 (ERO D/ACR 19/156) disposed of personal possessions etc. to son-in-law Thomas Wright, 'marriner' of East Donyland and left a bedstead with blue hangings to daughter Mary, wife of George Turner carpenter of Colchester. One of the executors was Peter Coveney (qv) brandy merchant.

Also see will George Holton, West Bergholt, NA PROB 11/1522 30 May 1811.

Subsequent innkeepers at the Angel to 1813 were John Bromley, Philip Hast and Joseph Rogers. The inn was owned by John Bawtree in 1813.

HOOKER STEPHEN [450]
Apothecary
fl. 1761-1776

Hooker was established in Colchester from 1761 when he appears in St Runwalds rates at 39 High Street (rated 20), though at that time he appears to have been trading from a smaller shop rated 10 on the downhill corner of the High Street and Pelhams Lane. He moved the business downhill to 39 High Street in 1765;

> Stephen Hooker. druggist and chymist, Removed from the corner of Pelham's Lane to the Glambers Head, four doors above the Red Lyon in the Gardeners Market. Sells all sorts of Drugs, Chymical and Galenical preparations, wholesale and retail, at the lowest Prices, Libeuse (?), Arabusade, Pyremont Spaw, ScarBorough, Tilbury, Bath and Bristol Waters, with a variety of Snuffs and Confectionary (sic).
>
> N.B. Various Articles in the Perfume, Dry Salting and Oil Way (*Ips*) 6 April 1765, viewed by JBB in hard copy, issue missing on microfilm).

He advertised again in 1773:

> Stephen Hooker
> Druggist, Chymist and Confectioner
> In the High Street, Colchester
>
> Being engaged with a considerable Confectioner in London, is enabled to sell Confectionery, at the following Prices; Macaroons, Savoy Biscuits, Naples Rolls, and Drop Cakes, at the London Wholesale Prices, allowing one Penny per Pound for carriage; at Retail, Macaroons &

H

> Savoy Biscuits at 1s 2d per Pound, Naples Rolls and Drop Cakes at 9d per Pound; with all other Articles in this Branch in Proportion. Likewise Mineral Waters, Foreign and English Perfumes, Wax, Sperma Coeti*, Candles, Snuffs and Spices.
>
> A Variety of Patent Medicines, all Kinds of Drugs, Chymical and Galenicals, truly prepared and sold in any Quantity.
>
> N.B. Small Quantities of each Kind will be sold in proportion to a larger, for the Benefit of the Poor (*Ips*] 16 January 1773).

*Sperma-Ceti: Solid white waxy substance, in oblong flakes, made from whale oil and taken medicinally. 'Its virtues are emolient and pectoral; it is good in coughs and other disorders of the breast; and is excellent in external applications, such as linaments, and the like', *Dictionary of Arts and Sciences*, (1784): 3022.

He married Miss Denny of Colchester on 2nd June 1774 (*Ips*] 4 June 1774).

According to Bland (Appendix 3, *Bland's Anecdotes*:84):-

> Hooker, a chymist and druggist, was for many years highly esteemed and respected by his neighbours. His propensity to thieve he indulged in a long time without suspicion, and many petty thefts were attributed to others, of which he was the perpetrator. He at last stole a gold watch of great value from Mr Nathaniel Hedge 1 (qv).
>
> Being from other circumstances suspected, a plan was laid to detect him, and at a Club at the Red Lion Inn, a wager was proposed by which everyone present was obliged to produce their watches. Hooker, not suspecting any design, and rendered callous to detection by frequent escapes, most inadvertently produced his among the rest. It was recognised and immediately claimed by Hedge. Hooker begged for mercy, and forbearance to expose him, delivered up the watch, and was suffered to retire to his

home. The next morning he quitted Colchester for America, and was never afterwards heard of.

He married a woman of the name of Jones who for many years after his departure carried on a little grocer's shop, and was respected and commiserated by all, and closed her life in useless repinings for the absence and conduct of her offending husband.

Though Bland is incorrect in the maiden name of his wife, Hooker certainly disappeared suddenly from Colchester between 1776 and 1780 (years for which parish rates are available) while Mrs Hooker remained. His death was not reported and Hannah Hooker is referred to as 'Mrs' not 'Wid.' in subsequent records. She was the owner of the property on the corner of Pelhams Lane and of 39 High Street in 1783 (Land Tax) but lived elsewhere. In 1784, for one year only she is occupier of 50 High Street (rated 10).

HOSSACK COLIN [453]
Physician
fl. 1764-1782

Dr Colin Hossack, 'of Colchester, and Physician to his late Royal Highness Frederick Prince of Wales' was author of *An Abridgement of Baron van Swieten's Commentaries on the Aphorisms of Dr Herman Boerhaave*. Moses Griffith MD (qv) also mentions consultations with Hossack in his own writings (nfr).

Colchester, March 7

Whereas it has been currently reported about the Country that Dr HOSSACK has left Colchester this is to give Notice, that he has only removed from St Martin's Lane into EAST STREET (*Ips*) 10 March 1764).

His house was on the north side of East Hill, near the bottom, modern-built when offered for sale (*Ips*) 27 February 1768).

To be SOLD, on EAST HILL, COLCHESTER

H

> A Modern built HOUSE with a Brick front and Sash-Windows; consisting of three Parlours wainscotted & hung with good Paper, Marble Chimnies and Slabs; the chambers large and ... a Garden well planted with Fruit-trees & walled round and a Stable for six or more Horses, all Freehold.
> For further Particulars enquire of Dr. Hossack in Colchester

It was described more fully on 8 December 1770 (*IpsJ*);

> Dr Hossack's House for Sale
>
> A very convenient House mostly Brick; consisting of a Hall wainscotted and hung with a neat Paper, two Fore Parlours, one wholly wainscotted, the other wainscotted chair-high, and hung with a neat Paper, a Back Parlour fitted up in the same Manner, with good Marble Chimney pieces, a very good Kitchen, Washhouse and a garden walled round ... Brick Stable ... 6 Bed chambers. ... Enquire of Mr Pilborough (qv).

It was taken by a Dr Hopson for some time, evidently let not sold, and seems to have been occupied by Hossack in 1776 when he insured his 'own dwelling house' for £200 with Sun Assurance (Policy 365831, 31 January 1776). It was for sale again 16 January 1783 (*IpsJ*).

Hossack was Senior Warden of the Unity Lodge of Masons, no. 402, meeting at the Red Lion (Henry Sadler, *Life of Thomas Dunckerley* (1891)). Amongst others he signed a smallpox notice of 22 May 1773 (*IpsJ*) stating the town had only 11 cases.

He died in 1782 when creditors of the late Dr Colin Hossack 'heretofore of Colchester, since of Kelvedon, and late of Braintree' were to apply to Mr Bullock (qv) attorney, acting executor (*IpsJ* 21 December 1782).

His will (ERO D/ABR 27/351 made 18 February 1773, proved 18 December 1782) names his brother James Hossack and son-in-law William Bullock (qv) as executors and trustees. It directs all his real and personal estate to be sold and the proceeds invested to pay interest to his wife for life, thereafter, £100 to his son James and the rest equally between his three daughters, Catherine Campbell Hossack spr., Charlotte Bullock and Mary Hossack spr.

His wife lived until 1791 (*IpsJ* 2 April 1791).

See also C. Hossack, Mayor of Sudbury in Aug 1754 (JBB Note, nfr); NA IR 1/54/143, 1762 Charlotte Hossack apprenticed to Lucia and Hannah Reeve (qv) spinsters and mantua makers for £20; 1767 Hossack and daughters Catherine Campbell Hossack and Charlotte Hossack witnessed the will of Elizabeth Mayhew (widow of William, made 1767, proved 1787, ERO D/ABR 28/40).

HOUSSAYE ISAAC AND TAMARY [454]
fl. 1750-1791

A Hugenot couple. Isaac seems to have been the son of 'Noé Houssaye et sa femme Marie Blondeau', baptised at the French Church, Threadneedle Street, London on 27 September 1685 (W. J. C. Moëns, *Registers of the French Church Threadneedle Street*, Vol. 2, (1896):279). The couple apparently came from Tours. Others recorded of that surname are Isaac and Claud Houssaye on 8 May 1697 (Hugenot Society Publications, *Denizatures*, 1911: 249).

Houssaye who seems to have traded as a Portugal merchant, was already a resident gentleman in Colchester, when his wife Tamary, originally of Georgia, was naturalised on 14 March 1749/50 (Hugenot Society, *Naturalisations*:151, 23 Geo II no 2, by Royal Assent). He subscribed to Morant's *Colchester* in 1748.

The Houssayes lived on East Hill, St James, the North side near the top (rated 17 with £50 personal estate in 1778 (Land Tax); JBB NB Red 2:53, note 'above Whaley'). Isaac made his will on 10 February 1755 (NA PROB 11/821, Glazier 72; witnessed Francis Perigal, Copthall, Merchant, Henry Stockdale, apothecary, Beauforts Buildings, William Mason (qv), attorney, Chancery Lane). It was proved on 31 March 1756. He left his 'dear and loving wife Tamary Houssaye the settlement already made of my estate in St James Colchester, now wholly in my

H

own occupation, but lately built by me and the Revd Mr Lynd' (Charles Lind (qv)) as well as two 'farms in Wigborough for life, thereafter to his nephew Anthony Martin, ensign in the Guards, then to Martin's sons if any, or daughters, failing whom to 'my cousin Mr Pezo Pilleau now of Chandos St, Covent Garden'.

The Wigborough property was Bumpsteads and Hill House farms, worth £3,600 in 1801. They were copyhold of the manor of Gt Wigborough with Salcott on whose rolls is noted the admission of the Houssayes on 25 August 1750. A copy of Isaac's will (also NA PROB 11/821, 31 March 1756) is entered on 12 February 1755 (Morant, Essex, Vol 1:221; ERO D/DU 4/14, Wigborough Court Books). The provisions of the will were followed, as shown by a copy administration for Maj General Anthony Martin in 26 October 1759 (after the death of Tamary) and of Mr Isaac Pilleau, Newington Surrey, gent in 30 October 1800, in default of issue of Anthony Martin.

The trustees and executors named by Isaac Houssaye were Edward Page Esq of Charterhouse Square London and Thomas Stonestreet Esq of Islington who both received £20 for mourning. Household goods were left to Tamary, as well as a life interest in:- her jewels and £50 for mourning, the interest on a Life Annuity no. 563 of £50 p.a., payable at the Exchequer, his entitlement to £1,700 on the death of Mrs Mary Mortal, wid., relict of Revd Charles Mortal, now residing in Dublin (the other trustees of this legacy being Revd Dr John Wynne and Sir Charles Benton both of Dublin), his book debts in Portugal and all other interest payments.

Anthony Martin was left £10 for mourning and Mrs Elizabeth Pritchard, Tamary's companion received £15. After Tamary's death, Susan Pilleau, daughter of 'Peze Pilleau aforesaid' received £200, if 21, failing whom to her father, failing whom to his son Isaac Pilleau.

£400 was left to the French Church, Threadneedle Street for the relief of the poor, similarly £50 to the Church of England Charity School in Colchester 'of which I was sometime Treasurer'. £50 was directed to George Wegg 2 (qv) and Revd

H

John Milton (qv) or his successor for the poor of St James, to be paid on Tamary's death.

The interest on the residue of the estate was left to Tamary for life, then to Anthony Martin, then to Isaac Pilleau, then between Elizabeth Page, goddaughter of Edward Page, Tamary Pritchard his wife's god daughter and niece of aforesaid Elizabeth Pritchard, Tamary Boch another goddaughter of his wife, and Elizabeth Pritchard herself.

The trustees were particularly requested to protect his wife 'to the utmost of their power, she having no relations of her own here in England'. Tamary continued to live quietly at Colchester. A letter to her from Edward Page, the trustee, survives (bound in the volume of the *Ipswich Journal* before the 15 January 1757, viewed by JBB in CPL, JBB NB Dec 71:45) dated 28 December 1756:

> Madam,
>
> I return you many thanks for your kind present. the Basket contained two firm Wild Ducks besides the Turkey, which as usual was the best I eat anywhere - Mr Stonestreet is with his Sisters at Islington from Friday till Tuesday and the rest of the week in Town at Mr Broughton's our apothecary in Aldermanbury - Francia executed his General Release last Thursday - have got one Mrs Whitehead a clergyman's widow to keep my house who was recommended to me by Mrs Chambers in our Square...'

Tamary's will (draft ERO D/Del B19 made 13 October 1778, witnessed John Halls (Revd), Thomas Boggis (qv), Saml Ennew (qv), NA PROB 11/1200/19, proved 19 January 1791) leaves to her nephew George Anthony Martin Esq, then a Lieut Colonel in the Light Infantry Company of the Brigade of Guards, now or late in America, (cf. American War of Independence 1776-783) all her plate except her silver teapot. To her cousin Susan Pilleau, the sole executrix who then lived with her she left, '... my bronze bust of Cosmo de Medicis, Grand Duke of Tuscany, purchased at Lisbon by my late Husband', as well as

H

all the household goods, the silver teapot, china etc and residue of the estate.

Tamary requested to be buried in the same vault as her husband. Her will was finally proved on 19 January 1791, several years after her death. The form follows that of the draft but with a codicil of 1 December 1780 (witnessed Jemima Freeman, Richard Freeman) which adds that; '...the Bronze Bust or Alto Relievo of Cosmo de Medicis, Grand Duke of Tuscany' was to be left to her nephew Col. George Anthony Martin of the Coldstream Regt of Guards for life, only if unmarried, then to her cousin Susannah Pilleau the sole executrix.

Tamary was buried in St James, 31 July 1789.

HOWE JOHN [977]
Innkeeper, Marquis of Granby
fl. 1790-95

Owned by Robert Wright (qv) during Howe's occupation.

HOWE R. [456]
Gunsmith
fl. 1806

Took over the 'old established shop' of Jackson and Hunt from Mrs Hunt in Head Street (*Ips*) 10 August 1806).

See also ERO P/Co R6, Examination Books, 19 October 1778, Daniel Jackson, Colchester, gunsmith lays complaint against William Hamilton, turner for assault.

HUDSON JOHN [457]
Innkeeper, Marlborough Head
fl. 1809

The Inn was for sale on 8 April 1809 (*Ips*) together with 5 tenements adjoining in Moor Lane and a house in Queen Street occupied by R. Dawes Esq (qv). Hudson acted as executor to John Hardy, gaoler in 1828/9 (ERO D/ABR 33/219).

HUMPHREYS, J. and W. YOUNGHUSBAND [980]
Drapers
1788-1790

Frequently advertised their drapers business in Colchester High Street from 1788 (e.g. *IpsJ* 17 February 1788). From 1790 they were established near the White Hart (no. 3 High Street) rated 21 where they succeeded Ebeneezer Cornell (qv).

HUNT JOHN [1218]
Carpenter
1755-1803

Apprenticed to William Lay (qv) of Lexden, 1770, £18 (NA IR 1/57/118).

1779 Married Mary Barns at Holy Trinity, being then of Great Clacton, carpenter (ERO ML D/ACL 1779).

In *Baileys British Directory* (1783) is listed as carpenter, Holy Trinity. One of the two Collectors of Land Tax for that parish, he and Mary Chignall occupied 'Corporation Estate' rated 9, which William Mayhew 1 (qv), annotating a Poll Book in 1747 (nfr), describes as 'messuage divid'd into Severall Wm Salmon, now W. Maples, £08.00.00'.

25 September 1784 (*IpsJ*), advertised for an apprentice also 3 or 4 journeymen joiners and carpenters.

Is listed in the 1791 *Universal Directory*, as Hunt and Barns.

1791 St Botolphs Overseers rates show him as the owner of properties including 27 rentals in the Lane including Stephen Candler (qv) (2), Wiseman Candler, and Candler junr.

1793 St Botolphs Land Tax, shows a similar listing, preceded by two Inns belonging to Mrs Barns, John Hunt owed property occupied by 'Barnes and others' rated 8 and land rated 2.

1803, however, John Hunt's will (ERO D/ABR 29/603) describes him as a brewer. His wife's father, Clark Barns (qv), brewer died in 1783, her brother Charles carried on till he died 1791. The brewery was on the site of what is now the Scheregate Hotel and the terrace in Abbeygate St.

JBB Note: the Barns or Barnes were a family of bricklayers etc. of whom Benjamin was paid £3 6s for the High St Obelisk in 1760.

HURLOCK MRS [459]
fl. 1785

IpsJ 18 June 1785: Sale of furniture, Head Street, late occupied Mrs Hurlock.

HUSSEY REVD NAPTHALI [460]
Rector of East Mersea
fl. 1737-1769

Resident in Colchester. In 1741 (*IpsJ* 3 October 1741) he lost from his house there a dozen fine Holland shirts marked NH, 2 pairs Holland and one pair Irish sheets marked NHA, 2 fine large Damask Table cloths marked NH and DH and two damask Napkins, four stocks etc. These were taken by a woman who pretended to tell the maid's fortunes. 2 gns reward was offered for the thief, described as Jane Mackbrian who said she was a Drummer's wife of Col. Poultney's regiment and commonly went about telling fortunes. She had a blue gown, short blue cloak, was of middle size with a round face, clear skin, hazel eyes and dark brown hair. She had drops in her ears 'newly bor'd' and was about 28 years old.

In 1748 (*IpsJ* 13 August 1748) with Albertus Bevan (qv), carpenter, he was to be inquired of regarding the sale of three brick houses over North Bridge for sale and demolition.

He lived in St Mary-at-the-Walls in a house owned by Thomas Lawrence, innholder (will ERO D/ACR 15/181, made 1744, proved 1745). His wife was left £10 in the will of Esther Pulston

(ERO D/ABR 23/400, 1749). He himself stood bond together with Revd John Halls (qv) for £2,000 in the administration of Martha Selly's estate, granted to her mother Elizabeth Selly (qv) the brewer (ERO D/ACWb52, 29 June 1749).

HUTCHINSON ABIATHER [466]
Tallow Chandler
fl. 1735-1744

Hutchinson is listed as a freemason of the Angel Lodge in 1735. He was a free burgess voting for Savage and Gray in 1741 (Tory) and the same year was Borough Chamberlain and Treasurer of the Workhouse Corporation.

His will of 1744 (ERO D/ABR 23/120) left his house in St Botolphs to 'his loving wife' Frances for life then 'to my right heir'. The residue of the estate was left to his wife and 'honoured mother' Sarah Hutchinson, who were co-executors.

HUTCHINSON RICHARD [461]
Goldsmith
1676-1746

One of a family with a longstanding trade in gold and silver-smithing in Colchester, London, Norwich and Chelmsford. The son of Richard Hutchinson, goldsmith of Colchester who died 18 July 1680, though his grandfather (also Richard) continued to trade in St Nicholas until his death in 1702.

A free burgess admitted 22 January 1700 and elected Assistant in the 1730s. Apparently the only member of the family to broaden his trade from goldsmith to clockmaker. Mason traced three long-case clocks of his manufacture in the 1960s. Occupied the family premises at St Nicholas until 1710 then moved opposite the Three Cups, St Runwald. Later occupied 24 High Street, rated 20.

A regular Grand Juror between 1717 and 1741, following a fine levied in 1716 on several Colchester individuals including Hutchinson, for non attendance (13 July 1716). Took the Oath

H

of Allegiance on 4 November 1723 (ERO D/B 5 R1) and voted in Borough elections in 1734 and 1741 and as a freeholder in the county in 1722 and 1734. A Guardian of the Poor between 1723 and 1734 and an Assistant between 1734 and 1738. A bill of his survives for mending the Borough Mace in 1728/9.

He died in 1746, aged 70 and is buried in St Peters.

His daughter Sarah married Revd Joseph Brockwell (qv) in 1751 and his son Thomas (qv) carried on the business until 8 September 1764 when the stock was advertised for sale opposite the Three Cups.

See also B. Mason, *Clock and Watchmaking in Colchester*, (1969): 236-242.

HUTCHINSON THOMAS [463]
Goldsmith
fl. 1747-1764

Son of Richard Hutchinson (qv). He voted in 1747 for Gray and Olmius. After his death in 1764 his stock in trade was advertised for sale at his premises opposite the Three Cups (*Ips]* 8 September 1764). The shop seems to have been in St Peters where no rate books are available for that date, as it does not appear in the relevant St Runwalds rates.

I/J

INGRAM REVD ROBERT [464]
Vicar of Wormingford and Boxted
fl. 1760-1804

Published a range of pamphlets including *Isaiah's Vision* (1784), *The Seventh Plague* (1785) and *An Improved Explanation of the Prophesy of Seven Vials of Wrath* (printed by Keymer, Colchester, 1780). The *Monthly Review* criticised his scholarship (JBB ms note). His will (NA PROB 11/1414/620, proved 13 September 1804) mentions two sons Robert Acklom Ingram (qv) and Rowland Ingram, a wife Catherine and property in Gracechurch Street.

INGRAM REVD ROBERT ACKLOM BD [465]
Curate of Wormingford and Boxted
fl. 1788-1809

Fellow of Queens College, Cambridge and curate to his father Revd Robert Ingram (qv). He preached the annual sermon for the Charity Schools at St James Colchester in 1788, later published by William Keymer 1 (qv), Colchester at 1s (*Ips]* 15 November 1788). In 1798 (29 April) he published a sermon to persuade the Congregations to form themselves into Military Associations and companies of Pioneers for the Defence of the Country addressed to his 'dear flock, who have been accustomed to look up to me for advice.'

The British Library Catalogue lists a range of his publications including the Charity School Sermon, *Disquisitions on Population* (in refutation of Malthus) of 1808 and *Parochial Benevolence* for the School of Industry at Boxted, published Colchester, 1800.

I/J

Later became Rector of Legrave, Leicestershire. His will is at NA PROB 11/1494, proved 30 March 1809).

See his entry in *ODNB*.

JACKLIN BENJAMIN [467]
Butcher and Innkeeper, Lamb
fl. 1775-1801

Jacklin was tenant at the inn but owned 5 adjacent tenements, probably in Rowes Yard behind. In 1781/2 Jacklin was executor to Rebecca Burgess, a relative (ERO D/ACW 34/5/35, 1782). His own will (ERO D/ACR 19/249, made 1785, proved 1801) left all his estate to his wife Sarah.

JACKLIN WILLIAM [1026]
Innkeeper, Fleur de Lys
w. 1762

After Jacklin's death the inn was offered for sale on 17 September 1763 (*IpsJ*).

> To be LETT & enter'd upon immediately. A good accustomed PUBLICK HOUSE, situate in the Parish of HOLY TRINITY in COLCHESTER, known by the Sign of the FLOWER DE LUCE with Brewing utensils & furniture and a good Stock of Beer. For further Particulars enquire of William Jacklin, Baker at Manningtree or at the house.

His will is at ERO D/ABR 25/209.

JACKSON DRUSILLA [468]
Ladies Boarding School, Dedham
fl. 1750

Drusilla Jackson from London took over the Ladies School from Elizabeth Wood (qv) in January 1750 (*IpsJ* 27 January 1749/50). She offered needlework and the French Tongue and lessons in writing, arithmetic, music and dancing from visiting masters. The school building was again offered for sale in 1816 (*Ips*J 8 June 1816) described as a substantial brick dwelling house in Dedham Street having been 'a Ladies Boarding School for more than half a century'.

JACKSON GEORGE [1303]
MP for Colchester 1790-6

Pro-Pitt Tory and the favoured candidate of the local Corporation Party. As Sir George Duckett, went on to a distinguished political career. See *ODNB*; Namier and Brooke, *The House of Commons*; Thorne, *The House of Commons*.

JACOB MRS [469]
fl. 1788-1801

Elizabeth Jacob was the widow of William Jacob who died intestate on 1 April 1799. At the time she thought he made a will in 1778 (*Ips*J 10 August 1799). They lived at 82 East Hill, on the north side near the top between J. B. Whaley (qv) and James Taylor a little uphill from Mrs Kersteman (qv), rated 14 with a personal estate of £100 per Land Tax Returns of 1778 (St James). She remained there until her death in 1801. Her furniture was offered for sale that November (*Ips*J 28 November 1801).

She had a ledger in St James church recording her death on 22 October 1801 aged 71, relict of William Jacob Esq as well as that of her mother Mrs Jane Betts (ob. 5 April 1775 aged 65).

JAMES JOHN 1 [1259]
Carpenter
fl. 1705-1728

Free burgess 1705 by apprenticeship to James Deane (father of James Deane (qv)) carpenter. Common Councilman, Assistant 1731, Chamberlain 1726-8. William Chisnall, free burgess, his apprentice, voted from London as a carpenter 1781 (perhaps with John Maples, Parker's Gardes, Lambeth) and 1784, but

I/J

was back in Colchester for the elections in 1788 and 1790. Not the same family as the Chignalls who were bakers.

JAMES JOHN 2 [470]
Surgeon
fl. 1778

James had the misfortune to have his nose pulled by a young Charles Shillito (qv), later the playwright and poet (Sessions Examinations, ERO P/CoR/7, 7 March 1778). The same month he married Hester the daughter of John Agnis (qv) gardener (CPL Crisp ML63, ERO D/ALL 1778 John James, St Runwalds, Colchester, surgeon to Hester Agnis of St Runwalds, 1778; *IpsJ* 15 March 1778, Mr James, apothecary to Miss Agnis, on Tuesday). The same year he took John Sharpe apprentice for 6 years for £52 10s (NA IR/1/61).

He had died by 1807, for in her father's will of 1807/8 (ERO) Hester is named as the wife of Jeremiah Daniell (qv) customs officer.

IpsJ 20 June 1778: For auction. East Hill properties (1) of James Taylor (qv) carpenter, (2) of Wilshire Wilson Esq (qv), and also those of John James, surgeon and James Taylor, Magdalen Street. Also for sale Cabinet goods and furniture of the same James Taylor who was going to leave the town.

St James Land Tax of 1790 has properties owned James Taylor but occupied by William Sparling (qv) rated 6 and another rated 2 owned and occupied by Taylor at the top of East Hill between East Hill House and the Ship.

JAMES WILLIAM [471]
Whitesmith and Bellhanger
fl. 1802

James' furniture and stock in trade including bellows, anvils, bellhanging tools etc. were sold at his premises on North Hill on 13 March 1802 (*IpsJ*).

JARROLD SAMUEL [472]
Baymaker
fl. 1757-1777

Had been apprenticed to Jonathan Tabor 1 (qv) baymaker for £80 in 1757 (NA IR 1/53/55) and later had premises in Queen Street on the site subsequently taken over by the Misses Lind (qv) for their school, from 1771 (*IpsJ* 29 June 1771). Jarrold had moved to Bury St Edmunds where he continued to trade until his death in 1777, when the *IpsJ* announced (17 May 1777):-

> GENTLEMEN in the Wool Trade are respectfully acquainted; that at the dying request of Mr SAMUEL JARROLD his business is continued by us, the widow and friends of the deceased ... situation of widow and orphans must excite your favourable regards ... The strictest honour and integrity may be relied on, and any future favour to the Halls will be highly esteemed by ... JARROLD, FROST & GREEN.'

JARVIS HENRY [473]
fl. 1802

IpsJ 13 March 1802; freehold estate in Hythe street for sale. Sometime occupied Wm Cook (qv) merchant, late of Mr Henry Jarvis.

JOHNSON GEORGE [475]
Innkeeper, Fencers
fl. 1779-1786

Witnessed the will of Samuel Smith, gent. in 1786 (26 May, ERO D/ABR 28/278). Succeeded at the Fencers by Ann Johnson, named as owner occupier.

I/J

JOHNSON HENRY [478]
Rower
fl. 1764-1785

Johnson had been set up in business with the aid of £25 from White's Charity in 1766 (Assembly Books – a bequest to assist deserving individuals connected with the wool trade in one of eleven English towns in rotation, Morant, *Colchester*, Book 3:1).

In the will of Thomas Boggis (qv) (1790) Johnson was left the value of his bond on this sum;

> To Henry Johnson the elder I give the sum of £25 to be paid him upon his delivering up the bond cancelled to my executors in which my said brother Isaac Boggis with others stand bond with me to the Corporation of Colchester in a matter called Whites Charity and that without any expense to my brother ...

Johnson was not successful and was declared bankrupt in 1785 (*IpsJ* 7 May 1785; ERO C47 CPL232, 1786, sale of bankrupt property by Johnson's assignees to Peter Devall 2 (qv)). After his bankruptcy, he became Clerk of the Market. A final dividend was declared at a meeting of creditors at the Red Lion (qv) in 1790 (*IpsJ* 27 November 1790).

Johnson voted from 1768, supporting the Rebow and Gray compromise. He was one of candidate Christopher Potter's (qv) supporters in 1784 and firmly pro-Pitt and the Corporation party.

His will (ERO D/ABR 31/1, made 1809, proved 1813, of All Saints, late baymaker now Clerk of the Market) left his messuage in All Saints to his daughters Sarah and Elizabeth Jane (spinsters) and a messuage in St Helen's Lane, St Nicholas, left him by his sister Sarah Draper to his son Henry Martin Johnson. Sarah Draper was his wife's niece (cf. will of Martin Bell (qv) Johnson's late master). Johnson's wife, Persis, survived him and died aged 78 on 7 February 1809.

See also will of Persis Eaton, widow of Messing, ERO D/ACR 17/103 1764/8, which left Persis Johnson £10 'and my new stays'.

JOHNSON THOMAS [1252]
Carpenter
fl. 1720s-70s

This name is shared by both carpenters and bricklayers probably related, and nonconformists. Several separate individuals have been identified.

1. Thomas Johnson, carpenter, will 29 March 1729, ERO D/ABR 20/277 has some bills in the Borough Chamberlain's accounts 1726-8, not explored.

2. Thomas Johnson, bricklayer voted for Brooksbank 1734; in 1734/5 was paid £64 10s for work on Winsley's Gift Houses (ERO D/Q/30); 1756, will ERO D/ACR 16/108, Revd Thomas Stanton (qv) executor, left all to wife Ann, (Ann Parker (qv)) who remarried John Parker (qv) perukemaker, and traded as a milliner when a widow later, St Nicholas parish. Thomas Johnson is buried with her at All Saints (headstone) with their only son, carpenter, see below.

3. Thomas Johnson, carpenter, voted for Houblon 1734, 1747 and was one of two of that name voting for Fordyce 1768, when an apprentice of his, Philip Woodthorpe, was made a freeman. 10 August 1765 (*IpsJ*) was one of the local carpenters advertising jointly for sawyers. 1765-6, was paid for windows for Octagon Chapel, 25 windows for £33 15s and again 'work and windows' £26 13s (ERO D/NC 52/5/2). *ChCh* 24 November 1769, fire burnt down his house at the Hythe. 29 June 1771, took Isaac Cook, apprentice, £9 (ERO D/B 5 Ta1). 5 August 1778, bankrupt (ERO TP 146/10). *ChCh* 21 August 1778, offered a large quantity of mahogany and cabinet goods to be sold by auction. 12 July 1779, Quarter Sessions, Thomas Adams discharged from apprenticeship to Johnson as bankrupt. John Howard, another apprentice was made free by right of service (nfr). 8 January 1780 *IpsJ*, advertised an auction of bankrupt stock at the Hythe. His widow was occupying the premises at St Botolph's Gate by 10 June 1780 (*IpsJ*). Johnson has a MI, All Saints, 1780 (CPL Crisp).

I/J

JBB note: 'Johnson's Square' on site of St Botolph's station may have something to do with him.

JONES EDWARD [481]
Grocer
fl. 1738-51

A free burgess who voted in 1747 for Nassau. One of those Whig tradesmen who gave evidence in support of George Gray (qv) when he was tried for sodomy during the political upheavals that resulted in the loss of the Borough Charter (D'Cruze, *Pleasing Prospect*:149-50).

He occupied a shop near the Mermaid in North Street (*Ips*) 4 October 1752). The will of Susannah Newton, spinster of St Martins, concerns Jones. She left her property to her mother, provided 'she provided thereouts according to her discretion for my unfortunate daughter or child, Susannah, the spurious offspring of that ungrateful and perfidious villain, Edward Jones of Colchester … grocer.' She also revoked all former wills, 'particularly that I made by the base Artifice and Insinuation of the said Edward Jones dated 17 October 1738' (made by William Mayhew 1 (qv), proved 1743, ERO D/ACR 15/147, spinster of Colchester).

Jones' own will of 1750/1 (NA PROB 11/786, 8 March 1751) left all his property to his sisters Rachel (qv) and Martha.

See also NA PROB 11/697, 27 August 1739, will of Edward Jones, grocer.

JONES RACHEL [1192]
Draper
fl. 1776-1780

Sister of Edward Jones (qv) who died 1750 and all of whose estate she inherited together with her sister Martha (whose will is NA PROB 11/786/82 proved 28 January 1750). Rachel Jones was in business in St Runwalds next Stephen Hooker (qv) rated 16 into the 1770s, in 1776-9 in St Nicholas near the church rated 12. At no. 30 High Street, rated 20 'or occupier' in 1780.

Her will is at NA PROB 11/1093, 13 July 1782, Rachel Jones, spinster.

JONES REVD WILLIAM [480]
Curate of Nayland
1727-1800

Prolific Tory anglican writer from mid-century. His publications include, *Catholic Doctrine of a Trinity* (1756), *A Letter to the Church of England* (1798) and *Consideration on the Religious Worship of the Heathen* (1799). Music was his field as well as theology, and in 1784 he wrote *A Treatise on the Art of Music*, printed by William Keymer 1 (qv) in Colchester and probably engraved by James Dunthorne 2 (qv). It was dedicated to the Directors of the Concerts of Ancient Music, and its 51 subscribers included Bamber Gasgoine snr. Esq., Revd Thomas Twining (qv), Revd Brooke Bridges (his brother-in-law), Edward Walker Esq of Gestingthorpe, Mr Alston and Mr James Dunthorne jun. (The British Library copy is inscribed ' to Doctor Burney with the compliments of the Author' and signed 'W. Jones No 35' – that is to Charles Burney the musicologist).

Jones participated in Colchester's musical life, and is mentioned in this connection in the correspondence of both Thomas Twining (qv) and Revd Nathaniel Forster (qv) (P. Holman, 'The Colchester Partbooks', *Early Music*, 28 (2000): 577-95; JBB, *EAE*:110, 177, 178; D'Cruze, *Pleasing Prospect*: 120, 124-5).

He was of Finedon, Northants when he married Elizabeth Bridges at Boxted on 10 July 1754 (by banns ERO D/P 155/1/4) and was perpetual curate of Nayland from 1776. He was buried there on 6 January 1800. His only daughter married Edward Walker Esq of Overhall, Gestingthorpe in 1781 (*ChCh* 14 September 1781).

See the fuller account of Jones in *ODNB*.

K

KEELING JOHN 1 [482]
China Merchant
1732-1783

On 6 September 1761 Keeling married Grace Lees (45) of Burslem, Staffs, at Burslem (nfr). His prospects were sufficiently good to enable him to marry, for he and Richard Hassells had taken over the business of the late William Hassells (qv) at Colchester and Bury St Edmunds (2 May 1761 *Ips*). They advertised from the premises in Wyre Street on 5 May 1764 (*Ips*). The partnership continued until 8 June 1765 (*Ips*) when it was dissolved by mutual consent. They announced that:-

> The said business will be still continued in all Branches by JOHN KEELING, at his Warehouse three Doors above the Red Lyon Inn in COLCHESTER, and at his Warehouse near the New Wool-Hall in BURY ST EDMUNDS ... The wholesale Warehouse is still continued by RICHARD HASSELLS, at the Bottom of Wire Street as of old.

Keeling's premises were at 39 High Street, previously occupied by John Rogers (qv) and rated 10. Keeling advertised the following week (*Ips* 15 June 1765) when he was trading from Bury on Monday and Thursdays only.

In 1767 (*Ips* 30 May 1767) he announced:-

> That he hath just come to Hand a large Assortment of all Sorts of Staffordshire Stone and Earthern Wares, with blue and white Holland Wares, Nottingham Ware, Delph, Glass, and Welch Wares both hollow and flat, with many other Articles, both useful and ornamental, made from the newest Fashions, which are to be sold wholesale and

retain at the most reasonable Rates ... N.B. Apothecaries served with Phials and Gally-Pots as cheap as in London, from his Warehouse in High Street, Colchester, and the best Price given for broken Flint Glass.

His wife Grace died on 21 February 1775 after a long illness (*ChCh* 1 March 1775) and was buried at St Nicholas. On 23 April 1779 (*ChCh*) described as a 'considerable chinaman', he married Miss Ann Ravens (cf Ann Minks (qv)). Keeling died on 8 February 1783 aged 51 'of the China and Staffs warehouse'. He shared a monument in St Nicholas churchyard with his son and daughter-in-law. His will (NA PROB 11/1101, 6 March 1783) left his wife, Ann all his books and £600 worth of stock in trade to enable her to carry on the business. She also received the St Runwalds messuage until his son John jun. inherited at 21, thereafter an annuity of £20 per annum. His two daughters Ann and Sarah both received £400 each at 21.

KEELING JOHN 2 [483]
China Merchant
fl. 1787-1846

On 1 September 1787 (*IpsJ*) took over the shop of his father, John Keeling 1 (qv) at 39 High Street. Under the terms of John Keeling 1's will the shop had in the interim been run by his second wife Ann (cf Ann Minks (qv)). In 1791 Keeling jun married Miss Page the daughter of Robert Page, Great Clacton (*IpsJ* 13 August 1791) and continued the business until 1806 when he retired and the stock was sold (*IpsJ* 9 July 1806). (The shop was later taken by George Rayner (qv), hatter – *IpsJ* 27 August 1808). Keeling jun died in 1846 aged 79 and Sarah his wife died in 1847 aged 73. They were buried in St Nicholas with John Keeling 1.

K

KEEP JOSEPH [484]
Woolstapler
fl. 1761-1804

A nonconformist woolstapler who is chiefly noted for being amongst the friends of the celebrated Taylor family. Ann Taylor recalled:-

> The plain, respectable household of the Keeps was almost within call of us. There were ten children, but Mary Keep was the only one near enough to our own age to become our associate. With her we soon reached bloodheat - fever heat on the thermometer of friendship. And through the Keeps we were next introduced to the Stapletons....

Mary and Betsy Keep became co members with the Taylor and Stapleton girls of their 'Umbelliferous Society' (Gilbert, *Memorials of Mrs Gilbert*, Vol. 1, (1874): 120; cf John Stapleton (qv)).

Joseph Keep had been apprenticed in 1761 to James Sommers of Kettling, Northants, woolstapler for £20 (NA IR 1/54/184). He was living in Bear Lane, St Martins, Colchester by at least 1776 however, when he insured his dwelling house &c for £300 (Sun Insurance policy 369571 of 5 June 1776). That same year he married Elizabeth Sewell of Little Maplestead (ERO ML D/ ALL 1776). In 1786 he became an assignee in Henry Johnson's (qv) bankruptcy together with Edmund Lilley (qv) and a Leicester woolfactor (ERO C47, CPL232, 22 March 1786). In 1796 St Leonard's overseers' accounts record a bill from him for a pair of blankets for the workhouse.

He died in 1804 and was buried in the Independent Churchyard on 11 January aged 54, with his wife Elizabeth who had preceded him there on 14 November 1799 aged 45. He was to be followed in June 1806 by his daughter Mary, the friend of Jane and Ann Taylor.

Keep's stock in trade including superfine broad and narrow cloths, coatings &c were for auction on 7 July 1804 (*IpsJ*). The house remained in the family until after Mary's death. The 'Substantial house and warehouse' in Bear Lane then let at £65 per annum were offered for sale on 15 August 1807 (*IpsJ*) when 'for the accommodation of the purchasor (sic) £400 may remain in mortgage' and the 'furniture of the late Miss Keep' was offered likewise on 17 January 1807 (*IpsJ*). The transaction was handled by Peter Daniell (qv) the nonconformist attorney.

See also (CPL Crisp) other Keep MIs in Independent Churchyard; Joseph Keep, 21 July 1812 aged 35, Isaac Keep, 6 November 1825 aged 35, Elizabeth Abell, late Keep, wife of Francis Tillett Abell (qv) 1 January 1807 aged 27; CPL Crisp ML89, ERO D/ALL 1804 Francis Tillett Abell (qv), St Runwald, gent. 28, to marry Elizabeth Keep St Martins (22), 1804.

KEMP WILLIAM [1122]
Wine Merchant
1804

Was declared bankrupt in 1804 (*Univ. Mag.* 26 October 1804).

KENDALL ELIZABETH [487]
Bookseller and Cabinetmaker
fl. 1725-1773

Born Elizabeth Garrett she married John Kendall (d. 1753) joiner and (for 58 years) quaker minister (Fitch, *Colchester Quakers*). They occupied a house at 51 High Street rated 13 where as a widow she entered into business as a bookseller and cabinet maker with her sons John (qv) cabinetmaker and Thomas (qv) bookbinder. She died in December 1773 (obituary *IpsJ* 18 December 1773).

John Garritt occupied 52 High Street, next door to Elizabeth Kendall, from 1780.

K

KENDALL JOHN [489]
Cabinetmaker, Bookseller
1726-1815

Son of Elizabeth (qv) and John Kendall. A quaker and active missionary for the Society of Friends (Fitch, *Colchester Quakers*, *ODNB*). Undertook religious tours of northern England and Scotland in 1750 and Holland in 1752 where he learned Dutch. Kendall snr died in 1758 and from 1759 John jun was more closely involved in the family business. In partnership with his brother Thomas (qv) they continued the bookselling trade offering to give full value for libraries (*IpsJ* 12, 19 May 1759). The business published numerous items including the 1747 and 1788 Poll Books for the Borough. (The 1741 Poll Book was also printed 'for John Kendall', presumably the father).

Kendall and his mother diversified the business (*IpsJ* 12 May 1759):-

> Elizabeth & John Kendall at the Desk and Bookcase in Colchester now make furniture (walnut-tree and Mahogony (sic)) and carry on as usual as Bookbinders and Stationers.... (they also sell) ... Medicines and Pills.

In 1764 Kendall married Ann Havens, daughter of Philip Havens 2 (qv). She died in 1805 aged 70 (Fitch). On 24 January 1764 he was created free burgess. He voted in 1768 (Rebow and Gray), 1780 (Rebow), 1781 (Affleck), April 1784 (Affleck, Potter) and 1790 (Jackson, Thornton) tending to support a 1 Whig/1 Tory representation.

Kendall was a noted local benefactor. Together with Ann he founded Kendall's Almshouses for eight poor widows in 1791 (*VCH Essex*, Vol. 9). He also instituted a trust for distribution of religious books in the town and a foundation to provide education for six poor boys.

According to *ODNB* he was well known for his 'kindly disposition and personal influence' as illustrated by his successful attempt to prevent a theatre performance in the town (offensive to his religious beliefs) by his powers of persuasion. He was well known to the Royal Family and was called on by the Prince of Wales when visiting a regiment in the vicinity. Kendall was the author of a range of religious works as well as a pious memoir, published posthumously. He died 27 January 1815 and was buried at the Friends' Burial Ground. Revd Yorick Smythies (qv) wrote a long epitaph on him beginning; 'Weep for a sage; a sage to us is lost...' (*Bland's Anecdotes*:62, Appendix 3, also JBB, *EAE*:183-4).

KENDALL ROBERT 1 [1012]
Draper and Upholsterer
1741-1803

Of the quaker Kendall family. Born 1741, the son of Robert 1 (d. 1777 aged 63, will ERO D/ACR 18/604, made 1774, proved 1777) and Elizabeth (d. 1773 aged 68) (Fitch, *Colchester Quakers*: 155-6). Received a life interest in half the dwelling house he occupied in St Runwalds in his father's will.

Kendall married Sarah Alefounder of St Martins in 1765 (CPL Crisp ML102). She was the daughter of John Alefounder 1 (qv) and died on Monday, 6 June 1803, aged 60, only a few months after her husband. Kendall was a Colchester free burgess, voting from 1768 onwards. He traded from premises in St Runwald, near the Red Lion.

Kendall is chiefly known for the case of Pattison v Kendall, which occurred after he seriously wounded Jacob Pattison (qv) (apprentice to a nearby apothecary) with a sword. Pattison frequently visited the Kendall household to treat the female apprentices' ailments. Though Kendall once warned Pattison off with a knife, he made no further objection as the visits continued. On one evening visit, Pattison and Mrs Kendall had left the apprentices' chamber. Kendall ascended the stairs. A scuffle followed in Mrs Kendall's bedchamber. Pattison fled, wounded in the chest. Kendall pursued him downstairs and stabbed him again. Pattison collapsed and a neighbour intervened to save further injury. Kendall argued that discovering Pattison in Mrs Kendall's bedchamber reinforced his earlier suspicions about his relationship with her. A detailed letter to the newspaper by 'Veritas' gave a picture more favourable to Pattison. Kendall was eventually tried at Chelmsford summer assizes in 1778. The jury found Kendall guilty of wounding Pattison, but gave him a minimal sentence of a shilling fine and was ordered to pay the £50 surgeon's bill (*IpsJ* Dec 1776, 3 and 10 January 1777, 4 and 18 April and 15 May 1778; JBB, *EAE*:144-7).

He seems to have moved premises in 1790. *IpsJ* 17 July 1790 advertised the auction of part furniture and effects of Robert Kendall at late dwelling house High Street, he having moved to 'Wier' Street.

Kendall died in January 1803 aged 62. Was buried at St James, 21 January 1803.

See also Rebow Account Book at ERO C47, Box 2; January 1775, Kendall provided goods value £83 10s 7½d for the Rebows (Isaac Martin Rebow (qv)) at Wivenhoe Park; in 1766, Kendall had been paid £200 on account.

KENDALL ROBERT 2 [492]
Brasier and Ironmonger
fl. 1755-1756

Probably one of the Bury family of quakers. He removed thence from Colchester in December 1755 (*IpsJ* 6 December 1755). In the same issue of the newspaper, William Kendall 3 (qv) opposite the obelisk advertised that he was selling off the stock in trade of a person declining the jeweller's and silversmith's way, at the King's Head. The following March (*IpsJ* 20 March 1756) Robert Kendall, then at the Sun near the Market Cross in Bury St Edmunds, advertised his late dwelling house near the Red Lion, Colchester and a shop near against the obelisk to let.

K

KENDALL THOMAS 1 [490]
Distiller
1727-1784

A quaker. The son of Thomas Kendall, distiller, died in 1752 and Sarah, *née* Spurgeon. He married Ann Sparrow of Coggeshall in 1751 and had two sons, Thomas Sparrow Kendall distiller (qv) and John, and two daughters Ann and Sarah (Fitch, *Colchester Quakers*). He was a free burgess and voted from 1768-84, supporting Potter in 1781 but returning to Smyth in 1784. He occupied premises at no. 40 High Street, 2 doors up from the Red Lion whence he advertised 'Good Old Raisin Wine' on 3 April 1756 (*IpsJ*) and where he remained until his death.

KENDALL THOMAS 2 [488]
Bookseller
1726-1791

A quaker (Fitch, *Colchester Quakers*). Born in 1726 to John and Elizabeth Kendall (qv). Traded at the family premises of 51 High Street together with his mother and brother John Kendall cabinetmaker (qv). Admitted free burgess on 7 March 1768. Voted in 1768 for Rebow and Gray; 1781 for Affleck, April 1784 for Affleck and Smyth, July 1784 for Smyth and 1788 for Tierney. Died in 1791 aged 62, apparently unmarried.

KENDALL THOMAS 3 [981]
Joiner
fl. 1697-1724

Free burgess, created in 1697, of St Nicholas, fee £7 (Assembly Book). A quaker, he married in 1712 to Ann Haskins, who died in 1744 (Fitch, *Colchester Quakers*:155). Took two apprentices, Humphrey Mayhew in 1719 (Monday Court) and William Mumford in 1718 (Thursday Court). His will is ERO D/ABR 19/239, 1726.

K

KENDALL THOMAS SPARROW [493]
Distiller
1758-1800

Son of Thomas Kendall 1 (qv) distiller and wife Ann *née* Sparrow. Married Patience Seaman in 1788 and had three daughters, one dying in infancy (Fitch, *Colchester Quakers*). A free burgess who followed his father in voting for radical candidates between 1781 and 1790. Succeeded his father at no. 40 High Street and acted as executor to his will (ERO C47, CPL 638, deeds 112 High Street).

KENDALL WILLIAM 1 [491]
Chairmaker, Appraiser
fl. 1730-1767

Born in 1730, a quaker (Fitch, *Colchester Quakers*). Son of John and Elizabeth (qv) and brother of John Kendall (qv) cabinetmaker and bookseller. In 1755 he married Ann Docra of Feering. (She died in 1772). In 1757 the couple sold up the Colchester cabinet making business and moved to Norwich (15 and 22 January 1757 *IpsJ*). Ten years later William again advertised in Colchester as an appraiser, an occupation often taken on by cabinetmakers and upholsterers (*IpsJ* 25 July 1767).

KENDALL WILLIAM 2 and ISAAC [494]
Baymakers
fl. 1767-1788

William Kendall was admitted free burgess 7 December 1767, described as a baymaker. Isaac Kendall, admitted free burgess that year was a merchant taylor but voted as a baymaker in 1788.

KENDALL WILLIAM 3 [485]
Goldsmith
fl. 1750s

Auctioned stock of jewellery from premises opposite the obelisk as Robert Kendall 2 (qv) was moving to Bury (*IpsJ* 6 December 1755, JBB note - probably before the moving of the obelisk from the centre of the High Street).

KENT JOHN [1280]
Cider Maker
fl. 1777

Of Black Boy Lane in 1777 where he had Fine Red-Streak Cyder ready for sale. This announcement comprised part of an advertisement for the auction of a messuage in Black Boy Lane tenanted by William Abbott (qv). Interested parties were to apply to Kent (*IpsJ* 2 May 1777, JBB NB Jun 64:64).

KERSTEMAN ANDREW [495]
Curate, St James
fl. 1790s

One of several representatives of the Kersteman family resident in Colchester. He was curate of St James where he signed the burial register in the 1790s.

He was married at Marks Tey in 1799 to Miss Margaret Waller daughter of late Revd D. Waller, Archdeacon of Essex (*IpsJ* 19 October 1799; CPL Crisp ML104, ERO D/ACL 1799).

KERSTEMAN JEREMIAH [1156]
Canewdon, Gent
ob. 1789

A relation of William and Ann Kersteman (qv) of East Hill, Colchester. Lived at the Manor of Lostmans (Morant, *Essex*, Vol. 1:316-7: 'now only a farm: upon which there is a very good

K

house' purchased 1746 by Mr Jeremiah Kersteman). Jeremiah Kersteman of Canewdon ob. 12 April 1789 (*Gents. Mag.*).

See also; CPL Crisp ML87, ERO D/AEL 1778, Jeremiah Kersteman, 22 of Prittlewell, Esq to Elizabeth Frost, 27, of Boreham, 1778; CPL Crisp ML100, ERO D/AEL 1835, Jeremiah Kersteman Esq of Canewden (sic) to Mary Spitts of Gt Burstead, 1835; CPL Crisp ML145, ERO D/ALL 1778, Thomas Kersteman of Canewden, gent to Dorothy Kersteman of St James, 1778.

KERSTEMAN WILLIAM AND ANN [496]
East Hill
ob. 1790, 1797

William and Ann Kersteman were wealthy Colchester residents. He was Charles Gray's (qv) grandson and received £20 in Gray's will. (cf. hatchment, All Saints, Mary Webster *née* Kersteman, mother-in-law to Charles Gray).

The Kersteman's house on East Hill was formerly occupied by Robert Parradine (qv), baymaker (JBB ms note). The Land Tax of 1778 gives Mr Kersteman rated 12, with a personal estate of £80, next door to Widow Aldus and Mr Taylor.

Kersteman also had property in Canewdon and Paglesham where other branches of the family lived. Morant (*Essex*, Vol. 2:316-7) notes that the Manor of Lostmans, Canewdon was 'now only a farm; upon which there is a very good house' purchased 1746 by Mr Jeremiah Kersteman ... William Kersteman, gent. and Mr Thos Edlyne &c. also have some lands in this parish.' On Paglesham, Morant mentions that, 'William Kersteman gent. has some lands here.' The Canewdon and Paglesham Kerstemans had ongoing connections with Colchester. Thos Kersteman of Church Hall, Paglesham (captain of Loyal Paglesham Volunteers) married Sarah Phillips (daughter of William Phillips (qv)) at St Mary-at-the-Walls, Colchester in 1800 (CPL Crisp ML 961; *IpsJ* 3 January 1801). This Thomas Kersteman died 27 April 1801.

K

The East Hill Kerstemans had at least two daughters. The eldest daughter married Lieutenant Benjamin Craven (qv) (*IpsJ* 10 November 1787, at St James) and Dorothy Kersteman of St James Colchester married Thomas Kersteman of Canewdon in 1778 (CPL Crisp ML 145). There may have been a third daughter; a Sophia Kersteman was buried in St James on 26 July 1797 together with William Kersteman of East Hill (2 August 1790) and Ann his widow who died 15 February and was buried 20 February 1797.

Mrs Kersteman's furniture and the house were auctioned by Barlow and Bunnell (qv) shortly after her death. The house was notable for having a 73ft front. Mr James Taylor (qv) builder (and neighbour) would show the premises which were 'well calculated for the baize manufactory' (*IpsJ* 4 March 1797).

KEY JOHN [498]
Writing Clerk
w. 1787

A nonconformist requesting in his will (ERO D/ACR 18/283, writing clerk, Colchester) to be buried in the Independent Churchyard with an inscription which he wrote himself.

The/ Immortal Soul/ left the Body of/ John Key/ on the 2nd Day of July 1787/ in the 51st year/ of his Age – and/ Here/ He Sleeps – Waiting for the/ Glories – or the Terrors/ of the Last Day./ Reader/ That Day will reveal what/ he was – and what/ Thou Art/ (CPL Crisp MIs).

Related to the Rouse family (uncle of John Rouse (qv)). Interesting chiefly because of his friendship with other leading nonconformists, e.g. Francis Freshfield 1 and Revd Giles Hobbes (both (qv)) and for his antiquarian and numismatic enthusiasm. He left Francis Freshfield two volumes of the *Customs and Institutions of Antient Nations* and a complete set of the *Spectator,* and to Hobbes, three canvas bags of ancient coins and medals.

K

KEYMER CHARLES GREAT [499]
Grocer
fl. 1815

Colchester Gazette 8 July 1815:

> We are happy to hear that the valuable receipt for Candied Eringo Root for the excellence of which this town has been so justly celebrated, has been transferred by Mr Charles Great Keymer, the representative of the late Mr Great, to Miss Crane (qv), druggist. A box of this excellent sweetmeat has always been deemed an acceptable offering to any of the Royal Family who have passed through Colchester.

His will is at NA PROB 11/1655, proved 7 March 1822.

See entries for the Great family for further explanation of their role in the production of this local sweetmeat.

KEYMER MARK [500]
Brasier
fl. 1768-1790

The son of Robert and Dinah Keymer of Hadleigh and brother to William Keymer 1 (qv) the High Street printer and stationer. Occupied a shop at no. 18 High Street, called the 'Hen and Chickens' from 1768 until 1783. In 1771 (CPL Crisp ML91, ERO D/ACL 1771) he had married Mary Cant (qv) of St Peters who ran one of Colchester's stagecoaches. From 1783 Keymer moved into the Cant's premises at the top of North Hill rated 18. He continued to own the High Street shop, and the business advertised from there as copper smiths and braziers 'almost opposite the 3 Cups' on 30 June 1768 (*IpsJ*) when he also held a shop in Hadleigh.

St Peters registers record the baptisms of four of the Keymers' children; Robert on 28 May 1775, Samuel (qv) on 25 March 1778, Mary on 23 July 1779 and Dinah on 20 September 1781. There are burials for another son, John (nfr) and a daughter Susannah (1 June 1788). Keymer himself died in 1790 and was buried at Hadleigh on 11 August 1790. His death on 'Friday last' and 'after a long affliction' was announced in *IpsJ* of 14 August 1790. His will of 1788/1790 (ERO D/ABR 28/214) leaves the bulk of the estate both real and personal to his 'loving wife Mary' for the maintenance of herself and their young children, between whom the estate was to be equally divided after her death. She advertised shortly after his death that she intended to continue the business (*IpsJ* 21 August 1790). It seems that Mary Cant was not Keymer's first wife, for he also leaves a small remembrance to Mark Keymer his eldest son, as he was already provided for. Also the co-executor named with Mary is Richard Leatherdale, Hadleigh, draper and Keymer's brother-in-law.

KEYMER SAMUEL [1004]
Brasier
bkt 1808

Baptised 25 March 1778, the son of Mark Keymer (qv) and Mary *née* Cant (qv). Was trading as a brazier and tinman in the High Street in 1808 (*IpsJ* 18 June 1808) when his stock, including black tin tea kettles, was sold for the benefit of his creditors.

There is a water colour portrait of him by E. P. Strutt in the possession of Colchester and Ipswich Museums.

KEYMER WILLIAM 1 and 2 [1016]
Printer and Bookseller
fl. 1757-1821

Father and son who ran a long-standing printing and bookselling business in Colchester High Street. Not Borough free burgesses, though William snr had a vote in Suffolk county for property at Stowupland. William 1 and Robert his brother were apprenticed to Charles Bathurst, stationer, in London for £20 each (NA IR 1/18/69). William 1's father was Robert Keymer, bookseller of Hadleigh, Suffolk (d. 11 November 1775) whose will of 1774/6 (ERO, Deanery of Bocking, D/APb

K

W3/203, JBB NB 79/1:9) left £20 to William, £100 to his brother Richard and another £100 to brother Mark Keymer (qv), brazier. William 1 was living in Colchester (St. Peter) when, aged 28, he married Ann Edward of St Runwald (aged 30) at St Nicholas (CPL Crisp ML91, 1760). His wife was sister to Mrs Mary Great, wife of Charles Great (qv) apothecary.

William snr was trading from premises at the Bible and Star, opposite the Three Cups from the late 1750s (*IpsJ* 22 October 1757). He was agent for the Militia Insurance in 1762 (*IpsJ* 23 January 1762) and for the *Wonderful Magazine* in 1764 (*IpsJ* 1 December 1764). Rival advertisements appeared between Keymer and incoming tradesman Samuel Gibbs (qv) in 1767. Keymer's stock included patent medicines (*IpsJ* 29 August, 13 September, 3 October). He sold Colchester's new Borough Charter in 1767, price 1s (*IpsJ* 29 August 1767). In 1771 (*IpsJ* 25 May 1771) he took over the printing office, previously occupied by John Pilborough (qv) at 25 High Street (St. Runwalds rates). Pilborough died the following year.

Keymer sold lottery tickets in the 1770s. In 1775 a ticket could win £500 (*IpsJ* 10 November 1770, 18 March 1775, 23 December 1775, *ChCh* 13 September 1776).

Publications, including those of local authors, were frequently advertised. For example: (*IpsJ* 4 November 1769) Henry Crossman's *The County Parishioner*, 1769; (*IpsJ* 26 April 1777), Clara Reeve's (qv), *Champion of Virtue*, with frontis. by Benjamin Strutt (qv) and; (*IpsJ* 7 February 1767) her *Progress of Romance*; William Cole (qv) *Psalmodist* - In *IpsJ* 29 July 1769 Keymer advertised that he was still selling this item at its original price. In 1779 the Keymers sold George Carter's portraits of Garrick (*IpsJ* 19 June 1779) and the architectural books of William Salmon 2 (qv), carpenter, in stock after his death (*IpsJ* 3 April 1779). Medical works by Loftus Wood (qv), including some printed by Keymer (see below), were advertised in 1791 (*IpsJ* 22 October 1791).

William 1 was held up by footpads wearing false noses in 1791 (*IpsJ* 12 February 1791, long account). The following year he retired from the business in favour of his son, who, as well as the printing and binding offices also advertised patent medicines. Keymer supplied 'a Parchment Register Book' to All Saints parish in 1793 for £1 16s (Churchwarden's Rate book, ERO D/P200/8/2, 24 May 1793).

William 2 took over the business and married in the same year. He was therefore of St Runwalds when he married Hannah Ram (CPL Crisp ML150, 1792) the daughter of Hythe merchant John Ram (qv). She died the following year (on 10 June 1793 aged 20) and is buried at St Leonards with her mother Hannah, herself the only daughter of Alderman John King (qv). In 1795 (CPL Crisp ML95) Keymer 2 remarried to Jane Salter (the daughter of Revd Nathaniel Salter (qv)), both of St Runwald.

For many years the Keymers ran a circulating library. A catalogue of 1797 (CPL) lists 3,316 volumes. Of many advertisements, see *IpsJ* 28 January 1786, or *IpsJ* 1 October 1791 when terms were 16s a year, 5s a quarter, or 1d an evening per volume. They were the leading printers in Colchester of their day, covering a wide range of work including Chapman and André's *Map of Essex*. This was printed by subscription. Keymer was sole proprietor in Colchester, per the Index Map of 1785; see also edition in Clacton Public Library and accompanying leaflet (viewed by JBB 1970s) and *IpsJ* 31 October 1789, 30 June 1792. The Keymers published various pamphlets by Defoe (E. M. Lawson & Co, catalogue 180, nfr).

Other examples include:-

IpsJ 21 August 1784, Major Henry Waller (qv), *Avaro and Tray or, the Difference between Reason (or the Human Soul) and Brutal Instinct: a genuine Tale*, 1s.

IpsJ 21 May 1785, Anon, *Memoirs of Sir Simeon Supple of Simeon Grove, Member for the Borough of Rotborough*, 1s 6d. A political satire, probably aimed at Sir Robert Smyth (qv). JBB believed it to be authored by Charles Shillito (qv) see discussion and extracts in JBB *EAE*:92-5.

IpsJ 31 March 1792, Revd Acklom Ingram (qv), *The Necessity of Introducing Divinity into the Regular course of Academical Studies*.

IpsJ 4 August 1792, William Cole (qv), *A Morning and Evening Service*, 12s to subscribers, 15s to others.

K

James Fisin (qv), *Ode to Charity*, written for the use of Sunday Schools, August 1790 (BL catalogue).

Ips] 5 April 1783, Loftus Wood (qv), *Observations on Air and Regimen*, (1782); *Enquiry into Fixed Air; Selection of Curious Medical Cases*, trans. from Memoirs of the Royal Academy of Sciences of Paris.

Charles Shillito (qv), *The Sea Fight, an elegiac poem from Henry, Lieut. RN, to Laura, founded on a correspondence between the parties in 1758, written at sea*, London, 1779 (BL); *A Country Book-Club, a poem*, 4º, 2s 6d, 1788 (BL); *The Man of Enterprise, a Farce*, performed by the Norwich company, 1s, 1789 (BL).

William Martin Leake (qv), Vicar of Fingringhoe, *A Masonic Sermon, preached at St Peters, June 1777*, 1778 (Colchester Public Library).

Dr Nathaniel Forster (qv), Rector of All Saints, 1762-1790, *Grace without Enthusiasm, A Sermon, Trinity Sunday*, 1781 (Colchester Public Library); *A Discourse on the Utility of Sunday Schools*, 1786 (Colchester Sunday School founded that year); *An Answer to Sir John Dalrymple's Pamphlet on the Export of Wool*, 1782 (BL).

J. Gibson, *Some Helpful Hints and Friends Admonitions to Your Surgeons on the Practice of Midwifery*, 1772.

Keymers printed the Colchester Borough Poll Books from 1780, changing to smaller type in 1790 (25 June 1790 *ChCh*).

Keymer's Essex Memorandum Book for 1767 (*Ips]* 6 December 1766) and succeeding years. The *Memorandum Book* for 1791 was advertised on 17 December 1790 (*ChCh*).

Printed *Catalogue and Rules* for Colchester Castle Book Society, 1816.

William Keymer snr. made his will in 1806 (NA PROB 11/1545/310, proved 30 June 1813). Witnesses included Benjamin Strutt (qv). Keymer left 2 small farms, 4 tenements, 2 meadows, his house with printing office adjoining in Culver Lane to his two sons, who were executors. He also left to his son William his 'admission ticket to Colchester Theatre which I purchased of William Ivory (qv) having thereon the name of Thomas Clamtree (qv) engraved with his interest in the

Theatre.' (cf James Thorn 2 (qv) for origin of these silver tickets for Colchester Theatre.)

William 2 finally sold the printing presses to Swinborne and Walter in 1821 (*Ips]* 13 October 1821).

See also wills of Charles Toll Keymer, Priscilla Keymer (ERO JBB NB 92/3).

KILBORN WILLIAM [501]
Barrister at Law
fl. 1762-1769

Deputy Recorder of Ipswich. Occupied the White House 50 Balkerne Lane from 1762 (Deeds of White House, Balkerne Lane, notes JBB NB June-67 and correspondence with R. Walker, ERO C905, Box 4, Box 10) when he first appears in the parish rate books. The house was probably built for him, and was sold to John Lupton (qv) gent before 1767 (cf Lupton's will of that date).

Kilborn then moved to St Nicholas where he occupied a mansion owned by Ruth Wallis (qv) (her will, ERO D/ABR 27/83 BR27, 1772, mentions a house later occupied by Shaw King (qv)) until he moved to Stratford (per his will, NA PROB 11/948, proved 9 May 1769) where he died on 6 April 1769. Clara Reeve (qv) the local poet and author wrote some lines in his memory in her *Original Poems* of that year (1769):74.

Kilborn was buried in Saffron Walden. He has a handsome ledger (viewed by JBB in 1992, NB 92/2:70) near his grandfather who was vicar there. The grandfather's will is at NA PROB 11/727, 13 July 1743.

KILBY REVD GEORGE [502]
Rector of Great Birch and St Leonard, Colchester
w. 1775/1777

Rector of Birch for 25 years and between 1742 and 1753 of St Leonard Colchester (Morant, *Colchester*). He was a founder member of the Castle Book Society. He was resident in All

K

Saints parish in old age, next Nathaniel Hedge 1 (qv) rated 12 in 1763 (house later occupied by Rees Harris (qv)). His will (see below) requested that he be buried with his wife in the chancel at Gt. Birch without very much ceremony. £10 was left to the poor to be distributed on the advice of John Hellen, son of his tenant, Elizabeth Hellen. His brother in law Charles Digby of Mile End, Old Town, Middlesex received £50 and also remembered were various poor London relatives including a weaver, a waterman and a salesman.

Guinea rings were left to his 'much esteemed friends', James and John Round (qv), Charles Gray (qv) and George Wegg 2 (qv) Esqs, Dr Moses Griffith (qv), Revd Nathaniel Forster (qv), Revd John Smythies (qv). The main beneficiaries were his sisters Elizabeth Knowles and Dorothy Brett and sister-in-law Sarah Kilby.

The will (NA PROB 11/1034, made on 11 November 1775, proved 12 September 1777) was witnessed by the nonconformist lawyers Peter Daniell and William Francis (both qv). He died on 1st September. (*IpsJ* 6 September 1777).

See also JBB note, NB 86/6:37: Kept the registers of St Nicholas very well.

KILNER REVD JAMES [503]
Rector of Lexden
w. 1769

A JP for Lexden and Winstree sessions. An original member of the Castle Book Society in 1752 (JBB NB 92/2:15). Rector of Lexden from 10 February 1729 and for Tolleshunt D'Arcy from 25 June 1741 (nfr). He married Elizabeth, daughter of Sarah Rawstorn (*née* Papillon) who died in 1768. Musgrave's *Obituaries* records him dying on 26 November 1769 aged 76. His will of 9 November 1769 proved at PCC 8 December 1769 (NA PROB 11/953) was purely monetary, leaving £200 apiece to his sons and £200 apiece to his daughters and grandchildren. It ordered that the Tithe Books were to be delivered to his successor.

KING ENOCH [1202]
Pavior
fl. 1775-1791

Appears to be a very specialist trade, and no other individual is mentioned in local sources as pursuing it. Premises in St Botolphs, Moor Lane, rated 2, March 1784, and in St Botolphs, Black Boy Lane, rated, 4 June 1791. William Beverley (qv) farrier left him £10 and clothes (1782).

Parish churchwardens accounts include bills from King, viz; All Saints, January 1775, £4 1s 4d for paving; St Leonards Hythe, 1794, £17 4s for 52 yards of pavement.

Also recorded as a cricket umpire. In 1778 a match between Nayland and Colchester resulted in long protests from both sides over a dropped catch, given out by King who was acting as umpire. Colchester replied to Nayland's protest with 32 lines of verse in *ChCh* 21 August 1778;

> But how could you dare upbraid our Umpire?
> Enoch King, we fear not his name
> The game knows so well, no one can excel
> In him we repose for the same.

Nayland responded by publishing a playlet in the following week's paper, satirising the Colchester team (*ChCh* 28 August 1778, JBB *EAE*:149).

See also CPL Crisp ML104, ERO D/ACL 1799, Enoch King of St Martins to Susan Smith of Holy Trinity.

KING JOHN [1203]
Miller
ob. 1790

A Table Tomb at St Leonards, Lexden commemorates John King, many years an Alderman and three times Mayor, who died 7 February 1790 *aet*. 69 and Hannah, his wife. who died 6 January 1780 *aet*. 58. Also in memory of John WHITMORE, his

K

grandfather, late of this parish who died 30 December 1722 *aet* 62.

King's first wife Hannah was the daughter of Abraham Wright (qv) bays-ticking miller (CPL Crisp ML103, ERO D/ALL 1745, John King of St Giles, Colchester and Abraham Wright, miller, bd. John (24) to Hannah Wright. See below for further connections between the King, Whitmore and Wright families).

27 August 1764, admitted free burgess by apprenticeship to William Whitmore. Created Common Councilman 10 September 1765, Assistant 29 August 1766, Alderman 29 August 1768. Was Mayor in 1771 and again in 1775 when both the elected Mayor, John Baker (qv) and his replacement Thomas Bayles (qv) had died in office. King served as Mayor again in 1779 and 1782 and was a Borough justice between 1776 and 1790. Voted for Rebow and Gray in 1768, plumped for Rebow in 1780, for Potter in 1781 when Potter had the support of the Corporation, though for Affleck and Smyth in April 1784 and for Smyth (not Potter) in July 1784, by which time Potter was an outsider. He supported Jackson rather than the radical Tierney in 1788. The only eighteenth-century Mayor whose portrait is in Borough possession, now at Tymperleys Museum, chubby-faced and perhaps corpulent, in his robe and chain of office (JBB note: never seemingly involved in anything scandalous, he is the sort of stolid reliable person much needed in day to day local government).

Overseer of the Poor for All Saints in 1765 and 1766. Churchwarden 1768-1772 and 1772-1788.

Took an apprentice, Jonas Cole, 1 December 1779, no fee, 7 years (nfr). Cole later voted from Ipswich as a miller, for Jackson in 1788.

See Benjamin Smith (qv) who owed King £150 at his bankruptcy, 1772.

Owned Middle (water) Mill (All Saints), by the Colne, rated 40 from at least 1763 (rates not recorded earlier) to 1780, rated £35 in 1785. (Overseers Rates of 1745/6 give John Bentall, Mill, £30 and Overshott Mill, £2). King was succeeded there by William Abbott, who signed King's will as witness, and occupied the

K

mill as his widow's tenant, till final settlement of John Ram's (qv), King's son-in-law's, bankrupt estate in 1809. N.B. not to be confused with Middle (wind) mill, St Giles, which was also owned by King - see Lot 1 in auction list below.

Much of King's real property became bound up in the Marriage Settlement of his only child Hannah to John Ram (qv) Hythe merchant, 31 May/1 June 1771. Ram later was bankrupted so the estate can be traced back from its final dispersal after Ram's death, bankrupt, at Fingringhoe, 26 September 1809. The sale was advertised the following November. The following table gives the sale details followed by further information from rate books and other local sources (indicated but not fully referenced).

IpsJ 4 November 1809

FREEHOLD WINDMILL, WATERMILL, LAND & ESTATES in COLCHESTER, Essex.

Auction at Woolpack by Hawes & Fenton.

1. Post-mill and dwelling, parish St. Giles, and 40 rods garden occ. Mr N. Ram, or tenants. Windmill, known as middle mill, on Golden Noble Hill in detached portion of St Giles. (John King's from 1745 rated 11 in 1786. John Ram left it to son Nicholas. Nicholas Ram bought it. Further details in K. G. Farries, *Essex Windmills*, Vol. 3:91.)

2. MIDDLE (water) MILL (All Saints) and acre of common meadow called King's Meadow occ. Mrs Mary King and Mr William Abbott. (John King's since 1763 rated 40. Left to second wife. William Abbott (qv) had had it since 1790. Wm. Abbott bought it.)

3. Meadow 2½ acres adjoining Dead Lane parishes St Peter and St Martin, adjoining Lot 2. occ. Thomas Andrews (qv), (Rates paid in both parishes, 6 and 6, 1773, 1783 when King had other properties, 12 and 11 St Peters (12 and 6, tenements, in 1795). Bought by Richard Patmore (qv).)

4. Sayers Farm and Quay, par St Giles. (Ram's properties in 1771).

K

5. Messuage divided 3 tenements, near the Plough, St Botolphs, incl. carpenter' shop and large yard, in several occs; George Mason, Wm. Chignall, Robert Simson, Robert Tabor Esq (qv) and Mr John Lingwood (qv). (Rates 1793, 7 and 9. The yard once Augustine Wayland's (qv) carpenter. Wm Chisnall votes 1768. Bought by Robert Tabor (qv)).
6. Several messuages near Anchor, St Giles occ. Cater, Ladbrook, Woolner, Orrin, Byford, Halls, Phillips, Nason, Baker and Ward. (Rates 1783, one 12 late Cocks (the Inn?). Bought by Orrin).
7. Fourth share of Quays etc. at Hythe. (Bought by William Dixon (qv).)

Note at head of advertisement states:-

> The above estates were all sold a few years since to the present occupiers, during the lifetime of Mr John Ram, who is lately deceased, and therefore the purchasers at this immediate possession.

For further details of the bankruptcy see John Ram (qv). He was of Berechurch when he married Hannah King in 1771 (*IpsJ* 8 June 1771, 'last Tuesday'). She died 26 June 1791 aged 44.

John King's death was announced, aged 69, in the *IpsJ* 13 February 1790 ('last Sunday'). His will, NA PROB/11/1189, 139 Bishop, was made by William Mason 2 (qv), 23 December 1789 and proved 19 March 1790, left:-

- £2,000 to be divided between Ram's six children and residue to Hannah Ram.
- £100 plus marriage settlement to second wife, Mary Mortier (CPL Crisp ML 91, married, both of All Saints, in 1782, hence her tenancy of Middle Mill, till after Ram's decease in 1809).

See also: Colchester Oath Book (ERO D/B 5 R1) includes 9 December 1728, William Whitmore, Lexden, miller; 24 February 1729 John Whitemore, W. Bergholt, miller; John Whittmore, miller, will ERO D/ABW 84/3/3, 1722/3 (refers to daughter Sarah King as widow with three children, Matthew, Sarah and John. But father's Christian name not given);

K

William Whitmore, miller, Lexden will ERO D/ABW/94, 1743 (son of John Whitmore's deceased brother Henry. Doesn't refer to John King). Henry Stow (qv) miller of Lexden married Elizabeth, daughter of Abraham Wright (qv) bays-ticking miller, sister to King's first wife Hannah.

KING SHAW [504]
Comarques, Thorpe le Soken and Colchester
w. 1792

Morant gives King's antecedents in detail when discussing his property in Thorpe and Kirby:-

> Comarques, a seat in Thorp, built by Capt Comarques and the Revd Mr Joshua Lisle; belongs to Shaw King Esq., who has also an estate ... (the Manor of Landermere) ... in this parish'.

Morant continues:-

> John Shaw of Colchester, gent., by Mary his wife, daughter of - Lufkin of Ardley, had - John, his son and heir; of Catherine Hall and Lincolns Inn; Member of Parliament for Colchester in 1659, 1660 and 1661; Recorder of that Town, knighted before 1664, created Sgt. at Law 26 Nov 1683, and who dyed in 1690, aged 73. He married Thamar daughter and heir of Samuel Lewis, of Roydon in Suffolk Esq; and had by her John, born in 1648; Samuel; Thomas; Jeremy; and six daughters Thamar; Mary wife of Joseph Thurston Esq; Abigail; Penelope; Hannah; Elizabeth. John, the eldest son, dyed 13th January 1681, before his father, without issue surviving; though he had three wives, namely, 1. Anne, daughter of Thomas Brame, of Kent, Esq 2. Penelope, daughter of Sir Thomas Dereham, of Norfolk, bart 3. ... Daniel, of Colchester wid. By the first he had John, Thomas, Joseph, Anne, which had all dyed before him. Samuel, the second son, was a Barrister at law, but dyed unmarried, 16 April 1677. Thomas the third son, was Rector of Greenstead, and Great Holland, and departed

K

this life 3 May 1692 aged 40 years. Jeremy Shaw Esq, the fourth son, seated at Kirby, was a Justice of the Peace for this County. He married first, Sarah daughter of Joseph Barbar of Bedfordshire, Esq: His second wife was Anne, daughter of - Hammond of Oxfordshire gent, widow of John Nicholas Esq; By the first he had - Gabriel Shaw Esq: many years a Justice of Peace. for this Country, By Anne his wife, daughter of Edward Cremer, of East Bergholt gent, he had his only daughter and heir, Elizabeth married first to John King Esq; by whom she had Shaw King Esq: by her second husband Mr George Pickard, merchant (qv) she had one son named Thomas.

Shaw King Esq succeeded his grandfather in this and other estates. He married first Mrs Catherine Slaney by whom he hath one daughter living. By his second wife - he hath several children (Manor of Grove House, Kirby – Morant, *Essex*, Vol 1:481, Thorpe le Soken and Kirby).

The marriage settlement between Shaw King Esq and Mrs Catherine Slaney settled the advowson of Steeple and Large Wickhouse Farm on her as well as property in Kirby le Soken. George Pickard (qv) was a party (ERO D/Del T2/40).

King later moved into Colchester and leased a mansion house in Culver Street, St Nicholas (see ERO D/ABR 27/83, will of Ruth Wallis wid., made 18 April 1772 which left to her daughter Elizabeth, married to James Ashwell (qv), mansion house in St Nicholas late occupied William Kilborn Esq (qv) and now Shaw King). He had moved to All Saints when he made his will in 1792 (NA PROB 11/1295, Exeter; Shaw King of Colchester Esq made 27 August 1792, witnessed William Mason jun (qv), Chas G. Keymer (qv), W Keymer jun (qv), codicil made 25 June 1795 witnessed P. H. Gretton (qv), John Ribbans, Thos Neverd, proved 21 August 1797).

The will reiterated and confirmed the terms of the marriage settlement (see above) to his first wife Catherine, of 'diverse messuages and tenements,' lands Kirby, Walton, Thorpe le Soken and Steeple.

The document then recites a long and complex entail of properties mentioned in the marriage settlement with Elizabeth 'my now wife,' made 16 April 1757, including her estates in Islys Doddington Magno, Burton Latimer Northants, Assingdon Much Wakering and North Shoebury, Essex. It continues:-

> And whereas I am seized of and entitled unto the Reversion in fee expectant on the decease of me and my said wife of and in seven undivided twelfth parts of a farm and lands in the parish of Addingdon (occ. Benj Palmer) purchased of the Revd Mr Bearblock (?) ... and the other five undivided twelfth parts were part of the Estate of my said present wife and are comprised in my last present named marriage settlement....

And similarly 'the expectant' of diverse lands in Clacton occupied by Samuel Day. He was also 'seized in fee simple ... of and in diverse Oyster Layings ... in or near Tollesbury and West Mersea....

> And whereas I have now living by my said wife Elizabeth four sons namely the Revd Shaw King (qv), Robert King, John King, Charles King who have all attained their ages of 21 years and no other child.

On the marriage of the Revd Shaw King to Elizabeth his present wife (CPL Crisp ML148, Shaw King of Thorp Clerk to Elizabeth Sturgeon of Trinity, Colchester, 1787) by a settlement of 2/3 November 1787, several estates in Thorpe le Soken, St Botolphs, St Giles and Ardleigh were settled on him plus a chaplainship of Dragoons or ecclesiastical preferment (and till then £100 p.a.) and a promise of £1,000 'on my decease.' The said chaplainship or preferment not having been purchased, he had been given the annuity and was now left £1,000 as promised, or alternatively an estate in Assingdon.

The oyster layings etc. were left to his wife Elizabeth for life and afterwards share and share alike between the four sons. The three younger sons were also to share the Assingdon estate if Revd Shaw King preferred the £1,000 legacy. In this case the

K

estate was to be sold and proceeds divided. Estates in Clacton to be similarly to be sold and divided between the sons and also the dwelling house in parish All Saints 'in which I now reside'.

His wife was also left £542 11s 3d Bank of England Stock to and for her own use and benefit.

And all other stock was left to his 3 younger sons to divide between them.

Revd Shaw King and Elizabeth 'my said dear wife' were named executors.

The Codicil left a messuage, Brightlingsea lately purchased of William Mihill of Little Baddow now occupied by son John King, to John King plus £30 to defray the expenses of taking up the same in the Manor Court.

The family are recorded amongst monumental inscriptions at Thorpe:-

>Here Lyeth the Body of
>John King of Comarques, Thorpe le Soken
>in the County of Essex Esq.
>Who departed this life
>12th July 1735
>In the 28th year of his Age
>Also of
>Shaw King Esq, son of the above
>Who died 23rd July 1797
>Aged 67 Years
>Also of Elizabeth his wife
>Who died 29th of March 1802
>Aged 67 Years
>Also of John King Esq.
>of Mersea Cottage in this County
>Son of the above Shaw King Esq.
>Who died 13th January 1827
>Aged 61 years

Tablet, Thorpe le Soken on North Wall of Tower:-

K

SACRED TO THE MEMORY OF
SHAW KING ESQ.

formerly of COMARQUES IN THIS Parish but later of Colchester who died the 17th July 1797 aged 67 years and was interned in Kirby Church Within le Soken

In a tomb the South side of the Parish Church of St Mary at Walls within the Borough of Colchester are deposited the remains of CHARLES KING ESQ attorney at law, fourth son of he above named SHAW KING, who departed this Life 26th September 1799 in the 32nd year of his Age.

In the Vault in Kirby Church are deposited the Remains of MRS ELIZABETH KING relict of the above named SHAW KING who departed this life on the 29th March 1802 aged 67 years.

Within a vault situated on the south side of this Churchyard are interr'd the Remains of ROBERT KING Esq, Captain in HM Royal Artillery and Second Son of the above named SHAW KING who departed this Life on the 2nd February 1802 aged 38 years

Also in the same vault are deposited the remains of the REV SHAW KING of Comarques in this parish eldest son of the above named SHAW KING who died the 17th January 1817 in the 57th year of his age

*Also the Remains of
ELIZABETH wife of the above mentioned
SHAW KING MA who died beloved and respected
30th August 1839
Aged 73 Years

*added later

See also will Revd Shaw King, clerk, Thorp-within-the-Soken, NA PROB 11/1593, proved 19 June 1817; *Ips]* 19 February 1791, Mansion, Trinity St, late of Mrs Sturgeon widow. Apply Mr Charles King atty or Revd Shaw King, Thorpe le Soken; 20 August 1791 (*Ips]*) Sale of house in Trinity St with gateway

429

K

sufficient for two carriages; *IpsJ* 29 November 1839, Comarques and two fields in St Botolphs for sale under the will of Revd Shaw King.

KIRBY JOHN [509]
Collector of Customs
fl. 1744-1777

Then a gent aged 26 of Colchester, Kirby married Ann Martin (16) of East Donyland in 1744 (ML ERO D/ALL 1744). His wife was the daughter of Robert Martin Esq (qv). Two of their sons, Robert Martin Kirby and William Leppard Kirby were baptised at St Leonards on 8 June 1755 and 30 April 1766. In the year of his marriage, on 22 August 1744, Kirby was appointed Collector of Customs at the Hythe, a position which entitled him to 'have a horse', and to premises at the Customs House. In 1749 he was named executor to Elizabeth Butler (spinster of Wivenhoe ERO D/ACR 15/329) who left rings to Captain Robert Martin (qv) and his wife Ann, and a damask table cloth and napkins to Ann Kirby.

In 1766 (*IpsJ* 29 March 1766) he acted as agent for the sale of his father-in-law's house at East Donyland (complete with 'fishponds, garden walled in &c') and succeeded to the manor of Great Holland following Robert Martin's death. (Morant, *Essex*, Vol 1:479)

See also John Kirby, probably son of above, buried All Saints churchyard; died Sunday 1 December 1809 aged 68, 'entitled to a Reward in Heaven for attention to religious and charitable duties' (CPL Crisp MIs).

KNOWLSON FRANCIS [986]
Hosier
bkt. 1798

Was declared bankrupt in 1798 (*Eur. Mag.* 12 June 1798).

KREBS CHRISTIAN [510]
Occulist
fl. 1790-1791

A travelling occulist from Hadleigh who in 1790 visited Colchester and set up to take consultations at Mr Malby's (qv) coachmaster (*IpsJ* 13 November 1790). The following year he visited Beccles (*IpsJ* 15 January 1791) and later advertised cures for deafness (*IpsJ* 26 March 1791).

L

LAVALLIN MICHAEL [513]
Cabinetmaker
fl. 1795-1821

In 1795 Lavallin married Ann Gilson of Holy Trinity, the same year (*Ips]* 31 October 1795) he took over the cabinetmaking side of William Bunnell's (qv) business at his premises at High St opposite the Dial Church. By Bunnell's death in 1808, Lavallin was occupying 'spacious and lofty' workshops in George Lane which were being sold with the rest of Bunnell's estate (*Ips]* 10 December 1808). Around the turn of the century Lavallin occasionally acted as auctioneer for various sales, including Bunnell's, usually in partnership with William Linton (qv). In 1821 (*Ips]* 24 February 1821) Lavallin gave up business in Colchester. He retired to Jersey where he died at St Helens in July 1834 (*Essex County Standard* 12 July 1834).

LAWRENCE NATHANIEL ESQ [514]
fl. 1730-1751

Whig Alderman at the time of the loss of the Charter in 1741/2. Was Mayor in 1696, 1704, 1710, 1719. Morant notes (1748) he was still alive, aged 88, and remarkable for having recovered the use of his legs after being lame 'above 7 years' (Morant, *Colchester*, Appendix, Book 3:52). He voted until 1747 (for the Whig, Olmius).

Lawrence made his will (NA PROB 11/786, 52 Busby, proved 12 February 1751) on 14 December 1730 (witnessed Robert Halls, Richard Hill, Nathaniel Richardson). A codicil was added on 31 August 1738 (witnessed Daniel Wall (qv), Mary Hobard, Robert Halls). It left his chariot and horses to his wife Lydia and his capital messuage St James to his daughters Bridget and Martha (see below for their wills). It also mentions

L

other properties in St James including the Rose and Crown inn (qv), the White Horse St Nicholas, other property including in Wire Street occupied by Edward Capstack (qv), in Lt. Maplestead, Raydon and Layham Suffolk, Halstead, also five acres in Skirbeck Lines.

Lawrence died in 1751.

Nathaniel Lawrence the elder was Mayor in 1672, 1679, 1683, and 1709. He died 5 May 1714, aged 87.

See also other Lawrence wills including; John Lawrence, butcher, Colchester NA PROB 11/893, proved 15 November 1763; Bridget Lawrence, spinster, Colchester, NA PROB 11/1011, 15 September 1775; Martha Lawrence, Colchester, NA PROB 11/979, 13 July 1772; John Lawrence, bricklayer, Colchester, ERO D/ABR 22/89, 1737; Thomas Lawrence, innholder, ERO D/ACR 15, made 1744, proved 1745.

LAWRENCE THOMAS [517]
Gunsmith
fl. 1763-73

Apprenticed to Thomas Cole, Dedham for £20 in 1757 (NA IR 1/52/203). In 1763 (*IpsJ* 26 November 1763) he took over the shop of the late Nathaniel Cole (qv) in Head Street. He was a free burgess who voted in 1768 for Fordyce. 1773 rates for St Mary-at-Walls show premises on the east side of Head Street near the Fleece occupied by William Taylor (qv) glazier, rated for 'part of Lawrences'.

LAWRENCE WILLIAM 1 [515]
Shuttlemaker
fl. 1739-1784

Married Judith Burton of Bocking in 1739 (ERO ML D/AML 1739). A free burgess who voted in 1781 and April 1784 supporting first Potter then Smyth. His son was William Lawrence 2 (qv) turner.

L

LAWRENCE WILLIAM 2 [516]
Turner
1744-1807

Son of William 1 (qv), a shuttlemaker and Judith, *née* Burton of Bocking. A free burgess and regular voter, in general for radical candidates. Lawrence leased premises from Thomas Kendall 1 (qv) distiller from 1779 until at least 1800 in Back Lane at the rear of Kendall's shop near the Red Lyon (rated 16). His wife Elizabeth received a legacy of £300 in the will of John Wall 1 (qv) (made 1781, proved 1783). Lawrence turned both columns and 'ballisters' for the new octagonal meeting house in Lion Walk and his bills of 1766 and 1767 survive (ERO D/NC 52/5/2). He died in July 1807 aged 63 and is buried at St Mary's.

LAY WILLIAM [1208]
Master Carpenter
c.1744-1814

Brother of Robert Lay Esq of Aldham Hall, farmer. They died within a week of each other in 1814, William being then of Stanway aged 70 (nfr). Robert's will (NA PROB 11/1567/194 Pakenham, proved 19 April 1815) leaves William the interest of 3% Consolidated Bank annuities for life.

William Lay's active career includes taking an apprentice John Hunt (qv) for £18 in 1770 (NA IR 1/57/118). Worked for the Martin family of Wivenhoe, billing largish sums; 1770, £173 4s 5d at Three Cups, and £15 16s at Alresford Hall (nfr, but cf ERO C47, Rebow Box 2). However an Examination in the Borough Sessions of Isaac Chaplin, carpenter of Lexden 18 March 1782 says Lay 'now or late of Lexden' owed him £2 1s 4d (ERO P/Co R10).

Lay married Eleanor, daughter of Thomas Elsden of Lexden in 1768, and had three children baptised there; Elizabeth 3 July 1768, William 4 January 1770, Thomas Elsden 13 November 1771.

Thos Elsden's will (ERO D/ABR 28/250) made in 1778 left nearly everything to Elizabeth. Lay was sternly forbidden to intermeddle, or use her money to meet his own debts. (Elizabeth failing to have heirs, next in line was her brother Thomas, only after him William). By 1776 Elsden had married again to Elizabeth Clark, widow, at Wormingford, and was living in her property, 'High Chimneys' in Stanway. The will was proved in 1792, and 'High Chimneys,' described as lately newly built in 1793, belonged to William Lay in the parish map of 1808, then occupied by William Willes. It is an elegant brick building, with the highest rooms on the first floor. A Mrs Pattrick, widow, lived there around 1820. She has connections also with William Phillips (qv), so one cannot affirm too confidently that Lay built it. Any other late possible work has not come to light.

See also, *Colchester Gazette* 27 March 1819, William Lay builder moving from N. Hill to Headgate owing to expiry of lease.

LECHMERE MARIA SOPHIA [518]
Winsleys, High Street
w. 1782

The Lechmere family occupied the house owned by Winsley's trustees at the top of East Hill.

Miss Lechmere made her will on 15 March 1782 (NA PROB 11/1130, 258 Ducarel, proved 4 May 1785; witnessed Peter Daniell (qv), William Francis (qv)). It mentions her sister Elizabeth Carolina Grimwood widow, nieces Maria wife of Mr Thomas Taylor and Elizabeth Newman widow and nephew Thomas Lutter Lechmere. The last was left the £800 already lent to him, for the use of his children Thomas and Lucy.

To the seven children of her sister Grimwood she left some gifts of silver. Gold rings of a guinea value went to Mrs Mary Keeling, her daughter Miss Mary Keeling, Mr James Wright, his wife Sally Wright, her great niece Maria Sophia Newman, now 4 years old who was left her gold watch on reaching the age of 6.

L

Martha Summersum, widow, received £10 as did Hannah the wife of William Hubbard, Colchester, butcher. The will also mentions monies recovered in a Chancery suit from Mr Petfield. Her five godchildren; John Matthew Grimwood (qv), Nicholas Waller, Lucy Lechmere, Maria Wright received £20 apiece. The bed and bedding in the servants garret was left to Hannah Hubbard.

The executors were Thomas Lechmere Grimwood and Thomas Luther Lechmere.

See also wills Rebeckah or Rebecca Lechmere, widow, Colchester, NA PROB 11/833, p. 19 October 1757; Lucy Lechmere, spinster, All Saints, Colchester, NA PROB 11/903, 13 November 1764; Richard Lechmere, ERO 1745, JBB NB Dec 71; D'Cruze, *Pleasing Prospect*: 34-5, 58-9.

LEE WILLIAM [519]
Carrier and Innkeeper, Wagon and Horses
fl. 1772-1790

Married Ann Stevens, daughter of Thomas and Elizabeth (qv) in 1772 (CPL Crisp ML205, ERO D/ALL 1772) around the time of her mother's death. The couple took over the Wagon and Horses and remained there until 1780 when James Stevens (qv), Ann's brother, took the premises. The Lees seem to have moved to St Marys since Lee is described as a waggoner of St Marys when, after Ann's death he married Mary Garrard of the same parish in 1783 (CPL Crisp ML166, ERO D/ALL 1783). Lee was declared bankrupt in March 1790 (*ChCh* 12 March 1790).

See also; CPL Crisp ML177, ERO D/ALL 1807, William Lee, St Peters, bookkeeper 22 to Mary Garrard of the same, 21; ERO P/CoR/5, 22 October 1774 William Lee, Colchester victualler complained at Petty Sessions that he had last night apprehended his apprentice Matthew Carpenter who had run away three months previously; ERO P/CoR/17 22 May 1794, Settlement Examination of William Taylor, who declared he had about 16 years earlier served for a year as servant to Mr William Lee, St Peter, victualler and carrier at £5 4s.

LEGGATT WILLIAM [520]
Innkeeper, Ship
fl. 1793-1802

Alehouse recognisances of 1793 name Leggatt. He still kept the house in 1799 when it was the venue for the bankrupt auction of John Mannall, gingerbread baker (qv) (*ChCh* 1 March and 12 April 1799).

He witnessed the will of Thomas Beswick (qv) scrivener in 1797 and in 1800 was named executor to John Lincet (qv) carpenter of St Marys, receiving £5 5s. The will was proved in 1802.

LEPINGWELL MARK [1243]
Carpenter
fl. 1750s-1790s

Three carpenters of this name in Colchester.

Henry Bevan 2 (qv) named Mark Lepingwell 1 first among the workmen who were to bear him to the grave (his will 1756). Lepingwell is also a beneficiary of Albertus Bevan's (qv) will made 1759 as nephew, repeated by his wife *née* Fitch 1770. He worked for Isaac Green (qv) 1749/50.

ERO ML D/ALL 1775 Mark Lepingwell 2 of All Saints, carpenter, to Sarah Armer of same. St Botolph's rates (nfr) give Mark Lepingwell 2, rated 2 two doors from Michael Hills in Queen St.

1791, Mark Lepingwell 3, was apprenticed to Nathaniel Wenlock (qv) £5. Free burgess by right of service 20 October 1806, of 18 Old Nicholas St Shoreditch. He was also 'of Shoreditch' when he married Mary Burton of Holy Trinity, 1803.

This curious name can hardly be missed, as it occurs frequently; e.g. Emmison's index to *Wills at Chelmsford*, 1721-1797 volume, gives twelve, in Yeldham, Castle Hedingham, Kelvedon etc. and there are marriage licences in the same area. Restricting notice to carpenters there are; ERO ML D/ABL1730, Daniel Leppingwell of Thorpe, Essex and Robert Cornwall of Bures carpenter bound, Daniel (26) to Margaret Dayman (24) of Bures (cf. will, 1739 Edward, carpenter, of Castle Hedingham ERO D/AMR/11/158).

LETTSOM Dr J COAKLEY [522]
Physician
fl. 1775-1786

Founder of the London Medical Society (*ODNB*) and member of the Colchester Medical Society from May 1786.

LEWIS MR [523]
Schoolmaster
fl. 1788

Ran an academy on North Hill in competition with the successful enterprise of Thomas White (qv) (*IpsJ* 16 August 1788). The undertaking appears to have been short lived, however, as there is no trace of it in the 1790 Land Tax return for the parish.

See also Mr P. Lewis of Colchester married Miss H. Hollingsworth of that town (*ChCh* 15 March 1799); St Peters Registers show James Lewis married Rose Berry 27 September 1798, burials show Elizabeth daughter John Lewis 28 September 1784, Charles son of B. Frederick Lewis 31 March 1789 and Abraham, son of Abraham and Elizabeth Lewis, 16 July 1795.

LEWIS SUSAN [524]
Innkeeper, Joiner's Arms
fl. 1813-1818

Named as occupier (a widow) in the Bawtree deeds (ERO D/DEl T16, 1813) and in the Cole and Hale survey of Holy Trinity (1818) where the cottage was occupied by Mrs Grice.

LIDGOULD BRIDGET [526]
w. 1773

Widow of Revd Charles Lidgould of Holy Trinity (qv). She built what was later (c1950s) Martins Bank in Head Street, next door to her niece Jane Smythies at Headgate House (wife of Frank Smythies 1 (qv)).

Bridget Lidgould died on 29 May 1773 aged 75 (cf wall tablet Little Bentley with her husband). Her will (NA PROB 11/990, proved 16 July 1773) made on 27 March 1773 (witnessed Mary Wright, John Foakes and Benjamin Johnson) was proved by her nieces Susannah Norfolk and Jane Smythies. It left £5,000 to her niece Elizabeth Burleigh (sister to the executrixes and daughter of William Norfolk of Cambridge). Jane Smythies received estates in Bromley subject to £100 to each of her sisters under the terms of Charles Lidgould's will and also the £15 p.a. Charles Lidgould's will left to Bridget Lidgould's faithful servant Susan Garood, to which she (Bridget) added £5 p.a. Susannah Norfolk received a gold watch and a cottage in Little Bentley subject to £10 p.a. to Susan Garood and to permitting Robert Goymer and his wife to dwell in it as long as they wish at 40s p.a. rent. Nieces Jane and Susannah were also left all her furniture in the two fore parlours and chambers over together with all plate and china equally. Susan Garood was left 'the little bed she now lies in my room and also all the furniture of my Back Chamber and Parlour under it' also kitchen furniture and everything in the cellar and pantries and 'cloathes and linnen' except two pair of best sheets.

Bridget's nephew John and his two sisters Martha Sedgwick, Elizabeth Lidgould and Jane Pye received £20 each and equal shares in the legacy which their 'dear uncle' had left them. Another servant Sarah Wash received one years wages if still in her service. Jane Smythies and her husband Francis were to provide Susan Garood with a house 'she shall chuse' at £6 p.a. Jane and Susannah were residuary legatees.

LIDGOULD REVD CHARLES [525]
Rector Holy Trinity and Little Bentley
w. 1765

Lidgould has an oval wall tablet at Little Bentley recording his death on 2 October 1765, aged 75. His will (NA PROB 11/913, Rushbrook 418) was proved on 9 November, 1765, having been made an 8 March 1764 witnessed by clergymen Richard Daniell (qv), John Smythies (qv) and Thomas Twining (qv). It stipulated that the bond given to his dear wife Bridget at their marriage was to be discharged and provide her jointure. She also was left a farm at Gt Bromley, his own house and the house adjoining. £15 annuity was left to his faithful servant Susan Garood out of the farm after his wife's death. £300 was left to the children of his brother-in-law Alderman William Norfolk of Cambridge, being Elizabeth the wife of Mr James Burleigh of Cambridge, Susan and James Norfolk (see will of his widow Bridget Lidgould (qv)). His bank stock and notes were left in the hands of trustees, John Pye Esq of Sparshot, Hants and James Burleigh. The interest was to be paid to his wife, then to the children of his late brother John.

Lidgould had a library of 2,000 books of which many were given to the Castle Library. Others were auctioned (5 April 1766 *IpsJ*).

LILLEY EDMUND [527]
Baymaker
fl. 1748-1798

One of the Aldermen created by the Borough Corporation party from honorary free burgess in one day on 29 August 1785 (for the surrounding politics see Frank Smythies 1 (qv), *VCH Essex*, Vol. 9) and served as Mayor for the Tory Corporation party in 1786 and 1790. Lilley recorded three votes in parliamentary elections in the Borough between 1788 and 1796, for Tory candidates.

He had risen from comparatively humble origins and was a rougher aged 17 when he married Sarah Woods of St Mary (25) in 1748 (bound by William Watson, weaver) (ERO D/ALL 1748, spelt 'Lilly'). By 1768 occupied one of the tenements in Trinity Street owned by John Richardson (qv) apothecary (sale of deceased Richardson's estate *IpsJ* 28 May 1768). Together with Joseph Keep, woolstapler (qv) and a Leicestershire wool factor acted as assignee in the bankruptcy of Henry Johnson (qv) in 1786 (ERO Acc C47 CPL232, sale of bankrupt property by assignees to Peter Devall 2 (qv)).

As Lilley's prosperity increased he progressed to occupy a mansion in Bear Lane which was offered for sale after his death (*IpsJ* 15 December 1798, full description; *ChCh* 14 December 1798). He was buried in St Martins, as Ald. Edmund Lilley JP, having died on 6 May 1798 aged 65. His second wife Hannah was later buried with him, dying on 7 January 1805 aged 52. His will, (ERO D/ACR 19/155 1798, Alderman of the Borough of Colchester) made the month he died, left all his estate entirely to Hannah, naming her, William Smith 2 (qv) wine merchant and Thomas Wood (qv) innholder as executors.

LINCE FRANCIS [529]
Woolstapler
fl. 1734-1792

Lived in premises in Black Boy Lane and voted as a free burgess from 1734, supporting one Whig and one Tory until 1788 when he voted for Tierney and again for Thornton in 1790.

He died aged 77 and was buried at St Peters on 6 January 1792. He had made his will on 21 November, 1788 (ERO D/ABR 28/291, woolstapler, proved 25 February 1792) leaving the messuage in Black Boy Lane to his son Morfee Lince (qv). His son Francis, in Norwich received £20; a son, Benjamin of Colchester received £15; a daughter Mary, wife of Joseph Coney (qv) (and a member of Lion Walk congregation from 1769 (Blaxill, *Lion Walk*)) £15; another daughter Elizabeth wife of William Lambell of Ballingdon (Suffolk) £15; and a similar amount to his housekeeper, widow Sarah Wright who was also to retain use of her chamber in his house for life and to have all household goods and wearing apparel. Morfee Lince was named sole executor.

LINCE MORFEE [530]
Cardmaker
fl. 1769-1807

Son of Francis Lince (qv) and a free burgess who voted from 1780 until 1807, in general for Whig or radical candidates. He married Sarah Lincoln of St Botolphs when a cardmaker of St Nicholas aged 23 in 1769 (CPL Crisp ML151, ERO D/ALL 1769). By 1789-1790 he was a prominent member of St James parish vestry. In 1792, on the death of his father he became chief heir and sole executor of the estate.

LINCET JOHN [1260]
Carpenter
w. 1800/1802

Free burgess, 1764.

Of St Mary-at-the-Walls, carpenter, married Mary Stradling of St Peters, 8 October 1755.

His premises were next door to Samuel Shead, Crouch St (Regal area) in 1768 and on the east side of Trinity St in 1776 (ERO D/DC 33/12 ff.).

Thursday Court affidavit 20 February 1778, against John Hills jun carrier, for £3 3s promissory note. Shaky signature.

Is included as a carpenter in the *Universal Directory* of 1791.

His will is ERO D/ABR 29/455, made 1800, proved 1802. Left his esteemed friend Daniel Chapman of Stanway, gardener, his tenement in St Mary's where he dwells, and messuage in 'Ellens Lane' St Botolphs. Codicil witnessed by William Cole (qv) leaves £10 to friend Fudgell Cook (qv) jun.

L

LIND REVD CHARLES [531]
Rector of Wivenhoe and West Mersea
fl. 1738-1771

Rector of West Mersea between 1738 and 48, of Wivenhoe from 1750 and of Paglesham from 1752. He was resident in All Saints, Colchester with his two daughters Letty and Mary (qv) and son John (qv). John later became a political pamphleteer and sometime tutor to the Polish Prince Stanislaus Poniatowski (*ODNB*). Lind was a friend of Jeremy Bentham the utilitarian and of Nathaniel Forster (qv) the scholarly Rector of All Saints.

He published two pamphlets in May 1769 *On the Guilt and Danger of Contracting Debts,* and, *Essays on the late Act against Clandestine Marriages* (London, Rivington, *Essays on Several Subjects*, BL 8403.k.3, *IpsJ* 20 May 1769). The latter essay remarks the cruelty of parting people improperly married if truly in love and on the severe penalties imposed on officiating clergymen (in part a response to Hardwicke's Marriage Act of 1752). In the introduction Lind says he has a palsy of the right side and cannot write these four years and has had to dictate to a person who cannot spell words of more than three letters. The essay topics may not have been entirely academic. A clergyman (unnamed) was committed to Chelmsford gaol by Charles Gray (qv), charged on his own confession with having unlawfully married a minor without the father's consent or Banns or Licence (*IpsJ* 2 August 1766, Chelmsford, 1 August).

Lind became insolvent and Charles Gray (qv) was named as a trustee for his creditors ('unluckily for me' as he wrote in 1762, 4 August 1762. BL Add Mss 33563, Bentham ms, re insolvency of Charles Lind, including accounts for 1760, power of attorney of 3 March, 1760, letter from Gray to Bentham of 4 August, 1762; J. Bentham, *Correspondence of Jeremy Bentham*, I. Christie (ed.), Vol. 3 (London, 1971).) Lind died on 6 March 1771, still in debt. His livings were sequestrated and his penniless daughters opened a school.

Lind's will (ERO D/ACR 17/165, made 26 February 1771, witnessed Revd John Halls (qv), John King (qv), Thomas Bayles (qv), proved 'late of St Botolphs Colchester 13 March

L

1771 by Mary and Laetitia Lind, spinsters, executrixes', asked that if he die at Colchester or Wivenhoe to be buried at Wivenhoe near dear wife and eldest daughter, Mary and Laetitia each received their choice of twenty of his books, a like number to his grandchildren to be chosen by their father.

The rest of the books and furniture were to be sold to meet 'the few debts I have contracted since my return from Chelmsford' any surplus to his daughters:-

> ... my intention never having been to have made any other use of the kind indulgence of my creditors in taking so small a composition but only to prevent expensive suits which I could not bear but to have paid the full Debt if God had enabled me so to do, but since that is not in my power I hope G will make up to them by the Riches of his bounty what they have lost by my Poverty, and I also hope they will not take amiss my leaving these trifles to my children which would be no service to my Creditors but a great advantage to my Daughters.

His donative of St Giles in Colchester, mortgaged for £200 and £100 to daughters, was to be sold giving three quarters of the proceeds to his creditors and a quarter to daughters 'and I hope this cannot be looked on as defrauding my creditors'.

> Item I leave to my son John the sum of Five Shillings in case he comes to England and demands the same and I pray God to bless my Son and to preserve him in the belief and practice of his Holy Religion.

His son-in-law William Borthwick was asked to assist his daughters as executrixes.

LIND JOHN [1302]
Political Writer
1737-1781

The son of Colchester resident Revd Charles Lind (qv) and sister to the Misses Lind (qv). Hence connected to the social circle in the town around Revd Nathaniel Forster (qv) which

L

also included Jeremy Bentham, sometime apprentice in Colchester and Lind's close friend.

See the comprehensive biography in *ODNB*.

LIND LETTY and MARY [533]
Schoolmistresses
fl. 1768-1775

These sisters, friends of the Revd Nathaniel Forster (qv) and, through him, of Jeremy Bentham, turned to keeping school due to the insolvency of their father, the Revd Charles Lind (qv). Jeremy Bentham senior, had remarried to Mrs Abbot, widow of Forster's predecessor at All Saints and became one of the trustees for Charles Lind's creditors.

They began the school in autumn 1768 in St Botolphs Street;

> At COLCHESTER in ESSEX, YOUNG LADIES are Boarded, and carefully educated by the MISS LINDS, upon the following Terms;
>
> Board and all Sorts of Needle Work with the English Language, at Fourteen Pounds a Year and an Guinea Entrance.
>
> The Terms for other Accomplishments; Dancing ½gn Entrance Half a Guinea per Quarter; Writing and Arithmetic, 10 shillings per Quarter. Musick if required (*IpsJ* 29 October 1768).

On the death of their father they moved the school to 'a more convenient house in Queen Street very near the church' (*IpsJ* 29 June 1771). Without the income from his livings their financial position seems to have worsened and the school became their only source of livelihood (Nathaniel Forster's correspondence, British Library, Add. Ms. 11277, 11 February 1781, for their money problems).

Matters were still unsettled in 1774, when they wrote to Bentham snr;

L

We Receiv'd last Night a Draught from you on Messrs Gines and Atkinson for Fifty Pounds made payable to our Order, and are much oblig'd to you Sir, for this punctual Performance of the Promise you were kind enough to make us, we thank you at the same time for the trouble you have taken about the sale of St Giles, and we are very glad it is at last dispos'd of so well. Our Brother has told us you have likewise given him a state of our Father's accompts & will deliver up to him the Bonds of the Creditors on the Trust for which you were Agents. We consider this as another Mark of your Friendship to us, for which we feel ourselves very Sensibly Oblig'd. Our best compliments to wait on Mrs Bentham: and we are, Sir, your oblig'd humble servts, Ma. Lind and L. Lind, Colchester April or May 8th 1774 (date unclear because this is a copy) to Jeremy Bentham Esq Queen Square Place Westminster (BL Add Mss 33563).

The sisters had become friendly with Bentham jnr and in 1774 acted as go-between between himself and his youthful sweetheart, Mary Dunkley (see Mrs Rudd (qv), J. Bentham, *Correspondence of Jeremy Bentham*, I. Christie (ed.), Vol. 1 (London, 1968), Letter 114, August 1774, Letter 127, 9 December 1774).

They remained at Queen Street for four years until they went to live with their celebrated brother, John Lind (qv) at Long Ditton. The house was re-let (*Ips*] 10 June 1775) described as 'a large messuage and near an acre of garden ground'. They did not loose touch with the circle of friends made in Colchester, however. In 1782 (Add. Ms. 11277, 25 June 1782) Forster was reporting that Miss Lind and her niece had been making a visit of several months to the household of Samuel Parr (qv) (late Master of the Free School) who had by then moved to Norwich.

L

LING JOHN [532]
Innkeeper, Rose and Crown
fl. 1781-1799

Ling was servant to Sarah Thornton (qv) and received £50 in her will of 1781/9. At some time during the 1790s he took over the inn from her son Robert (qv). In 1799 Ling retired and the inn was advertised for sale on 29 March 1799 (*ChCh*) comprising a bar, three parlours, seven bedrooms etc. The stock and contents were advertised for auction on 7 June 1799 (*ChCh*) and included household goods, dairy utensils, linen, hay, corn and beans.

LINGWOOD ISABELLA [535]
Innkeeper, Golden Fleece
fl. 1783-1805

Listed as sole proprietor in 1793 after the death of her husband John Lingwood (qv). In 1795 (ERO ML D/ALL 1795) married William Bateman (qv) and continued to run the inn with him.

LINGWOOD JOHN [534]
Innkeeper, Golden Fleece
fl. 1783

Listed in rates and recognisances. Tenant of Mary Pamphling (qv).

See also his son John Lingwood who died in 1834 (will ERO D/ABR 23/40) and was executor to William Thorp, saddler in 1823 (ERO D/ACW 40/6/13).

LINTON WILLIAM [1018]
Auctioneer
fl. 1813

Traded as an auctioneer and appraiser in the Napoleonic period, often in partnership with Michael Lavallin (qv). Also acted alone for example, sale of bankrupt stock of Mr Groves

L

(qv) gunsmith, and also the sale of freehold premises, St Mary, both 1813 (*IpsJ*, JBB NB Jan 65:56, 58, nfr). Not researched further by JBB.

For his partnership with James Lovett (qv) see under Lovett, also D'Cruze, *Pleasing Prospect*:96, 99.

LISLE JORDAN HARRIS [536]
Apothecary
fl. 1781

The Lisles traced their ancestry to Sir George Lisle who was executed following the siege of Colchester in 1648. Lisle's father was a Colchester apothecary who had married Sarah Harris from nearby Gt Horkesley. They married at Wormingford (Registers 24 August 1718; CPL Crisp ML 221, ERO D/ACL 1718 George Lisle of Colchester, apothecary and William Lisle of Colchester iron merchant bound, George (27) to marry Sarah Harris (19) of Great Horkesley, 1718. George Lisle's will is at NA PROB 11/718, 19 May 1742). The family connections with Horkesley were confirmed by William Lisle's marriage (CPL Crisp ML239, ERO D/ABL 1719, William Lisle, Colchester, Merchant and Robert Middleton bound, William (24) to marry Isabel Middleton, 1719; Great Horkesley registers, 24 August 1718). According to Morant (*Essex*, Vol. 2:238) a 'Jordan Harris' had an estate at Great Horkesley including 'very valuable meadows' in 1748.

Jordan Harris Lisle himself married in 1743 to a woman from slightly farther afield (ML249; D/ALL 1743 Jordan Lisle (22) of Colchester, apothecary, married Catherine Hills (22) of Chattisham, Suffolk at Lawford, 1743).

Lisle was in business at 28 High Street, opposite the Moot Hall, then in Queen Street until 1781. The St Runwalds premises were taken by John Fiske (qv) around 1772. Lisle was a founder member of the Colchester Medical Society (see Appendix 2). He took Horatio Cock (qv) into partnership in June 1781 (*IpsJ* 25 August 1781) and moved to Copdock, selling the 'old accustomed Apothecary's shop, with fixtures, drugs &c, the owner retiring from business.' (*IpsJ* 23 June 1781).

The Queen Street premises were advertised again on 14 June 1782 (*IpsJ*):-

> To be SOLD: All those Two Brick Messuages, being Freehold, with the gardens and appurtenances in Queen Street in the parish of All Saints, Colchester, now in the several occupations of Mr Horace Cock, Surgeon and Mrs Bradstreet; each house consisting of two parlours, a kitchen, three chambers and three garrets over the same, with a good pump and other conveniences.
>
> Also six freehold tenements called The White Houses in Queen Street, parish of St Botolphs occupied by William Sherman, Samuel Johnson and others.
>
> Apply Mr Lisle at Copdock or Mr Ennew (Samuel Ennew (qv)) at Colchester.

The shop continued as an apothecary's for some years (c.f. will of Lydia Hawes (qv), widow, ERO D/ACR19/621, 1814 and *IpsJ* 30 October 1813, when a substantial brick mansion in the middle of Queen Street with a 111 ft. frontage 'including former surgery and apothecary's shop adjoining' were sold).

Lisle was a Borough voter who voted from 1747 to 1784 (Olmius and Nassau 1747, Gray and Rebow 1768, Potter 1781, Smyth 1784). He had been nominated Alderman under the Charter of 1763 and was Mayor 1769-70. He resigned from the Corporation 'now of Copdock' on 4 July 1782.

His will made 18 March 1784 (witnessed i.a. by Horatio Cock (qv)) was proved 19 June 1788 (NA PROB 11/1167). It leaves properties in Thorpe, Ardleigh and Norfolk to his sister Ann Lisle, faithful friend Mrs Margaret Flaske of Copdock, spr., and cousin Mrs Ann Malden, wife of Isaac Malden. His house was offered to let at Copdock on 30 August 1788 (*IpsJ*). He has a table tomb in Copdock churchyard, not easily decipherable.

L

LISLE WILLIAM [1186]
Iron Merchant
fl. 1695-1756

Son of Joshua Lisle, Vicar of Thorpe-le-Soken 1666-99, baptised 11 February 1695/6. He was apprenticed (NA IR 1/41/20, 1710) as William, son of Joshua Lisle clerk, deceased to John Lumpkin 1 (qv) of Colchester, ironmonger, £36. Free burgess by apprenticeship, 1717.

His brother George Lisle, Apothecary (bapt. Thorpe 18 March 1690/1, mar. Sarah Harris at Gt. Horkesley 1718 (ML221) was the father of Jordan Harris Lisle (qv), apothecary.

He married in 1719 (CPL Crisp ML239) to Isabel Middleton, bound by Robert Middleton, clerk.

In 1734 as an 'Officer' voted for Brooksbank. For his vigorous career as Supervisor of Riding Officers, see Hervey Benham, *Smuggler's Century* (ERO, 1986):132-4. He was eventually dismissed 1750.

He was one of the rioters on Charter Day 1741, as the Borough Charter was lost (ERO C905, Box 2:*IpsJ* Notes). In the 1741 election, voted for Whigs Martin and Olmius (the unpopular party) and plumped for Nassau in 1747 (For the loss of the Charter, see *VCH, Essex*, Vol. 9, D'Cruze, *The Middling Sort*, Chapter 6).

IpsJ 10 July 1756;

> Wanted at COLCHESTER:
>
> A GARDENER that can mow well, and understands the pruning of Fruit Trees. It matters not much whether he can raise Melons or Cucumbers, but he must be very sober, honest and industrious. Such a one may apply to Mr Wm. Lisle.
>
> At the same Place an experienced Coachman is wanted, to drive four Horses.

IpsJ 19 March 1757: To be Sold. The Timber Frames of several Buildings, one 100 x 20 ft. another 80 x 23, another 70 x 15, the rest smaller, but all of two storeys and extremely well timbered, at the bottom of East Hill. Likewise a large Quantity of old Tiles. Enquire of Mr Wm. Lisle. (This building is pictured in the Map in Morant's *Colchester*).

Date of decease not found.

LOAN(E) JEREMIAH and family [1248]
Bricklayer
fl. 1700-1730

Bricklaying family. Free-burgesses since 1654

1700, ERO D/P129/13/1: Indemnity settlement certificate from Rochford parish to Colchester for Robert Loane, wife and 4 children.

1710, Jeremiah, son of Robert, bricklayer, takes freedom. Another son, Thomas, became a free burgess in 1721. By 9 October 1731 Jeremiah Loan was seventh senior Common Councilman, in Assembly list.

Chamberlain's vouchers, ERO D/B 5 Ab1/26, 1718-21, payments include: 3 December 1719 (22) 2s 6d; January-July 1719 (55) £2 17s 1d; 1733-34 (57) £8 15s 4½d; March 1736 (work done since 1735) £281 6s for rebuilding Hythe Bridge (illustrated, *VCH, Essex*, Vol 9:296), also further bill 1737/8 (80) with John Godfrey for £500 plus (work not identified). (John Godfrey was junior warden at foundation of Angel Lodge of freemasons 1735; his apprentice, John Limmer was made free 1740. Buried 4 February 1752, at St Mary's, 'out of Holy Trinity.')

Rebow vouchers, ERO C47, Box 2; 1730, £23 5s 6d for surveying Rebow estates (Mr Loan).

Cromwell, *History of Colchester*, Vol 2:424 mentions that on 12 March 1725/6 there occurred the collapse of two wine-vaults in St Mary's, four men trapped; Baker, Parker, Loane bricklayers, and two others. Appleby was dug out and survived many years.

Jeremiah Loane of Colchester bricklayer married Susannah Lock of Elmsted, ERO ML D/ACL 1718; Jeremiah Loane of St

L

James married Susannah Bluit of Copford, ERO ML D/ALL 1732.

Will of Jeremiah Loan, Jan/Apr 1755 (ERO D/ACR 16/77); a short will listing much mortgaged property. Proved by widow Susan. Her will is of 1766 (ERO D/ACW 32/2/15).

Note from Nancy Briggs (ERO) 29 October 1962: ERO D/DL E9. Letter from Robert Loane, dwelling by Sir Isaac Rebow's wall in Colchester 29 July 1706, about white marble pavements a foot square made in Suffolk.

Apprentices of Jeremiah Loane:-

- John Barnes, made free 1711 (for Barnes see John Hunt (qv) and Thomas Garnett (qv)).
- Peter Cuffley (qv), made free 1764 (bankrupt at the Hythe, 2 March 1765 (*IpsJ*), lime kiln taken over by Joseph Green (qv)).

LODGE HENRY [538]
Upholder and Auctioneer
1709-1796

Son of William Lodge, saddler (qv) who died in 1738 leaving Henry a messuage in St Nicholas, probably no. 55 High St rated 16 where Lodge remained throughout his life. Married twice; to Mary Johnson of Witham (21) (ERO ML D/ACL) in 1737 and after her death to Elizabeth Oddy of Messing, (22) in 1740 (ERO ML D/ALL).

Lodge's apprentices were; William, son of William Halbrun, Ipswich in 1743 for £30 (NA IR 1/50/167); George son of John Eyles, in 1751 for 25 gns (NA IR 1/51/127); Nathaniel Barlow (qv) in 1755 for £30 (NA IR 1/52/93); Daniel Osborne in 1769 for £25 (NA IR 1/26/76).

A free burgess who voted between 1747 and 1790. Served as High Constable until succeeded by John Pilborough (qv) on 13 January 1756. Voted in support of the radical, Robert Smyth (qv) in 1784 when the Corporation party, including his late apprentice Nathaniel Barlow 1 (qv), deserted to the rival candidate, Christopher Potter (qv), but returned to the

Corporation interest in 1788 and 1790, supporting Jackson. He was elected Common Councillor in 1740, Assistant in 1763, Alderman on 27 August 1764 and was Mayor between 1764 and 6 when he gave an 'elegant entertainment' at the Three Cups to the 'Body corporate' (*IpsJ* 6 October 1764). Lodge's brother, William, was Clerk of the Market when, in 1764 (10 November 1764, nfr) William's sight was restored by Chevalier Taylor the occulist. For many years Henry Lodge was churchwarden of St Nicholas, with Samuel Nockolds (qv) hatter. According to Bland, Lodge was, 'a most professed gourmand, who went to Rotterdam ... (with James Ashwell (qv)) ... to eat fish dressed in a peculiar way' (Appendix 3, *Bland's Anecdotes*).

Lodge was active as an auctioneer, especially between the 1750s and 1770s (amongst many advertisements, see. *IpsJ* 1 May 1756, 6 October 1770). He was notable for his elegant descriptions of property, for example, (*IpsJ* 6 May 1769);

> To be sold at Colchester in Essex
>
> A Good New-built HOUSE, with Brick Front, sash'd, with a handsome Frontispiece and good Entrance, with Parlours on each side, one of them neatly wainscotted and hung with a good Paper, a neat Chimney-piece and two Beaufets* hung with a good Paper, several Bed-chambers hung with new papers, with all desirable conveniences: a handsome good Dining-room wainscotted in the newest Taste, hung with one of the best Papers, and an elegant Chimney-piece; a Kitchen with Store-room and Pantries &c. Sundry rooms for Servants, a Laundry and Cellars, a good Brew Office with Terras-Cistern and Lead Pump fixed in the Brew Office; in the Yard another Pump well supplied with water; a Garden well laid out, with a good Brick Wall, some good Wall-fruit and Espaliers, a neat Summerhouse and a Grotto, with a curious piece of Roman Pavement in the Garden; Coach-house and Stables and many other conveniences without doors. The above House situated in

the best Part of the Town for the Conveniency of Markets &c, a pretty Prospect from the Backside of the House.

Many other Recommendations might be advanced in favour of the House; as Bells hung, Locks on Doors &c, the Rooms all being ready to fit up with Furniture directly.

For further Particulars enquire of Henry Lodge in Colchester.

*Open cupboards each side of the fireplace.

N.B. This was a house rebuilt on the site of the Old Queens Head next the Moot Hall cf Thomas Bayles 1 (qv) and John Eglonton Wallis (qv) for more of the history of this house.

Lodge died on 20 June 1796 aged 87 (St Nicholas mon.). On 24 September (*Ips*] 24 September 1796) his premises at 55 High Street, opposite the George Hotel were offered for sale.

LODGE WILLIAM [537]
Saddler
w. 1738

His will (ERO D/ABR 22/176) left a messuage St Nicholas to his son Henry Lodge (qv) subject to a payment of £50, which together with the residue of the estate, was to pay debts and funeral expenses, the remainder to be divided between the children of his son William jun and son-in-law John Mason.

LOVE EDWARD [1025]
Grocer
fl 1768-88

In 1765, aged 28, a grocer of Colchester, married Ann Hills of West Ham aged 25 (CPL Crisp ML207, ERO D/ALL 1765). Advertised from St Botolphs Street in 1767 (*Ips*] 18 July 1767) selling Teas including Fine Souchong, 8s a lb., Finest Hyson 14-16s a lb. and Chocolate at 4s a lb.

Love was a free burgess whose votes disclose not only his changing political adherence but also his changing address. He voted for Fordyce in 1768 from Colchester, from Ostend for Affleck in 1781, from Deal for Smyth in July 1784, and as a gentleman from the Spreadeagle, Gracechurch Street, London for Jackson in 1788.

See also: George Love, voted in 1734/5 and 1741.

LOVETT JAMES [542]
Grocer
fl. 1777-1810

In 1777 married Ann Nash of St Nicholas (CPL Crisp ML265, ERO D/ACL 1777). Originally traded in St Leonards where he occupied property rated 13 and with a personal estate estimated at 20. In the early 1780s was active in St Leonards' Vestry and acted as churchwarden and as overseer in 1783. In 1784 he moved to premises in St Nicholas at 108-9 High Street. *Benham's Guide to Colchester* (1874) includes an illustration of the frontage, then Joslins. Listed as bankrupt in 1810 (*IpsJ* 23 June 1810). His estates including a Hemp Cloth Factory in St Helens Lane were sold (*IpsJ* 28 July 1810).

For a full discussion of Lovett's bankruptcy and business partnerships including with William Linton (qv) see D'Cruze, *Pleasing Prospect*:84, 95-9.

LOW THOMAS [543]
Innkeeper, Cock and Blackbirds
fl. 1778-80

Low was listed in the 1778 Alehouse Recognisances. He was still landlord (named as Thomas Law) when this inn amongst a number of others in the town were offered for sale on 4 November 1780 (*IpsJ*). Samuel Ennew (qv) attorney was agent for the sale.

L

LOWTEN THOMAS [544]
Attorney, Kings Bench
fl. 1780s–1814

Lowten worked as attorney to the Colchester Corporation from the 1780s and is also found acting in other matters in association with Frank Smythies (qv). Colchester Corporation were far from good payers, however. Lowten died in 1814 (obit. *Gents. Mag.*) but as late as 1817 his executors were suing the Corporation for £796 13s 8d in unpaid bills incurred for for Smythies' defence in disputed Recordership case (cf J. M. Grimwood (qv)).

See also JBB, *EAE*:150; D'Cruze, *Pleasing Prospect*:198.

LUES NICHOLAS [545]
Innkeeper, Wagon and Horses
fl. 1724-51

The son of George Lues, grocer and his wife Susannah, an apparently prosperous trading family. His maternal grandparents were Robert Nichols, glazier and wife Susannah. He was related to John Proctor merchant taylor (qv), and like Proctor, had close associations with the Wegg family (Samuel Wegg junior was Proctor's godson).

Lues was apprenticed to William Sherman, baymaker in 1717 for £35 (NA IR 1/6/41). He was a free burgess voting in 1741 for Savage and Gray and in 1747 for Gray and Olmius. His first documented association with the Wagon and Horses was on 22/23 November 1724 (Deeds ERO D/Dht T337/12) when a mortgage indenture between Lues and his wife Mary, John Proctor and Samuel Wegg raised £200 on the Wagon and Horses, as well as on nearby tenements in St Peters and 2 in Holy Trinity. Proctor's will of 1739 (ERO D/ACR 15/29) leaves £50 to Lues as well as a fourth reversionary interest in the three St Peters tenements to Lues and Samuel Wegg. On 13 September 1739 the butchers' stalls in the town market were let to him at £55 per annum (Morant, *Colchester*, Vol. 1:76) which were sold after his death (*IpsJ* 15 June 1751). Lues mortgaged his remaining interest in these properties for £60 to Wegg on 23/4 October 1747. The Wagon and Horses was then occupied by Anthony Whitney. By this time Lues already owned and was living at the Griffin in the High Street, as his will of August 1747 (made by William Mayhew 1 (qv)) details. (In 1748 he was rated 15 for the Griffin and 17 for the butchers' stalls). He remained there until his death in 1751 (will ERO D/ABR 24/54, made 1747, proved 31 August 1751). His will leaves the Griffin as well as the reversion of a farm in Suffolk, and personal estate including beer and farming stock to John and Mary Pain, shoemaker of Colchester since 'the greatest part of my substance is the produce of the money and labour of the said John Pain and Mary his wife.'

LUGAR JOHN [1261]
Carpenter
fl. 1710-1742

JBB has the following notes on this family, not fully researched:

1710, Edward Lewgar, maltster of Ardleigh, bought 38 East Hill for son John, carpenter, who resold 1714.

1741, William, carpenter, son of John, made free burgess. He died 30 March 1747/8.

5 September 1742, John Lugar widr. married Susannah Watts wid. both of Ardleigh (by banns ERO D/P 263/1/3).

28 March 1749, Nathaniel Deeks (qv) married Susan Lugar wid. (by banns ERO D/P 263/1/3). He was admitted a free burgess 1768, by apprenticeship to Lugar. Voted from Ardleigh in 1780.

ROBERT LUGAR, architect 1774-1855, comes of this family. Father is Edward, gent in 1768 poll book. Free burgess, as son of Edward in 1812. Probably designed *Villa Franca*, late *The Turrets* in 1817 for Francis Smythies 2 (qv).

See also *IpsJ* 24 September 1791, sale of farming stock and household furniture of Mr Edward Lugar, leaving Badley Hall, Ardleigh; *IpsJ* 20 January 1791, sale of household furniture of

L

Philip Lugar, Ardleigh, deceased; *Ips]* 22 September 1798, sale of property of William Lugar, Ardleigh deceased.

LUMLEY VALENTINE [546]
Clergy, Bungay
fl. 1743-1794

Became sizar at Jesus College Cambridge in 1743. Was vicar of Ilketshall St Lawrence and St Margaret 1755-1794 and of Stockton, Norfolk 1758-1794, when he died aged 70 (Venn, *Alumn. Cantab.*).

His will of 1794 (Norwich Consistory Court, 136) left the presentation and patronage of the living of St Margaret Ilketshall and Stockton to his kinswoman Sarah Purson (?) Cam(m)ell, wife of his sole executor, Robert Camell, surgeon, Bungay, with the request that she should present them to his nephew Valentine Lumley Barnard (qv). Robert Lumley Barnard received the south end of a cottage in Bungay and £13 annuity. Rebecca Barnard was left the north end of the cottage and £5 annuity. Rebecca Wright, spinster, then living with him, received a farm at St Andrew, Ilketshall. His trustee was Richard Nelson Burstall of Bungay.

See also the will of Anne Lumley, wife of Valentine, Norwich Consistory Court, 82, 1786, JBB NB 75/9:35.

LUMPKIN JOHN 1 and 2 [1027]
Ironmongers
fl. 1730-1755

These two John Lumpkins were uncle and nephew. They are both buried at St Peter's in an altar tomb with inscriptions to Mr John Lumpkin, sen. died 6 May 1745, aged 59; Mr John Lumpkin, jun. son of Robert Lumpkin, died 24 December 1754, aged 50, and three of his children, who died in their infancy; Rachel daughter of John Lumpkin, died 9 April 1763, aged eleven (Strutt, *Colchester*, Vol. 2:16).

NA IR 1/41/20, 1710, William (qv), son of Joshua Lisle clerk, dec'd. apprenticed to John Lumpkin 1 of Colchester ironmonger, £36.

Chamberlain's Vouchers (ERO D/B 5 Ab1/32, 33) include several long bills in a pleasant small hand from John Lumpkin 1 including; 1736 (100) £2 1s 2d, 1737/8 sum not noted but includes nails for (John) Alefounder 1 (qv) and William Salmon 1 (qv).

Was created Assistant in 1731 and voted for Houblon in 1734/5 and for Gray and Savill in 1741. John Lumpkin 2 voted for Gray and Savill 1741, like his uncle, and for Gray and Olmius 1747.

John Lumpkin 1's will (NA PROB 11/739/146 Seymer) was made 11 March 1742, proved by nephew John 2, sole executor and residuary legatee 30 May 1745. He left:-

- £100 to loving brother Robert.
- £100 to niece Mary Draper the now wife of Mark Draper (qv) of Witham, clockmaker.
- £50 to Mark Draper.
- £100 each to their three children, John, William and Mary Draper at 21.

For Mark Draper, see also B. Mason, *Clock and Watchmaking in Colchester*, (1969):407-10. Draper bought his freedom 24 February 1729 though Mason states he was apprenticed to Barnaby Dammant (qv).

John Lumpkin 2's will (NA PROB 11/814, 50 Paul) was made when he was sick and proved 3 February 1755. He left his wife Rachel a life interest in all his tenements in St Peter's occ. Mr Afflick (cf Edmund Affleck (qv) and notes on Deeds of 59 North Hill, JBB NB Blue 2:17-21) and one empty formerly occupied by John Cranmer (qv), and copyholds in Lexden. After his wife's death these properties were left to daughter Rachel and heirs, failing whom sister Mary Draper's children. The will directed that John Sebborn (qv) seedsman, and William Lisle (qv) gent (earlier apprenticed to John Lumpkin 1) should sell stock in trade, and invest the proceeds, interest to daughter Rachel till 21, for whom wife was named guardian.

The daughter Rachel's death in 1763 aged 11, led to a very interesting 'Deed to lead to the Uses of a Fine - 30 June 1763' in the deeds of 'Cullingford's' 156 High St (JBB notes 1971, ERO C905, Box 8) In this the beneficiaries for numerous properties on North Hill were Mark Draper of Witham, John Draper of Maldon, and Elizabeth his wife, Mary Bright of Witham widow (the son William evidently dead). On a later deed of 1795, Mary was named as wife of Robert Atkinson, of City of London, packer.

Re the High St premises, *Ips]* 22 February 1755, advertised the shop of Mr John Lumpkin, (2) ironmonger, dec'd, 'opposite the White Hart' which had also been in his uncle's possession, 'formerly the King's Arms, afterwards the Sun.' These premises had been sold by Elizabeth Selly (qv) brewer for £150 in 1750. Joseph Wallis (qv) the next occupier after Lumpkin, finally bought them in 1795 from John Draper and Mary Atkinson for £875 plus £175, and established his iron foundry there. Part of the site had been bought by Revd William Smythies 2 (qv), 1763, who built St Peter's vicarage on it (destroyed by fire in the 1840s).

LUPTON DR JOHN [547]
Apothecary
ob. 1770

Lived at the White House, 50 Balkerne Lane (Deeds of White House, Balkerne Lane, notes JBB NB June-67 and correspondence with R. Walker, ERO C905, Box 4, Box 10).

Died in 1770, a 'retired apothecary from London' at Colchester (*Ips]* 13 October 1770).

His will (NA PROB 11/961, Jenner, made 12 August 1767, proved 17 November 1770) named his brother Thomas Lupton, City of York, upholder as executor. He left the house and contents to his wife for life, then to his brother. Mourning rings were left to apothecaries in London, and the Revd Richard

Rycroft. His grandson Nelson Rycroft received £10 for books and a 'metal watch which is not a bad one ... when his father shall think it fit for him.'

The deeds of the property include a Lease/Release of 30/31 May 1781 which transferred the property from Thomas Lupton executor (John Lupton and his wife both being dead) to Revd Thomas Twining (qv) for £170, being:-

> All that capital messuage or tenement and that messuage of tenement (next adjoining the said capital messuage) ... St Mary at the Walls ... in the several occupations of Mary Warner, widow and Samuel Farrin, afterwards William Kilbourn Esq (qv) and Nicholas Harrison, since of John Lupton and Nicholas Harrison ... now or late Mary Lupton, widow and James Bennall.

LYONS JOHN [535]
Ostler, George Inn
w. 1801

Bland (Appendix 3, *Bland's Anecdotes*:74-7) recalls Lyons as 'a singularly honest and upright man. He wore a black old hunting cap, and a full-bottomed wig, which from long service had attained a yellow hue'. His old drab coat with large silver buttons was his Sunday best which he 'possessed more than half a century'. Bland's story is that for many years Lyon courted Abigail Arthy, the servant of Francis Snell (qv) tailor whose shop was across the road from the George. She had had the smallpox and lost an eye, but apparently had a *tendresse* for Snell and, it seems, had an illegitimate child by him (see under Francis Snell (qv)).

Bland says that he had been told by Thomas Kendall (presumably Thomas Sparrow Kendall (qv) (who lived next door to Snell) that he had overheard Lyons confronting 'Nabby' with the rumours about Snell. In Bland's words:-

> When John Lyons heard this, he reproached his Nabby, and she wept bitter tears and denied it. But he vowed he would have nothing more to do with her unless she

L

would immediately wish that her one eye might drop into his cap, which he held out for that purpose ... if she were false. She called all the pride of her sex to her aid, spurned with contempt the proposition, and John took his leave, and thus escaped the trammels of matrimony.'

Lyons died aged 64 on 19 August 1800. He was buried in St Nicholas. As Bland comments 'broken hearts die slow'. Lyon had saved his money and left a legacy 'for the education of six poor boys' as well as a 'donation to the dissenting meeting which he regularly attended during his lifetime.' In fact he left £5 per year to those living in the Culver Street almshouses, provision for twelve 3d loaves each Sunday to twelve people including those living in St Nicholas almshouses and a similar number to those attending the Methodist meeting, as well as £5 to the minister annually (ERO D/ACR/19/239, 1801).

Index to Volume 1

This index is a straightforward listing of dictionary entries in this volume. The third volume of *Colchester People* includes fuller cross-referenced indexes across all volumes, including by trade or profession.

A

ABBOTT REVD JOHN DD [1], Rector, All Saints, w. 1759/60, 1
ABBOTT WILLIAM [1280], Woollen Draper, Tailor and Shopkeeper, w. 1804, 1
ABELL FRANCIS [4], Saddler and Tanner, fl. 1762-77, 2
ABELL FRANCIS TILLETT [3], Attorney, fl. 1785-1838, 2
ABSOLON CHARLES [4], Hythe Merchant, fl. 1786-1795, 3
AFFLECK Sir EDMUND, R.N., MP [5], MP for Colchester Borough, ob. 1788, 4
AGNIS BENJAMIN [8], Gardener, w. 1763/5, 8
AGNIS JOHN [7], Gardener, fl. 1751-1808, 8
AGNIS ROBERT [9], Gardener, w. 1782, 9
AGNIS THOMAS [6], Gardener, w. 1733, 9
ALDUS JOHN 1 [10], Gardener, fl. 1741-1767, 10
ALDUS JOHN 2 [11], Gardener, fl. 1767-1807, 10
ALEFOUNDER ALICE [17], Schoolmistress, fl. 1750-1801, 11
ALEFOUNDER JOHN 1 [1223], Carpenter, 1701-1763, 12
ALEFOUNDER JOHN 2 [1224], Architect and Surveyor, 1731/2-1787, 13
ALEFOUNDER JOHN 3 [1225], Portrait Painter, 1758-1794, 16
ALEFOUNDER JOHN 4 [1283], Naval Surgeon, ob. 1787, 17

ALEFOUNDER ROBERT [14], Linen Draper and Grocer, fl. 1738-1784, 17
ALEFOUNDER UPCHER [12], Customs Officer, late Baymaker, 1725-1785, 19
ALVIS PETER [16], Cordwainer, w. 1743, 20
ANDERSON THOMAS [18], Linen Draper, fl. 1791, 20
ANDREWS THOMAS [19], Brewer, fl. 1769-1815, 21
ANGIER BEZALIEL 1 [991], Miller, ob. 1783, 22
ANGIER BEZALIEL 2 [1286], Miller, Mayor 1788, ob. 1801, 24
ARDLEY THOMAS [1255], Carpenter, will 1798, 27
ARGENT WILLIAM [22], Baymaker, fl. 1784-1820, 27
ARNOLD JOSEPH [24], Man Midwife, fl. 1786, 29
ARUNDELL ROBERT MONCKTON [25], 4th Viscount Galway, 1752-1810, 29
ASHFORD RICHARD [976], Candlemaker and Grocer, fl. 1780-1815, 30
ASHWELL JAMES [27], Grocer and Wine Merchant, fl. 1754-1791, 31
ASHWELL JAMES WALLIS [28], Merchant, ob. 1817, 33
AUSTON EDWARD [30], Gardener, fl. 1789-1806, 35
AYLMER MR [31], Colchester Dancing School, fl. 1757, 36

465

B

BAAS LUCY [1278], Gentry, 1745-1809, 37
BACON RICHARD [1301], Upholsterer, w. 1733, 38
BACON SIR RICHARD [33], Attorney, 1695-1773, 38
BAGNALL JOHN [1113], Printer, fl. 1725 in Colchester, 39
BAINES JOSEPH [992], Baker, w. 1785, 39
BAINES PETER [34], Innkeeper, George, fl. 1790-9, 40
BAKER JOHN 1 [36], Baymaker, fl. 1759-74, 40
BAKER JOHN 2 [35], Carrier, fl. 1755, 41
BANCILHON ANTHONY [1250], Mason, fl. 1753, 42
BANISTER JOSEPH [38], Watch and Clockmaker, 1778-1875, 42
BARKER THOMAS [40], Innkeeper, Castle, All Saints, fl. 1781-1787, 43
BARKER THOMAS RUTLEDGE [41], Victualler, Castle, All Saints, fl. 1787-1791, 43
BARLOW NATHANIEL 1 [42], Upholster, Auctioneer and Appraiser, c. 1740-1798, 43
BARLOW NATHANIEL 2 [43], Grocer, fl. 1779-1802, 45
BARNARD JOHN [45], Surgeon, ob. 1768, 46
BARNARD REVD JOHN [44], Clergy, ob. 1767, 47
BARNES ANN [46], Victualler, Cross Keys, w. 1792/3, 48
BARNS CLARK [49], Brewer, w. 1783, 48
BARNS THOMAS 1 [50], Brewer, ob. 1791, 49
BARNS THOMAS 2 [51], Saddler, fl 1794-1808. ,49
BARSTOW REVD THOMAS [52], Rector, St Mary-at-the-Walls, fl. 1771-1788, 50
BARTHOLOMEW EDWARD [1247], Carpenter, d. 1744, 50
BARTHOLOMEW JOHN [1249], Stonemason, 1711-1782, 51
BARTON ROYSTON [53], Captain 67th Foot, ob. 1802, 52
BATEMAN WILLIAM [54], Innkeeper, Golden Fleece, fl. 1795-1805, 53
BAWTREE JOHN [55], Brewer, w. 1772/3, 54
BAYLES THOMAS 1 [58], Grocer, w. 1726/7, 54
BAYLES THOMAS 2 [56], Grocer, w. 1727/8, 55
BAYLES THOMAS 3 [57], Attorney, fl. 1745-1775, 55
BELL MARTIN [61], Grazier, Broker and Rower, fl. 1734-1772, 56
BERNARD REVD VALENTINE LUMLEY [63], Curate Great Holland, Rector of Frinton and Stockton, Norfolk, 1746-1816, 57
BERNEY BOWN JOHN [93], Innkeeper, White Hart , fl. 1773-1775, 58
BEST THOMAS CAPT [1273], Captain in East India Company, c. 1715-1775, 58
BEST THOMAS 2 [64], Clothier, ob. 1789, 60
BEST THOMAS 3 [1193], Grocer, fl. 1790-1809, 60
BETTS STEPHEN [65], Tinman, fl. 1764-1809, 61
BETTS WILLIAM [66], Attorney, fl. 1784-1834, 62
BEVAN ALBERTUS [1204], Master Carpenter, d. 1766, 62
BEVAN HENRY 1 [1205], Master Carpenter, 1675-1728, 63
BEVAN HENRY 2 [1206], Master Carpenter, 1705/6-1766, 64
BEVAN ISAAC [67], Attorney, fl. 1745-72, 66
BEVERLEY WILLIAM [68], Farrier, w. 1782, 67
BIGG WILLIAM REDMORE, RA [1179], Painter, fl. 1749-1828, 67

BLACKWELL WILLIAM [72], Innkeeper, Black Boy, fl. 1796-1805, 67
BLAND CHARLES [1197], Hosier, ob. 1775, 68
BLAND EDWARD 1 [74], Hosier, fl. 1775-1797, 69
BLAND EDWARD 2 [73], Tobacco Pipemaker, fl. 1735-55, 70
BLAND HENRY DANIEL [1198], ob. 1851, 71
BLAND JOEL [1285], Salesman, w. 1780, 72
BLATCH JAMES ESQ [75], (formerly Smythies), fl. 1770-1812, 72
BLITHE FRANCIS [1114], Bookseller, d. 1718, 74
BLOMFIELD BEZALIEL [76], Farmer and Maltster, fl. 1755-1799, 74
BLOWER BARWELL [77], Baymaker, Bocking (Essex), fl. 1752-1776, 75
BLYTH ANN OATHWAITE [86], Merchant, fl. 1777-1814, 76
BLYTH CLARK [82], Cabinetmaker and Joiner, later Woolcomber, fl. 1754-1768, 77
BLYTH DANIEL 1 [81], Merchant, 1753-1799, 78
BLYTH DANIEL 2 and MARY [85], Perukemaker and Milliner, fl. 1765-1780s, 79
BLYTH DANIEL OATHWAITE [87], Merchant, fl. 1799-1835, 80
BLYTH JOHN [80], Perukemaker, d. 1803, 81
BLYTH SAMUEL 1 [79], Tailor, fl. 1756-1782, 81
BLYTH SAMUEL 2 [84], Innkeeper, Castle, All Saints, fl. 1763-68, 81
BLYTH THOMAS [83], Perukemaker, fl. 1759-1802, 82
BOAD HENRY [88], Schoolmaster, fl. 1732-1759, 82
BOGARD CORNELIUS [89], Draper, ob. 1756, 84

BOGGIS ISAAC 1 [1118], Baymaker, fl. 1731-1762, 85
BOGGIS ISAAC 2 [1119], Merchant, 1740-1801, 87
BOGGIS JAMES [1292], Gent, ob. 1787, 90
BOGGIS JOHN 1 [1294], Baker, ob. 1728, 92
BOGGIS JOHN 2 [1293], Baker, ob. 1752, 92
BOGGIS JOSEPH [976], Baker, fl. 1760s, 93
BOGGIS THOMAS [1120], Baymaker, 1739-1790, 94
BORROWS WILLIAM [90], Corkcutter, fl. 1759-1806, 97
BOUTELL EDWARD [91], Innkeeper, Bricklayers Arms, fl. 1783-90, 98
BOWLAND JOHN KILLINGWORTH [1180], Hatter and Wine-Merchant, fl. 1789-1818, 98
BOWLER RICHARD [92], Cardmaker, fl. 1717-1754, 99
BOYLE MICHAEL and MARY [94], Ribbon and Silk Manufacture and Millinery, fl. 1775-1809, 101
BOYS JAMES [1289], Merchant, w. 1745, 102
BOYS MARY [1141], ob. 1792, 104
BOYS REVD RICHARD [1291], Rector, W. Bergholt, ob. 1784, 105
BOYS WILLIAM 1 [1288], Alderman, w. 1714, 105
BOYS WILLIAM 2 [1290], Rector W. Bergholt and Easthorpe, w. 1734, 106
BRAME BENJAMIN [96], Innkeeper, Marquis of Granby, fl. 1778-1789, 106
BRAMSTON THOMAS ESQ and son [1276], Gent, fl. 1729-1802, 106
BRAZIER MARY [97], Hatter, fl. c. 1750, 107
BREAM JAMES [98], Saddler, 1730-1780, 107
BREE REVD JOHN [100], Rector, Marks Tey, fl. 1753-1780, 108

467

BREE REVD WILLIAM [99], Rector, Marks Tey, fl. 1721-1753, 108
BRIDGE JOHN [1221], Carpenter, 1778-1845, 110
BRIDGES THEOPHILUS [103], Victualler, Cross Keys, fl. 1792-1800, 111
BROCK JOHN [104], Saddler, fl. 1768, 112
BROCKWELL JOSEPH [106], Baker, w. 1755/7, 112
BROCKWELL REVD JOSEPH [105], Rector, W. Mersea and Steeple, fl. 1735-1797, 112
BROOKER JAMES [115], Innkeeper, Chaise and Pair, later Castle, St Peters, fl. 1795–1802, 114
BROOKER JOHN [110], Innkeeper, King's Arms, and Tulip Grower, fl. 1753-1802, 114
BROWN EDWARD [1215], Carpenter, 1721-1790, 115
BROWN JACOB [119], Staymaker, fl. 1768, 116
BROWN JOHN 1 [124], Victualler, w. 1793/4, 117
BROWN JOHN 2 [123], Innkeeper, Duke of Marlboro, fl. 1780-9, 117
BROWN JOHN 3 [120], Innkeeper, Joiners Arms, fl. 1783, 117
BROWN JOHN 4 [121], Distiller, fl. 1808, 117
BROWN JOHN 5 [1254], Stonemason, fl. 1812, 118
BROWN ROBERT [122], Perukemaker, fl. 1719-1778, 119
BROWNE ABRAHAM [125], Baymaker, w. 1729, 120
BRUNWIN LAYZELL [128], Surgeon, Apothecary and Man Midwife, fl. 1752-62, 120
BUFFETT JOHN [1166], Clockmaker, 1692-1758, 120
BULLOCK WILLIAM ESQ [131], Attorney, c.1749-1822, 122
BUMSTEAD JOHN [133], Colchester Academy, fl. 1784-1796, 124

BUNNELL WILLIAM [132], Upholsterer, Auctioneer &c, fl. 1785-1808, 125
BURNHAM JOSEPH 1 and 2 [1191], Drapers, fl. 1726-1775, 126
BUTCHER JOHN [1256], Carpenter, fl. 1768, 127
BUTLER [134], Brazier, fl. 1807, 127
BUXTON JAMES [135], Wine Merchant and Distiller, fl. 1746-95, 128

C

CAGE JOHN [123], Collarmaker, w. 1760, 130
CAMPLIN BISHOP [136], Coachmaker, fl. 1773-76, 130
CANDLER STEPHEN [1222], Carpenter and Auctioneer, 1738-1812, 131
CANNING FRANCIS [1143], Gent, w. 1783, 135
CANT GEORGE 1 [138], Gardener, fl. 1728-1747, 136
CANT GEORGE 2 [139], Gardener, fl. 1740-1780, 136
CANT GEORGE 3 [143], Gardener, fl. 1772-1809, 136
CANT JOHN [137], Coachmaster, fl. 1718-1741, 137
CANT MARY [142], Coachmaster, fl. 1760–1768, 137
CANT THOMAS [140], Coachmaster, fl. 1741-1760, 138
CANT WILLIAM 1 [141], Gardener, 1742-1805, 138
CANT WILLIAM 2 [144], Gardener, fl. 1779-1831, 139
CANT WILLIAM SAMUEL [145], Gardener and Sergeant-at-Mace, fl. 1802-31, 140
CAPSTACK EDWARD [146], Currier and Tanner, fl. 1768-1808, 140
CAREW THOMAS [147], Apothecary, fl. 1721-1740, 142

CARLETON CATHERINE [148], Clergyman's widow, w. 1763/64, 142
CARLETON HUMPHREY [149], Gent, fl. 1775-1805, 143
CARR SAMUEL [151], Grocer, 1733-1806, 144
CARTER ALEXANDER [994], Miller, w. 1801, 145
CARTER JAMES [153], Tailor, fl. 1800-32, 146
CARTER STOWERS [995], Miller, w. 1791, 146
CATCHPOOL RICHARD [155], Staymaker, 1722-1790, 147
CATCHPOOL WILLIAM [1220], Carpenter, 1714-1798, 147
CAUTLEY REVD JOHN [157], Rector, St Runwalds and Messing, fl. 1777-1797, 148
CHAMBERLAIN THOMAS [159], Innkeeper, Bear Inn, fl. 1790-5, 148
CHEEK JOHN [1120], Stagecoachman, fl. 1750, 149
CHIGNALL JOHN [161], Maltster, Felsted, w. 1771, 149
CHIGNELL THOMAS 1 [166], Baker, fl. 1742-59, 149
CHIGNELL THOMAS 2 [163], Baker, fl. 1768-75, 150
CLAMTREE ISAAC SAMUEL [165], Attorney, fl. 1777-1823, 150
CLAMTREE THOMAS [164], Customs and Excise, fl. 1741-84, 151
CLARKE ANN [162], Innkeeper, Joiners Arms, fl. 1780, 152
CLARKE JOHN 1 [168], Baymaker, fl. 1734-1767, 152
CLARKE JOHN 2 [167], Victualler, Joiner's Arms, w. 1780, 153
CLARKE WILLIAM [169], Physician, 1698-1778, 153
CLUBBE JOHN REVD [1181], Rector, Whatfield, Suffolk, 1703-1773, 154
CLUBBE JOHN [170], Apothecary and Surgeon, fl. 1780, 155

COCK DANIEL [174], Brewer, fl. 1750s, 155
COCK HORATIO [173], Surgeon, fl. 1783-1831, 156
COCK JOHN [172], Innkeeper, Sun, fl. 1784-96, 157
COLCHESTER WILLIAM [1182], Schoolmaster, Dedham, fl. 1730-1773, 158
COLE EDWARD [1196], Tanner, ob. 1759, 159
COLE GEORGE WILLIAM [183], Wine Merchant, fl. 1773-1807, 160
COLE JOHN 1 [174], Coal and Corn Merchant, fl. 1758-1773, 160
COLE JOHN 2 [175], Merchant and Gentleman, fl. 1773-1789, 161
COLE NATHANIEL [1154], Gunsmith, fl. 1760, 162
COLE WILLIAM [184], Composer and Landsurveyor, 1737-1824, 162
CONEY JOSEPH [185], China Dealer and Cooper, fl. 1768-80, 162
COOK FUDGELL [187], Papper, fl. 1791, 163
COOK WILLIAM [189], Merchant, fl. 1786-1795, 163
COOKE SAMUEL [190], Merchant, fl. 1795-1806, 164
COOPER THOMAS [191], Fingringhoe and Langenhoe, fl. 1809-1839, 165
COOPER WILLIAM [117], Clockmaker (and Brasier), 1706-1757, 166
CORNELL EBENEEZER [193], Draper, fl. 1775-1790, 167
CORRY JAMES [1167], Clockmaker, fl. c.1718, 167
CORSELLIS NICHOLAS ESQ [194], Wivenhoe Hall, 1697-1761, 168
CORSELLIS NICHOLAS CAESAR [196], Donyland Hall, ob. 1806, 169
CORSELLIS REVD NICHOLAS [195], Rector, Wivenhoe, 1744-1828, 170
COURTNEY MRS ESTHER [197], Muffmaker, fl. 1766, 173

469

COWELL JOHN [1183], Watchmaker, London, fl. 1761, 173
COWLEY JOHN [198], Wine Cooper, fl. 1767, 174
CRABB ROBINSON HENRY [697], Scrivener, fl. 1790-1795, 174
CRACKANTHORP SAMUEL [200], Merchant, fl. 1776-1799, 174
CRANE MRS MARY RACHEL [201], Druggist, ob. 1820, 176
CRANE ROBERT [1200], Army Officer, fl. 1782-1805, 178
CRANFIELD GEORGE [202], Innkeeper, Golden Cann, fl. 1783, 178
CRANMER JOHN [203], Innkeeper, Kings Arms, St Peters, w. 1759, 178
CRAVEN CAPTAIN BENJAMIN [204], Barrack Master, fl. 1787-1802, 178
CREFFIELD PETER [1282], Gent, fl. 1735-1748, 179
CREFFIELD SIR RALPH [205], Ardleigh, w. 1732, 180
CRICKETT PETER [206], Draper and Tailor, fl. 1768-84, 181
CRICKITT C. A. [1145], High Steward, fl. 1736-1803, 182
CROSS BENJAMIN [208], Surgeon, w. 1709, 182
CROSS EDMUND [207], Cabinetmaker, Chairmaker and Joiner, 1705-1793, 183
CROWE JAMES [210], Innkeeper, Bear, fl. 1789, 183
CUFFLEY PETER [212], Ironmonger, fl. 1763-5, 184
CULLUM JAMES [213], Innkeeper, White Hart, fl. 1786-8, 184
CUNNINGTON JOHN and ROBERT [214], Scriveners, fl. c. 1800, 184
CUTTER THOMAS [215], Clerk to the Justices, ob c. 1772, 185

D

DAMMANT BARNABY [1168], Clockmaker, 1683-1738, 186
DAMMANT WILLIAM [216], Surgeon, fl. 1712-1714, 187
DANIEL THOMAS [221], Attorney, 1712-1775, 187
DANIEL WILLIAM [220], Attorney, 1703-1771, 188
DANIELL JEREMIAH 1 [223], Gent, 1670-1742, 190
DANIELL JEREMIAH 2 [979], Gent, 1697-1766, 190
DANIELL JEREMIAH 3 [222], Wine Merchant, fl. 1802, 191
DANIELL PETER [224], Attorney, 1732-1792, 191
DANIELL RICHARD MD [218], Physician, ob. 1772, 193
DANIELL REVD RICHARD [219], Rector, Colchester St Martin, Mistley and Bradfield, w. 1778, 193
DANIELL SAMUEL [217], Milliner, ob. 1758, 194
DANIELL SAMUEL 2 [225], Attorney, fl. 1792-1828, 195
DARBY CHARLES [1184], Bookseller, fl. 1745-1756, 195
DARE MRS JULIAN [226], fl. 1765-1785, 196
DAVIS GEORGE [229], Wheelwright, w. 1790, 200
DAVIS HENRY 1 [228], Innkeeper, Horse and Groom, w. 1772, 200
DAVIS HENRY 2 [230], Innkeeper, Horse and Groom, fl. 1783-1796, 201
DAVIS SAMUEL [1161], Man Midwife, 1728, 201
DAWES RICHARD [231], Surgeon, fl. 1742-1776, 201
DAY CATER [233], Surgeon, fl. 1754-1799, 202
DEANE JAMES [1146], Builder and Architect, 1698-1765, 203
DEBOYS CHARLES [235], Staymaker, w. 1742, 203
DeHORNE JOHN [238], Hill House, Lexden, fl. 1810, 204

DELIGHT MICHAEL [239], Weaver, fl. 1791, 204
DENNIS PHILIP ESQ [241], fl. 1782, 205
DENNIS WILLlAM [240], fl. l773, 205
DENTON THOMAS 1 [242], Innkeeper, Goats Head, fl. 1784-1812, 205
DENTON THOMAS 2 [243], Liquor Merchant, Goats Head, fl. 1793-1813, 206
DESBROSSES PETER [244], Wine Merchant, fl. 1780s, 206
DEVALL PETER 1 [245], Weaver, ob. 1767, 207
DEVALL PETER 2 [246], Wool Sorter, fl. 1767-1828, 207
DEVALL PETER 3 [247], Baymaker, fl. 1790s-1834, 209
DIBDIN CHARLES [248], Ipswich Composer and Musician, fl. 1764-1787, 210
DIKES ROSE [250], Wine Merchant, fl. 1765-1782, 213
DINGLEY MRS [251], fl. l815, 213
DINGLEY REVD ROBERT HENRY [252], Rector, Beaumont-cum-Moze, w. 1792/3, 213
DISS ISAAC [253], Scrivener, 1740-1814, 218
DIXON THOMAS [254], Merchant, fl. 1761-1809, 220
DIXON WILLIAM [255], Merchant, fl. 1795-1810, 221
DOBBY HENRY [256], Woollen Draper and Tailor, fl. 1768-1786, 222
DOBSON ROBERT [257], Cheesemonger, Tea Dealer and Grocer, fl. 1768-87, 222
DOWNS NATHANIEL [261], Staymaker, fl. 1777-1784, 223
DRAKE REVD RICHARD [262], Rector of Gt. Oakley and Hadleigh, w. 1737/8, 223
DRAPER MARK [1005], Clockmaker, 1729-1776, 223
DRAWBRIDGE JOSEPH [263], Exciseman, fl. 1787, 224
DUDDELL REVD [264], Coggeshall School, fl. 1768-79, 224
DUFFIELD JOSEPH 1 [265], Cardboardmaker, fl. 1710 -1717, 225
DUFFIELD JOSEPH 2 [266], Cardboardmaker, fl. 1717-1747, 225
DUFFIELD THOMAS and MARY [267], Lime and Coal Merchants, fl. 1717-1750, 227
DUKE ROBERT [1019], Draper, fl. 1750-1780, 228
DUNKLEY THOMAS [270], Surgeon, fl. 1754-1767, 229
DUNNINGHAM JOSEPH [271], Cardmaker, 1695-1771, 230
DUNTHORNE JAMES 1 [1185], Limner, 1730-1815, 231
DUNTHORNE JAMES 2 [1110], Limner and Musician, c.1758-1794, 233
DUNTHORNE REVD JOHN [272], Baptist Minister, fl. 1733, 238
DUNTHORNE RICHARD [273], Attorney, fl. 1765-c.1845, 238
DUPRÉ Mr [275], Dancing Master, fl. 1761-67, 239
DURRELL ROBERT [997], Brandy Merchant, fl. 1750, 239
DYE THOMAS [276], Scrivener, fl. 1747-76, 239
DYER BENJAMIN [278], Clothier, fl. 1734-52, 240
DYER REVD MR [277], Clergy, fl. 1767, 240

E

EARDLEY JOHN [279], Surgeon and Apothecary, fl. 1764-1787, 242
EDGAR CAPTAIN [280], fl. 1779, 242
EDWARDS JOHN [282], Surgeon, fl. 1736-1756, 243

EISDELL THOMAS [283], Baptist Minister, Colchester, fl. 1758-1772, 243
ELDRED JOHN [284], Gent, fl. 1782, 244
ELLINGTON LEONARD [285], Bayfactor, fl. 1766, 244
ELLIOTT Adm GEORGE [286], Gent, w. 1795, 244
ELLIS THOMAS [1100], Exciseman, fl. 1739-1784, 245
ENNEW SAMUEL [287], Attorney and Clerk of the Peace for Essex, 1717-1795, 245
ENNIFER JOHN [288], Innkeeper, Golden Lion St Peter, fl. 1754, 248
ESSEX JOHN [291], Gardener, fl. 1799-1812, 249
ESSEX THOMAS [290], Gardener, w. 1796/9, 249
EVANS REVD TRISTRAM [292], Rector, Beaumont-cum-Moze, fl. 1723-1777, 250
EVATT ROBERT [293], Surgeon, c. 1709-1755, 251
EYRE JOSEPH [297], Musician and Composer, ob. 1789, 253

F

FALYARD WILLIAM [1300], Gent, w. 1784, 254
FANE RODNEY [1275], Counsellor at law, ob. 1733, 254
FARRAN JOSEPH [298], Gardener, d. 1791, 254
FAUNCE COLONEL [299], fl. 1815, 254
FENNING JOHN 1 [301], Gent, fl. 1806, 256
FENNING JOHN 2 [1301], Blacksmith, w. 1736, 256
FENNING JOHN 3 [302], Coachsmith, fl. 1783-90, 256
FENNING SAMUEL [1002], Butcher, bkt. 1798, 256

FENNO JOHN [1015], Stationer, Printer, Bookseller, fl. 1777-1790, 257
FENWICK ROGER [303], Mariner, fl. 1737-1747, 258
FIELD JOHN 1 [304], Gunsmith, fl. 1784, 258
FIELD JOHN 2 [305], Weaver, fl. 1791, 258
FIRMIN JOHN [306], Surgeon, fl. 1676, 259
FISIN JAMES [309], Musician, 1750-1847, 259
FISKE JOHN [310], Surgeon and Apothecary, fl. l763-1773, 259
FITCH JAMES [1236], Glazier, fl. 1768, 261
FLACKE HORATIO [311], Sea Bathing Proprietor, Wivenhoe, fl. 1734-1754, 261
FOAKES THOMAS and SARAH [315], Coastal Trade, fl. 1746-1788, 262
FORDYCE ALEXANDER [316], Banker, fl. 1768-1780, 263
FORSTER REVD DR NATHANIEL [1115], Rector All Saints, 1726-1790, 265
FOWE ELIZABETH [319], Innkeeper, Angel, fl. 1773-6, 266
FOWE WILLIAM [318], Innkeeper, Angel, fl. 1766-74, 266
FOWLER REVD CHAPPELL [320], Rector of Frating, 1704-1781, 267
FOX JOHN [321], Surgeon and Apothecary, Dedham, fl. 1730-1747, 267
FRANCIS GEORGE [1231], Plumber and Glazier, ob. 1788, 268
FRANCIS JAMES [325], Clerk, fl. 1780-1836, 269
FRANCIS MRS [323], Draper, fl. 1790s, 269
FRANCIS WILLIAM [324], Attorney, fl. 1770-1816, 270
FRANKLYN JOHN [326], Surgeon, fl. 1730-1767, 271
FREEMAN RICHARD [328], Attorney, fl. 1742-1780, 271

FRESHFIELD FRANCIS 1 [331], Salt Merchant, 1711-1773, 272
FRESHFIELD FRANCIS 2 [333], Salt Merchant, fl. 1773-1808, 273
FRESHFIELD RICHARD 1 [330], Salt Merchant, 1688-1756, 274
FREWEN DR EDWARD [13], Rector of Frating, fl. 1744-1831, 274
FROST M. [334], Mantua Maker, fl. 1780-1, 276
FROST SAMUEL 1 and 2 [1271], Carpenters, Beaumont, ob. 1781, 1789, 276
FROST WILLIAM [332], Surgeon and Apothecary, Kelvedon and Colchester, fl. 1763-1773, 278
FULLER Major [335], fl. 1807, 279

G

GALE ABRAHAM [336], Innkeeper, Sailor and Ball, fl. 1768-73, 280
GANSEL DAVID ESQ [338], Architect, fl. 1730-1770, 280
GARDENER LT COL HON W. H. [339], Commander Royal Artillery in Colchester, fl. 1816, 281
GARLAND JOHN [340], Innkeeper, Colchester Paquet, fl. 1780-7, 282
GARLAND THOMAS [1134], Scrivener, fl. 1709-c.1749, 282
GARNETT THOMAS [1219], Bricklayer, ob. 1769, 282
GARRARD JOSEPH [341], Carrier, fl. 1791, 284
GIBBON REVD CHRISTOPHER [343], Curate All Saints Colchester, Tollesbury, fl. 1733-1760, 284
GIBBON ELEANOR and SARA [1102], Boarding School, fl. 1764, 284
GIBBON MARY [344], Milliner, fl. 1753-62, 285
GIBBS SAMUEL [980], Bookseller, 1730-1816, 286
GIBSON GOLDEN LEE [985], Tailor, 1803-1805, 289
GIBSON JOHN [345], Tailor, d. 1796, 289

GIFFORD HOPE [347], Gent, fl. 1685-1719, 290
GILSON BENJAMIN [1296], Baker, fl. 1734-1786, 292
GILSON CHARLES [1295], Baymaker, ob. 1770, 294
GILSON REVD DANIEL [1272], Minister, fl. 1691-1738, 294
GILSON DANIEL 2 [1273], Gent, ob. 1769, 294
GILSON THOMAS 1 [1297], Baker, 1727-1768, 295
GILSON THOMAS 2 [1298], Baker, w. 1804, 295
GLANDFIELD WILLIAM [1244], Plumber and Glazier, ob. 1798, 296
GLIDE THOMAS 1 and 2 [1201], Pot Makers, Thorpe, fl. 1750s, 296
GODFREY JOHN [350], Surgeon, Coggeshall, fl. 1767, 297
GONNER JOHN [356], Seed Merchant, fl. 1774-1799, 298
GONNER THOMAS [355], Chairmaker, 1705-1788, 298
GOODAY SAMUEL [1238], Carpenter, w. 1692, 299
GOODWIN THOMAS AND WILLIAM [359], Boot and shoemakers, fl. 1760s-80s, 299
GOOSE NAPTHALI [360], Chymist and Druggist, fl. 1806-1826, 300
GOSLIN JOHN 1 [1270], Carpenter, fl. 1749-1757, 300
GOSLIN JOHN 2 [364], Innkeeper, Bear, fl. 1782-8, 301
GOSLIN JOHN 3 [361], Glover and Breechesmaker, fl. 1785, 301
GOSLIN JOHN 4 [366], Gent, Beverley Lodge, fl. 1813, 301
GOSLIN STEPHEN [363], Innkeeper, Goat and Boot, fl. 1768-1783, 302
GOUDE ANTHONY and SARAH [365], Wagon and Horses, fl. 1751, 302
GRAY CHARLES ESQ [423], MP, 1696-1782, 303
GRAY GEORGE [1299], Glazier, w. 1747, 303

473

GRAY T. [1163], Baker, bkt. 1804, 304
GREAT CHARLES [369], Grocer, fl. 1762-1797, 304
GREAT SAMUEL [367], Apothecary, ob. 1706, 307
GREAT THOMAS [368], Apothecary, fl. 1747-1762, 308
GREEN EDWARD ESQ [373], Sudbury and Lawford Hall, Essex, w. 1814, 310
GREEN ISAAC [1207], Master Carpenter, 1721-1799, 310
GREEN JAMES [374], Innkeeper, Seahorse, fl. 1763-1789, 313
GREEN JOHN 1 [377], Woolcomber, fl. 1783-1815, 313
GREEN JOHN 2 [371], Coach harness maker, fl. 1771, 314
GREEN JOSEPH [375], Merchant and Lime Kiln Proprietor, fl. 1765-1808, 314
GREEN MRS [372], Saddler, fl. 1794, 315
GREEN SARAH [376], Innkeeper, Seahorse, fl. 1789-1801, 315
GREEN WILLIAM [370], Draper, fl. 1760s, 316
GRETTON REVD CHARLES [379], Rector, Springfield, w. 1779/1783, 316
GRETTON PHILIP [378], Surgeon and Man Midwife, fl. 1786-1834, 316
GRIFFITH COL EDWARD [383], 4th Rgt Dragoons, ob. 1781, 317
GRIFFITH MOSES MD [381], Physician, 1698-1785, 318
GRIGSON THOMAS [386], Ironmonger, ob. 1762, 318
GRIMWOOD JOHN MATTHEW [388], Barrister, Recorder and High Steward, fl. 1787–1832, 318
GRIMWOOD THOMAS [387], Dedham Grammar School, fl. 1750-66, 319
GROVES [389], Gunsmith, fl. 1813, 319
GUSTERSON HENRY 1 [1257], Carpenter, 1739-1803, 319

GUSTERSON HENRY 2 [391], Innkeeper, Golden Lion St Mary, fl. 1780-1783, 320

H

HADLEY JOHN [392], Gent, fl. 1774-1814, 321
HAGON JOHN [33], Gingerbread Baker, w. 1784, 321
HAINES HEZEKIAH [394], Copford Hall, w. 1763, 322
HALL BENJAMIN [396], Merchant and Baymaker, bankrupt 1795, 322
HALL THEOPHILUS [397], Wine Merchant, fl. 1747-1772, 323
HALLEY REVD THOMAS [398], Vicar, St Peters, fl. 1739-1759, 324
HALLS JAMES [401], Fishmonger, fl. 1765-1784, 324
HALLS JAMES ESQ [400], c. 1753-1847, 325
HALLS REVD JOHN [399], Rector of Easthorpe, 1708-1795, 328
HAMILTON JAMES [402], Coachmaster, New Kings Head, Innkeeper White Hart, formerly Draper, fl. 1764–1803, 329
HAMILTON WILLIAM [404], Hardwood Turner, fl. 1778-9, 331
HARBOTTLE LUCKIN [406], Messing, ob. 1766, 331
HARRIS REES [407], Minister, St Helen's Lane Chapel, fl. 1782-1795, 332
HARRIS ROBERT [1277], Apothecary, fl. 1780-1788, 332
HARRIS STEPHEN [999], Miller, 1788, 332
HARRISON Family [410], Surgeons, 333
HARRISON WILLIAM [408], Innkeeper, King's Head, fl. 1753, 333
HARVEY CAPT DANIEL [411], Customs, fl. 1778-1795, 333
HASSELLS WILLIAM [412], China Dealer, fl. 1759-61, 334

HATTON JOHN [413], Gardener, ob. 1756, 334

HAVENS PHILIP 1 [414], Baymaker, 1692-1769, 335

HAVENS PHILIP 2 [415], Baymaker, 1732-1782, 336

HAVENS PHILIP 3 [416], Baymaker and Gentleman, fl. 1768-1796, 337

HAWES MRS LYDIA [41], ob. 1813, 337

HAWKE MARTIN hon. [418], fl. 1804, 337

HAWKINS WILLIAM [1246], Timber and Deal Merchant, c. 1757-1812, 337

HAYWARD HENRY [1210], Builder and Architect, 1754-1829, 340

HAYWARD HENRY HAMMOND [1211], Builder and Architect, fl. 1812-1862, 342

HEARD GRANGE 1 [419], Woolcomber and Baymaker, c. 1731-1815, 344

HEARD GRANGE 2 [420], Baymaker, fl. 1769-1812, 345

HEARSUM JEREMIAH [1258], Carpenter, fl. 1734-c.1780, 346

HEATH CHARLES [422], Baymaker, Baker and Army Contractor, 1754-1828, 346

HEATHFIELD JOHN [424], Tinman, fl. 1735-1757, 348

HEDGE CHARLES [431], Silversmith, fl. 1773-1808, 348

HEDGE JACOB [430], Watchmaker, fl. 1769-1794/8, 349

HEDGE JOHN [477], Watch and Clockmaker, 1737-1778, 349

HEDGE MARTHA [429], Milliner, fl. 1765-75, 350

HEDGE NATHANIEL 1 [425], Clockmaker, 1710-1795, 351

HEDGE NATHANIEL 2 [426], Clockmaker and Jeweller, 1735-1821, 351

HEDGE THOMAS [428], Clockmaker and Coachmaster, 1744–1814, 352

HEMSTED STEVEN [433], Surgeon and Apothecary, Haverhill, fl. 1784, 354

HEWES BYAM [1000], Miller, w. 1793, 356

HEWES JOHN [432], Baker, fl. 1754, 357

HEWES ROBERT [1169], Clockmaker, 1711-1769, 358

HEWITT REVD CHARLES [435], Master of the Free School and Rector St James and Greenstead, fl. 1779-1840, 358

HICKERINGILL REVD EDMUND [437], Rector, All Saints, resident Pond Hall, Wix, w. 1708/1709, 359

HICKERINGILL THOMAS [436], Pond Hall, Wix, w. 1771/1794, 360

HICKERINGILL WILLIAM AND MARY [438], Brewers, Lime and Coal Merchants, fl. 1750-1775, 361

HICKS GEORGE [440], Innkeeper, Three Cups, fl. 1753-1763, 362

HICKS WILLIAM [441], Maltster and Coal Merchant, fl. 1798-1808, 363

HILLS ABIGAIL [444], w. 1788, 363

HILLS CHARLES [443], Baymaker, fl. 1768-1780, 363

HILLS FRANCES and CELIA [1283], fl. 1788-1830s, 365

HILLS MICHAEL [446], Baymaker, fl. 1731-1786, 366

HILLS MICHAEL ROBERT [445], Colne Park, w. 1788, 368

HILLS THOMAS [442], Carrier, fl. 1754, 374

HITCHCOCK WILLIAM [1245], Carpenter, c.1721-1792, 374

HOBBS GILES [1155], Minister, Lion Walk, 1775-1808, 376

HOLBOROUGH THOMAS [1170], Clockmaker, 1676-1727, 376

HOLME JOHN [447], Landsurveyor, ob. 1813, 377

HOLMSTED JOHN [448], Surgeon, fl. 1706, 377

HOLTON BARKER [449], Innkeeper, Angel and Carpenter, 1695-1778, 377
HOOKER STEPHEN [450], Apothecary, fl. 1761-1776, 379
HOSSACK COLIN [453], Physician, fl. 1764-1782, 381
HOUSSAYE ISAAC AND TAMARY [454], fl. 1750-1791, 383
HOWE JOHN [977], Innkeeper, Marquis of Granby, fl. 1790-95, 386
HOWE R. [456], Gunsmith, fl. 1806, 386
HUDSON JOHN [457], Innkeeper, MarlBorough Head, fl. 1809, 386
HUMPHREYS, J. and W., YOUNGHUSBAND [980], Drapers, 1788-1790, 387
HUNT JOHN [1218], Carpenter, 1755-1803, 387
HURLOCK MRS [459], fl. 1785, 388
HUSSEY REVD NAPTHALI [460], Rector of East Mersea, fl. 1737-1769, 389
HUTCHINSON ABIATHER [466], Tallow Chandler, fl. 1735-1744, 389
HUTCHINSON RICHARD [461], Goldsmith, 1676-1746, 389
HUTCHINSON THOMAS [463], Goldsmith, fl. 1747-1764, 390

I/J

INGRAM REVD ROBERT [464], Vicar of Wormingford and Boxted, fl. 1760-1804, 391
INGRAM REVD ROBERT ACKLOM BD [465], Curate of Wormingford and Boxted, fl. 1788-1809, 391
JACKLIN BENJAMIN [467], Butcher and Innkeeper, Lamb, fl. 1775-1801, 392
JACKLIN WILLIAM [1026], Innkeeper, Fleur de Lys, w. 1762, 392

JACKSON DRUSILLA [468], Ladies Boarding School, Dedham, fl. 1750, 392
JACKSON GEORGE [1303], MP for Colchester 1790-6, 393
JACOB MRS [469], fl. 1788-1801, 393
JAMES JOHN 1 [1259], Carpenter, fl. 1705-1728, 393
JAMES JOHN 2 [470], Surgeon, fl. 1778, 394
JAMES WILLIAM [471], Whitesmith and Bellhanger, fl. 1802, 394
JARROLD SAMUEL [472], Baymaker, fl. 1757-1777, 395
JARVIS HENRY [473], fl. 1802, 395
JOHNSON GEORGE [475], Innkeeper, Fencers, fl. 1779-1786, 395
JOHNSON HENRY [478], Rower, fl. 1764-1785, 396
JOHNSON THOMAS [1252], Carpenter, fl. 1720s-70s, 397
JONES EDWARD [481], Grocer, fl. 1738-51, 398
JONES RACHEL [1192], Draper, fl. 1776-1780, 398
JONES REVD WILLIAM [480], Curate of Nayland, 1727-1800, 399

K

KEELING JOHN 1 [482], China Merchant, 1732-1783, 400
KEELING JOHN 2 [483], China Merchant, fl. 1787-1846, 401
KEEP JOSEPH [484], Woolstapler, fl. 1761-1804, 402
KEMP WILLIAM [1122], Wine Merchant, 1804, 403
KENDALL ELIZABETH [487], Bookseller and Cabinetmaker, fl. 1725-1773, 403
KENDALL JOHN [489], Cabinetmaker, Bookseller, 1726-1815, 404
KENDALL ROBERT 1 [1012], Draper and Upholsterer, 1741-1803, 405

KENDALL ROBERT 2 [492], Brazier and Ironmonger, fl. 1755-1756, 406
KENDALL THOMAS 1 [490], Distiller, 1727-1784, 407
KENDALL THOMAS 2 [488], Bookseller, 1726-1791, 407
KENDALL THOMAS 3 [981], Joiner, fl. 1697-1724, 407
KENDALL THOMAS SPARROW [493], Distiller, 1758-1800, 408
KENDALL WILLIAM 1 [491], Chairmaker, Appraiser, fl. 1730-1767, 408
KENDALL WILLIAM 2 and ISAAC [494], Baymakers, fl. 1767-1788, 408
KENDALL WILLIAM 3 [485], Goldsmith, fl. 1750s, 409
KENT JOHN [1280], Cider Maker, fl. 1777, 409
KERSTEMAN ANDREW [495], Curate, St James, fl. 1790s, 409
KERSTEMAN JEREMIAH [1156], Canewdon, Gent, ob. 1789, 409
KERSTEMAN WILLIAM AND ANN [496], East Hill, ob. 1790, 1797, 410
KEY JOHN [498], Writing Clerk, w. 1787, 411
KEYMER CHARLES GREAT [499], Grocer, fl. 1815, 412
KEYMER MARK [500], Brazier, fl. 1768-1790, 412
KEYMER SAMUEL [1004], Brasier, bkt 1808, 413
KEYMER WILLIAM 1 and 2 [1016], Printer and Bookseller, fl. 1757-1821, 413
KILBORN WILLIAM [501], Barrister at Law, fl. 1762-1769, 417
KILBY REVD GEORGE [502], Rector of Great Birch and St Leonard, Colchester, w. 1775/1777, 417
KILNER REVD JAMES [503], Rector of Lexden, w. 1769, 418
KING ENOCH [1202], Pavior, fl. 1775-1791, 419
KING JOHN [1203], Miller, ob. 1790, 419

KING SHAW [504], Comarques, Thorpe le Soken and Colchester, w. 1792, 423
KIRBY JOHN [509], Collector of Customs, fl. 1744-1777, 428
KNOWLSON FRANCIS [986], Hosier, bkt. 1798, 428
KREBS CHRISTIAN [510], Occulist, fl. 1790-1791, 429

L
LAVALLIN MICHAEL [513], Cabinetmaker, fl. 1795-1821, 430
LAWRENCE NATHANIEL ESQ [514], fl. 1730-1751, 430
LAWRENCE THOMAS [517], Gunsmith, fl. 1763-73, 431
LAWRENCE WILLIAM 1 [515], Shuttlemaker, fl. 1739-1784, 431
LAWRENCE WILLIAM 2 [516], Turner, 1744-1807, 432
LAY WILLIAM [1208], Master Carpenter, c.1744-1814, 432
LECHMERE MARIA SOPHIA [518], Winsleys, High Street, w. 1782, 433
LEE WILLIAM [519], Carrier and Innkeeper, Wagon and Horses, fl. 1772-1790, 434
LEGGATT WILLIAM [520], Innkeeper, Ship, fl. 1793-1802, 435
LEPINGWELL MARK [1243], Carpenter, fl. 1750s-1790s, 435
LETTSOM Dr J COAKLEY [522], Physician, fl. 1775-1786, 436
LEWIS MR [523], Schoolmaster, fl. 1788, 436
LEWIS SUSAN [524], Innkeeper, Joiners Arms, fl. 1813-1818, 436
LIDGOULD BRIDGET [526], w. 1773, 437
LIDGOULD REVD CHARLES [525], Rector Holy Trinity and Little Bentley, w. 1765, 438
LILLEY EDMUND [527], Baymaker, fl. 1748-1798, 438
LINCE FRANCIS [529], Woolstapler, fl. 1734-1792, 439

LINCE MORFEE [530], Cardmaker, fl. 1769-1807, 440
LINCET JOHN [1260], Carpenter, w. 1800/1802, 440
LIND REVD CHARLES [531], Rector of Wivenhoe and West Mersea, fl. 1738-1771, 441
LIND, JOHN [1302], Political Writer, 1737-1781, 442
LIND LETTY and MARY [533], Schoolmistresses, fl. 1768-1775, 443
LING JOHN [532], Innkeeper, Rose and Crown, fl. 1781-1799, 445
LINGWOOD ISABELLA [535], Innkeeper, Golden Fleece, fl. 1783-1805, 445
LINGWOOD JOHN [534], Innkeeper, Golden Fleece, fl. 1783, 445
LINTON WILLIAM [1018], Auctioneer, fl. 1813, 445
LISLE JORDAN HARRIS [536], Apothecary, fl. 1781, 446
LISLE WILLIAM [1186], Iron Merchant, fl. 1695-1756, 448
LOAN(E) JEREMIAH and family [1246], Bricklayer, fl. 1700-1730, 449
LODGE HENRY [538], Upholder and Auctioneer, 1709-1796, 450
LODGE WILLIAM [537], Saddler, w. 1738, 452
LOVE EDWARD [1025], Grocer, fl 1768-88, 452
LOVETT JAMES [542], Grocer, fl. 1777-1810, 453
LOW THOMAS [543], Innkeeper, Cock and Blackbirds, fl. 1778-80, 453
LOWTEN THOMAS [544], Attorney, Kings Bench, fl. 1780s–1814, 454
LUES NICHOLAS [545], Innkeeper, Wagon and Horses, fl. 1724-51, 454
LUGAR JOHN [1261], Carpenter, fl. 1710-1742, 455
LUMLEY VALENTINE [546], Clergy, Bungay, fl. 1743-1794, 456
LUMPKIN JOHN 1 and 2 [1027], Ironmongers, fl. 1730-1755, 456
LUPTON DR JOHN [547], Apothecary, ob. 1770, 458
LYONS JOHN [535], Ostler, George Inn, w. 1801, 459

Printed in Great Britain
by Amazon.co.uk, Ltd.,
Marston Gate.